# Ghanaian Politics and Political Communication

# Africa: Past, Present, & Prospects

Series Editors: Toyin Falola (University of Texas at Austin) and
Olajumoke Yacob-Haliso (Babcock University)

This series collates and curates studies of Africa in its multivalent local, regional, and global contexts. It aims fundamentally to capture in one series historical, contemporary, and multidisciplinary studies that analyze the dynamics of the African predicament from deeply theoretical perspectives while marshalling empirical data to describe, explain, and predict trends in continuities and change in Africa and in African studies.

The books published in this series represent the multiplicity of voices, local, and global in relation to African futures. It not only represents diversity but also provides a platform for convergence of outstanding research that will enliven debates about the future of Africa while also advancing theory and informing policymaking. Preference is given to studies that deliberately link the past with the present and advance knowledge about various African nations by extending the range, breadth, depth, types, and sources of data and information existing and emerging about these countries.

The platform created proceeds from the assumption that there is no singular "African experience," nor is it possible to, in any way, homogenize the identities, histories, spaces, and lives of African people.

### Titles in the Series

*Ghanaian Politics and Political Communication.* Edited by Samuel Gyasi Obeng and
    Emmanuel Debrah.

# Ghanaian Politics and Political Communication

Edited by
## Samuel Gyasi Obeng
## Emmanuel Debrah

ROWMAN &
LITTLEFIELD
————— INTERNATIONAL
London • New York

Published by Rowman & Littlefield International, Ltd.
6 Tinworth Street, London SE11 5AL
www.rowmaninternational.com

Rowman & Littlefield International, Ltd. is an affiliate of
Rowman & Littlefield
4501 Forbes Boulevard, Suite 200, Lanham, Maryland 20706, USA
With additional offices in Boulder, New York, Toronto (Canada), and London (UK)
www.rowman.com

**British Library Cataloguing in Publication Information**
A catalogue record for this book is available from the British Library

ISBN: HB 978-1-78661-369-1
ISBN: PBK 978-1-5381-5883-8
ISBN: ebook 978-1-78661-370-7

**Library of Congress Cataloging-in-Publication Data**

Names: Obeng, Samuel Gyasi, editor. | Debrah, Emmanuel, editor.
Title: Ghanaian politics and political communication / edited by Samuel Gyasi Obeng, Emmanuel Debrah.
Description: New York : Rowman & Littlefield, 2019. | Series: Africa: past, present & prospects | Includes bibliographical references and index.
Identifiers: LCCN 2019014327 (print) | LCCN 2019017507 (ebook) | ISBN 9781786613707 (electronic) | ISBN 9781786613691 (cloth) ISBN 9781538158838 (pbk)
Subjects: LCSH: Ghana—Politics and government—2001– | Elections—Ghana—History—21st century. | Communication in politics—Ghana. | Politics, Practical—Ghana.
Classification: LCC JQ3036 (ebook) | LCC JQ3036 .G427 2019 (print) | DDC 324.709667—dc23
LC record available at https://lccn.loc.gov/2019014327

# Contents

# Preface

This book brings together scholars in the social sciences (especially political science and history), media studies (particularly mass communication and journalism), discourse analysis, text grammar, folklore, performing arts, and linguistics to think about, synthesize, and analyze issues related to democratization and policy in an African context as elucidated and explicated via elections and election campaigns. Other issues of political content, context, cotext, and intertext discussed by the contributors to this volume include ways political actors (especially presidents or members of Parliament) and the media speak about important policy issues such as health care, infrastructure, education, finance, and agriculture in the context of a sessional address to Parliament or political campaigning and the discursive strategies employed to communicatively deliver and interactionally manage such policy issues. Additional major areas of coverage include how political ecology affects democratization (especially general elections), issues that political parties and their actors lean on and highlight during elections, and split-ticket voting (especially what causes it to happen and its impact on who gets elected and the consequent impact on party unity or disintegration).

On political communication, important areas of coverage include how much communication is in political actors' speeches and the extent to which governments and political actors actually stay in communication with the electorate and how medium (written and spoken, especially the use of a foreign tongue) can render communication useless and ineffectual and cause communication breakdown. Pragma-linguistic issues related to language, power, ideology, and representation are also discussed, as are issues deemed politically nerve-wracking and potentially dangerous given their ability to entrap political actors and cause the citizenry to either lose confidence in them (the political actors) or even call for their resignation. Music has always been part and parcel of African traditional political communication, and it is refreshing to see some of the contributors to this volume discuss the role of music in contemporary African political communication in relation to topics such as patriotism, mobilization, and stance-taking.

There is no doubt that politics, philosophy, and language are entwined on matters relating to liberty given how powerful actors often intrude the liberty of non-powerful actors thereby preventing them from active communicative engagement in the communal and state discourse ecologies; it is therefore refreshing that the entwining of language and liberty in an African political ecology is given some elucidation and explication in this book.

The contributors have used specific African (Ghanaian) political, historical, and sociocultural crosscurrents to shed light on themes that run through the Ghanaian political ecology in order to help readers follow through the logic of their arguments; this helps to prevent their analysis from being insulated from any rigorous public inspection and/or criticism. Analytical assertions and claims are fully supported by verifiable data gathered from authentic sources. All the contributors have firsthand knowledge of the political ecology in which they operate, and they write about it in a manner that gives further authenticity and credence to the description and elucidation of their analytical assertions.

It would have been impossible to put this volume together without the scholars and media professionals (contributors) agreeing not only to contribute chapters to this volume but to share their research and professional experience with us. Their selflessness and professionalism are truly appreciated.

Toyin Falola, a doyen of African history, Africanity, and African intellectualism, deserves our sincere thanks. His painstaking editing of the volume and his encouragement to one and all are highly treasured. We are also grateful to Dr. Samson Lotven for copyediting the chapters for grammar, content, and cohesion.

# Prologue

This polity, our polity,
Has a history of holding peaceful democratic elections.
But our Strength and our Peace
Are rooted in the hearts of respected statesmen and women
Who possess the Wisdom to solve inter-party hostility and struggle.
Since the Path, Our Path,
Was constructed to meet the River of Democracy,
Our Religious Leaders and Chiefs
Have always been on hand to help provide Peace, Security, and Tranquility.
The Voices, those of our Civil Society,
Cannot and have not, for the most part, been muted.
It is interventions from the Wise Women, Men of Honor, and Faith-Based Leaders
That have contained the tension
Brought by our inter-party Games and Machinations.
Our Media, Our Mouthpieces,
Have produced and distributed News
That keeps our political actors in check.
And if you want to know where we are heading,
Look at our past actions
And how we have conducted our elections
For without the Past, there can be no Future.
Our Democracy, our Elections,
Are impacted by our Philosophies and Pecuniary Realities.
If the Umbrella cheats,
The Elephant trounces the Umbrella and All,
At the next elections!
If the Elephant becomes swollen-headed and pays no attention to fairness,
The Umbrella's protesting voice for justice can be heard loud and clear.
If those in power dance too skillfully,
By singing songs to outplay the Dominated Voices,
Their skillful dance brings nothing but Defeat!

ix

The spoken word, they say,
Can make or break on the spur of the moment!
So political actors and their parties
Employ Verbiage that makes their promises and platforms tellable.
In this part of the World,
Knowing what to say is important!
But even more important
Is knowing how to say it!
Singing about issues seen as relevant to our lives
Gets Our Political Actors and Social Institutions
Our Listening Ears!
Indeed, singing about such an important issue as Our Healthcare
Gets Our Ears and Our Voting-Hearts!
The Tongue used in bringing one's message
Is critical in reaching the citizenry
Campaign in a bombastic language and in the language of the colonialists and invaders,
And Shame and Defeat are brought to your doorstep instantly.
Focusing on the so-called Elite, the Rich, and the Suit-and-Tie-Wearing Nut-Heads
Brings nothing but Failure!
A Chief who refuses advice
Gets a headless vulture for dinner.
Those who hear these words of wisdom and communicate wisely
Are rewarded with a four-year Representational Glory!
Indeed, those actors who sing and act against
Infrastructural Development, the Economy, and Corruption
Live to see four more years in Parliament and at the Presidency.
Those who sing the Correct Tune
Are viewed as more persuasive
Than those who merely shout Insults and Spill Venom!
Remember, Voters in this part of the world
Are as rational as, if not more rational than,
Their counterparts in the so-called Western World.
Play the tune the mass of the population calls,
And they show up in their numbers in your support.
Call and play your own tune,
And witness trouncing never seen before in this Ecology, our Political Ecology!
When the weakness of our economy and wealth
Show on the faces of the Masses,
They carry this stressful condition with them into the Ballot Booth.
In this part of the world,
Eating all and leaving none for your Neighbor
Constitutes both a Moral and an Electoral Offense;
An offense that results in being booted out of office.
And believe me,
In this land that we call ours,
We have had the privilege of observing
The Cheats, The Arrogant, and The Irresponsible
Sent to the Political Gallows
Never to emerge from their Political Graves.

We are never oblivious to what happens around us!
The hard lessons from our neighbors,
Those who call Africa their place of origin,
Have ingrained in our political minds and brains
The need to avoid Trouble at all cost!
Lessons learned from the experiences of our Friends,
Those from Kenya, Liberia, Rwanda, Sierra Leone, and many others,
Caution and counsel us to avoid Conflict and Outright War!
Indeed, in this part of the world,
War spares No One!
Death, they say, Has No Friends!
Big-Wigs who once failed to make their party's nomination process transparent
Saw their demise via their own kith and kin.
Their own political family members engaged in,
And advocated for ticket-splitting.
Indeed, those who keep other actors waiting in perpetuity
See their political fortunes and wealth vanish into thin air.
For not only does Waiting Political Actors' patience run out,
They abandon or jump ship,
And join other Parties or stand as Independent.
Do not make the Ones who hold all the cards to your survival angry;
For by so doing, they support your opponent financially,
Thereby hastening your swift entry into Political Hell.
Greed, Arrogance, and Disappointment
Spare no Politician!
Indeed, like Death,
Greed, Arrogance, and Disappointment spare No One!

*Chapter One*

# Introduction

## Samuel Obeng and Emmanuel Debrah

The Republic of Ghana, previously called Gold Coast during British colonization, is located between latitudes 4°45'N and 11°N, and longitudes 1°15'E
and 3°15'W. It has a land mass of 92,099 square miles (238,535 kilometers
square). Ghana's south is occupied by the Atlantic coastline, which stretches
350 miles (560 kilometers or) on the Gulf of Guinea. It shares an eastern
border with the Republic of Togo, a western border with Cote D'Ivoire, and
is bounded on the north by Burkina Faso. Prior to colonization, different
ethnic groups and kingdoms occupied present day Ghanaian territory but
these ethnic groups and kingdoms were forcibly brought together under British rule and named Gold Coast because of the discovery of abundant gold
deposits.

So much is written about Ghana's history and politics that there is no
need to reinvent the wheel and/or rehash already-known historical and political discourse. What is important, for the purpose of this volume, is that the
United Gold Coast Convention (UGCC) was the main liberation force that
championed the fight for Ghana's independence. However, the ideological
divide in the direction of Ghana's independence movement between Kwame
Nkrumah and Joseph Boakye Danquah led Nkrumah to split from the UGCC
to form the Convention People's Party (CPP). In the first general election of
1951, the CPP won the majority of votes in the Gold Coast Legislative
Council and Nkrumah became leader of the Gold Coast's government business. After the attempt to reorganize for future political engagements, the
UGCC disbanded in 1951 and became the United Party (UP), the main
opposition party.

On March 6, 1957, Gold Coast declared independence from Britain and
established the nation of Ghana. The name Ghana was proposed by Dr. J. B.
Danquah, the doyen of Ghanaian politics and the leader of the UGCC; the

proposed name was accepted by the legislative council. The name Ghana is from the ancient Ghana Empire (sixth century to thirteenth century) that was located south of the Sahara, northwest of the Niger River in present day Mauritania and Mali. It is believed that some of the ethnic groups that occupy present-day Ghana emigrated from the old Ghana Empire, hence the name Ghana.

Following Ghana's constitutional referendum and presidential election on July 1, 1960, Nkrumah declared Ghana a republic and he became Ghana's first president. The passage of the *Avoidance of Discrimination Act, 1957 (C.A. 38)* eventually led to the declaration of Ghana as a one-party state. Nkrumah willfully and wrongly considered the United Party, the Anglo Youth Organization, the Ga Shifimopke, the Muslim Association Party, the National Liberation Movement, the Northern People's Party, and the Togoland Congress, as being confined to or identifiable to specific ethnic or religious groups and were thus not broad-based enough to be "accepted" as true representations of all the ethnic and religious groups in Ghana. Even though the ban took effect on December 31, 1957, Ghana officially became a one-party state in 1964.

Ghana's current executive branch of government has, since January 7, 2017, been made up of President Nana Addo Dankwa Akufo-Addo (who is both head of state and head of government), Vice President Mahamudu Bawumia, and cabinet ministers (also referred to as the Council of Ministers) who are nominated by the president and approved by Parliament. The legislative branch consists of a unicameral Parliament of 275 seats whose members were directly elected in single-seat constituencies by a simple majority vote. Elected members of Parliament serve four-year terms and are eligible for reelection. In the December 7, 2016, elections, the New Patriotic Party won 171 seats in Parliament (54 percent of the total votes cast) followed by the National Democratic Congress which won 104 seats (with 44 percent of the total votes cast). The other minority parties (the main ones being the Convention People's Party, the People's National Convention, and the Progressive People's Party) together won 2 percent of the total votes cast.

Ghana's judiciary branch of government is made up of the Supreme Court (the highest court of the land, with Sophia Akuffo as the chief justice) and twelve other justices. Sophia Akuffo succeeded Georgina Wood (Ghana's first female chief justice). The "subordinate" courts consist of the court of appeal, the high courts, the circuit courts, the district courts and the regional tribunals.

Since independence, Ghana has, for the most part, enjoyed peaceful democracy with nonviolent elections and peaceful transfer of power. However, it has also had its democracy interrupted by coup d'états and military uprisings during which times the nation's constitutions have been suspended and people tried by kangaroo courts and unfairly imprisoned or killed in public planned executions.

Despite the mostly peaceful transfer of power, election results in Ghana have sometimes been challenged or contested in courts. It comes as no surprise that all the chapters on politics in this volume are about elections; especially its nature, conduct, the campaign platforms of its political actors, the issues upon which the electorate based their voting decisions, and the election results.

This book is thus about Ghanaian party politics as well as political text and talk (i.e., political communication). Structurally, the book is divided into two halves. The first half draws on the expertise of some of the distinguished political scientists who have lived in Ghana's political ecology and studied Ghanaian politics from an emic perspective. Their papers draw on, and from, different theoretical and methodological orientations to synthesize and analyze issues related to the political environment, elections, and the democratic process. Others examine political campaigning, whether or not political actors and political parties lean on issues pertinent to the lives of the electorate during political campaigning, issues of split-ticket voting, and a determination of the extent of responsiveness on the part of the political elite and policy makers (members of Parliament or MPs) to their constituents in policy making such as the making of Ghana's National Health Insurance Scheme.

The second half deals with Ghanaian political communication in its broadest sense from cross-disciplinary and interdisciplinary perspectives and from different theoretical and methodological viewpoints. The authors, all distinguished in their fields of study, draw from such disciplines as media studies, linguistics, discourse analysis, pragmatics, and ethnomusicology in investigating the speeches of Ghanaian political actors. Also critically exemplified and thoroughly illuminated is the type of language(s) used in political communication, the electorates' linguistic and communicative competence in such language(s), and the extent to which incompetence in the language(s) impedes communication between political actors and the citizenry as well as the extent to which it intrudes the citizens' liberty. Important linguistic-pragmatic strategies examined include political actors' use of *pronouns of power* as well as *inclusive* and *exclusive* political pronouns (especially, the first-person pronoun deictic usage), of different sentence types and their discursive and communicative import, of *inferencing*, of *collocation*, of *graphology*, and of the use of *factive constructions* to show credence, emphasis, and amplify cogent facts. Discourse-pragmatic features identified, exemplified, and explicated include the performance and enactment of representation, power, domination, and manipulation. Others include the role of music in Ghanaian political communication, especially how songs reflect and refract Ghanaian political thought and political practice and how music is used in political criticism, civic education, and nurturing and encouraging patriotism among Ghanaians. Some of the papers examine communication as a social practice as well as a political and juridical process. Others question the extent (if any) to which Ghanaian presidents' State of the Nation addresses can be said to involve a real communication given the problems posed by medium, tone, tenor, genre, and key, which tend to prevent intended communication outcomes from being realized and/or achieved. One paper examines political discourse in a completely different domain; that of student politics.

In chapter 2, Debrah discusses Ghana's political ecology and its impact on the 2016 general elections. Specifically, he closely examines the political and economic drives that influenced the outcome of Ghana's 2016 elections and discovers that the incumbent National Democratic Congress's (NDC) political campaign strategy aimed at outplaying those of the New Patriotic Party (NPP) achieved obverse results. Debrah observes that the tension that the interparty games generated was contained through what he refers to as *a peaceful bargaining that was made possible through the intervention of the Inter-Party Advisory Committee* (IPAC) and *the efforts of eminent Ghanaian chiefs and leaders of faith-based organizations*. Debrah also discovered that Ghana's economic conditions at the time of the election helped to reinvent the wheel of political fortune by propelling the opposition NPP candidate Nana Akufo-Addo and his party to victory.

Debrah establishes the fact that Ghana has a unique record of holding peaceful democratic elections in its Fourth Republic and that its democratic institutions are resilient and remain a critical factor that has pulled the country from the brink of virtual collapse over the years. This, Debrah argues, is due in part to (a) the presence of respected statesmen and stateswomen who stand above partisan politics and who can be reached out to in times of interparty hostility and struggle; (b) religious leaders and chiefs who assist in providing security against political upheavals; (c) vocal civil society, vociferous media anchors, and social and political commentators; and (d) Ghana's historical precedents of the 1992 and 2012 elections during which rising political tensions resulting from colossal fraud in the presidential elections and the accompanying protracted election petition (at Ghana's Supreme Court) led to opposition parties coming together and boycotting parliamentary polls. These historical episodes reminded the political parties, political actors, and the citizenry to continue opting for and remaining in a democracy where they could have competitive elections rather than to move backward into state collapse. Indeed, the hard lessons and social anarchy that happened in other African countries like Liberia, Sierra Leone, Rwanda, and Kenya, among others, served as a reminder to reject disorder and to opt for democracy and the constitution of order.

In chapter 3, Alidu writes about the election campaign in Ghana's 2016 national elections, examining how political parties and candidates running for political office interact with the Ghanaian electorate to obtain their votes.

In particular, Alidu asks about the nature and dynamics of the political parties' campaign strategies, the salient issues raised in the campaigns, and how the parties disseminated campaign issues to the electorate. In answering the above-mentioned questions, Alidu uses both secondary data (a desk review of the literature on elections and campaigns with the view to contextualizing the debate and providing the necessary theoretical underpinning for explaining his central question) and primary data that was taken from a nationwide post-election survey conducted by the Centre for Social Democracy (CSD) and the Department of Political Science of the University of Ghana.

Alidu demonstrates that in order to make an informed decision at the polls, it is incumbent for political parties and actors seeking office to provide important messages via their campaigns. Based on his collected and scrutinized data, Alidu notes that the New Patriotic Party (NPP) presented a clearer policy message to the voters than did the National Democratic Congress (NDC). Specifically, the NPP's campaign message was in sync with the voters' expectations. Furthermore, NPP's mode and medium of message delivery as well as its four-year campaign platform superseded those of the NDC in terms of content and expression. In particular, whereas the NPP employed a grassroots-led and door-to-door campaign strategy, the opposition NDC implemented an elitist and extravagant approach; a campaign strategy that Alidu discovered alienated the majority of the NDC's principal followers.

Alidu cautions political parties and their candidates against unnecessarily focusing on the so-called elite and to refrain from urban-style campaigns that involve the deployment of such sophisticated media tools as billboards and the use of celebrities; he recommends the employment of efficient sociological factors like ethnicity and regionalism. He specifically calls on political parties and political actors to pay attention to context-specific campaign strategies and the stature of candidates they elect to lead and/or represent their parties.

In chapter 4, Asante, also writing about Ghana's 2016 elections, examines the extent to which the political parties and their candidates leaned on so-called "established" and "projected" issues in their political platforms that were seen as being relevant to the lives of the citizenry. In pursuing the above objective, Asante relies on both primary and secondary data to examine Ghana's political campaign landscape with the view to determining how the political parties and their candidates interacted with the voters on important national issues. Important issues elucidated include the untested assumption that Ghanaian voters are nonrational in their choices at the polls. In particular, Asante attempted to find out the content of the political parties' and the political actors' campaign messages, which particular messages influenced the electorates' choices of candidates at the polls, and what lessons could be learned from them.

Asante discovered that issues related to infrastructural development, the economy, and corruption influenced voters' choices in the 2016 general elections. The main opposition political party (the NPP) was viewed as being capable of rescuing the Ghanaian economy and that led to the rejection of the incumbent NDC. Also, personal issues that were not connected with the daily economic routines of the people were rejected by voters who looked for rational response to post-election policy decisions that would positively impact their lives. In fact, he discovered that mere identification of critical issues without an attractive messaging strategy yielded poor results. The opposition NPP's ability to successfully label President Mahama as incompetent, corrupt, and a failed manager of the Ghanaian economy, as well as their presentation of Nana Akuffo Addo (the opposition's presidential candidate) as a problem solver, an anti-corruption crusader, and one with the ability to provide each and every district with a factory, made their message sellable to the electorate.

Asante concludes by showing that Ghanaian voters are as rational as their counterparts in the Western World and that their decisions at the ballot box are shaped by the most important socioeconomic issues affecting their lives.

Darkwa, in chapter 5, addresses the question of split-ticket voting by attempting to find out why political party elites advocate for ticket-splitting or find out which candidates will split their ballot and then advocate the same. He also examines how and the extent to which split-ticket voting has affected the current distribution of votes and seats in the Ghanaian Parliament. Darkwa discovered that as long as a political party's nomination process is transparent and democratic, Ghanaian political actors and party elites do not engage in or advocate for ticket-splitting. However, if political actors find out that adhering to the status quo would mean waiting in "perpetuity" to be nominated by their parties, they accuse other political actors of irregularities in the nomination process (Ichino & Nathan, 2013, 2017) and use that excuse to get party officials to make decisions in their favor or to leave the party with other supporters to contest as independent. Supporting the work of Frempong and Asare (2017), Darkwa expounds that political actors who have parliamentary and presidential ambitions are capable of incapacitating their party's candidates from winning an election with the sole purpose of winning such a candidate to their fold. Darkwa notes further that in most cases of ticket-splitting, the smaller parties support the bigger ones in the presidential race whereas the bigger ones yield or defer some parliamentary seats to the smaller parties enabling the smaller parties to pick up a few seats in Parliament and also offering them ministerial and other governmental appointments. Darkwa notes, however, that split-ticket voting results in political actors incurring the anger of their parties and of the general public.

Also discovered by Darkwa was the extent to which the financing of electioneering campaigns contributed to the phenomenon of ticket-splitting.

Specifically, he discovered that some politicians finance the campaigns of their opponents with the hope that the recipients of such financial support will find fault with their own party's nomination process and will consequently create confusion that will trigger recognizable indicators of intraparty coordination failures and subsequently enhance the fortunes of the campaign financier to triumph in the election.

In chapter 6, Wahab, drawing evidence from Ghana's National Health Insurance Scheme, examines whether or not members of the Ghanaian Parliament were responsive to their constituents in policy making. In pursuing the above objective, Wahab examined the historical pathways of Ghana's health care policy landscapes and how elected political actors responded to widely held wishes of the citizenry for Parliament to pass a national health insurance legislation (an issue which Wahab contends was a fiercely deliberated campaign issue in Ghana's 2000 election). In particular, synthesizing and analyzing data principally pulled from Ghana's official parliamentary records (that is, parliamentary floor speeches), Wahab makes the case that on the most important issue of health care reform, elected officials demonstrated that they took interest in, and hence cared about, the health needs of their constituents. The citizenry and civil society required action to be taken on health care reform, and the elected political actors and the political parties promised to take steps to make it happen by making it an important campaign issue.

Wahab concludes that the Ghanaian MPs (members of Parliament; especially those of the NPP) prioritized the interests of the electorates and consequently took action to promote the electorates' interests regarding policy making on issues that directly affected the electorates' lives and upon which they (the electorates) based their ballot-casting decisions. Thus, the elected political actors met the needs of their electorate, providing evidence to demonstrate democracy at work. Wahab contends that even though NDC MPs boycotted the vote on the issue, suggesting they might have been less responsive to the citizenry's concerns, their (the NDC MPs) comments outside Parliament helped straighten the rough edges of the bills thereby helping to improve the quality of the health care legislation in Ghana at the time.

The study by Amoakohene and Ansu-Kyeremeh in chapter 7 details when a government becomes unaware that it is not in communication or is unwilling to communicate with the citizenry. The authors note that becoming out of touch with the citizenry proves that despite the fact that Ghanaian governments may have owned and monopolized the media, their uncritical examination of the communication environment as relates to needs, characteristics, or nature of the audience and the audience's linguistic and communicative competence, preferences, and habits (particularly in the age of multiple media types and outlets), most likely led to the alienation of a section of the Ghanaian citizenry to whom the government become incommunicado. The authors analyze official documents for responses to issues of communication incongruences. Of particular concern, the authors note, is the tendency for Ghanaian governments to "communicate" messages in a foreign language, the English language; a medium the audience may not patronize because of their lack of both linguistic and communicative competence in English. This communicative infraction, the authors note, has consequences in, for example, a communication shut-out of citizens who do not speak or understand English. Amoakohene and Ansu-Kyeremeh note that governments preferred to encourage consensus journalism as if they are unaware of their non-communication or mis-communicative situation. Either the governments resort to censorship where conceivable, the journalists working for the state-owned medium resort to employee self-censoring, or the government pursues what Amoakohene and Ansu-Kyeremeh refer to as "predatory private media space appropriation," a situation that inadvertently drifts into a government not being in communication with the citizenry.

Agyekum, in his chapter (8), analyzes the first person pronoun deixis used by Ghana's president, Nana Akuffo Addo, in his 2018 State of the Nation address delivered to Ghana's Parliament. He examines the discourse of pronominal deixis from semantic, pragmatic, and discourse analytic perspectives. Working within the theoretical framework(s) of Critical Discourse Analysis (CDA) and its offshoot Political Discourse Analysis (PDA), Agyekum synthesizes and analyzes the major sociopolitical facets of the president's speech that touched Ghana's economy, education, health, agriculture, transport, energy and power, and security, among others. Agyekum identifies and elucidates the political lexicon and jargon in the president's text as well as the rhetorical devices used by the president to mention and augment his government's achievements. Speech acts and deixis are also elucidated with particular focus on the first-person singular ("I") and plural ("we") deixis. He discusses the pronominals inherent in the speech and their roles in the speech acts of expressives, assertives, commissives, declaratives, and directives.

In chapter 9, Sarfo-Kantankah examines the discursive constructions of *the representative claim* (one's claim to represent or to know what represents the interests of a group of individuals or a group of things) in the United Kingdom and Ghanaian parliamentary discourse. Using a corpus-assisted discourse studies approach, Sarfo-Kantankah notes that parliamentarians perform a representative function, where they represent, at least in principle, their constituents' interest, the party's interest, the country's interest, their own interest, and other interests. He makes an empirical exploration of the ways in which the United Kingdom and Ghanaian parliamentarians constructed their claims of representation (i.e., as representatives of the people). He established the fact that parliamentarians construct their representative claims in the following ways:

- Explicitly/directly through transitivity, whereby MPs construe representation as comprising different kinds of experience by specifying the mandate of parliamentarians (relational processes); representation is verbalized (verbal processes) and acted out (material processes). The explicit constructions employ two main expressions, the first person singular and plural pronoun constructions—*I*-represent and *we*-represent constructions.
- Implicitly/indirectly, which is achieved through deictic/indexical referencing; namely, personal, temporal, and spatial referencing. Sarfo-Kantankah demonstrates how parliamentarians display levels of attachment to the people they represent through the use of person references such as "our." He notes that such expressions as *our country, our nation,* or *our people* indicate inclusiveness, and the idea of sharing in the citizenries' plight and needs, as well as an emotional bonding with them. The personal deictics, Sarfo-Kantankah notes, are used to create trustworthiness, goodwill, and closeness to the people, which implies empathy and working in the interest of the people. The time or temporal deictics are used to index current periods and their associated social activities and to relate them to historical periods and their associated events in order to compare, contrast, or amplify such events' sociopolitical magnitude and/or importance. This by and large enables the political actors to showcase their performance and achievements as being better than those of past administrations and political actors. Thus, use of temporal deictics helps the parliamentarians to paint a picture of where their nations have come from and where they are, as well as to project into the future. Use of the place/spatial deictics, according to Sarfo-Kantankah, makes it possible for the political actors to make references to their constituencies or other towns, cities, or geographic areas needing one form of attention or another.

Sarfo-Kantankah draws an important conclusion, the fact that, whereas political actors on the side of the ruling government construct their representations in a positive frame, which enables them to justify their government's political achievements, actions, and policies as valid, those in opposition construct their representations in a negative frame to delegitimize the ruling government's policy decisions and actions. Sarfo-Kantankah emphasizes the assertion regarding the different ways in which parliamentarians construct such representativeness and accountability. He notes that parliamentarians, by making claims that they represent the people, portray themselves as the embodiment of the people's interests.

In chapter 10, Amoakohene, in her study on the extent of communication in Ghanaian presidents' State of the Nation addresses, cites chapter 8, article 67 of Ghana's Fourth Republic Constitution that enjoins all presidents to present a State of the Nation address (a major policy directional statement or policy proposals expected to cover all sectors of the economy) to Parliament at the beginning of each parliamentary session and on the occasion of Parliament's dissolution as a prelude and the basis of her study. She explicates the fact that the State of the Nation addresses constitute an important way through which presidents communicate their policy priorities to citizens through their elected representatives. This chapter resulted from an examination of the State of the Nation addresses of five presidents representing the two political parties that have formed governments in Ghana's Fourth Republic over a period of twenty-six years. Using content and textual analyses as well as twelve search words, the author examined texts of all twenty-six State of the Nation addresses for their mention of and the importance attached to communication/media as a sector, government priority/emphasis, and as a mark of attention paid to difficulties of telling governments' success stories. These include the posture toward communication (and the media), and structures developed to facilitate effectively communicating the government's agenda. In all, the National Democratic Congress (NDC) governments' sixteen State of the Nation addresses paid greater attention to the media/communication than the ten delivered by the New Patriotic Party (NPP). In relation to other sectors covered in all addresses, however, media and communication occupied an insignificant space usually embedded in and subsumed under telecommunications and information communication technology (ICT) or technology which were unduly emphasized. It is recommended that equal attention be given in State of the Nation addresses to demonstrate commitment to all sectors. Regarding the media/communication sector, it is important to note that ICTs are only ways to influence the media/communication and should therefore not replace them in importance.

In a study that has implications for critical discourse analysis and student political discourse, Edu-Buandoh and Nkansah, in chapter 11, explore political discourse in a completely different political ecology, that of student politics. Their study, which examines power, domination, and manipulation in students' parliamentary discourse in a Ghanaian university (the University of Cape Coast), explicates the contextual and discursive features employed by the student political actors to enact power, domination, and manipulation in what the authors refer to as pseudo-political discourse. Using an eighty-seven-minute recorded discourse from the University of Cape Coast Students' House of Parliament, the authors make use of Fairclough's three-tier critical discourse analysis approach as a qualitative research design to bring out linguistic features that mark inequalities in the discourse. They employed the theory of social power as their analytical model and discovered that the linguistic and discursive features used in their studied unique political discourse context projected manipulation, polarization, domination, and sources of power in the discourse ecology.

The object of chapter 12 is a synthesis and an analysis of the role of music in Ghanaian political communication. The authors, Agyekum, Amuah, and

Wuaku, rightly note the undeniable importance and inseparable nature of music in human life in general, and in Ghanaian political life in particular. Working within the broad tenet of ethnomusicology and explicating the texture and content of transcripts of twelve Ghanaian songs with strong political orientation and content, the authors situate their discussion under political anthropology. They discovered that clear articulation and management of songs has the potential to ward off conflicts and animosity among Ghanaians, to ensure their linguistic and communicative liberties, and to affirm their right to participate in the governance of their country. Furthermore, the authors demonstrate the fact that music has the power to help individuals to commit important social, cultural, and political issues to memory, thereby helping to create self-awareness and instant ability to challenge, protest, and/or support government policies as was the case of the *Operation Feed Yourself* agricultural policy of the 1970s. Their study also expounds the role of music in the expression of ideologies, political propaganda, political commendations, and criticisms as well as patriotism and disloyalty among the citizenry. The authors warn that music, like the spoken word, can make or break an individual or political actor if not performed in the right rhetorical context. An important sociolinguistic issue discussed by the authors is the role of multilingualism in political communication. Specifically, Agyekum, Amuah, and Wuaku explain the fact that political criticism (praise, among others) done through music employs Ghanaian English, Akan, and Ewe code-switching; and that these languages are involved as a result of being the most widely spoken languages in Ghana, thereby making the political songs reach as many Ghanaians as anticipated by the musicians and their associated political actors. The authors conclude that the content and texture of the studied politically oriented songs helped to unearth the songs' reference to patriotism, political campaigning, praise, and sociopolitical resistance.

In chapter 13, Sikanku, Boadi, Aziz, and Fordjour take a close look at the current Ghanaian president's (President Akufo-Addo's) address to the nation on an alleged military cooperation between Ghana and the United States, an agreement that was rumored to give the United States a military base in Ghana but that turned out to be either untrue or extremely exaggerated. The speech was televised live nationally on April 5, 2018, to the Ghanaian populace. The authors identified dominant frames present in the president's address and explicated the communicative and/or image repair strategies employed by the president. Also synthesized and analyzed is a subjection of the president's speech to Benoit's concept of *the functions of political communication* with the view to determining what communicative functions the president's speech was used to perform. The authors couched their study within the notions of framing, image repair, and functional theory within political communication. Quantitative analysis (content) and qualitative analysis (textual) were employed as the methodological approaches to this research. The major frames identified by the authors were as follows:

**Deepening democracy**—where President Akufo-Addo saw the cooperation agreement as open and transparent thus enhancing the country's democratic processes. His use of such key vocabulary items as "accountable," "open," and "transparent" emphasizes his perception of democratic ideals and enables him to play to his base and to appeal to the wider Ghanaian population.

**Veiled attacks**—by which the president strongly denounced his political opponents who he framed as "nation wreckers" who want to "destabilize" the nation's peace. He also framed their political posture as deleterious to the country's progress.

**Comparison**—whereby the president set his ruling New Patriotic Party (NPP) against the opposition National Democratic Congress (NDC) and then framed the NPP as being better than the NDC. Through comparison, the president projected his decision as a good one by comparing his party's record to that of the opposition NDC, which he described as secretive and undemocratic.

**Enhancing bilateral relations with the United States**—where the president uses his speech to enhance Ghana's image at home and abroad by framing the cooperation agreement as a way to reinforce Ghana's standing in the world citing Ghana's commitment to peacekeeping efforts.

Concerning image repair, the president characterized the process leading up to the agreement as transparent and open, denied the fact that a military base had been set up, evaded responsibility by comparing it to agreements by previous regimes, and highlighted the positive aspects of the agreement. The president highlighted his reputation as a human rights and democracy advocate and champion by placing it within the wider context of international peace and security.

In the final chapter (chapter 14), Obeng recapitulates and extends his earlier studies on free speech and the interlacing of language and liberty in the Ghanaian political sphere, especially, how Ghanaian political actors, social commentators, journalists, and the news media have used language in their pursuit of and for liberty (Obeng, 2018, 2019). In particular, he makes a synthesis and an analysis of the concepts of *censorship* and *free speech* and a determination of the extent to which Ghanaian political actors, critics, and the media have enjoyed or been denied them within Ghana's post-independence political domain. Obeng contends that the dominated Ghanaian voices' strategy of protesting injustice visited upon them by dominant persons or institutions amplifies power imbalance within the Ghanaian political ecology. He demonstrates that an observation of the interconnectedness between language and liberty in the Ghanaian political ecology shows Ghana's languages and linguistic situation, its politics, history, law, and culture affecting each other in a web of constellation, all shaping the fight for liberty.

Obeng elucidates an important point, the fact that liberty for Ghanaians is made a reality by both the dominant voices and the voices of the dominated Ghanaian political actors, social commentators, and journalists irrespective of their unique philosophical and ideological orientations, their histories, and their sociocultural distinctiveness. He notes further that all the voices deem Ghana's democratic development, the constitution of order, and associated economic development as a function of the exercise by all Ghanaians contributing their unique talents to shaping liberty for all Ghanaians. Ghanaians, Obeng notes, view the intrusion on their negative and positive liberty as preventing them from playing their unalienable role in the socioeconomic and political life of Ghana. The persons and institutions whose liberties are intruded see the intrusion as objectionable, and therefore adopt linguistic and discursive strategies to challenge the intrusion in order to free themselves and to ensure their right to participate in the process of governance and to share in the political power and social life of their communities.

Obeng maintains that working within his theory of *language and liberty* requires scholars to establish the fact that liberty has its roots in Ghana's law, politics, languages, and its overall philosophical traditions, and that liberty depends on language to become a reality. He notes that demonstrating how language and liberty impact each other charges us to find out what kind of language is used by actors seeking liberty. On this, Obeng identified *factivity formulae* like *as you know we all know,* and *you will recall,* which presuppose the truth of a following complement clause (Kiparsky & Kiparsky, 1979), as well as the use of conditional sentences, political pronouns (usually *us* versus *them,* also referred to as inclusive and exclusive pronouns), physical verbs (which denote destruction/harassment/injury), collocation, adverbs and adverbial constructions (which describe the extent of oppression and how badly/urgently the victims need liberty) (Obeng, 2018, 2019), and graphology (especially the use of uppercase letters) as some of the linguistic strategies for challenging the dominant voices and fighting for liberty. Furthermore, Obeng identifies *contrastive pairs* also called *antithetic constructions,* deferential modes of address and reference, various politeness strategies, candor, inferencing, glittering generalities, emotional valence, intertextuality, and delegitimization (Chilton, 2004) of each other's action leading to the creation of an "other" worldview as some of the discourse-pragmatic markers that index the entwining of language and liberty in the Ghanaian political ecology.

Obeng concludes by noting that the fight for liberty becomes reality through language and that one's understanding of the law on liberty within the Ghanaian political ecology as well as one's recognition of the rights of individuals and the need to challenge dominant voices' illegitimate actions within a polity help to actualize the fight for liberty. Obeng calls attention to the fact that language behavior in Ghana's political ecology, as measured in terms of the candor of political actors like J. B. Danquah, Adu Boahen (a former presidential candidate of the New Patriotic Party), Paul Victor Ansah (a university professor and sociopolitical commentator), Elizabeth Ohene (a distinguished journalist), and many others, is complexly in sync with their stance on liberty and how liberty relates to law, ideology, and political power.

## REFERENCES

Chilton, Paul A. (2004). *Analysing Political Discourse: Theory and Practice.* London: Routledge.

Frempong, Alex Kaakyire Duku, and Bossman Asare. (2017). *Elections in Ghana (1951–2016)*, rev. and updated ed. Tema, Ghana: Digibooks Ghana Ltd.

Ichino, Nahomi, and Noah L. Nathan. (2013). "Do Primaries Improve Electoral Performance? Clientelism and Intra-Party Conflict in Ghana." *American Journal of Political Science* 57(2): 428–441.

Ichino, Nahomi, and Noah L. Nathan. (2017). "Primary Elections in New Democracies: The Evolution of Candidate Selection Methods in Ghana." Working paper. Ann Arbor: University of Michigan.

Kiparsky, Paul, and Carol Kiparsky. (1979). "Fact." In Donna Jo Napoli and Emily Norwood Rando (eds.), *Syntactic Argumentation*, 328–368. Washington, DC: Georgetown University Press.

Obeng, Samuel Gyasi. (2018). "Language and Liberty in Ghanaian Political Communication: A Critical Discourse Perspective." *Ghana Journal of Linguistics* 7(2): 199–224.

Obeng, Samuel Gyasi. (2019). "Grammatical Pragmatics: Language, Power and Liberty in African (Ghanaian) Political Discourse." *Discourse and Society* 33(5).

*Chapter Two*

# Ghana's Political Environment and the 2016 General Election

## Emmanuel Debrah

Ghana is widely regarded as an example of a successful democracy in Sub-Saharan Africa (Gyimah-Boadi, 2009; Ninsin, 2016; Ayee, 2017). Since making a transition from authoritarian to democratic rule in 1992, the political system has been consolidated through regular elections, albeit some have expressed concerns about growing weaknesses of some of the institutions and structures of governance (Gyimah-Boadi, 2009; Agyeman-Duah, 2005; Ayee, 2016). Except the contested 1992 founding election that ended in the opposition parties' boycott of the parliamentary election on the charge of a "stolen verdict," subsequent elections have produced relatively acceptable outcomes (Ayee, 2017; Debrah, 2015; Gyimah-Boadi, 2009). The December 7, 2016, poll was the seventh in Ghana's Fourth Republic, which began in 1992 when a liberal constitution was overwhelmingly adopted by the electorates in a well-attended referendum. Hence, of the studies reviewing Ghana's democratization, there is a concentration on the electoral mechanics and the institution for achieving credible elections (Debrah et al., 2018; Debrah, 2011; Agyeman-Duah, 2005; Gyimah-Boadi, 1999; Ayee, 1998; Lindberg & Morrison, 2008). Other scholars have spent significant time on the role that the nascent political parties have played in the democratic process. In particular, the National Democratic Congress (NDC) and the New Patriotic Party (NPP) have fielded candidates to contest all the elections and alternated power at several junctures (Ninsin, 2016; Gyimah-Boadi, 2009; Debrah, 2009; Nugent, 2001a). Analysis of the outcome of the elections has not escaped those who have undertaken empirical research into popular perceptions about intra-party democratic ethos of the political parties and electorates' choices at the polls (Debrah, 2015; Oquaye, 1995; Osei, 2013; Nugent, 2001b; Kelly & Benning, 2013; Jeffries, 1998).

However, the environmental context within which elections have been held and political parties have undertaken their electoral activities has been overlooked in the growing body of knowledge that has flooded the democratic literature. It is therefore professionally and academically necessary to devote valuable effort to probe the environmental context within which the political forces and the important actors made the debates and mobilized their supporters to make electoral decisions at the polls. Referencing the 2016 election is appropriate not only because it was the most competitive of all the elections, but also it was the first time that a woman chairperson was presiding over the Electoral Commission (EC) to conduct an election in the Fourth Republic following the retirement of Dr. Kwadwo Afari-Gyan, who conducted six elections. While the incumbent John Mahama was seeking a reelection, the fierce and astute opposition candidate Nana Akufo-Addo was contesting for president for a third time. Also, there were speculations in the media, though not based on founded empirical data analysis, that the Progressive People's Party (PPP) candidate Dr. Paa Kwesi Nduom could push the election to a second round. Against this backdrop, the chapter examines the political and electoral ambience that shaped the conduct and outcome of the election. Depending largely on secondary data sources, the chapter reviews information buried in the archives, electoral and print media reports, and articles from books and journals, among others, in order to explain how the environmental forces shaped the outcome of the election.

## THE LEGISLATIVE FRAMEWORK FOR ELECTIONS IN GHANA

Ghana's democracy has evolved significant and enduring legislations and instruments on which the conduct of elections has been anchored. The body of laws that has undergone periodic reforms is partly responsible for the relatively successful delivery of credible elections. Key among the statutes and instruments for managing competitive and peaceful elections are the following:

- Constitution of Ghana (1992, as amended)
- Representation of the People Act (1992, as amended)
- Presidential Elections Act (1992, as amended)
- Electoral Commission Act (1993, as amended)
- Political Parties Act (2000)
- Representation of the People (Constituencies) Instrument (2004)
- Public Elections (Registration of Voters) Regulations—C.I.72 (2012)
- Public Elections Regulations—C.I. 75 (2012)

- Public Elections Act—CI 75 (2012)
- Political Parties Code of Conduct (2012)

The electoral laws and systems that have been developed to direct Ghana's election are strict on the tenure of the president. In particular, the 1992 Fourth Republic Constitution unequivocally stipulates, "the President of Ghana is elected for a four-year term and can serve a maximum of two terms in office" (Republic of Ghana, 1992, p. 25). The electoral laws further stipulate that "the President shall be elected in a single national constituency on the basis of a majority system" (Republic of Ghana, 1992, p. 27). According to the electoral system, to win the presidential election, a candidate should obtain 50 percent + 1 of the total valid votes cast. The law adds that "if no candidate secures such a majority then two candidates that obtained the most votes go to a run-off election until a winner emerges" (Republic of Ghana, 1992, p. 26). The law designates the chairperson of the Electoral Commission (EC) as the returning officer for the election of the president. This means that the whole country is demarcated as a single electoral area in the presidential elections, which makes it easy for any voter to cast the ballot in any preferred polling station to choose the president (Republic of Ghana, 1992, p. 27).

On the other hand, in the parliamentary election, the country is delimited into several electoral constituencies and each voter chooses a candidate in a designated constituency. This provision conforms to the prevailing single-member constituency electoral system. Based on this rule, the EC divided the country into 275 constituencies. Therefore, voters elected 275 candidates—each representing a constituency—into Parliament to represent them. The electoral system is based on the *first-past-the-post*. The elected president holds office for four years and is eligible for reelection for another term, while members of Parliament (MPs) have unlimited tenure (Republic of Ghana, 1992, p. 25).

The EC that is mandated to conduct credible elections is the creation of two laws, namely the 1992 Constitution and Act 451, promulgated in 1993. The EC is a seven-member body comprising a chairman who is the image of the institution, two deputy chairpersons (who are responsible for operation, and finance and administration respectively), and four other non-portfolio members. The seven members in charge of the policy making constitute the body that manages the electoral processes by enacting policies as rules to guide the elections (Republic of Ghana, 1992). The policy is reduced into guidelines to direct several inter-related activities intended to regulate the behavior of the political actors and the professional election staffs that administer the process. All members of the EC are appointed by the president based on the expert advice of the Council of State (partly elected and partly appointed members of eminent statesmen), but it is largely perceived by the public as a dumping place for favorites of the government, rather than an "eminent chamber of non-partisan citizens" (Gyimah-Boadi, 1999, p. 23; Debrah, 2011). But the Council of State functions only in an advisory role and the president is not bound by its counsel. This limitation on the powers of the Council of State in the appointment process has heightened popular perception that the EC members are politically appointed because there are no real checks on those the president selects. Despite popular apprehensions about the objective recruitment of EC members, the institution is often regarded as independent, and has acted to inspire public confidence in its work even though the periodic expression of distrust of the EC persists (Gyimah-Boadi, 1999; Debrah, 2011).

Ghana's parent law and other subsidiary legislations outline, in considerable detail, the legal requirements and qualifications for participants who contest elections and citizens wishing to vote:

- Universal adult suffrage for citizens who are eighteen years of age and older
- Only citizens who are of sound mind, not ex-convicts, and who honor their tax obligations are eligible to contest or and vote in elections
- Registration of qualified voters and exhibition of the voter roll even though voting is not a compulsory obligation
- Registration and certification of political parties
- Holding of presidential and parliamentary election on the same day except the 1996 elections
- Holding of presidential run-off within twenty-one days where no winner emerges in the first round
- Secret balloting
- Appointment of returning and presiding officers and polling officials
- Monitoring and observation of the electoral process by representatives of political parties and candidates
- Counting of ballots immediately when polls close (Republic of Ghana, 2012)

In line with Article 42 of the Constitution that "every citizen of Ghana of eighteen years of age or above and of sound mind has the right to vote and is entitled to be registered as a voter for the purposes of public elections and referenda" (Republic of Ghana, 1992, p. 25), the EC enacted the Registration of Voters Regulation (C.I. 72) in 2012, a Constitutional Instrument that directed the registration of voters, including those who turned eighteen years, or more, in 2016.

However, there were controversies over the voter roll. The question was whether the process could lead to the cleaning of registered voters from the voter roll. The opposition parties led by the NPP demanded a fresh voter registration rather than a limited registration (Oquaye, 1995; NPP, 1992; Jeffries, 1998). It argued that the voter roll was inaccurate and flawed with double, underaged, and foreigners' registration. The uncertainties about getting a credible register loomed large because the EC could not come out clearly on how to deal with the cleaning of the voter roll (Citifmoline, 2016). The opposition contended that the issue of how to validate the voters' list (*no verification, no vote* in 2016) was pending at the Inter-party Advisory Committee (IPAC)—a forum that brings representatives of the parties and EC with donors as observers to dialogue on vexed issues regarding the management of the electoral process (Debrah, 2015; Gyimah-Boadi, 1999), but the EC indicated its preference for voters' validation at the exhibition of the register. The disagreement was worsened by an application filed at the Supreme Court, which prayed the apex court to order the EC to register all diaspora voters. By 2016, the diaspora voting legislation was only implemented for citizens in the Ghana Government Missions abroad, such as international peace keepers, embassy officials, persons on official duties, and students on scholarships through the Ministry of Foreign Affairs.[1]

The fear of the opposition was further informed by the revelations at the Supreme Court on how the EC handled the 2012 election and the final declaration of Mahama as having been validly elected even though unscientific public opinion gave the verdict to the opposition candidate, Nana Akufo-Addo (Modernghana.com, 2013). Besides, by the time the limited-registration-of-voters exercise commenced, none of the recommendations advanced by the Supreme Court for achieving a credible election had been implemented by the EC. For instance, in the limited-registration exercise, citizens continued to identify their status by using national health insurance cards, which the Supreme Court ruling discouraged (see Pulse.com, 2016). The appointment of the chairperson of the EC proved to be problematic because she was "lifted/transferred" from another independent constitutional body to chair the EC when Afari-Gyan retired. It was a novel practice in the governance system and sparked a huge public uproar. Regarded as a nonentity, immature, and inexperienced, she came under constant attacks from civil society and opposition parties—only the NDC and the government showered praises on her. Perceived to be overly confident and excited about her new role, several civil society groups and opposition parties dealt with her in a contemptuous manner because she seemed to be oblivious of the many lapses her actions and inactions created in the management of the electoral process (Clottey, 2016). For instance, she led the EC to propose a change of election date from December 7 to November 7, 2016, without recourse to the authority of Parliament. Also, the EC faced financial difficulties because the government did not respond to its request for the release of funds to implement the election time table. Yet, the EC concealed this valuable information from the public—which the public interpreted as a strategy of shielding the government from public backlash (Myjoyonline.com, 2015). Opposition-EC conflict worsened when the EC consistently ignored the opposition's suggestions on electoral reform by leaning on its independence—and arrogantly insisting that it could not be forced to act (Mensah, 2016). As the unresolved issues about compilation of fresh voter roll lingered, the opposition parties vowed to create their own parallel monitoring strategies outside the EC's framework (Mensah, 2016).

Mounting pressure on the EC from the opposition parties and civil society forced it to introduce electoral reforms. The EC set up a panel of experts to listen to the parties' positions on whether a new voters' register was necessary or not. In the end, a majority of the stakeholders did not accept a compilation of a register of new voters but agreed that since there were flaws in the register, there should be a clean-up exercise (Electoral Commission, 2016). The experts weighed two options: they argued that the periodic limited voter registration had not succeeded in cleaning the roll and backed the verification system because it could potentially eliminate registration errors. The EC further boosted voter confidence by promising to decentralize the transmission of election results from the election headquarters to subnational levels in order to allow for the public airing of election results as they came in from the regions. The EC also amended the legislation on handling of electoral offenses. It promised to make the provisional register available to each party after the exhibition period and to continue with the tradition of implementing measures for ensuring the transparency of the voter registration process by allowing agents of the parties to observe the daily registration at the centers and to authenticate daily records (Electoral Commission, 2016).

## THE POLITICAL CONTEXT OF THE ELECTION

In contrast to the one-party system adopted by Kwame Nkrumah and his CPP in the early 1960s (Chazan, 1983), Ghana propagated a liberal multi-party system in the Fourth Republic democratic dispensation, which has close to thirty registered political parties, including the following:

- National Democratic Congress (NDC)
- National Patriotic Party (NPP)
- Progressive People's Party (PPP)
- National Democratic Party (NDP)
- Convention People's Party (CPP)
- People's National Convention (PNC)
- Democratic People's Party (DPP)
- United Front Party (UFP)

- Independent People's Party (IPP)
- United Renaissance Party (UPP)
- New Vision Party (NVP)
- Ghana Freedom Party (GFP)
- Great Consolidated Popular Party (GCPP)
- All Peoples Congress (APC)
- Yes, People's Party (YPP)

Of these, the NDC and NPP have dominated the political landscape by alternating power in January 2001, 2009, and 2017. At every election, their cumulative popular votes have hovered around 90 percent of the total valid votes cast.[2] Yet, there is no state funding for their political programs (Arthur, 2017; Debrah, 2014; Kelly & Benning, 2013). In the preparation for the 2016 election, the governing NDC seemed well organized in terms of financial resources and party organization.

Formed in 1992 as a "social democratic party," the NDC's logo was an umbrella with the head of a dove at the tip with a blend of red, white, green, and black. Its motto is "Unity, Stability, and Development." The NDC won the 1992 and 1996 general election respectively under J. J. Rawlings. It lost in 2000 to the NPP but made a comeback in 2008 when Atta Mills defeated Nana Akufo-Addo in the presidential race. John Dramani Mahama won the 2012 presidential election with 50.7 percent of the votes (Morrison, 2004). In early intra-NDC contest in November 2015, Mahama was nominated as the presidential candidate for the 2016 general elections. On the other hand, the NPP, a liberal conservative center-right party having as its emblem the African elephant, with red, white, and blue symbols, was formed by the remnant of the politicians of yesteryear who controlled the economy and politics after the overthrow of Kwake Nkrumah's government by the NLC assisted by the CIA. Its leader, John Agyekum Kufuor, who took over from Albert Adu Boahene after the 1992 election, won in 2000 and was reelected in 2004, becoming president of the Republic (Morrison, 2004). The NPP rode back to power after its presidential candidate Nana Akufo-Addo won overwhelming popular support in the 2016 general election. Thus, the 2016 election was a two-party affair that pitted the incumbent John Mahama against opposition candidate Nana Akufo-Adddo. In the end, Akufo-Addo received 53.83 percent of the popular vote while Mahama garnered 50.7 percent (Electoral Commission, 2016).

## GOVERNMENT BEHAVIOR (ABUSES OF INCUMBENCY)

The incumbent president, John Dramani Mahama, who hails from Bole-Bamboi in the northern region of the country, was a former legislator and vice president under Professor E. A. Mills's administration and was sworn into office in June 2012 as the substantive president following the demise of the then president. Therefore, incumbency weighed heavily in favor of Mahama in the December 2012 elections. Even so, he narrowly won over Nana Akufo-Addo, the NPP presidential candidate, amidst accusations of election fraud by the incumbent's agents (Electoral Commission, 2012; Modernghana.com, 2013). The perennial abuse of incumbency (assumed or proven) is one of the sources of election controversies (Debrah, 2004, 2014; Cheeseman et al., 2017). This is because the electoral laws are silent on the commencement of election campaigns. Hence, the incumbent would often seize every opportunity in the course of performing state duties to launch his campaigns for the next election. These are often reflected in presidential speeches and visits to rural communities (Cheeseman et al., 2017; Myjoyonline, 2017). For instance, the NDC unveiled its election logistics such as campaign vehicles and multi-dollar party headquarters to the consternation of all. It utilized the services of state institutions such as the Non-Formal Education Program, National Commission of Civic Education, security agencies, local government officials such as regional ministers, district chief executives, and other state functionaries to mobilize mass support for its candidate John Mahama—the then president (Ghana Integrity Initiative, 2016).

Under the pretext of engaging the people or what was code-named "accounting to the people tour," the president John Mahama (the NDC presidential candidate) initiated a nationwide political campaign to showcase himself to the electorate. But the character of the country tours could not be divorced from political campaigns, as everywhere (communities) visited, he solicited the electorate's support for his reelection bid. The huge presidential entourage, including the profligate spending of public resources on campaign tours, were a financial cost to the state, yet the opposition candidates were denied the oxygen of state campaign funds—a real abuse of incumbency (Cheeseman et al., 2017; Myjoyonline, 2018).

President Mahama's grand campaign objectives included a plan to mobilize a lot of money through awarding contracts to his cronies—as many of the contracts had been executed through sole-sourcing rather than competitive tendering (Danquah Institute, 2016; Ghanamma.net, 2016). Members of the opposition accused the president of exploiting the public procurement process to buy off political clients in order to amass funds to oil the wheel of his political campaign. Next, the president turned to court the support of the influential groups and leaders in the society. Among them were prominent religious leaders (charismatic church pastors), paramount chiefs and sub-chiefs, students, and media anchors. To these groups and leaders (journalists, chiefs, celebrities, university girls), the president distributed cars to support their activities (Pulse.com, 2016; Ghanaweb.com, 2016). These presidential actions terrified the opposition parties and candidates. Also, senior NDC executives engaged in outreach missions to all the ten regions of the country to collect data to finalize the party manifesto. They had adequate resources to train party foot soldiers to undertake house-to-house canvassing, held town hall and workplace meetings, and bought allegiances of some charismatic pastors to rally their members in support of Mahama's candidature (Cheeseman et al., 2017).

Mahama, who rode to power on the promise of "A Better Ghana" and prosperity for the people, presided over an ailing economy, and at the time he was sworn in as president, the economy was already in a bad shape. He did little to turn it around and brought no real improvement in the living conditions of the people (Mbaku, 2016). Inflation soared; so too did lending rates from the banks. This poor management of the economy led to a severe energy crisis that accelerated the collapse of many businesses and imposed hardship on the population. With industries folding due to the protracted energy crisis, many private sector workers faced redundancy punishments from their employers. Even in the period where oil revenue was expected to help stimulate economic growth and development, there was a general complaint by state institutions of inadequate financial resources to carry out their responsibilities (Kontoh, 2016). But the government had been mindful of its campaign promises and so began talking to the International Monetary Fund (IMF), which in 2007 Kufuor's government had weaned itself from, for a possible recapitalization of the economy through a loan agreement (Kontoh, 2016). After signing onto the IMF bailout, the government received funding to resuscitate the economy, which facilitated the provision of some infrastructure projects in certain parts of the country albeit inadequate to transform the lives of the people, a majority of whom were poor (Ghanaweb.com, 2016). At the same time, the IMF conditionality restrained the government from opening up the public sector to the many youths that had graduated from polytechnics, universities, and other institutions. Even teacher and health professional trainees were denied employment. As a result, the country witnessed many industrial actions by public sector employees, which opposition forces hijacked to their political advantage (Ghanaweb.com, 2016; Myjoyonline.com, 2016).

Poor economic management was connected to corruption in government. The Mahama-NDC government was labeled as the one that had contracted more external loans than any other government; yet, the public believed that the resources leaked out through official corruption (Ghanaweb.com, 2018). His junior brother was widely perceived as the principal conduit for channeling state resources into the family's private accounts (Myjoyonline, 2016). A majority of the people thought that Mahama and his cronies benefited from the so-called "unprecedented" development projects the government claimed to have undertaken through contract inflations and kickbacks.

Furthermore, his critics (political opponents) attacked his opulent nepotism and ethnocentrism. He was accused of filling the legions of top bureaucratic and political posts with his family and ethnic group members (Ghanaweb.com, 2014). A few months before the December polls, the president "forced" the resignation of the governor of the Bank of Ghana, an Ewe, and replaced him with his tribe's man from the North. He extended the tenure of the Inspector General of Police (IGP), who also hails from his home region, after his retirement. In the ministerial sector, either the substantive minister or the deputy was from his ethnic group or the northern sector of the country. Also, the president and his NDC were accused of instigating intra-NPP conflict between the old guards and the youth, which led to the suspension of the party's chairman and general secretary; ethnocentric feeling was framed around the claim that a Nana Akufo-Addo win would deny the prospect ofr an Ashanti becoming president sooner, as well as another falsehood alleging that the NPP presidential candidate would not concede defeat if he lost the election (Myjoyonline.com, 2018).

It must be emphasized that the above narratives helped generate tension in the body politic and raised the political temperature extremely high. In part, the interparty conflicts occurred because the political parties lacked the internal capacity to nurture orderly civic actions in a sustainable manner. Indeed, the political parties were the cause of the violent attacks within and outside their parties' structures (Citinewsroom.com, 2016). The parties' uncontrolled actions were not surprising because it is commonplace that the parties incubate and train their own thugs, which they would then use to unleash terror on their opponents (Ghana News Agency, 2016). Known as "machomen," each party entertains "this paramilitary or security squad" to protect its core party members—perhaps, a sign of the lack of confidence in the police—as there is a general perception that state security is a politicized institution (Pulse.com, 2016). Again, violence was imminent because political parties' propaganda machinery taught the public that "every president runs for two terms." Hence, one of Mahama's campaign messages was to invoke the unwritten tradition of reelecting the incumbent president. His action suggested that it would be unfair for the electorate to deny him the benefit of the precedence of eight years mandate—therefore, the behavior of the president was perceived as a desperate attempt to enforce the two-term tradition. On its part, the opposition NPP regarded the election as a do-or-die affair. Its message to the electorate was that the NDC had completed the supposed eight years—that, the two-term mandate applied to the party rather than the president. Thus, counting from President Atta Mills the opposition charged that Mahama's four years completed the party/NDC's eight years and reminded the voters that the 2016 election was Nana Akufo-Addo's turn to ascend to political power. According to the NPP, just as Atta Mills stood for the third time before winning, it was Nana Akufo-Addo's third time of contesting as a presidential candidate and so must be made the next president (Newpatrioticparty.org, 2016).

Whereas the interparty anxieties pictured a political volatile environment and created doubts about the possibility of achieving a peaceful election, many politicians and political observers were optimistic that the political system has in-built mitigating factors that are self-regulating to absorb the tensions and preelection acrimonies. In the past, the political entrepreneurs had counted on the goodwill of the Electoral Commission (EC) and the Judiciary as "reliable conflict resolution bodies." The Ghanaian public continued to look up to these constitutional bodies to address any election-related conflicts despite the scandal that hit the judiciary via the discovery by international investigative journalist Anas Arimiyaw Anas, which revealed that corruption was deeply rooted in the judiciary, the evidence Anas provided about the extent to which corruption had undermined the administration of justice, and the resultant public disillusionment regarding the manner in which the Supreme Court ruled on the legitimacy of the 2012 presidential election (Clottey, 2016). Also, the political parties continued to value the role of the Inter-Party Advisory (IPAC) body to resolve interparty disagreements. Moreover, even after the Supreme Court's ruling on the election petition, the many legal litigations brought by the opposition groups against the EC and other state elements suggested growing popular trust and confidence in the judiciary.

Furthermore, the existence of some domestic not-for-profit and nonpartisan groups, such as religious groups and traditional rulers (chiefs), and the recently established Peace Council served as institutionalized structures for incubating peace in the body politic. Given that chiefs and religious leaders are highly revered by a majority of the population (even if some have shown partisanship tendencies), their interventions and advocacies brought peace and cohabitation among the differing groups and the people. In the wake of the interparty acrimonies, some prominent chiefs, Christian leaders, and Muslim leaders admonished their members and nonmembers to commit to a peaceful election. They ensured that politicians whose actions could undermine peace were publicly rebuked (Modernghana.com, 2016).

In the end, the voters rejected Mahama's second-term push and pronounced the NPP's Nana Akufo-Addo the next president of the Republic of Ghana with the announcement by the chairperson of the EC that the former had obtained 44.35 percent compared with the latter's 53.79 percent of the valid votes cast in the December 7, 2016, polls. Thus, Nana Akufo-Addo's win was made possible by the prevailing environmental forces and conditions, such as abuses of incumbency that proved to be counterproductive, as well as by the economy. Indeed, throughout the Fourth Republic the economy has always wielded an invisible foot in shaping the elections' outcome. In 2000 and 2008, similar economic difficulties faced the incumbent but while the nation survived the turbulence, it led to the political downfall of the incumbents—history was repeated in the 2016 elections (Debrah, 2009).

## CONCLUSION AND LESSONS

The chapter has highlighted the political and economic forces that shaped the outcome of the 2016 elections. The country's democratic culture, which supports multiparty politics, has produced significant interparty competition. The election saw many parties participating in the contest. Each party and candidate had the opportunity of selling their products to the electoral consumers or customers. The incumbent's political maneuverings aimed to outplay its opponents did not achieve their objective. The tension that the interparty games generated too was contained through peaceful bargaining made possible through the intervention of the IPAC and the efforts of eminent chiefs and faith-based groups' leaders. But the economic conditions helped to reinvent the wheel of political fortune by propelling the three-time opposition NPP candidate Nana Akufo-Addo to victory.

It has further shown that Ghana has a unique record of holding peaceful elections in the Fourth Republic. Its institutions are also resilient and remain a critical factor that has pulled the country from the brink of collapse over the years. Indeed, many stakeholders believe that there are to be found in Ghana a number of respected statesmen and women who stand above partisan politics and can be relied upon whenever society feels threatened by internal disorders (interparty tension and conflict). The presence of a growing number of religious leaders and chiefs provides security against shocks from political upheavals. Supported by a sea of vocal civil society and vociferous media anchors, the election process changed from the tide of imminent conflict to peaceful political bargaining and collaborative engagements. Above all, the experiences with the 1992 and 2012 elections, where rising political temperatures led to the opposition coalition's boycott of parliamentary polls after detecting massive fraud in the presidential election and a protracted presidential election petition at the Supreme Court, respectively, reminded voters and political parties to remain in the democratic tradition of competitive election instead of retrogressing into state collapse as was witnessed in Liberia, Sierra Leone, Rwanda, and Kenya, among others.

## NOTES

1. The application was brought by members of the Progressive Alliance Movement (PAM)—a New York State incorporated nonprofit organization that sought a Declaration that Applicants have fundamental human rights under Articles 17(2), 42, and 33(5) of the 1992 Constitution of the Republic of Ghana, the Representation of the People (Amendment) Act 2006 [Act 699] Article 13 of the African Charter on Human and People's Rights, Article 25 of

the International Covenant on Civil and Political Rights, Article 21 of the Universal Declaration of Human Rights and Protocol 1 (article 3) of the European Convention on Human Rights. The Court ruled on 2017.

2. As it was in previous elections, the total percentage votes of the opposition parties in the 2016 election was 1.86.

# REFERENCES

Agyeman-Duah, B. (2005). *Elections and Electoral Politics in Ghana's Fourth Republic.* Accra: Centre for Democratic Development.

Arthur, P. (2017). "Political Parties' Campaign Financing in Ghana's Fourth Republic: A Contribution to the Discourse." *Journal of Asian and African Studies* 52 (8): 1124–1140.

Ayee, J. R. A. (1998). Assesing the progress of Democacy and Good Goverannce in Africa: The Case of Ghana. unpan1.un.org/intradoc/groups/public/documents/cafrad/unpan008718. pdf.

Ayee, J. R. A. (2016). "Ghana Continues to Be a Beacon for Democracy in Africa." https:// blogs.lse.ac.uk/africaatlse/2016/12/12/ghana-continues-to-be-a-beacon-for-democracy-in-africa/.

Ayee, J. R. A. (2017). "Ghana's Elections of 7 December. 2016: A Post-Mortem." *South African Journal of International Affairs* 24 (3): 311–330.

Chazan, N. (1983). *An Anatomy of Ghanaian Politics: Managing Political Recession, 1969–1982.* Boulder, Colorado: Westview Press.

Cheeseman, Nic, Gabrielle Lynch, and Justin Willis. (2017). "Ghana: The Ebbing Power of Incumbency." *Journal of Democracy* 28 (2): 92–104.

Citifmonline.com (2016). "NDC Abusing Sole-Sourcing Rule for Personal Gain—NPP." https://www.ghanamma.net/2016/10/10/ndc-abusing-sole-sourcing-rule-for-personal-gain-npp/.

Citinewsroom.com. (2016). "Injured Victim of Election 2016 Violence Begs NPP for Help." https://citinewsroom.com/2018/09/11/injured-victim-of-election-2016-violence-begs-npp-for-help/.

Clottey, P. (2016). "Ghana Electoral Commission Ordered to Clean Up Voter Lists." https:// www.voanews.com/a/ghana-electoral-commission-ordered-clean-voter-lists/3317071.html.

Dailyguidenetwork.com. (2016). "EC Gave Us Voter's Register with 'Corrupted' Files—NPP." https://dailyguidenetwork.com/ec-gave-us-voters-register-corrupted-files-npp/.

Danquah Institute. (2016). "Ghana Loses $2bn in Sole-Sourced Contracts—Danquah Institute." https://www.graphic.com.gh/news/general-news/ghana-loses-2bn-in-sole-sourced-contracts-danquah-institute.html.

Debrah, E. (2004). "The Politics of Elections: Opposition and Incumbency Factor and the Ghanaian 2000 Elections." *African Insight* 2/3: 3–15.

Debrah, E. (2009). "The Economy and Regime Change in Ghana, 1992–2004." *Ghana Social Science Journal* 5 & 6 (1 & 2).

Debrah, E. (2011). "Measuring Governance Institutions' Success in Ghana: The Case of the Electoral Commission, 1993–2008." *African Studies* 70 (1): 25–46.

Debrah, E. (2014). "Intra-Party Democracy in Ghana: The Case of the NPP and NDC." *Journal of Power, Politics & Governance* 2 (3&4): 10–25.

Debrah, E. (2015). "Reforming Ghana's Electoral Process: Lessons and the Way Forward." *Journal of Law & Politics* 8 (1): 3–18.

Debrah, E. (2016). "The Ghanaian Voter and the 2008 General Election." *Politikon* 43 (3): 371–387.

Debrah, E., et al. (2018). "Does the Use of a Biometric System Guarantee an Acceptable Election's Outcome? Evidence from Ghana's 2012 Election." *African Studies* 77: 1–24.

Electoral Commission. (2012). Presidential Election Results. Accra: Electoral Commission.

Electoral Commission. (2016). "EC Implements 27 Reforms for Better Elections." http://www. ghana.gov.gh/index.php/en/media-center/news/2721-ec-implements-27-reforms-for-better-polls.

Ghana Integrity Initiative. (2016). Election 2016. GII cites NDC for vote buying, incumbency abuse. https://www.pulse.com.gh/.../election-2016-gii-cites-ndc-for-vote-buying-incumbency-a...

Ghana News Agency. (2016). "EU Expresses Concern over Clashes between NDC and NPP Supporters." https://www.ghanabusinessnews.com/2016/11/17/eu-expresses-concern-over-clashes-between-ndc-and-npp-supporters/.

Ghanaweb.com. (2014). "Ethnic Cleansing of Ashantis in Mahama's Government." https://www.ghanaweb.com/GhanaHomePage/features/Ethnic-Cleansing-of-Ashantis-in-Mahamas-Government-323258.

Ghanaweb. (2016). "Mahama Bribing Chiefs with V8s for Endorsements—NPP." https://www.ghanaweb.com/GhanaHomePage/NewsArchive/Mahama-bribing-Chiefs-with-V8s-for-endorsements-NPP-483530.

Ghanaweb.com. (2016). "TEWU Declares Strike Over." https://www.ghanaweb.com/GhanaHomePage/NewsArchive/TEWU-declares-strike-over-408139.

Ghanaweb.com. (2017). "Court Clears Ghanaians in Diaspora to Vote in 2020." https://www.ghanaweb.com/GhanaHomePage/NewsArchive/Court-clears-Ghanaians-in-diaspora-to-vote-in-2020-610657.

Ghanaweb.com. (2018). "Corruption Ranking Covered Corruption Cases under Mahama Gov't." https://www.ghanaweb.com/GhanaHomePage/NewsArchive/Corruption-ranking-covered-corruption-cases-under-Mahama-Government-628485#.

Ghanaweb.com. (2018). "Report: The Fall and Rise of Ghana's Debt." https://www.ghanaweb.com/GhanaHomePage/NewsArchive/Report-The-fall-and-rise-of-Ghana-s-debt-478949.

Gyimah-Boadi, E. (1999). "Ghana: The Challenge of Consolidating Democracy," In Richard Joseph (ed.), *State, Conflict and Democracy in Africa*. Boulder, CO: Lynne Rienner.

Gyimah-Boadi, E. (2009). "Another Step forward for Ghana." *Journal of Democracy* 20 (2): 138–152.

Jeffries, Richard. (1998). "The Ghanaian Elections of 1996: Towards the Consolidation of Democracy?" *African Affairs* 97 (387):189–208.

Kelly, Bob, and R. B. Benning. (2013). "The Ghanaian Elections of 2012." *Review of African Political Economy* 40 (137): 475–484.

Kontoh, Eric Kofi. (2016). "Will Economy Impact Ghana's Presidential Election?" citifmonline.com/2016/11/.../will-economy-impact-ghanas-presidential-elections-articl...

Lindberg, Staffan I, and Minion K. C. Morrison. (2008). "Are African Voters Really Ethnic or Clientelistic? Survey Evidence from Ghana." *Political Science Quarterly* 123 (1): 95–122.

Mbaku, J. M. (2016). "The Ghanaian Elections: 2016. African in Focus." https://www.brookings.edu/blog/africa-in-focus/2016/12/15/the-ghanaian-elections-2016/.

Mensah, N. Y. (2016). "Courting Controversies: Ghana's Electoral Commission under Fire Ahead of Close Elections." https://africanarguments.org/2016/10/31/courting-controversies-ghanas-electoral-commission-under-fire-ahead-of-close-elections/.

Modernghana.com. (2013). "How the Supreme Court Judges Ruled in the Election." https://www.modernghana.com/news/487157/how-the-supreme-court-judges-ruled-in-the-election-petition.html.

Modernghana.com. (2016). "Traditional Rulers Set Measures to Ensure Peaceful Election." https://www.modernghana.com/news/391959/traditional-rulers-set-measures-to-ensure-peaceful-election.html.

Morrison, M. K. (2004). "Political Parties in Ghana through Four Republics: A Path to Democratic Consolidation." *Comparative Politics* 36 (4): 421–442.

Myjoyonline.com. (2015). "Electoral Commission's Elections 2016 Budget Hit by ¢400m Cut." https://www.myjoyonline.com/politics/2015/December-21st/electoral-commissions-elections-2016-budget-hit-by-400m-cut.php.

Myjoyonline.com. (2016). "Day 3 of ECG workers' Strike: Consumers Denied Service." https://www.myjoyonline.com/news/2016/August-26th/day-3-of-ecg-workers-strike-consumers-denied-service.php.

Myjoyonline.com. (2016). "Mahama Is Buying Votes, Abusing Incumbency—GII." https://www.myjoyonline.com/politics/2016/August-17th/mahama-is-buying-votes-abusing-incumbency-gii.php.

Myjoyonline.com. (2016). "CORRUPTION: An Everlasting Item on Ghana's Elections Agenda." https://www.myjoyonline.com/opinion/2016/May-27th/corruption-an-everlasting-item-on-ghanas-elections-agenda.php.

Myjoyonline.com. (2018). "A Critique of Friends and Family Government." https://www.myjoyonline.com/opinion/2018/February-28th/a-critique-of-friends-and-family-government.php.

New Patriotic Party (NPP). (1992). *The Stolen Verdict*. Accra: NPP.

Newpatrioticparty.org. (2016). "Change Your Voting Pattern This Year—Akufo-Addo Appeals to Obom-Domeabra Residents." https://www.myjoyonline.com/politics/2016/September-22nd/change-your-voting-pattern-this-year-akufo-addo-to-obom-domeabra-residents.php.

Ninsin, K. A. (2016). *Issues in Ghana's Electoral Politics*. Accra: African Books Collective.

Nugent, Paul. (2001a). "Ethnicity as an Explanatory Factor in the Ghana 2000 Elections." *African Issues* 29 (1/2): 2–7.

Nugent, Paul. (2001b). "Winners, Losers and Also Rans: Money, Moral Authority and Voting Patterns in the Ghana 2000 Election." *African Affairs* 100 (400): 405–428.

Osei, Anja. (2013). "Political Parties in Ghana: Agents of Democracy?" *Journal of Contemporary African Studies* 31 (4): 543–563.

Oquaye, Mike. (1995). "The Ghanaian Elections of 1992: A Dissenting View." *African Affairs* 94 (375): 259–275.

Pulse.com. (2016). "Corruption: Mahama Accused of Bribing Chiefs with V8s." https://www.pulse.com.gh/ece-frontpage/corruption-mahama-accused-of-bribing-chiefs-with-v8s/ckvmmxx.

Pulse.com. (2016). "Election 2016 Ghana: Limited Voter Registration Exercise in Pictures." https://www.pulse.com.gh/ece-frontpage/election-2016-ghana-limited-voter-registration-exercise-in-pictures/qby733j.

Pulse.com. (2016). "Election 2016: Clean Voters' Register with Limited Registration." https://www.pulse.com.gh/ece-frontpage/election-2016-clean-voters-register-with-limited-registration-danquah-institute/qk1j2ys.

Pulse.com. (2016). Election 2016: Police: NDC Supporters under Violent Attacks from NPP." https://www.pulse.com.gh/ece-frontpage/election-2016-police-ndc-supporters-under-violent-attacks-from-npp-fanatics/h085q34.

Pulse.com. (2016). "JUSSAG: Judicial Service Workers Call Off Strike." https://www.pulse.com.gh/ece-frontpage/jussag-judicial-service-workers-call-off-strike/k09hlqt.

Republic of Ghana. (1992). *Constitution of Republic of Ghana*. Accra: Assembly Press.

Republic of Ghana. (2012). *Registration of Voters Regulation (C.I. 72)*. Accra: Assembly Press.

*Chapter Three*

# Election Campaign in Ghana's 2016 National Elections

## Seidu Alidu

After witnessing the quality of democracy that has emerged in the continent over the past two decades, scholars have become pessimistic about the prospect of a consolidated democracy for Africa (Lindberg and Morrison, 2008; Jeffries, 1998; Jeffries and Thomas, 1993; Gyimah-Boadi, 2015; Diamond, 2015; Aryee, 2011; Bratton, 1999; Levitsky & Way, 2015; Kurlantzick, 2011; Debrah, 2016). Scholars are particularly disappointed about the gradual erosion of democratic values in the earlier triumphant countries that became democratic when the Third Wave of democratization began (Huntington, 1991; Diamond, 2015). The waning in optimism occurred as the number of countries hitherto recognized as electoral democracies reduced from 120 to 116 in 2009, with no net improvement in the number of countries that practiced good democracy (Diamond, 2015). This development triggered anxiety and the sounding of the alarm bell. There was a creeping period of democratic recession in the world, and Africa in particular (Kurlantzick, 2011). The growing insurgence by terrorist cells, intra-tribal wars that have led to losses of personal liberties, lives, and displacement of the critical mass of the population, have helped to intensify the pessimism (Diamond, 2011).

Notwithstanding democratic decline, Ghana has consistently proved to be an example of electoral democracy. Since 1992, elections have become a four-year cycle ritual. Hence scholars dealing with the analysis of Ghana's democracy have paid glowing tributes to the elections rather than the dynamics of political communication—how the political parties and candidates have connected with the electorate (Lindberg, 2012; Jeffries, 1998; Gyimah-Boadi, 2011; Diamond, 2015). Of the number of studies that have examined elections in Ghana, the question of why the electorate has voted has received much attention (Debrah, 2016; Aryee, 2011). These scholars attributed the motivation for voting in the elections to political parties, government policies and programs, party loyalty, and ideological identities (Gyampo & Debrah, 2013; Aryee, 2011; Obeng-Odoom, 2013). While these explanations are relevant to our understanding of the voters' choices at the polls, they overlooked the critical and complex issues regarding how the potential duty bearers chose to connect with the electorate. Addressing political campaigning is crucial for our understanding of the election and its processes because many scholars believe that the nature of the electoral campaign determines, to a large extent, the direction of citizens' votes (Elischer, 2012). In particular, political campaign messages are used by voters to distinguish among the competing candidates in terms of their ability to communicate their policies to them (Heywood, 2007). For instance, the functionalists have argued that election campaigns are used by candidates that are very certain of losing an election to state a specific point of view; and for those that are certain of winning, it becomes nothing less than a tool for victory (Freeman, 2012). These theorists believe that voting is a comparative act in which electorates assess the campaign messages of competing political parties and their candidates and then vote for the candidate or party whose message appears convincing. Two factors are often important in the assessment: the caliber of candidates who contest for elections and the political party that each candidate represents (Freeman, 2012; Heywood, 2007).

Against this background, this paper answers three salient questions of how political parties and candidates interact with the electorates in order to obtain their votes. It accomplishes this goal by addressing these three interrelated questions. First, what was the nature and dynamics of the political parties' campaigns? Second, what were the salient issues in the campaign? Third, what was the messaging technique, how the parties disseminated the campaign issues to the electorate? Section one reviews the literature on democratization in order to set the theoretical and empirical context for interrogating these issues. Section two discusses the strategies used by the parties to engage the electorates. Section three concludes the paper with lessons for effective election campaigns in Ghana.

This paper relied on two major sources of data: secondary and primary. The secondary data was mainly a desk review of the literature on elections and campaigns in order to contextualize the debate and provide the necessary theoretical underpinning for explaining the central question. The primary data was extracted from two major sources: a nationwide post-election survey conducted by the Centre for Social Democracy (CSD) and the Department of Political Science of the University of Ghana of which the author was a member of the researcher. For the CSD research, 3,000 questionnaires were administered in all the ten administrative regions and targeted, at least, three constituencies in each region. This was complimented by focus group discussions of twelve to fifteen participants and a total of eighteen elite interviews. In the Department of Political Science survey, 5,000 questionnaires were administered in fifty constituencies across the country (i.e., 100 question-naires were administered per constituency). Electoral areas were selected using probability and simple random sampling techniques, five electoral areas were randomly selected per constituency, and 20 questionnaires were administered in each electoral area. Both surveys used the Statistical Package for the Social Sciences to analyze the data and followed strict ethical proce-dures during the data collection stage.

## THE PARTIES' CAMPAIGN STRATEGIES

As already indicated, the success of a political party in an election is depen-dent on the rigor campaign message it carries out to the electorate. This is because an effective and well-organized campaign could mitigate many elec-toral pitfalls (Heywood, 2007). Ghana's 1992 Constitution prescribes that national elections should be held once every four years (Republic of Ghana 1992). The national election is preceded by the choice of candidates to con-test on the ticket of the competing parties, or an individual may nominate himself/herself as independent (Republic of Ghana, 1992). The selection of the presidential candidate is also preceded by the election of party executive that in turn starts with the selection of local executives at the ward or branch, constituency and regional executives. The flagbearer of a party is mandated by the Constitution to pick a running mate to partner with him or her to engage the electorate in a national campaign. The running mate eventually becomes the vice president, should the political party secure victory in the election.

Both the Constitution of the National Democratic Congress (NDC) and the New Patriotic Party (NPP) prescribe that the election of the flagbearer should occur two years prior to the general election any time the party falls into opposition, and one year if it is the incumbent government. The party believes that these measures give adequate time to market the presidential candidate to the electorate. It is the choice of the party candidates to contest the presidential and parliamentary elections that generate internal political campaigns.

The two major political parties used different campaign methods and strategies to market their respective candidates to the voters. The NDC's campaign was largely elitist in character. The party's campaign was influ-enced by parallel campaign groups that operated with little coordination. (Stiftung, 2018; Alidu & Aggrey-Darkoh, 2018). The NDC created a multi-plicity of groups with personal agenda to stress in the election. They included groups such as "Celebrities for Mahama," "I Choose JM," "Scholars for

Mahama," "Babes for Mahama," "Zongo for Mahama," "Toaso Democrats," "Medics for Mahama," "*Boys Boys* for Mahama," "*Girls Girls* for Mahama" to mention a few (Alidu & Aggrey-Darkoh, 2018). Resources were channeled through these mushroomed and hurriedly established campaign machines even though they lacked direction and tenacity. To a large extent, these groups spent a greater part of their efforts and time on personal adoration and on immortalizing John Mahama's legacy rather than delivering the hard message to the voters. These complex groups were perceived as rival lobbyists seeking to capture a greater part of the post-election political bargaining—distribution of scarce national resources (Stiftung, 2018). The NDC elitist campaign was further evident in the caliber of people that composed the campaign team. While the NPP put the candidate and his running at the center, the NDC surrendered the campaign to renowned artists or celebrities, who were popular musicians, media anchors, and prominent businessmen (Department of Political Science Survey Report, 2017).

Another feature of the NDC's mode of campaign was its extravagant texture. The campaign, which began with a flamboyant manifesto launch, featured wealthy foreign celebrities from Nigeria including Chief Mamadu Dele of Ovation and Nkem Owoh of the popular "Osofia in London" movie fame who were not registered Ghanaian voters, yet they propagated the campaign agenda of the NDC presidential candidate. This was quite offensive to some voters (Stiftung, 2018). Compared to 2008 and 2012, the NDC embarked on a door-to-door campaign and addressed the needs and worries of the electorate; they moved from house to house, market to market, and community to community. Thus, the enthusiasm, which the previous elections generated in the voters, was completely missing in 2016. Some of the members of the party's top campaigners were accused of being hungry money seekers and of being snobbish for refusing to answer voters' phone calls on pertinent campaign issues (Stiftung, 2018).

The fact that the high-profiled NDC figures campaigned in luxurious vehicles fueled the perception that the NDC and its presidential candidate had become corrupt with the agenda to siphon the state's meager resources (Department of Political Science Survey Report, 2017). Yet, the paradox of the NDC campaign was that while it was resource-drawing, the teeming supporters looked for economic relief. Thus, the ostentatious campaign of the NDC was widely repudiated by a cross-section of the electorate. The opposition contended that at a time when the country was experiencing grave economic disorder, growing unemployment and poverty rates, the NDC could run lavish campaigns with taxpayers' money (Stiftung, 2018).

Furthermore, supporters of the party accused the campaigners of failing to manage and distribute campaign resources equitably (CSD, 2017). The manner in which the NDC distributed resources was not beneficial to the party in the 2016 elections. They were of the belief that the party spent too many resources trying to win the votes of electorate in the swing regions, knowing very well that those voters are influenced largely by the dominant party model and nothing will swing their votes from the traditional party they have always voted for (CSD, 2017). The consequence of this action was the complete neglect of the regions that have always been loyal and have voted for the NDC. For instance, voters compared the huge developmental investments made in the Ashanti, western, eastern, and central regions that usually (except Ashanti and eastern) swing to the meager investment made in the three northern regions and Volta region. Though it makes sense for a party to direct its campaign to win swing regions through investment, the NDC overly did it to the disadvantage of regions that have been its traditional stronghold (CSD, 2017). The net effect was that the NDC lost in these regions in whose development they had invested so much. In the Volta region for example, leading members of the NDC complained about the government's last-minute attempt to win their votes by dumping sand and construction equipment on the Accra-Ho highway. The discerning electorates were swayed by the NPP message of hope (Alidu & Aggrey-Darkoh, 2018).

The NDC campaign sought to market its presidential candidate, John Mahama, even though it constituted a small proportion of the strategy it adopted. Instead of a focus on the content of the party's manifesto, the campaigners of John Mahama concentrated on the personality of the candidate. He was presented as a successful president who deserved another term as did presidents Rawlings and Kufuor. Therefore, in line with the tradition of electoral politics in the Fourth Republic, the NDC campaign team was convinced that the reelection of Mahama was a "cool-chop" phenomenon (CSD, 2017).

On its part, the opposition NPP resorted to a grassroots-led, door-to-door campaign strategy. The party divided its campaign into three zones to reflect the geopolitical characteristics of Ghana's electoral politics, namely coastal, savannah, and middle belt. Prominent party figures and candidates rotated the three zones even though each had a particular campaign assignment to deliver in the designated campaign zone (Stiftung, 2018). The flagbearer, Nana Addo Danquah Akufo-Addo, pitched his camp in the coastal area of the country. The running mate, Dr. Mahamudu Bawumia, and other prominent party members from the three northern regions concentrated their campaign in the Savannah area. The third team was led by the former finance and education minister under the previous NPP government. Yaw Osafo Marfo took the middle belt. The three-pronged strategy was designed to hook the party and its candidate to grassroots electorate. In each of the zones, the core campaign team was joined by the regional, constituency, and ward executive members whose assignments included provision of the grassroots campaign infrastructure. The NPP campaign took the form of town hall meetings, encounters with voters at local events and ceremonies such as traditional festivals and church or mosque programs. Rarely did the campaign teams hold major rallies and durbar (and other public gatherings). These forms of campaigns were both suitable for the rural communities and cities: in the villages, the campaign teams reached out to the voters in the market squares, and church annual harvesting ceremonies, among others. In the urban and peri-urban communities, the campaign teams met voters at the town and council halls. The party's outreach campaigns extended to the youth, largely students in tertiary and secondary schools to excite them about the Free Senior High School agenda (CSD, 2017).

The NPP campaigners resorted to a strategy to neutralize the two-term syndrome that John Mahama sought to promote in his campaign. To do this, the NPP adopted an approach to suggest that there was a distinction between the party and candidate. Since John Mahama took over from president Atta-Mills, the NDC had served the maximum two terms the 1992 Constitution prescribed for a president (Stiftung, 2018; CSD, 2017). While the NDC sold its message to the urban areas through celebrities' pomp and pageantry, the NPP penetrated the rural and suburban communities with its campaign of a "finished term for Mahama." It responded heavily to the NDC campaign that sought to portray Mahama as a successful president by attacking the so-called Mahama's achievement (CSD, 2017). The NPP created the perception that John Mahama was corrupt and incompetent. The "Toaso" slogan was therefore seen as a continuation of corruption and incompetence; neither the NDC nor John Mahama (JM) was able to shake off this tag. This mode of campaigning affected both JM and the party's parliamentary candidates (PCs) (Alidu & Aggrey-Darkoh, 2018).

## DISSEMINATING THE CAMPAIGN MESSAGE TO VOTERS

There is consensus among scholars that the quality of a campaign is measured by the manner in which the message is delivered to the electorate (Freeman, 2012; Boafo-Arthur, 2004; Bob-Milliar, 2011; Debrah, 2004). According to these scholars, campaign messages may be delivered through a variety of methods including personal, electronic, print, and social media. Since democratic rejuvenation in 1992, the Ghanaian political parties and their candidates have utilized several channels to communicate to their supporters. In the run-up to the 2016 elections, in particular, the majority of the parties resorted to the electronic media. Findings from this study revealed that television was the most effective political campaign medium (37.7 percent), followed by radio (30.3 percent), even though the parties also resorted to social media (13.1 percent) and door to door (10.4 percent). Table 3.1 provides detailed responses from interviewees.

While the political parties and candidates that participated in the election used the media to reach out to the electorate, not all of them administered their messages effectively. For instance, a majority of the respondents (60 percent) said the NPP was more effective in the delivery of their campaign messages than the NDC. Only 28 percent claimed that the NDC's campaign message was effective (see table 3.2).

Asked why they think that the NPP delivered the most effective campaign message to the voters, 72 percent indicated that the party's policy information was concise, catchy, self-convincing, and related to their living conditions than that of the NDC. A minority of the respondents (21 percent) insisted that the NDC delivered an inspiring campaign message. Also, 67 percent of respondents affirmed the fact that the NDC's social media campaign was floppy. They observed that the NPP policy-led campaign captured the social media spaces to the extent that it set the agenda for the NDC and the government. According to 67 percent of the respondents, the social media campaign was especially apt and resonated with the youth and the new voters, which helped them to make informed decisions at the polls. The NPP strategy involved picking the most touted NDC policies in the area of infrastructural development and demonstrated the falsehood in the NDC advertised achievement to the voters. While the NPP spent time engaging with the rural voters through door-to-door campaigning with proven policy interventions that have the capacity to mitigate their economic woes, the NDC mounted loud speakers on top of pickup vehicles amid pomp and pageantry—which was much more of a fanfare than an aggressive policy message to voters (CSD, 2017).

**Table 3.1.   Which of these mediums was more effective to you in the messages that were delivered?**

| Valid Media | Frequency | Percent | Valid Percent | Cumulative Percent |
|---|---|---|---|---|
| Radio | 821 | 30.7 | 30.7 | 30.7 |
| TV | 998 | 37.3 | 37.3 | 68.0 |
| Newspaper | 57 | 2.1 | 2.1 | 70.1 |
| Posters | 45 | 1.7 | 1.7 | 71.8 |
| Social media | 350 | 13.1 | 13.1 | 84.9 |
| Billboards | 31 | 1.2 | 1.2 | 86.1 |
| Door-to-door | 278 | 10.4 | 10.4 | 96.4 |
| NR | 95 | 3.6 | 3.6 | 100.0 |
| Total | 2675 | 100.0 | 100.0 | |

Source: CSD (2017).

**Table 3.2.  Which party was more effective in the delivery of its campaign message?**

| Valid Parties | Frequency | Percent | Valid Percent | Cumulative Percent |
|---|---|---|---|---|
| NPP | 1630 | 60.9 | 60.9 | 60.9 |
| PPP | 127 | 4.7 | 4.7 | 65.7 |
| NDC | 769 | 28.7 | 28.7 | 94.4 |
| PNC | 7 | .3 | .3 | 94.7 |
| CPP | 22 | .8 | .8 | 95.5 |
| NDP | 4 | .1 | .1 | 95.7 |
| NR | 116 | 4.3 | 4.3 | 100.0 |
| Total | 2675 | 100.0 | 100.0 | |

Source: CSD (2017).

Furthermore, whereas the NPP resorted to close-contact campaigning by visiting the voters in town halls and market places, the NDC erected giant billboards across the country which showcased its presidential candidate in dramatic joyous mood—celebrating victory that was not imminent. Hence when asked to assess the effectiveness of the NDC style of campaigns, a whopping 78 percent described it as wasteful and a drain on state resources, even though there was no clear evidence that state resources were involved in the advertisements.

In terms of using party manifesto to motivate the electorate, the differences between the NDC and NPP were clear. The NPP promised a wide range of economic programs, which the NDC ridiculed as unrealistic but resonated well with the voters' overwhelming socioeconomic aspirations (Department of Political Science, 2017). The NPP manifesto articulated in simple terms how the policy proposals would be executed and their benefits for the voters. On the other hand, the NDC manifesto that was captured in the "Green Book" merely focused on what the government had accomplished even though a large amount of the population suffered from poverty-related conditions (Department of Political Science, 2017). While it may be a good campaign strategy to explain the achievements of the government to the electorate, the NDC mode of communicating the message through billboards, among others, spelt doom for it at the polls. Hence, of the total 669 respondents in the study, 509 said they voted for the NPP because it ran a focused campaign. They brought the issues to the doors, homes, and compounds (face-to-face), which excited the imaginations of the voters about a better and more prosperous Ghana than the NDC, who delivered its campaigns through billboards, pickup vehicles, loudspeakers, dancing, and music, blurring their understanding of the real message (CSD, 2017; Stiftung, 2018).

## CONCLUSION

This paper has attempted to show that voters need to be fed through campaign messages in order to make their voting decision at the polls. From this study, it is obvious that the NPP had a clearer policy message to the voters than the NDC. The former carefully chose its campaign message that related very well with the expectations of the voting population. Besides, the party's mode of delivering its campaigns and platforms placed it over the NDC in the popular assessment of the capability of the two to lead the people to the next four years. While the NPP resorted to a grassroots-led and humble door-to-door campaign strategy, the NDC adopted an elitist and flamboyant approach, which alienated the majority of its core supporters who are grass-roots-based.

In terms of recommendation and policy, this chapter draws attention to an already important factor that potentially influences electoral victory but with less attention than has been given to it in previous literature. The tendency of political parties and their candidates to focus on the elite by engaging in urban-style campaigns that deploy sophisticated media tools such as billboards and the deployment of celebrities is a counterproductive to an efficient campaign because it produces little impact on voters. Rather, investing confidence in sociological factors including ethnicity and regionalism as well as the political parties that present them the platform to win elections has reduced the level of attention paid to electoral campaigns and the role of the media in them. Moving forward, equal attention should be given to the media and electoral campaign strategies just as it is done to the policies and the caliber of candidate elected to lead the party.

## REFERENCES

Alidu, S., and Aggrey-Darkoh, E. (2018). "Rational Voting in National Elections: The 2012 and 2016 Elections in Perspective." *Ghana Social Science Journal* 15(1): 98–121.

Aryee, Joseph R. A. (2011). "Manifestos and Elections in Ghana's Fourth Republic." *South African Journal of International Affairs* 18(3): 367–384.

Boafo-Arthur, K. (2004). "The 2004 General Elections: An Overview." In Boafo-Arthur, K. (ed.) *Voting for Democracy in Ghana: The 2004 Elections in Perspective* (Vol. 1), Accra: Freedom Publications.

Bob-Milliar, G. M. (2011). "'Tenygeyng gbengbeng! (We are holding the Umbrella very tight)': Explaining the Popularity of the NDC in the Upper West Region of Ghana." *Africa: Journal of the International African Institute* 81(3): 455–473.

Bob-Milliar, George M. (2012). "Political Party Activism in Ghana: Factors Influencing the Decision of the Politically Active to Join a Political Party." *Democratization* 19(4): 668–689.

Bratton, M. (1999). "Second Elections in Africa." In L. Diamond and M. Platner (eds.), *Democratization in Africa*. Baltimore: John Hopkins University Press.

Chazan, N. (1983). *An Anatomy of Ghanaian Politics: Managing Recession 1969–1982*. Boulder, CO: Westview Press.

CSD (2017). "The 2016 Post-election Survey: Accounting for the Defeat of the NDC (The Youth Perspective) (unpublished).

Debrah, E. (2004). "The Electoral Process and the 2000 General Elections in Ghana." In T. Lumumba-Kasongo (ed.), *Liberal Democracy and Its Critics in Africa: Political Dysfunction and the Struggle for Social Progress*. London: Zed Books.

Debrah, E. (2016). "The Ghanaian Voter and the 2008 General Election" *Politikon* 43(3): 1–17.

Department of Political Science. (2017). "Post-2016 Election Survey" (unpublished).

Diamond, L. (2011). "Why Democracies Survive." *Journal of Democracy* 22(1): 17–30.

Diamond, L. (2015). "Facing Up to the Democratic Recession." *Journal of Democracy* 26(1): 141–155.

Dunn, J. 1975. "Politics in Asunafo." In D. Austin and R. Luckham (eds.), *Politicians and Soldiers in Ghana*. London: Frank Cass.

Elischer, Sebastian. (2012). "Measuring and Comparing Party Ideology in Non-Industrialized Societies: Taking Party Manifesto Research to Africa." *Democratization* 19(4): 642–667.

Freeman, P. (2012). *How to Win an Election: An Ancient Guide for Modern Politicians*. Princeton: Princeton University Press

Gyampo, R. E. V., and Emmanuel Debrah. (2013). "The Youth and Party Manifestos in Ghanaian Politics: The Case of the 2012 General Elections." *Journal of African Elections* 12(2): 96–114.

Gyampo, R. E. V. (2012). "The Youth and Political Ideology in Ghanaian Politics: The Case of the Fourth Republic." *Africa Development* 37(2): 137–165.

Gyimah-Boadi, E. (2015). "Is Democracy in Decline?" *Journal of Democracy* 26(1).

Heywood, A. (2007). *Politics*. (3rd ed.). Palgrave MacMillan Press.

Huntington, S. (1991). *The Third Wave: Democratization in the Late Twentieth Century*. Norman: University of Oklahoma Press.

Ishiyama, John. (2012). "Explaining Ethnic Bloc Voting in Africa." *Democratization* 19(4): 761–788.

Jeffries, R. (1998). "The Ghanaian Elections of 1996: Towards the Consolidation of Democracy." *African Affairs* 97(387): 189–208.

Jeffries, R., and Thomas, C. (1993). "The Ghanaian Elections of 1992." *African Affairs* 92(368): 331–366.

Konteh, R. (2007). "The Role of Youth in Ensuring Peaceful Elections." Report on a conference of West African political parties organized by the IEA-Ghana in Accra, April 2.

Kurlantzick, J. (2011). "The Great Democracy Meltdown: Why the World Is Becoming Less Free." *New Republic* 242(4903): 12–15.

Levitsky, S., and L. Way. (2015). "The Myth of Democratic Recession." *Journal of Democracy* 26(1): 46–53.

Lindberg, S., and M. C. K. Morrison. (2008). "Are African Voters Really Ethnic or Clientelistic? Survey Evidence from Ghana." *Political Science Quarterly* 123(1): 95–122.

Obeng-Odoom, F. (2013) "The Nature of Ideology in Ghana's 2012 Elections." *Journal of African Elections* 12(2): 75–95.

Republic of Ghana. (1992). Constitution of the Republic of Ghana.

Stiftung, Friedrich Ebert. (2016). *Elections 2012*. Accra: Friedrich Ebert Stiftung Ghana.

Stiftung, Friedrich Ebert. (2018). *Elections 2016*. Accra: Friedrich Ebert Stiftung Ghana.

Wayo-Seini, A. (2006). "Does Party Philosophy Matter?" Report of conference of political parties organized by the IEA-Ghana at Akosombo, October 28.

*Chapter Four*

# Communicating with the Electorate in the 2016 Elections

*Did the Political Parties and Their Candidates Lean on the Issues?*

## Richard Asante

The literature on Western democracy projects the electorate in older democracies as rational in their choices of candidates at the polls (Down, 1957; Dalton, 2000; Dalton & Klingemann, 2011; De Vries, 2016). These Western scholars claim that voters in developed democracies regularly cast their votes to choose leaders based on policies presented to them by the candidates. In particular, Downs (1957) insisted that voters in the United States calculate benefits they obtain from voting before they cast their ballot for a candidate (i.e., voters' choices are based on the expected benefits from candidates' campaign messages). Political parties in developed democracies, therefore, develop comprehensive manifestoes with which they conduct their political campaigns (Thimsen, 2017; Swoyer, 2016; Southwell, 2016; Werner, 1997). For instance, in developed democracies, political parties' platforms capture the most salient national issues that relate to the economy such as health, education, employment, and family issues, among others (Lewis-Beck, 1988; Nadeau, Lewis-Beck & Bélanger, 2013; Dassonneville & Dejaeghere, 2014). The economic-voting thesis postulates that when the economy is good, the rational Western voters will reward the incumbent with their votes. Conversely, when the economy is bad, the voters will punish the incumbent by casting their votes for the opposition (Tufte, 1978; Key & Cummings, 1966; Fiorina, 1981; Lewis-Beck & Stegmaier, 2007). According to Anthony Downs (1957: 39), voters look to the future: "[W]hen a man votes, he is helping to select the government which will govern him during the coming election period. He makes his decisions by comparing future performances he expects from the competing parties." Thus, the orientation of the Western scholars regarding voters' voting decision is that they look to both the past and future economic conditions and vote according to the improved living conditions over the years or expected benefits to be gained. The question is left unanswered on issues relating to race, gay rights, abortion, the Supreme Court, and many others issues that significantly impact elections in such developed democracies.

On the contrary, for a long time, most Western political scientists that carried out studies on African democratization presented conclusions suggesting that African voters are irrational in their choices of candidates at the polls. They observed that the African political parties and the campaigns they pursue during elections are neither programmatic nor issue-based in content. Rather voters' choices are driven largely by identity politics (Bates, 1974; Sadie, Patel, & Baldry, 2016; Weitz-Shapiro, 2012) or what Lonsdale (1994) referred to as political tribalism and ethnic censuses (Horowitz, 1991). Guelke (1996) and Ferree (2006), for example, have described elections in South Africa as nothing more than "racial" census. A growing number of some African scholars have also revealed the prevalence of ethnicity in the voting patterns of elections that have been held under Ghana's Fourth Republic (Nugent, 1999; Frempong, 2001; Gyimah-Boadi & Asante, 2006; Asante, 2013; Jockers, Kohnert, & Nugent, 2009; Lindberg & Morrison, 2005; Debrah, Seidu, & Owusu-Mensah, 2016).

Similarly, while praising the sustained momentum of democratic practice and consolidation through the immense role of political parties, as well as print and electronic media, some scholars observed that candidates and parties' campaigns have been characterized by personality attacks, insults, the use of inflammatory language, derogatory remarks, hate speech, and violence (Anebo, 2006; Gyimah-Boadi, 2009; Asante, 2013; Gyampo & Debrah, 2013). It has been contended that the non-issue-based politics often perpetrated by the two dominant parties in Ghana's politics, namely the New Patriotic Party (NPP) and National Democratic Congress (NDC), heightened suspicion, fear, panic, and tensions in the body politic (Commonwealth Observer Group, 2016; European Union Election Observation Mission, 2016), and the opposition parties have proven to be incapable of convincing voters to "take them as the alternative" (Gyimah-Boadi, 2009; Asante, 2006; Young, 2002; Posner, 2005; Bratton, 2013; Bratton, Bhavnani, & Chen, 2012; Aryee, 2011).

Against this backdrop, this paper examines the Ghanaian political campaign landscape in order to determine how parties and their candidates interacted with the voters. Specifically, it examines the plausibility of the claim that Ghanaian voters are nonrational in their choices at the polls. It also examines the extent to which political parties and their candidates were able to communicate with voters on the salient national issues. What were the contents of the parties and candidates' campaign messages? It asks what particular messages influenced the voters' choices of candidates at the polls and what lesson can be learned from communication of Ghanaian political parties and candidates with voters. It draws data from secondary sources such as published books, articles from journals, and speeches by politicians (documented and recorded for newspaper, television, radio, and Internet sources, among others). The information obtained from these various sources were synthesized to establish whether the political parties' message delivered on the campaign platforms were issue-based or not.

## THE PARTICIPANTS AND CONTEXT OF THE 2016 ELECTION

The 2016 election was Ghana's seventh general election held since returning to a multiparty democracy in 1992. The 1992 Constitution and the Political Parties Act established the legal framework for conducting elections in Ghana. These laws seek to guarantee an independent electoral commission with the responsibility of organizing elections that would be free and fair, the right to vote and be voted for, and freedom of assembly, association, expression, and movement (Republic of Ghana, 1992). By the time official political campaigns commenced in June 2016, all the political parties had conducted their primaries to choose their presidential and parliamentary candidates. Seven presidential candidates made up of six allied political parties and one independent were cleared by the Electoral Commission (EC) to contest the 2016 polls. They were as follows:

1. Nana Akufo-Addo—New Patriotic Party (NPP)
2. John Dramani Mahama—National Democratic Congress (NDC)
3. Papa Kwesi Nduom—Progressive People's Party (PPP)
4. Ivor Kobina Greenstreet—Convention People's Party (CPP)
5. Edward Mahama—People's National Convention (PNC)
6. Nana Konadu Agyeman—Rawlings National Democratic Party (NDP)
7. Jacob Osei Yeboah—Independent

The stakes in the 2016 presidential and parliamentary elections were much higher than the previous elections due to the political and environmental dynamics. Since 1992, elections in Ghana have become a two-horse race between the NPP and NDC. Election 2016 was to test whether the ruling social democratic/center-left NDC would solidify its hold as a dominant party in Ghana or the main opposition center-right NPP that governed the country from 2001 to 2008 was resilient enough to wrestle power from the

NDC. The election was also about which of the minor opposition parties would emerge as a third force or whether the independent candidate could cause an upset. Also, the NDC had enjoyed two full terms in power from 1993 to 2000, and from 2009 to 2016 compared to the NPP, 2001–2008. The opposition NPP was determined to return to power. Its presidential candidate, Nana Akuffo-Addo, was contesting elections for the third consecutive time (2008, 2012, 2016—in each of these, he was unsuccessful) and at seventy-two years of age, it could possibly be his last chance to bid for political power. The NDC, on the other hand, had some significant advantages over the NPP: the party enjoyed tremendous incumbency advantages. Having been forced into opposition by the NPP after the 2000 elections, losing all the perks that come with political power and office, leading members of the party frequently expressed their frustration and complained that life in opposition was a "hell" (Asante, 2013). As a result, since regaining power from the NPP in 2009, the party was determined to consolidate its grip on political power. Furthermore, the incumbent NDC president, John Mahama was determined to complete a second four-year term (two full terms) in office. A loss would be embarrassing and will be the first time a sitting president had failed to win a second term. Besides, Mahama had beaten Akuffo-Addo by about 300,000 votes in the contested 2012 presidential election.

These aside, it is important to point out that an important feature of elections in Ghana since 1992 is that political parties mount spirited and fierce campaigns by crisscrossing the country to canvass for votes (Asante, 2013). The political parties that satisfy the requirements often develop and launch their manifestos with which they set out to market or sell their policies and programs as well as presidential and parliamentary candidates (products) to the electorates (customers/political clients) (National Democratic Congress, 2016; New Patriotic Party, 2016). The laws governing elections in Ghana do not define the official date of starting political campaigns; however, parties are required to end campaigning twenty-four hours before polling day (Republic of Ghana, 2000). Since 1992 political parties' campaign activities in the election year often start slowly around May then gather momentum in October and intensify in November until the polling day on December 7. The campaign period is always preceded by parties' primaries to elect their presidential and parliamentary candidates.

## PERSONALISM, SLOGANISM, AND INSULTS AS CAMPAIGN MESSAGE

Did the political parties and their candidates that contested the 2016 general elections resort to non-issue campaigns? The thesis that African politics is dominated by personalized campaign was somewhat evident in the candidates' campaign platforms, albeit minimally. Thus, aspects of the political parties' campaigns were devoted to personal attacks even though it constituted a small proportion of the overall activities of the candidates. In particular, the NDC and its presidential candidate were caught in an erroneous "feeling of continuity in power" slogan. John Mahama consistently deployed slogans in local languages, such as "Nooooo abaa baser" (to wit) "we are not going back" (Myjoyonline, December 17, 2016). In order to communicate to the opposition that it had gone ahead of them to the seat of government (i.e., run faster than them in the political race) he resorted to the celebrity Usain Bolt's style of declaring his track race victory by stretching his arms long to say that "I am ahead of all of you." In similar fashion, Mahama turned his campaigns to victory songs rapped in local slogans captured in a Ga dialect, "*ehejorbodorr*" meaning, "we are going forward." The most dramatic of all catchphrases used by the NDC campaigners was a song composed in Ga dialect, "*Onaapo*" that is to say, "you wouldn't even get" (Peacefmonline, March 27, 2017). The most debilitating part of the non-issue campaign was the collection of artistic impressionistic infrastructure pictures in the blue book published by the Ministry of Communication (Ministry of Communication, 2015) in which the NDC did something close to photoshopping of nonexisting infrastructural projects to convince voters of a good job done (Peacefmonline, April 11, 2008; Ghanaweb, May 22, 2018). The non-issue-focused campaign advanced by the NDC was captured in the post-election defeat inquiry committee set up by the party to identify the forces and events that spelled doom for the presidential candidate who trailed behind the NPP Nana Akufo-Addo by over a million votes (Myjoyonline, December 17, 2016). One of the party's stalwarts, Ekow Spio-Grabrah, a communication expert, lamented how "the 2016 NDC campaign was reduced to insults and slogans instead of the salient issues that occupied center stage of the NPP campaign" (Myjoyonline, October 27, 2017).

Next, the parties' campaigns were denigrated with interpersonal insults with the NDC launching the heaviest scathing attacks on his arch rival Nana Akufo-Addo, the NPP presidential candidate. The Mahama campaigners denigrated Nana Addo with derogatory phrases such as "the short man" to convey the message to his supporters that the seat of government is not available for those with height challenges (Ghanaweb, January 28, 2017). Nana Akuffo-Addo was presented in the mass media aligned to the incumbent as politically nonperforming, power-hungry, and a promoter of violence (Myjoyonline, March 27, 2016). The NDC resorted to a replay of old campaign rhetoric, which the NPP candidate used in previous elections, namely "all die be die" (every means by which one dies is death). The NDC further ridiculed the NPP candidate as an old man who is not fit for a presidential job that demands sharpness, youthful strength, and charisma, qualities that were not available to the NPP candidate but were present in the NDC candidate

(Todayghana, December 5, 2016). According to the NDC, a vote for Nana Akufo-Addo implied a wasted resource since the old man would not survive one term—and Ghanaians would be called to go to the polls to elect a new leader (Ghanaweb, October 24, 2016). The NDC media anchors descended on the NPP candidate on a daily basis with personal attacks. The NDC communicators labeled Nana Akuffo-Addo as a weak man who could not promote peace, order, and stability in the NPP (Graphiconline, August 27, 2017). They accused him of presiding over a fragmented party, cleaved by factionalists who would extend the disunity to the government and destroy the developmental gains achieved under the NDC first term (Asante, 2016). Also, instead of focusing on the issue, the NPP turned its attention on Amisah-Arthur, the vice presidential candidate of the NDC and an economist chosen to neutralize the NPP Bawumia's effect, describing him as an incompetent man bereft of ideas about the solution to the economy's woes, intellectually offline, and a liability to the NDC campaign (Myjoyonline, December 17, 2016).

## DEBATING THE SALIENT NATIONAL ISSUES

Personalism aside, did the candidates' campaigns address the critical national socioeconomic issues that voters expected from them? The above discourse would sway even the most sanguine political analyst to conclude that politics in Ghana is largely non-issue. However, a thorough examination of the campaign landscape shows that it was issue focused. The parties' campaign discourse was steeped in the essential socioeconomic and political issues that voters look up to the candidates to address when they secured the popular mandate.

## THE ECONOMY AS VALANCE VOTING ISSUE

Despite the party's claim of maintaining stability, vast improvements and a facelift of the construction sector, and the rehabilitation of infrastructure, the NDC carried significant liabilities going into the 2016 elections. Ghana's 2016 presidential and parliamentary polls were conducted in an environment characterized by economic decadence—all of which were laid at the door step of the incumbent president John Mahama's administration. A major issue that dominated the 2016 general elections was the economy, which largely revolved around energy production and supply, education, infrastructure, health, poverty, and unemployment, among others. High cost of living, rising inflation, and rising unemployment left many Ghanaians frustrated (Asante, 2016). With the discovery of oil in 2010, some governance experts predicted that Ghana would be one of Africa's economically successful countries. However, Ghanaians were yet to enjoy the oil dividends and the benefits of growth, which were touted by the NDC government (Bertelsmann Stiftung, 2016; Gyimah-Boadi & Prempeh, 2012). Ranked 138th out of 187 countries in the 2014 Human Development Index, the country suffered after the fall in global prices of some key export commodities, such as oil, gold, and cocoa (Bertelsmann Stiftung, 2016). A three-year-long electricity crisis popularly referred to as *dumsor* (unstable power supply), led to the shutdown of industries leading to job losses with debilitating effects on the economy (Asante, 2016). It is not surprising that the 2016 elections were dominated by the country's deteriorating economy. The ailing economy, which was later grounded in the intensive care unit, could not even be resuscitated by the IMF bailout plan. Recognizing that the economy underpinned the campaign, President Mahama resorted to what he claimed was his excellent and unparalleled record of infrastructural development including the water supply in Accra; the construction of roads, bridges, and expressways, including the Nkrumah Interchange in Accra; and the rehabilitation of hospitals and airports (Ghanaweb, August 16, 2016). His campaign on continuity urged the voters to give him another term to complete his infrastructural projects. Throughout the campaign period, the president with the party's communicators and campaign team marketed the party's blue book, a document the government had put together cataloguing several infrastructural projects initiated by the Mahama administration (Ministry of Communication, 2016).

Bolstered by a failing economy characterized by deteriorating living conditions, the opposition parties attacked Mahama's disappointing economic management record that included microeconomic deficiencies, namely slow economic growth, excessive borrowing and indebtedness, high currency depreciation, high inflation and interest rates (see tables 4.1–4.4), and rising cost of living caused in part by the hikes in tariffs on utilities (Asante, 2016). The Ghana cedi depreciated by 14.8 percent, 12.6 percent, and 7.8 percent against the U.S. dollar, the pound sterling, and the euro, respectively, compared to a much higher depreciation of 31.2 percent, 29.3 percent, and 23.6 percent recorded in the corresponding period of 2014 (table 4.2). The public debt stock stood at 69.12 percent of gross domestic product (GDP) as at the end of September 2015, a slight decline from 70.15 percent of GDP in December 2014 (table 4.3). The provisional debt stock as of September 2015 stood at US$24,285.07, US$14,357.91 million for external debt and US$9,927.16 million for domestic debt (table 4.4). Inflation for the month of November shot up to 17.6 percent from 17.4 percent in October (table 4.1). The economic malaise was blamed on incompetence of the government.

Thus, in the context of these severe economic challenges with disillusioned and anxious voters looking for an economic savior, the NPP's Nana Akufo-Addo emerged as the candidate with the hope campaign message. The NPP manifesto was catchy, forward-looking, and framed around economic

Table 4.1.    Selected macroeconomic indicators.

| Macroeconomic Indicators | Percentage (%) | Year |
|---|---|---|
| Inflation | 17.4 | October 2015 |
| Interest rate | 25 | September 2015 |
| Treasury bill | 25.9 | September 2015 |

*Source:* 2016 *Budget of The Republic of Ghana.*

liberation, which captured the voters' overwhelming economic aspirations. Indeed, the opposition campaign message focused on "bread and butter issues" that were intended to leave a relatively lasting and memorable impression on the anxious voters. The NPP presidential candidate captured the economic development issues in catchphrases such as "One-District-One-Factory"; "One-Village-One-Dam"; "Free Senior High School"; and "One-District-One-Million-Dollars"; and others. In particular, the NPP candidate promised to reverse the Accra-Kumasi-Takoradi development model, where major infrastructure development and investments had been concentrated in these three major cities to the disadvantage of the rural and suburban areas (Myjoyonline, October 19, 2016). The promise to spread the national cake evenly across the country to bring real economic benefits to the excluded communities was all the more portentous. Nana Akufo-Addo excited the voters that the One-District-One-Factory concept was carefully designed to build at least one factory in each district for the purpose of creating jobs for the unemployed in the 216 local government units, a program geared toward reversing the north-south and rural-urban inequality in the country (Myjoyonline, August 31, 2016; Graphiconline, September 12, 2017).

It also promised to reactivate social protection and intervention programs such as the National Health Insurance (NHIS), School Feeding Programme (SFP), and National Youth Employment Programme that had been run down under the NDC-Mahama administration (Peacefmonline, September 18, 2017). The NPP promised to allocate one million dollars to each of the 275 constituencies for poverty alleviation (Myjoyonline, August 31, 2016). According to Nana Akufo-Addo, the mismanagement and incompetency of the Mahama-led government was evident in the failing NHIS, which was saddled with a huge debt of about GH¢1.2 billion (US$249,066,000) resulting in the virtual withdrawal of most healthcare service providers. Similarly, the School Feeding Programme (SFP) was in huge debt to warrant the cessation of food supplies to the schools (Peacefmonline, June 14, 2017). The NDC and Mahama's response to the NPP's promise of One-Village-One-Dam was to describe the program unachievable, and as a bad policy that will end up in failure thereby creating breeding grounds for mosquitoes in the targeted communities. Also, Dr. Mahamadu Bawumia, the running mate of Nana Akufo-

**Table 4.2. Rate of depreciation of the Ghana cedi.**

| Currency | 2015 (%) | 2014 (%) |
|---|---|---|
| US Dollar | 14.8 | 31.2 |
| Pound Sterling | 12.6 | 29.3 |
| Euro | 7.8 | 23.6 |

*Source:* 2016 Budgets of Republic of Ghana.

Addo, used lectures, town hall meetings, and rallies to show dexterity in evidence-based research (statistical data instrument) to engage in public discourse over economic conditions (largely pictured as standing on weak foundation) caused by the NDC incompetence (Peacefmonline, July 11, 2016). The opposition NPP chastised the NDC manifesto theme—Changing Lives, Transforming Ghana—as "deforming Ghana, deforming lives" (Ghanaweb, September 20, 2016). At a press conference captioned "Promises made, promises broken," the NPP slammed President John Mahama and his NDC for the poor handling of the economy during the past four years (Ghanaweb, September 20, 2016). President Mahama was described as the worst manager of the cedi in the last fifteen years (Ghanaweb, September 20, 2016). The NPP argued that the prospects of another four years under incompetent Mahama and the NDC would be catastrophic, with dire consequences for the livelihood of Ghanaians (Ghanaweb, September 20, 2016). For his part, Dr. Paa Kwesi Nduom, the presidential candidate of the Progressive People's Party (PPP), attacked Mahama's economy as being "sick and getting sicker" (Peacefmonline, November 2, 2015).

In reference to economic management comparison, the NPP recounted its record of steady economic growth characterized by social reliefs and welfare incentives for the poorest of the poor (Ghanaweb, December 4, 2016). According to the NPP, when it assumed power in 2001, the economy inherited from the Rawlings-led NDC was in a bad shape (such as macroeconomic instability, high inflation, depreciation of the currency, high cost of living, and huge debt stock), yet under John Kufuor's efficient leadership, the government implemented far-reaching economic policies that restored macroeconomic stability—a measure that was responsible for the boost in investors' confidence in the economy (Gyimah-Boadi, 2009; Debrah, 2009). The NDC campaigns also attacked the NPP's past economic record. It drew its attention to the baggage of economic deprivation suffered by Ghanaians during Kufuor's eight years tenure (2001 to 2008). According to the NDC, in the run-up to the 2008 elections, the economy had plummeted with inflation souring to create a high cost of living and unemployment, calling the economic management team failures (Ghanaweb, April 22, 2016). The NDC criticized the NPP for its complicity in the murder of Ya-Na, the overlord of

**Table 4.3.   Debt stock as a percentage of GDP.**

| 2015 | 2014 |
|---|---|
| 69.12 percent of GDP as at the end of September | 70.15 percent of GDP as at the end of December |

*Source:* 2016 Budget of Republic of Ghana.

Dagbon, thereby escalating the Dagbon conflict in the Northern Region that led to human and material loses (Modernghana, April 26, 2010).

## THE CORRUPTION CONUNDRUM

Political campaigns targeting political corruption have always been phenomenal in Ghana's electoral politics (Gyimah-Boadi, 2009; Asante, 2016). Throughout the history of democracy, opposition candidates have used corruption as a weapon to unseat incumbents (Asante, 2016). As in previous elections, the incumbent faced a barrage of criticisms directed at its activities that, according to the opposition parties, smacked of corruption. On assumption of office, Mahama made a public declaration to deal with corruption, that is, investigate and punish officials from the previous administration (Bratton & Gyimah-Boadi, 2015). But the opposition parties rather attributed the faltering economy to Mahama's promoted "create, loot, and share phenomenon" (Asante, 2016; Bratton & Gyimah-Boadi, 2015). The opposition parties portrayed the Mahama-led government as one of the most corrupt in Ghana's history (Graphiconline, November 30, 2016). Indeed, in the run-up to the 2016 elections, the ruling NDC was hit by high profile corruption scandals. For instance, Alfred Woyome, the NDC party financier, was in the news for having taken a GH¢51 million dubious "judgement" debt awarded against the state, ostensibly for wrongful termination of state contracts (Bratton & Gyimah-Boadi, 2015). The Mahama government's reputation suffered further humiliation following Joy FM's journalist Manasseh Azure's corruption exposé of 952 million cedis (US$196,354,760 at today's exchange rate) at the Ghana Youth Employment and Entrepreneurial Development Agency (GYEEDA) that upset many Ghanaians (Ghanaweb, April 22, 2016). This was followed by the heinous corruption discovery by some journalists regarding the management of the 200 million Ghana Cedis (US$41,251 at today's exchange rate) of the Savannah Accelerated Development Authority (SADA) project (Ghanaweb, April 22, 2016); the 2015 Smartty Bus Branding affair—a government contract to rebrand 116 Metro Mass Transit Buses at the cost of GH¢3.6 million (US$8.5 million) (Ghanaweb, April 22, 2016; Peacefmonline, January 29, 2016). It was contested by the opposition that the

**Table 4.4. Provisional debt stock (nominal).**

| 2015 | Internal | External |
|---|---|---|
| US$24,285.07 at the end of September | US$9,927.16 | US$14,357.91 |

*Source:* 2016 budget of Republic of Ghana.

cost of branding was more than the cost of purchasing the entire fleet of buses (Ghanaweb, April 22, 2016).

Other corruption cases included what the Bureau of National Investigation (BNI) uncovered at the National Service Secretariat involving an amount of GH¢7,000,000 (US$1,640,933 at the June 2019 exchange rate) paid to 22,212 ghost service personnel in more than a hundred districts (Ghanaweb, October 2, 2014); and the $60,000 Ford Expedition Vehicle from Burkinabe contractor Djibril Kanazoe given as a gift to President Mahama (Myjoyonline, June 15, 2016). Kanazoe had earlier won a contract of US$656,246.48 to construct a fence wall over the Ghana Embassy in Burkina Faso. The Public Account Committee (PAC) of Parliament described the cost of the project as outrageous and ordered the Bank of Ghana to investigate the project (Myjoyonline, June 15, 2016). Dr. Nduom rejected Mahama's infrastructure claims, arguing that the cost of most of the infrastructural projects was inflated and insisted that investments in infrastructure did not translate into growth and employment opportunities, whereas Nana Akuffo-Addo criticized the amount of monies in three NDC corruption scandals, which stood at a whopping 200 million cedis (US$41,251,000 at today's exchange rate) (Myjoyonline, April 19, 2015).

The corruption charges leveled against the NDC by the opposition parties and their candidates could not be mere allegations. The intra-NDC committee established to identify the factors that caused the party's defeat observed that "there were different groups taking money to organize the campaign" (Myjoyonline, October 19, 2016). The report noted that resources including money did not reach the grassroots or the polling agents that were assigned the duty of monitoring the polls. Rather, some of the leading party officials diverted the money for their personal use (Myjoyonline, October 19, 2017).

While throwing the searchlight of corruption on Mahama, the NDC campaigns also appealed to history to launch its attacks on the NPP. Mahama argued that despite Kufuor's declaration of zero tolerance for corruption, a number of corruption scandals rocked the NPP government. The Kufuor government's reputation in office was tarnished by allegations of narcotic trafficking, including the arrest and imprisonment of the sitting Member of Parliament Mr. Eric Amoateng in the United States (Gyimah-Boadi, 2009). Also, the minister of finance presented loan proposals to Parliament that contained inaccurate information; the spending of lavish celebration of the "Ghana at 50 Anniversary"; and the purchase of presidential airplanes and construction of a presidential office complex, the cost of which was twice the amount originally approved by Parliament (Gyimah-Boadi, 2009).

In the end, the voters went to the polls to choose the NPP presidential candidate Nana Akufo-Addo over the NDC's John Mahama, the incumbent president. The voters gave Nana Akuffo-Addo 53.7 percent of the vote while the NDC's John Mahama garnered 44.5 percent of the vote (Electoral Commission, Ghana, 2017). The result of the election was a resounding victory for the issue-based over the non-issue voting paradigm, and suggestive of the rationality of the Ghanaian voter in the choice of candidates in general elections in Ghana.

## CONCLUSIONS

This article has highlighted issues as central to parties' political campaigns. Important developmental issues were the salient factors that influenced voters' choices in the 2016 general elections. It has shown that the major issues that dominated the election campaigns were the economy and corruption. In times of economic despondency, voters are likely to be influenced by a candidate who addresses or speaks to their economic concerns and gives hope about how their plight will be addressed. Voters who think that the government is on the wrong path and has no hope in its ability to salvage the economic woes will reject the incumbent. On the other hand, voters who envisage a better economy under an opposition candidate are likely to vote for a change. This makes it compelling for political parties to speak to voters on the most critical national issues that concern them. The reliance on personal issues that are not connected to bread and butter might not be attractive to voters. Therefore, it makes it trite to say that campaigns rooted in valence issues, which voters expect candidates and their parties to provide rational responses to in post-election policy decisions, are most attractive to the voters.

This paper further shows that although it is important to identify the critical issues in the election year, the success or otherwise of a party's campaign to win power also hinges on the packaging of the message and how they are effectively communicated to voters. This has become even more important in light of the increasing dependence on issues that are already in the public domain. The NPP tagged Mahama as an incompetent, corrupt, and failed economic manager. Nana Akufo-Addo launched a strong attack on NDC's records (Mahama's infrastructure success story documented in the blue book) by highlighting the prevalence of corruption in the government. Unlike the NDC, the NPP focused on the bigger economic questions (issues) that resonated very well with the disillusioned voters. The party's campaign message to the voters indicated alternative solutions to the country's ailing economy and deteriorating infrastructure. The NPP's campaign message of "One-District-One-Factory," "One-Village-One-Dam" were cogent and excited the imaginations of the voters, suggesting that unlike the NDC, the NPP has the ideas and strategy to wrestle the economy from the morass of collapse.

This article has revealed that political parties are the principal agents for bringing up critical national issues for voters to appreciate the reality of the country's economic problems as well as the way forward to deal with them. Thus, only through parties' campaign platforms can the issues confronting society be highlighted and packaged for redress. While messaging is central to a party's campaign, the content of the message counts toward victory. The 2016 elections were about the Mahama government and NDC's track record in office. The voters demonstrated that it was the NPP rather than the NDC that could lift the national issues (problems confronting the people) to allow the voters to make their electoral decisions.

The Ghanaian voter has come of age. Rational as the voter of the developed democracies has been portrayed, it is evident that the Ghanaian voters' voting decisions have been shaped largely by salient socioeconomic issues. This implies that parties can make electoral impacts when they produce their platforms (manifestos) with which to inspire the electorate. Thus, manifestos may prove to be important policy documents with which political parties need to instruct their voters. This is because the manifestos encapsulate the overwhelming national issues that must be teased out for voters' information and the making of their voting decisions at the polls.

## REFERENCES

Anebo, F. (2006). "Issue Salience versus Ethnic Voting in the 2004 Elections." In K. Boafo-Arthur (ed.). *Voting for Democracy in Ghana: The 2004 Elections in Perspective*. Accra: Freedom Publications.

Asante, R. (2006). "Local Factors That Shaped the 2004 General Elections in the Ejura-Sekyedumase, Mampong and Effiduase-Asokore Constituencies." In K. Boafo-Arthur (ed.), *Voting for Democracy in Ghana: The 2004 Elections in Perspective*. Accra: Freedom Publications.

Asante, R. (October 2013). "Making Democracy Work? Quasi-Public Entities and the Drama of Elections in Ghana." *Journal of African Elections* 12(2): 56–74.

Asante, R. (2016). *Ghana Political Watch Brief*. Institute for Security Studies, Dakar Senegal.

Aryee, J. R. A. (2011). "Manifestos and Elections in Ghana's Fourth Republic." *South African Journal of International Affair s* 18(3): 367–384.

Bates, R. (1974). "Ethnic Competition and Modernization in Contemporary Africa." *Comparative Political Studies* 6(4): 457–484.

Bertelsmann Stiftung (2016). *Ghana Country Report*. Gütersloh: Bertelsmann Stiftung. https://www.bti-project.org/fileadmin/files/BTI/Downloads/Reports/2016/pdf/BTI_2016_Ghana.pdf.

Bratton, M. (2013). *Voting and Democratic Citizenship in Africa*. London: Lynne Rienner Publishers.

Bratton, M., R. Bhavnani, and T. Chen. (2012). "Voting Intentions in Africa: Ethnic, Economic or Partisan?" *Commonwealth & Comparative Politics* 50(1): 27–52.

Bratton, M., and E. Gyimah-Boadi. (May 2015). "Political Risks Facing African Democracies: Evidence from Afrobarometer." Afrobarometer Working Paper No. 157.

Commonwealth Observer Group. (2016). Reports of the Commonwealth Observer Group, Ghana General Elections, December 7, 2016.

Dalton, R. J. (August/September 2000). "Citizen Attitudes and Political Behavior." *Comparative Political Studies* 33(6/7): 912–940.

Dalton, R. J., and H. Klingemann. (2011). "Overview of Political Behavior: Political Behavior and Citizen Politics." In Robert E. Goodwin (ed.), *The Oxford Handbook of Political Science*. Oxford University Press.

Dassonneville, R., and Y. Dejaeghere. (2014). Bridging the Ideological Space: A Cross-National Analysis of the Distance of Party Switching. *European Journal of Political Research* 53: 580–599.

De Vries, C. (November 22, 2016). "Modern Elections and Voting Behavior in Europe." Oxford University Press. Retrieved from http://www.oxfordbibliographies.com/view/document/obo-9780199756223/obo-9780199756223-0093.xml.

Debrah, E. (2009). "Assessing the Quality of Accountability in Ghana's District Assemblies, 1993–2008." *African Journal of Political Science and International Relations* 3(6): 278–287.

Debrah, E., A. Seidu, and I. Owusu-Mensah. (2016). "The Cost of Inter-Ethnic Conflicts in Ghana's Northern Region: The Case of the Nawuri-Gonja Conflicts." *Journal of African Conflicts and Peace Studies* 3(1).

Down, A. (1957). *An Economic Theory of Democracy*. New York: Harper and Row.

Electoral Commission, Ghana. (2017). 2016 Presidential Results. Retrieved from http://www.ec.gov.gh/reports-and-publications/election-results/71-2016-presidential-results.html. Accessed on September 3, 2018.

European Union Election Observation Mission (EU EOM). (2016). Ghana Presidential and Parliamentary Elections 2016 Final Report.

Ferree, K. E. (2006). Explaining South Africa's Racial Census. *Journal of Politics*, Vol. 68, No. 4, November, pp. 803–815.

Fiorina, M. P. (1981). Retrospective Voting in American National Elections. New Haven, CT: Yale University Press.

Frempong, A. K. D. (2001). "Ghana's Election 2000: The Ethnic Undercurrent." In J. R. A. Aryee (ed.), *Deepening Democracy in Ghana: Politics of the 2000 Elections*. Accra: Freedom Publications.

Ghanaweb. (October 2, 2014.) "Fraud at NSS: About GH¢7.9m Paid to Ghost Personnel in a Month." Retrieved from https://www.ghanaweb.com/GhanaHomePage/NewsArchive/Fraud-at-NSS-About-GH¢7-9m-paid-to-ghost-personnel-in-a-month-328558. Accessed on August 15, 2018.

Ghanaweb. (April 22, 2016). "Corruption under Mahama Unbearable—Truth Forum." Retrieved from https://www.ghanaweb.com/GhanaHomePage/politics/Corruption-under-Mahama-unbearable-Truth-Forum-432871.

Ghanaweb. (August 16, 2016). "Infrastructural Development under Me 'Unprecedented'—Mahama." Retrieved from https://www.ghanaweb.com/GhanaHomePage/NewsArchive/Infrastructural-development-under-me-unprecedented-Mahama-463023. Accessed on May 21, 2019.

Ghanaweb. (September 20, 2016). "NDC Slogan Should Be 'Deforming Ghana, Deforming Lives'—NPP." Retrieved from https://www.ghanaweb.com/GhanaHomePage/NewsArchive/NDC-slogan-should-be-deforming-Ghana-deforming-lives-NPP-470944 Accessed on May 21, 2019.

Ghanaweb. (October 24, 2016). "'Nana Addo Too Old to Govern Ghana like Mahama'—Asiedu Nketia." Retrieved from https://www.ghanaweb.com/GhanaHomePage/

NewsArchive/Akufo-Addo-too-old-to-govern-Ghana-like-Mahama-Asiedu-Nketia-480222. Accessed on September 3, 2018.

Ghanaweb. (December 4, 2016). "Playback: NPP Holds Final National Rally for Election 2016." Retrieved from https://www.ghanaweb.com/GhanaHomePage/NewsArchive/ PLAYBACK-NPP-holds-final-national-rally-for-Election-2016-492240/. Accessed on September 3, 2018.

Ghanaweb. (May 22, 2018). "Nana Addo's 'Ghost Projects' Claim Dishonest—Mahama." Retrieved from https://www.ghanaweb.com/GhanaHomePage/NewsArchive/Nana-Addo-s-ghost-projects-claim-dishonest-Mahama-653831. Accessed on May 21, 2019.

Graphiconline. (November 30, 2016). "NPP Accuses Prez of Bribing BugriNaabu." Retrieved fromhttps://www.graphic.com.gh/news/politics/npp-accuses-prez-of-bribing-bugri-naabu. html. Accessed on August 18, 2018.

Graphiconline. (August 27, 2017). "'People Think I'm an Old Man'—President Akufo-Addo." Retrieved from https://www.graphic.com.gh/news/politics/people-think-i-m-an-old-man-president-akufo-addo.html. Accessed on September 3, 2018.

Graphiconline. (September 12, 2017). "Implications of Govt's 'One-District, One-Factory' Policy on Job Creation." Retrieved from https://www.graphic.com.gh/business/business-news/implications-of-govt-s-one-district-one-factory-policy-on-job-creation.html/. Accessed on September 3, 2018.

Guelke, A. (1996). Dissecting the South African Miracle: African Parallels. *Nationalism and Ethnic Politics* 2(1), 141–154.

Gyampo, R. E. V., and E. Debrah. (2013). "The Youth and Party Manifestos in Ghanaian Politics." *The Case of the 2012 General Elections* 12(2): 96–114.

Gyimah-Boadi, E. (2009). "Another Step Forward for Ghana." *Journal of Democracy* 20(2): 137–151.

Gyimah-Boadi, E., and R. Asante. (2006). "Ethnic Structure, Inequality and Public Sector Governance in Ghana." In Y. Bangura (ed.), *Ethnic Inequalities and Public Sector Governance.*" Basingstoke: Palgrave Macmillan.

Gyimah-Boadi, E., and H. Prempeh. (July 2012). "Oil, Politics, and Ghana's Democracy." *Journal of Democracy* 23(3): 94–108.

Horowitz, D. (1991). *A Democratic South Africa: Constitutional Reengineering in a Divided Society.* Berkeley and Los Angeles, CA: University of California Press.

Jockers, H., D. Kohnert, and P. Nugent. (September 2009). "The Successful Ghana Election of 2008: A Convenient Myth: Ethnicity in Ghana's Elections Revisited." GIGA Working Papers, 109: 1–21.

Key, V. O., Jr., and M. C. Cummings. (1966). *The Responsible Electorate: Rationality in Presidential Voting.* Cambridge, MA: Belknap Press.

Lewis-Beck, M. S. (1988). *Economics and Elections: The Major Western Democracies.* Ann Arbor: University of Michigan Press.

Lewis-Beck, M. S., and M. Stegmaier. (2007). "Economic Models of Voting." In R. Dalton & H.-D. Klingemann (eds.), *The Oxford Handbook of Political Behavior*, 518–527. Oxford, UK: Oxford University Press.

Lindberg, S., and Morrison, K. C. (2005). "Exploring Voter Alignments in Africa: Core and Swing Voters in Ghana." *Journal of Modern African Studies* 43(4): 565–586.

Lonsdale, J. (1994). "Moral Ethnicity and Political Tribalism." In F. Kaarsholm and J. Hultin (eds.), *Inventions and Boundaries: Historical and Anthropological Approaches to the Study of Ethnicity and Nationalism.* Occasional Paper 11. Roskilde: Department of International Development Studies, Roskilde University.

Ministry of Communication Publication. (2015). *Accounting to the People: Changing Lives and Transforming Ghana.* Accra: Ministry of Communication Publication.

Modernghana. (January 28, 2017). "And the Short Man Became the President of Ghana." Retrieved from https://www.modernghana.com/news/751672/and-the-short-man-became-the-president-of-ghana.html. Accessed on September 3, 2018.

Modernghana. (April 26, 2010). "NPP Are Exposing Their Complicity in Ya Na's Murder—Okudzeto Ablakwahhps." Retrieved from https://www.modernghana.com/news/273119/

npp-are-exposing-their-complicity-in-ya-nas-murder-okudze.html. Accessed on September 3, 2018.

Myjoyonline. (April 19, 2015). "NDC Corruption Scandals Cost ₵1.8bn, Supercedes IMF bailout—Akufo-Addo." Retrieved from https://www.myjoyonline.com/politics/2015/april-19th/ndc-corruption-scandals-cost-18bn-supercedes-imf-bailout-akufo-addo.php. Accessed on August 18, 2018.

Myjoyonline. (March 27, 2016). "'I Am Not Violent'; Nana Akufo-Addo Fights Back." Retrieved from http://www.myjoyonline.com/politics/2016/March-27th/i-am-not-violent-nana-akufo-addo-fights-back.php. Accessed on September 3, 2018.

Myjoyonline. (June 15, 2016). "Burkinabe Contractor Offers Controversial Gift to Prez Mahama." Retrieved from https://www.myjoyonline.com/news/2016/June-15th/burkinabe-contractor-offers-controversial-gift-to-prez-mahama.php. Accessed on May 21, 2019.

Myjoyonline. (August 31, 2016). "Akufo-Addo Will Implement $1m, 1 Constituency Poverty Policy without Sweat—Karbo." Retrieved from https://www.myjoyonline.com/politics/2016/august-31st/akufo-addo-will-implement-1m-1-constituency-poverty-policy-without-sweat-karbo.php. Accessed on September 3, 2018.

Myjoyonline. (October 19, 2016). "NPP Promises One Region, One Theater." Retrieved from https://www.myjoyonline.com/entertainment/2016/october-19th/one-region-one-theater-npp.php. Accessed on September 3, 2018.

Myjoyonline. (December 17, 2016). "Election 2016 Postmortem: Reasons the NDC Lost the 2016 Election." Retrieved from https://www.myjoyonline.com/opinion/2016/december-17th/election-2016-postmortem-reasons-the-ndc-lost-the-2016-election.php. Accessed on September 3, 2018.

Myjoyonline. (October 27, 2017). "2016 Election: NPP's Slogans Were Better Than NDC's –Spio-Garbrah Admits." Retrieved fromhttps://www.myjoyonline.com/politics/2017/October-27th/2016-election-npps-slogans-were-better-than-ndcs-spio-garbrah-admits.php. Accessed on August 18, 2018.

Nadeau, R., M. S. Lewis-Beck, and É. Bélanger. (2013). "Economics and elections revisited." *Comparative Political Studies* 46(5).

National Democratic Congress. (2016). *Changing Lives and Transforming Ghana. 2016 Manifesto*. Accra: National Democratic Congress.

New Patriotic Party. (2016). *Change an Agenda for Jobs Creating Prosperity and Equal Opportunity for All: 2016 Manifesto*. Accra: New Patriotic Party.

Nugent, P. (1999). "Living in the Past: Urban, Rural and Ethnic Themes in the 1992 and 1996 Elections in Ghana." *The Journal of Modern African Studies* 37(2): 305.

Peacefmonline. (April 11, 2008). "PIAC Exposes NDC over 'Ghost' Oil Projects." Retrieved from http://www.peacefmonline.com/pages/politics/politics/201804/349201.php. Accessed on September 3, 2018.

Peacefmonline. (November 2, 2015). "PPP Elects New Officers and Unveils 2016 Slogan." Retrieved from http://www.peacefmonline.com/v12/tools/printnews/news.php?contentid=259299. Accessed on August 27, 2018.

Peacefmonline. (January 29, 2016). "Cover-Up in GH 3.6m Bus Branding Scandal." Retrieved from http://www.peacefmonline.com/pages/local/news/201601/268365.php. Accessed on May 21, 2019.

Peacefmonline. (July 11, 2016). "Bawumia Mocks Mahama over NDC's Campaign Slogan." Retrieved from http://www.peacefmonline.com/pages/politics/politics/201607/285035.php. Accessed on September 3, 2018.

Peacefmonline, (March 27, 2017). "I Have Banned 'Onaapo' Song in My House—NDC Chairman." Retrieved from http://www.peacefmonline.com/pages/politics/politics/201703/310107.php?storyid=100&%20. Accessed on May 21, 2019.

Peacefmonline. (June 14, 2017). "Govt Releases GH¢78.5m to Pay School Feeding Caterers." Retrieved from http://www.peacefmonline.com/pages/local/news/20170 6/317478.php?storyid =100&. Accessed on August 27, 2018.

Peacefmonline. (September 18, 2017). "NHIA Clears NDC Huge Debt." Retrieved from http://www.peacefmonline.com/pages/local/news/201709/328125.php. Accessed on August 27, 2018.

Posner, C. (2005). *Institutions and Ethnic Politics in Africa*. New York: Cambridge University Press.

Republic of Ghana. (1992). Constitution of the Republic of Ghana, Tema, Ghana Publishing Corporation.

Republic of Ghana. (2000). *Political Parties Act, 2000*. Accra: Assembly Press.

Sadie, Y., L. Patel, and K. Baldry. (2016). "A Comparative Case Study of the Voting Behaviour of Poor People in Three Selected South African Communities." *Journal of African Elections* 15(1): 113–138.

Southwell, Priscilla L. (2016). "Tenor of Modern Political Campaigns: Alienation and Voter Turnout." In B. A. King and K. Hale (eds.) *Why Don't Americans Vote? Causes and Consequences*, 173–183. Santa Barbara, CA: ABC-CLIO.

Swoyer, Alex. (2016). "NYT Compares Trump to Sanders, 'Fueled by Small Donations.'" Breitbart, August 4. http://www.breitbart.com/2016-presidential-race/2016/08/04/nyt-compares-trump-sanders-fueled-small-donations/.

Thimsen, A. Freya. (2017). "Did the Trumpian Counter Public Dissent against the Dominant Model of Campaign Finance?" *Javnost—The Public* 24(3): 267–283.

Todayghana. (December 5, 2016). "NDC Holds Final Campaign Rally Today." Retrieved from https://www.todaygh.com/ndc-holds-final-campaign-rally-today. Accessed on May 21, 2019.

Tufte, E. R. (1978). *Political Control of the Economy*. Princeton: Princeton University Press.

Weitz-Shapiro, R. (2012). "What Wins Votes: Why Some Politicians Opt Out of Clientelism." *American Journal of Political Science* 56(3): 568–583.

Werner, Brian L. (1997). "Financing the Campaigns of Women Candidates and Their Opponents." *Women & Politics* 18(1): 81–97.

Young, C. (2002). *Ethnicity and Politics in Africa*. Boston, MA: Boston University Press.

*Chapter Five*

# (Mis)coordination

*Why Would Ghanaian Political Actors and Political Parties Strategically Encourage Split-Ticket Voting?*

## Samuel Darkwa

"Ghana stands to gain, and parliament will produce results for the people through give and take negotiations and proper debates devoid of insults . . . if we vote wisely and vote skirt and blouse."—Festus Lartey-Adjei (December 7, 2012)

"As you go out to vote on Sunday, I am urging my friends and anyone who really cares about the growth of democracy in Ghana to vote *skirt and blouse*. I'd like to have a situation where the president is from *Party A* but parliament is controlled by *Party B* or *Party C*."—Ato Kwamena Dadzie (December 5, 2008)[1]

Political parties usually have a strong incentive to encourage straight-ticket voting so that voters support all their candidates on the ballot. In Ghana, split-ticket voting is so common that it has a special name, "skirt and blouse voting," denoting a two-piece dress instead of one straight dress (Daddieh, 2009). It is associated with voting for a presidential candidate from one political party and for a parliamentary candidate from a different political party at the same set of elections (Asunka, 2016; Lindberg, 2013; Ichino & Nathan, 2013, 2017; Weghorst & Lindberg, 2013). The concept also refers to a split electoral outcome where the winners of the presidential and parliamentary contests within a given constituency (electoral district) are not from the same political party (Boafo-Arthur, 2006, 2008; Daddieh, 2009; Frempong, 2017). Finally, it also refers to instances where supporters of a political party will vote for the party's presidential candidate but also for a parliamentary candidate who is not on their party's ticket (Boafo-Arthur, 2006, 2008; Debrah & Gyampo, 2013).[2] Not only do we see evidence of split-ticket voting in some constituencies, but we also see some evidence that parties strategically encourage split-ticket voting under certain conditions. Further, civil society and media hulks may encourage split-ticket voting to achieve certain goals. The above two quotes are mere crumbs of what political party elites and other Ghanaians feed the electorates on in public and in private. This chapter will explore the reasons for this phenomenon and, thus, contribute to our understanding of split-ticket voting, elite (party leaders) behavior, and Ghanaian electoral politics within Ghana's Fourth Republic.

Why would party elites and supporters of a political party want either the party's presidential or parliamentary candidate to lose the election in a particular constituency? Why would a presidential and/or parliamentary candidate of a political party advocate either overtly or covertly for split-ticket voting? Again, why would a supporter, a member, or an official of a political party indeed vote to split the ballot, "roll-off" the ballot, or abstain? Finally, how has this phenomenon shaped the current distribution of votes and seats shared by the parties in Ghana? Using fieldwork conducted in Ghana that sampled 303 party elites as well as a few media hulks, civil society leaders, and members of academia in 2017, this chapter argues that political party officials and politicians will always do what they feel will serve their best interest. They will do so especially in situations where coordination breaks down. They may also deliberately frustrate coordination by finding it to be the most expedient means of facilitating their political goal at a given time. It stands to reason that we can have the conventional coordination, which is a harmonious interaction or relationship within a group or among groups of people working together, and the reverse (miscoordination), and therefore, we can represent both as (mis)coordination (Cox, 1999; Navia & Saldaña, 2015). I prefer to use *strategic coordination* instead of *(mis)coordination* in because whichever aspect of coordination option is employed by political actors, they do so with certain mindsets, and in response to their expectations of what other players are doing or will do. The bottom line is that political actors are strategic in their choices; meaning they make their choices in response to (in anticipation of) what other actors (competitors and voters) are doing (will do). Employing Cox's (1997, 1999) coordination theory, this chapter further argues that (mis)coordination is a two-pronged mechanism that political actors employ to communicate their intentions about the direction they expect the election to go. The electorates or their constituents are capable of reading between the lines where political actors communicate through (mis)coordination mechanisms because they come with certain observable indicators that provide their intended recipients with the appropriate cues. It is instructive to note that strategic coordination is carried out within party (intraparty) and between party (interparty). This chapter will identify the observable indicators of intraparty and interparty coordination cues that party elites create as they engage in strategic coordination. Following this, the chapter will generate testable hypotheses, test them, and then draw conclusions about how the political situation helps to promote split-ticket voting and split-district outcome in helping to enhance our understanding of ticket-splitting.

This chapter proceeds as follows: the next section presents Strategic Coordination Theory which is this study's contribution to the ticket-splitting literature. Strategic Coordination Theory is a two-pronged theoretical model used to analyze the phenomenon of ticket-splitting, especially from elites' perspective as it relates to intraparty and interparty coordination problems that they face in enacting their political agenda. Each of these will introduce and discuss the appropriate testable hypotheses that capture the observable indicators of intraparty and interparty coordination problems faced by party elites. The section that follows discusses alternative explanations with their associated hypotheses. These are partisanship, the educational level of the respondents, and whether or not the parties/candidates that respondents identify with contest in a given constituency. Another section touches on the data and how it was collected, how relevant it is to the questions and the theory, and how the variables are measured. Thus, the section discusses the dependent and independent variables as well as the control variables. The penultimate section models the interparty and intraparty coordination theory and presents the results from the logistic regression. This will connect to the discussion segment of the chapter by buttressing the results with stories of coordination problems in Ghana's Fourth Republic. The final section summarizes the discussions, reiterates the importance of this chapter, and proposes recommendations for future research in the subfield.

## STRATEGIC COORDINATION THEORY

To address the questions raised above, this section explores Cox's (1997, 1999) coordination theory to analyze split-ticket voting in the Ghanaian general elections between 1996 and 2016. Ghana presents the appropriate kind of context to investigate the link between coordination problems and split-ticket voting in emerging democracies. Though what pertains to Ghana may not wholly be generalizable to all emerging democracies, it represents an ideal research laboratory to systematically analyze the nexus between coordination problems and split-ticket voting in emerging democracies. Thus, this section seeks to advance the study of split-ticket voting by taking advantage of what the case of Ghana provides.

Cox (1997, 1999) developed a general theory of electoral coordination that was aimed at ensuring coordination within a single party (intraparty coordination) and coordination between and among parties (coalition/inter-party coordination). Cox observed that electoral systems of any kind determine how votes are translated into seats and are replete with coordination problems for electoral competitors. Such coordination problems emerge because there are more potential competitors vying for fewer seats. That is, there are fewer seats to be filled by several potential competitors (independent candidates, single parties' candidates, and candidates from parties in a coalition). Thus, within a single political party there may be several contestants, and within an ideological bloc, such as social democratic parties (center-left parties), there could be several capable candidates prepared and determined to enter the election fray in pursuit of fewer seats. This situation poses a coordination problem, especially to the political parties involved in the sense that they will need to limit the number of competitors. Cox contends that this could be done by "either limiting the number of actual competitors (e.g., via joint lists or fusion candidacies), limiting the number of competitors for whom voters actually vote (strategic voting), or both. The process of limiting either entry or vote dispersion entails coordinating the actions of more than one person" (Cox, 1999, pp. 145–146). The central thrust of Cox's (1999) general theory of electoral coordination goes as follows:

> Electoral systems affect the coordination of political forces at two main levels: (a) within individual electoral districts when candidates and lists enter the electoral fray and voters distribute their votes among them; and (b) across these districts (within the nation as a whole) as potentially autonomous candidates and lists from different districts ally with one another to form regional or national parties. A third and final stage of coordination is less directly affected by electoral rules, namely the forming and sustaining of governments . . . district-level electoral coordination problems for the simplest electoral systems . . . two different $M+1$ rules apply. First, the number of candidates or lists entering a given race tends to be no more than $M+1$; second, when more than $M+1$ candidates or lists do enter a race, votes tend to concentrate on at most $M+1$ of them. (p. 160)

From the long quote above, there are three levels of coordination per Cox's general theory of coordination. The first level involves political interaction within a local district or districts that cover strategic entry and strategic voting decisions at the district level, which he referred to as the two $M+1$ rules. The foremost $M+1$ rule deals with strategic entry decisions, which are expected to be coordinated by party elites. The next $M+1$ rule is referred to as $M+1$ candidate rule, which implies that where party elites fail to coordinate, voters who only care about the current elections will concentrate their votes on at most $M+1$ of the competitors. The second form of coordination, political interaction across districts, is what he refers to as linkage decisions among political actors (candidates and political parties contesting the election in different districts). Thus, the second form of coordination deals with the interaction between a presidential and a parliamentary candidate's joint efforts in prosecuting an electoral campaign aimed at gunning for victory. The third phase of coordination has to do with political interaction for setting up and maintenance of governments which deals with the distribution of offices (legislative and executive) to public officials. The first two levels are associated with elections and are directly affected by electoral rules, while the third level deals with formation and maintenance of governments. In applying how the coordination problems identified by Cox can explain split-ticket voting, I will restrict my discussion of the theory to the first two levels of coordination (but especially to the second level, which deals with elite interactions) and I consider the third level to be a bargaining chip that top political actors can use to facilitate how they overcome the coordination problems they face. As political actors are interested in votes, policy, and office (Golder, 2006; Kadima & Uteem, 2006) it is easier for them to employ Cox's third-level of coordination (office and government formation) as a negotiation chip to address their coordination problems.

It is worth pointing out that coordination problems faced by party elites and candidates are at times problems they deliberately create or encounter as they interact with other players in the pursuit of their political agenda. These problems are associated with certain identifiable indicators observed by Cox (1999), Benoit (2001), and Golder (2006). For the sake of clarity, I classify them into intraparty and interparty coordination successes and failures, as doing so will give a clear gauge to assess how party elites (candidates and parties) do in respect to the coordination problem they are confronted with. Coordination is necessary for party elites who are goal oriented and work together as a team in meeting those goals. Since they depend on one another to pursue a common goal, they will need to do things in a way that a single person pursuing similar goals will not normally do. Malone aptly captured this when he defined coordination as "the additional information processing performed when multiple, connected actors pursue goals that a single actor pursuing the same goals would not perform" (Malone, 1988, p. 5).

## Intraparty Coordination

Intraparty coordination deals with how party elites negotiate their interdependent relations within a given political party. According to scholars such as Cox (1999), Benoit (2001), and Golder (2006), intraparty coordination has associated observable indicators, as shown in table 5.1 below. When successful, the first observable indication is that political parties limit nomination or they coordinate on a single candidate (nominee). This is what Cox (1999) refers to as nomination control. He argues that nomination control could be done through primary elections or any internal party procedures that are transparent and democratic. The consequence of nomination control is that the party runs fewer candidates. Where there is nomination control or fewer candidates are presented on a party's ticket, it is highly probable that some aspirants might for one reason or the other withdraw their decision to contest or might lose to an in-party competitor. Therefore, the third observable indication of a successful intraparty coordination success is the ability of party elites to prevent losing (or disappointed) nomination seekers from entering the general election as independent candidates. This could be done by negotiating policy concessions and/or office positions with disappointed nomination seekers in exchange for their support prior to the elections. Thus, a promise of a government position to a losing in-party contestant is enough to secure their support for the election. This is where Cox's third level of coordination (government formation) becomes relevant in this section. The view is that government formation predates electoral victory and that it acts as a catalyst for inducing internal party cohesion for electoral success. The fourth observable indication of a successful intraparty coordination deals with linkage decisions among political actors from different districts within the same political party. This involves the creation of a common or joint electoral platform between the presidential and legislative candidates of a given party. This may include the use of marketing strategies such as billboards, as well as sponsoring joint advertisements for the purpose of making electoral impact. The presence of these in any political party points to intraparty coordination success. Where there are intraparty coordination successes, all things being equal, there will be straight-ticket voting. As such, under normal conditions where there is successful intraparty coordination, we do not expect ticket-splitting.

Contrary to the above are the indications of intraparty coordination failures as shown in the right quadrant of table 5.1. The first signal of intraparty coordination failure is over-nomination which happens where there exist factions, especially "competitive and degenerative types" (Boucek, 2009, p. 479). Cox (1999) observed that Japan's Liberal Democratic Party (LDP) often had over-nomination due to the existence of factions. In Ghana, the tendency of having about five independent parties from the Nkrumahist tradition contesting the election is a perfect example of intraparty coordination failure since their main ideological difference is a show of who is a true Nkrumahist (Jonah, 1998; Osei, 2012). The second sign of intraparty coordination failure is undemocratic ways of conducting a party's nomination process. Emanating from this is the third sign, the inability of party elites to prevent or persuade disappointed nomination seekers from contesting the election as independent candidates. Normally, internal party competition is good for the bigger national or subnational contests (Crutzen et al., 2009; Cox, 1999), but when it leads to the degenerative type referred to as a race to the bottom (Boucek, 2009; Crutzen et al., 2009; Volden, 2002), then mobilizing support for the bigger elections is bound to suffer. The fourth sign of intraparty coordination failure flows directly from the third, and it is the existence of splinter groups and defections from the party either to join another party or to create a new one. Analogous to this is fighting for supremacy among leading members of the party. There are also cases where there is no proper linkage between the presidential and legislative candidates of a given party. Thus, the existence of parallel structures within a political party that produce duplication of, say, campaigning of candidates, or the existence of animosity between the presidential and legislative candidates are all indications of intraparty coordination failures. Intraparty coordination failures are likely to produce ticket-splitting all things being equal. From the aforegoing discussions, we expect the following hypotheses as markers of intraparty coordination failures, all things being equal.

Where a party's nomination process is democratic, all things being equal, we expect both losers and winners to be gracious to each other and to see the result as a victory to democracy and to the party. This sense of victory of democracy and of the party is expected to unite the party toward the general elections and is, therefore, likely to reduce ticket-splitting. However, where a party's nomination process is tinted with accusations and counter-accusations because the process is undemocratic, or someone chose to make it so, then we expect the aggrieved contestants to express their displeasure. If their concerns or grievances are not satisfactorily resolved, then we are likely to see ticket-splitting. Hence, Hypothesis 1A: *the more contentious a party's nomination process is, the higher the likelihood of ticket-splitting.* Thus, a higher incidence of unsuccessful party primaries is likely to be associated with higher levels of ticket-splitting and vice versa. Consequently, both the magnitude and direction of contentious primaries and ticket-splitting is positive.

When the party primaries become contentious, but party elites are able to resolve the issues, all things being equal, we expect the aggrieved nomination seekers to remain in the party, and at best offer to their support to the success of the party. However, where party elites are not able to resolve the

**Table 5.1.   Observable indicators of intraparty coordination success and failure.**

| Intraparty Coordination Success | Intraparty Coordination Failure |
| --- | --- |
| Limiting nomination | Over-nomination |
| Running fewer candidates | Contentious primaries (independent contestants) |
| Ability to prevent independents | Existence of splinter groups |
| Creation of joint platform | No proper linkage between candidates |

*Sources:* Authors' own compilation from Benoit (2001), Cox (1999), and Golder (2006).

concerns of aggrieved persons, such persons are more likely to threaten to leave the party or to actually leave the party. Where aggrieved persons threaten to leave the party, all things being equal, it will affect party cohesion and if not properly handled, it is likely to produce ticket-splitting. Thus, Hypothesis 1B: *the more unsuccessful party nomination seekers threaten to leave the party, the higher the chances of split-ticket voting.* Like the effects of contentious primaries, aggrieved primary seekers' threats to leave the party are likely to induce ticket-splitting if not handled well; and if handled well, the process is expected to harmonize the party. It may also depend on whether the threat is credible or not. The status of such persons in the party will also determine how party elites respond to such threats. Therefore, unresolved credible threats to leave the party, which are not handled well, are likely to produce ticket-splitting with the direction being positive while those that are handled well are expected to be negative, all things being equal. Suffice it to say here that a threat to leave the party could be considered credible if the person has the capacity to leave and draw others along, or where the person actually leaves to contest as an independent.

Where there is internal wrangling in a party as a result of a contentious primary and the dust settles, is the party a united one or a factious type? Where the party becomes fragmented because some aggrieved members are defecting to contest the elections as independent candidates, there will be a high likelihood of ticket-splitting. As such Hypothesis 1C: *ticket-splitting is likely to peak as unsuccessful nomination seekers in a party contest the elections as independent candidates.* This often happens where in a particular electoral district or constituency the aggrieved unsuccessful primary seekers decide to contest the parliamentary race as independent candidates. In such instances, persons who defect or contest an election as independents will advocate for ticket-splitting and will want the party's candidate to lose even if that will mean another party's candidate winning the election. Thus, the direction and the magnitude of a party member contesting a parliamentary election as an independent candidate will be positively related to ticket-splitting.

Finally, where there exists proper party linkage such that there is a cordial relationship between the presidential and parliamentary candidates' campaign at the constituency level, especially where they rely on the party structures, ticket-splitting is likely to be low, all things being equal. However, in instances where there exists a disconnect between the presidential and parliamentary candidates' campaign or they abandon the party structures in their campaigns, we expect to see more split-ticket voting, all things being equal. Hence, Hypothesis 1D: *the more harmonious the interaction between a presidential and legislative candidate of a party is, the lower the likelihood of ticket-splitting.* Thus, where the candidates adopt a common pool and conduct their campaigns in a harmonious manner, all things being equal, split-ticket voting is likely to reduce. We expect a negative relationship between split-ticket voting and harmonious party relations such as the adoption of a common pool.

**Interparty Coordination**

Interparty coordination (pre-electoral coalition or electoral alliance) is any attempt by two or more political parties to harmonize their efforts jointly at the polls to maximize their mutual electoral benefits (Golder, 2006).[3] Interparty coordination is easier where two different parties with similar political ideologies forge an electoral alliance (Golder, 2006). However, unlike intraparty coordination that must be forged by political parties with same/similar ideology, interparty coordination could be forged by parties with different ideologies with the view of eliminating or defeating an "undesirable" party. Just like intraparty coordination, interparty coordination success is marked by observable signals. Benoit (2001) observed that party elites, through their coordination, sent cues to voters who rightly responded to such signals. The first observable signal of a successful interparty coordination is that the parties involved do not contest the elections independently. This is done using joint nomination, running of joint list or fusing of candidates. The essence is to present fewer candidates and they do this by way of coordination. In a single word, successful interparty coordination is characterized by mergers. Second, related to the above is strategic withdrawal of candidates. In some instances, parties that enter alliance negotiate on which candidates should step back. Benoit (2001) saw this as the strength of the Hungarian politicians in electoral coalition. Thus, the ability of parties to negotiate on step-back arrangements points to signals of successful interparty coordination. Third, parties in interparty alliance can negotiate and overcome the commitment problems faced by coalitions. Golder (2006) observed that due to the repeated interaction among pre-electoral partners, the commitment problem in practice is very easy. In South Korea for instance, due to term limits, presidential pre-electoral alliances are easy to form. Fourth, partners in interparty alliance coordinate on their campaigns, ensure that they run joint campaigns, and coordinate all their marketing strategies. Fifth, the ability of coalition partners to secure the support of their members is key to successful interparty coordination (Benoit, 2001).

Interparty coordination failures are characterized first by over-nomination. Cox (1999) argues that there will be a coordination failure if an ideological bloc enters the electoral fray with all possible competent candidates contesting. Second, related to the preceding point is what Golder (2006) refers to as a fight for supremacy. She observed that in France, members of the leadership group in the rightist party were fighting for leadership supremacy instead of fighting to defeat the leftist party. Third, conflict over policy, ideological differences, and distributional problems are clear signs of inter-party coordination failure. Golder (2006) found that distributional problems such as indivisibility of office impede pre-electoral coalitions in presidential systems especially in France. Although parties fail to form alliances due to policy and ideological divergence, Golder (2006) found that in France following the end of the Cold War, the center-left and center-right parties no longer have radical ideological differences, and as such they do not care much who wins. Thus, center-left parties, for instance, run many candidates and do not make compromises, so in the 2002 presidential elections, there were nine candidates representing the Left. The fourth sign of interparty coordination failure is the inability of coalition parties to secure the support of their members or support base (Benoit, 2001; Golder, 2006). Securing the support of coalition partners is crucial to the success of the coalition and this requires efficient and effective coordination. In fact, it is not enough to sign documents entering electoral agreement to ensure the success of coalitions but rather the support of those whose vote is also needed.

Flowing from the above discussions on interparty coordination, this section tests two hypotheses to falsify the credibility and reliability of the interparty coordination among coalition partners as far as Ghana is concerned. First, we expect that coalition partners will do their best to limit nomination by any available means anchored in transparent and democratic principles, ensuring that they put their best foot forward. That is, they coordinate on the most viable candidate(s) that can secure them the needed electoral victory or lead them in making electoral impact for future victory. Where the parties are able to coordinate on a single or required number of candidates, they need to endorse the coalition candidates and secure the support of their members. Thus, for a successful interparty coordination, party elites in alliance are required to endorse coalition partners even those from another party who have been accepted as coalition candidates. Hence Hypothesis 2A: *the more party elites endorse candidates of other parties, the higher the likelihood of ticket-splitting.* Thus, ticket-splitting is expected to increase in such circumstances where parties do not necessarily contest the election as a coalition but

**Table 5.2.   Observable indicators of interparty coordination success and failure.**

| Interparty Coordination Success | Interparty Coordination Failure |
| --- | --- |
| Joint nomination/campaigns | Fight for supremacy |
| Strategic withdrawal | Over-nomination |
| Effective negotiations | Conflict over policy/ideology |
| Ability to secure members' support | Inability to secure members' support |

*Sources:* Authors' own compilation from Benoit (2001), Cox (1999), and Golder (2006).

agree to support other parties in areas and in races; they do not contest the elections. The direction of the endorsement of split-ticket voting is expected to be positive, all things being equal.

Emanating from the preceding paragraph is the issue of strategic withdrawal of candidates to facilitate the performance of another candidate or party's performance. As stated earlier, Cox (1999) argues that electoral coordination is necessary because there are more potential contestants than the available number of seats. Parties that do well are those that are able to coordinate on the most viable candidates. To be efficient in that requires some form of modality of agreeing on a viable or suitable candidate as discussed above. However, in the event that parties have already agreed on their candidates before the coalition or electoral arrangement, there will be the need for some parties to withdraw their candidates in certain constituencies or voting districts where their chances of winning are comparatively weak for those with better chances of winning to have even more promising chances. In fact, Benoit (2001) observed that in Hungary, coordination also took the form of strategic withdrawal of candidates known as "stepping back" ostensibly to facilitate the chances of the contesting candidate. Consequently, the more such arrangements are done, the higher the likelihood of split-ticket voting given that party elites are able to secure the backing of their supporters. Therefore, Hypothesis 2B: *the more widespread strategic withdrawal of candidates, the higher the likelihood of ticket-splitting.* Thus, we expect strategic withdrawal and ticket-splitting to be positively related; that is, the higher the instances of strategic withdrawal, the higher the likelihood of split-ticket voting and vice versa.

## ALTERNATIVE EXPLANATION

Aside from the theory of strategic coordination and the accompanying hypotheses introduced above that evaluate my main arguments about coordination-induced ticket-splitting, this section considers several alternate explanations used in the literature as they pertain to split-ticket voting. These include candidate quality, partisanship, restricted menu of choice, and education to ensure that alternative explanations are not overlooked. Among these alternative explanatory variables, we expect candidate quality to belong to the fold of coordination because the essence of it is to settle on the most viable candidate or to harmonize a party's material and human resources to make the most of a current or future election.

### Candidate Quality

The literature on candidate-level factors of ticket-splitting has identified variables such as incumbency, campaign spending, and issue positioning as responsible for the phenomenon. In the United States, incumbents are said to often face unmatched contestants (Box-Steffensmeier, 1996). As a result, voters whose preferred congressional candidate is weak, for instance, will vote for their presidential candidate and either roll-off or vote for a more experienced candidate who is often the incumbent (Born, 1994; Burden & Kimball, 2009). This is the case because incumbency is frequently associated with candidate quality (Benoit et al., 2006; Burden, 2009; Scheiner, 2005). Conversely, it has also been found that incumbency can also be a liability instead of being an asset (Burden, 2009; Roscoe, 2003; Scheiner, 2005). Incumbents also at times lose their party's primaries to in-party challengers or lose the bigger contest to unpopular competitors. It has also been argued that the predominant cause of ticket-splitting is campaign spending (Burden & Kimball, 1998, 2009; Roscoe, 2003). Thus, in the United States, for instance, a candidate who is able to spend beyond $200,000 has a greater chance of getting the attention of the electorates and therefore can cause ticket-splitting (Burden, 2004; Burden & Kimball, 1998; Roscoe, 2003). It is also a common knowledge that some candidates often spend less than some incumbents and yet they win (Frempong, 2017; Roscoe, 2003). That incumbents do not always win and that high-spending candidates lose to less-spending competitors suggests candidate quality works best with coordination.

The final candidate-level variable identified to be responsible for ticket-splitting is issue positions. Proponents of issue positions argue that candidates can create ticket-splitting by moving closer to their opponent's issue position or moving away from their party's position (Frymer, 1994; Petrocik & Doherty, 1996). The line of this argument is elucidated by Key and Cummings (1966), who argue that when there is a clear difference between the parties or candidates contesting the elections, voters can make distinct choices but where the contestants look alike on ideological grounds and issue positions, voters do not have unique choice; therefore, they will split their votes. Burden and Kimball (2009) found a strong statistical association between a candidate's issue position and ticket-splitting. In a nutshell, the fundamental argument of proponents of candidate quality to ticket-splitting is that variations in candidate quality among contesting parties and or candidates can cause ticket-splitting. Therefore, we expect higher variations in candidate quality among contesting parties to be associated with ticket-splitting, all things being equal. Consequently, Hypothesis 3: *the higher the disparity in candidate quality between and among the contesting parties, the higher the likelihood of ticket-splitting.*

We expect candidate quality to be associated with ticket-splitting, but it worth pointing out that a party's ability to attract and field the most viable candidate boils down to the issue of coordination because where coordination fails, a party may fail to nominate the most qualified candidate or can have the most qualified candidate, but most splitters will likely split away from that candidate. However, with effective coordination, candidate quality is expected to be associated with positive splitting toward the most qualified candidate.

## Partisanship

It has been found that, partisanship intensity is inversely related to split-ticket voting (Beck et al., 1992; Campbell et al., 1960; Campbell & Miller, 1957). The argument is that persons who identify with parties will vote for their political parties irrespective of the candidate quality of their parties. These are often the core support base of a party. They often suffer from what international relation theories will call confirmation bias (Bennett, 2004; Jervis, 2017; Moravcsik, 2001) because once they have made their mind for a particular party, they will lock their minds from alternative views. In contrast, Maddox and Nimmo (1981) found that all partisans split their ballots; however, weak partisans do split more than other partisans. Thus, the position of Maddox and Nimmo (1981) gives clues that there are certain instances that even strong partisans may involuntarily split their ticket. This chapter asserts that one such circumstance is where coordination problems faced by candidates and parties are not well handled. However, the conventional wisdom is that weaker partisans are more likely to split their tickets, all things being equal. Therefore, we expect weak partisanship to be positively correlated with ticket-splitting, all things being equal. Thus, Hypothesis 4: *the weaker the partisan leaning of the electorates (in this case, party elites/ card-bearing members), the higher the chances of ticket-splitting.* It must be stressed, however, that voter level factors for ticket-splitting are different from elite level factors since normally elites will support and vote for all their candidates but will do so when coordination breaks down.

## Restricted Choice

Candidate availability has been identified as one of the candidate-level factors of ticket-splitting. It has been argued that two voters with diametrically opposed characteristics may have different choices. However, if, for instance, no Republican is running, voters cannot be able to vote for or against a Republican candidate (Roscoe, 2002). Benoit, Giannetti, and Laver (2006) refer to this situation as a *restricted choice menu*. In their study of ticket-splitting in the Italian mixed-member system, Benoit, Giannetti, and Laver (2006) observed that, although in mixed-member electoral systems voters are required to cast ballots simultaneously in single-member districts and multi-member PR districts, because some parties do not have candidates in both constituencies, their supporters have to vote for different parties. They describe these voters as frustrated because they are forced to split their votes between their most preferred parties and others. This similar situation confronts the members and supporters of the smaller parties in Ghana who do not have candidates contesting all races in all constituencies. In my fieldwork in Ghana where I surveyed party officials and members, about 26 percent of respondents cited the inability of their parties to have candidates in all constituencies as the motivation for voting skirt and blouse. If party officials who are supposed to think and act in party terms give such reasons as their motivation for voting skirt and blouse, then the electorates would not act differently when it comes to the effect of restricted choice menu on split-ticket voting. Thus, Hypothesis 5: *as the proportion of constituency nominations covered by political parties decreases, the higher the likelihood of ticket-splitting.* We expect a positive relationship between restricted choice and split-ticket voting, meaning the more restricted choices faced by members and supporters of smaller parties, the higher the likelihood of ticket-splitting. As is shown in the study, the reverse is also true.

## Education

Research has found a correlation between education and ticket-splitting (Beck et al., 1992; Dalton, 2013; DeVries & Tarrance, 1972). Some scholars have found a positive association between education and ticket-splitting, meaning higher-educated voters are more likely to split their ticket than their lesser-educated counterparts (De Vries & Tarrance, 1972). On the contrary, Campbell and Miller (1957) assert that a lower level of education is associated with ticket-splitting. As more recent scholarship has supported the positive relationship between higher levels of education and ticket-splitting (Beck et al., 1992; Dalton, 2013), this chapter will expect a positive correlation between education and ticket-splitting. Therefore, Hypothesis 6: *the higher the level of education of the electorates, the higher the likelihood of ticket-splitting.* Thus, the more educated the respondent/voter is, the higher the likelihood of ticket-splitting.

To sum up, based on the Strategic Coordination Theory and the literature related to split-ticket voting reviewed above, I expect the following: (1) contentious primaries are most likely to be positively related to ticket-splitting while successful primaries will be negatively associated to splitting, (2) instances where disappointed nomination seekers do threaten to leave the party or contest the election as independent candidates are likely to lead to ticket-splitting, thus (3) instances where aggrieved members leave the party to contest as independents are likely to trigger ticket-splitting, (4) strategic withdrawals and endorsements are likely positively related to splitting especially in instances where parties and candidates who do the endorsement or the strategic withdrawal do not contest the election on the same party label/

ticket but do so to facilitate the performance of one another, and (5) weak partisanship, higher level of education, and candidate quality are all expected to be positively related to splitting. On the contrary, where the presidential and parliamentary candidates of a political party harmonize their campaign, use the party structures, and adopt a joint platform, we expect a negative relationship with ticket-splitting.

## DATA AND MEASUREMENT

The data for this chapter were based on fieldwork carried out in Ghana in March 2017. The fieldwork sampled seven constituencies. In selecting the cases, this chapter considered how electoral scholars and analysts have divided the country based on the parties' strengths and the volatility of voter behavior in Ghana. Ghana is dominated by two major political parties; the New Patriotic Party (NPP) and the National Democratic Congress (NDC) who together account for over 90 percent of the votes since 1992 (Agyeman-Duah, 2005; Frempong, 2012, 2017; Lindberg, 2013; Osei, 2012). In the 2016 elections, for instance, there were six political parties and one independent candidate contesting the presidential slot. The outcome indicated that the NPP and NDC pulled 98.3 percent against 1.7 percent for the rest of the contestants. Also, the 275 parliamentary seats were all won by the two major political parties (Frempong, 2017).

Administratively, Ghana is divided into ten regions (with six new ones created this year, 2019) that are further classified into Southern Ghana, Northern Ghana, and the Middle Belt. Since the two major parties dominate the electoral landscape, electoral students and analysts have divided the ten administrative regions into how they relate to the two major parties. Four regions, Brong Ahafo, Central, Greater Accra, and the Western Region, are referred to as swing regions (Agyeman-Duah, 2005; Frempong, 2012, 2017; Lindberg, 2013).[4] The Ashanti in the Middle Belt and Eastern Region are the stronghold of the NPP, while the three northern regions (Northern, Upper East, and Upper West) as well as the Volta Region are the stronghold of the NDC (Agyeman-Duah, 2005; Frempong, 2012, 2017).

With this background, to avoid the problem of selecting constituencies based on the dependent variable, the selection of cases was based on the following criteria: (1) constituencies that have and those that have not witnessed a skirt and blouse outcome, and (2) constituencies that have experienced interparty electoral alliances. Also, constituencies that are (3) cosmopolitan, (4) swing constituencies, (5) party strongholds, (6) large in population size (having more than 60,000 registered voters[5]), and (7) constituencies won by a formerly party-affiliated candidate who protested by going independent. These criteria were used to ensure that consideration is given to swing regions, party strongholds, north-south-middle belt concerns, and demographic as well as other peculiarities. Thus, the seven selected constituencies were identified based on how they fit into the criteria above. Listed in alphabetical order, they are Ablekuma South, Bantama, Ellembelle, Evalue Ajomoro Gwira, Ketu South, Klottey Korle,[6] and Wulensi. Out of the seven constituencies selected, four were selected from the Greater Accra and the Western Regions (that is, two constituencies were selected from each of these two regions). In each case, the two constituencies selected from the Greater Accra and the Western Regions were contiguous. The selection was deliberately done to facilitate data collection and to save cost, given that the selected constituencies satisfy all the criteria listed above.

Alphabetically, the first constituency, Ablekuma South, is in the Greater Accra Region (one of the swing regions). This constituency fits the criteria in many ways: first, it is a swing constituency, urban and cosmopolitan, and it has a large population density as shown in table 5.3 below. Again, as shown in table 5.4 below, in 1996 and 2008, the constituency witnessed a skirt and blouse outcome. In the 1996 general elections, the NDC won the presidential vote while the NPP won the parliamentary seat. Again in 2008, the constituency witnessed a skirt and blouse outcome, but the two parties switched places in the sense that the NPP won the presidential vote while the NDC took the parliamentary seat. The second constituency is Bantama in the Ashanti Region, which is the stronghold of the NPP. Bantama is significant for its population density, unique voting pattern (voting about 80 percent straight-ticket), and ethnic dominance. It has never experienced a skirt and blouse outcome. Also, in the 2016 general elections, the incumbent parliamentary candidate of the NPP, who had lost the party's primary, filed to contest as an independent candidate, but the party was able to dissuade him, and he withdrew from contesting as an independent candidate. The third constituency is Ellembelle in the Western Region, which has experienced three skirt and blouse outcomes (1996, 2000, and 2004). It is a constituency where the NPP never contested the parliamentary elections between 1996 and 2008 but supported the Convention People's Party (CPP) candidate to win the election three consecutive times. Interestingly, the CPP candidate for the Ellembelle, Mr. Freddie Blay, has left his party to join the NPP and is now the national chairman of the NPP. Thus, the Ellembelle constituency satisfies four out of the seven criteria, as illustrated in table 5.3.

Table 5.3. Cases (constituencies) and their fitness for the selection criteria.

| Constituency | Skirt & Blouse Outcome | Experienced Interparty Alliance | Cosmopolitan | Swing Constituency | Party Stronghold | Huge Population Size +60,000 votes | Won by Independent Protester | Sample Size |
|---|---|---|---|---|---|---|---|---|
| Ablekuma South | Yes | No | Yes | Yes | No | Yes | No | 37 |
| Bantam | No | No | Yes | No | Yes | Yes | No | 51 |
| Ellembelle | Yes | Yes | Yes | Yes | No | Yes | No | 39 |
| Evalue A. Gwira | Yes | Yes | No | Yes | No | No | No | 39 |
| Ketu South | No | No | No | No | Yes | Yes | No | 46 |
| Klottey Korle | Yes | No | Yes | Yes | No | Yes | No | 38 |
| Wulensi | Yes | No | No | Yes | No | No | Yes | 46 |
| Other | | | | | | | | 7 |

The fourth constituency is Evalue Ajomoro Gwira, also from the Western Region that adjoins the Ellembelle constituency. This constituency has witnessed a total of four skirt and blouse outcomes out of the six elections considered under this project. In general, Evalue Ajomoro Gwira has witnessed the highest number of skirt and blouse outcomes between 1996 and 2016. It fits the selection criteria in many ways. Though, with a smaller population size, the constituency has produced skirt and blouse outcomes between the two major parties (NPP-NDC) and has also produced a CPP (a smaller party) member of Parliament through alliance with the NPP. The fifth constituency, Ketu South in the Volta Region, is a stronghold of the NDC often referred to as the NDC "world bank" (Agyeman-Duah, 2005; Frempong, 2012, 2017). Like Bantama, Ketu South is significant for its huge population density, unique voting pattern (voting about 90 percent for the NDC), and ethnic dominance. It has also never observed a skirt and blouse outcome. Albert Kwasi Zigah, who was the NDC legislator for two terms between 2005 and 2012, lost his third term bid and contested the 2012 and 2016 elections as independent, losing both attempts. Also, Mr. Jim Yao Morti, an NDC parliamentary aspirant who contested the incumbent NDC legislator but was disqualified, went independent in the 2016 election but lost. Thus, two independent candidates from the same party contested the party's candidate in the constituency in the 2016 election but they both lost to the party's candidate. This shows how strong the party is at the constituency. The sixth constituency is Klottey Korle constituency in the Greater Accra Region. This constituency has witnessed only one skirt and blouse outcome, which occurred in the 2016 elections as a result of a protest from an NPP candidate who lost the party's primaries and decided to go independent. As per table 5.3 above, the Klottey Korle constituency satisfies four out of the seven criteria; it is a swing constituency (alternating between NPP and NDC. Also, the winner of this constituency wins the presidential slot), and it is cosmopolitan with a large population density.

Finally, Wulensi, the seventh constituency in the Northern Region, is a swing constituency that has also witnessed three elections with split outcomes (1996, 2004, and 2008). This constituency has voted for the ruling government, the opposition, and independent candidates to get to Parliament. It has also produced outcomes where the winning presidential candidates were from different parties at different times. Finally, it also marked an instance where a candidate who could not get the party's nomination in 2008 went independent and won the parliamentary seat.

**Table 5.4.   Selected constituencies: Winning candidates and parties between 1996 and 2016.**

| Consti-tuencies | Region | 2016 | | 2012 | | 2008 | | 2004 | | 2000 | | 1996 | | Freq. |
|---|---|---|---|---|---|---|---|---|---|---|---|---|---|---|
| | | Pres. | Parl. | Pres. | Parl. | Pres. | Parl. | Pres. | Parl. | Pres. | Parl. | Pres. | Parl. | |
| Ablekuma South | Greater Accra | NDC | NDC | NDC | NDC | NPP | NDC | NPP | NPP | NPP | NPP | NDC | NPP | 2 |
| Bantama | Ashanti | NPP | NPP | NPP | NPP | NPP | NPP | NPP | NPP | NPP | NPP | NPP | NPP | 0 |
| Ellembelle | Western | NDC | NDC | NDC | NDC | NDC | NDC | NPP | CPP | NPP | CPP | NDC | CPP | 3 |
| Evalue A. Gwira | Western | NDC | NPP | NDC | NDC | NPP | NPP | NPP | CPP | NPP | NDC | NPP | CPP | 4 |
| Ketu South | Volta | NDC | NDC | NDC | NDC | NDC | NDC | NDC | NDC | NDC | NDC | NDC | NDC | 0 |
| Klottey Korle | Greater Accra | NPP | NDC | NDC | NDC | NDC | NDC | NPP | NPP | NPP | NPP | NDC | NDC | 1 |
| Wulensi | Northern | NPP | NPP | NDC | NDC | NPP | IND | NDC | NPP | NDC | NDC | NDC | NPP | 3 |

*Source:* Compilation from Electoral Commission, 1996–2016.

*Samuel Darkwa*

In administering the surveys, I did part of the fieldwork by myself and others were done by trained persons (professionals) whom I briefed on the goals of the research as well as the sampling frame. The research targeted the following: party chairs (either national, regional, district, or zonal), secretaries, women's organizers, youth leadership, campaign coordinators, treasurers, directors of elections, grassroots actors also referred to as cadres, research team members, results analysts, polling agents, and communication team members. Also sampled were eight parliamentarians whose constituencies experienced a split outcome (skirt and blouse outcome) or were threatened with skirt and blouse voting. Further, fifteen candidates defeated in their parties' primaries (of whom eight did not defect, one defected but was later persuaded by the party to come back, and six who contested the election as independent candidates) were interviewed. Also interviewed were five leaders of civil society organizations, one deputy chairman (operations) of the National Commission for Civic Education, three faculty members at the Department of Political Science at the University of Ghana[7] and nine media practitioners. In all, 303 respondents were surveyed through administered questionnaires (230 participants) and face-to-face interviews (73 participants) in March 2017. This was done to ensure that respondents fit the research question. Details of survey respondents are in the chapter appendix (table 5.7).

To ensure that this research sampled all the relevant political parties fairly, it was decided that political parties whose parliamentary candidates pulled at least 10 percent in any of the 275 constituencies in the 2016 general elections should be sampled. In this way, five political parties were selected. They were, in alphabetical order, the Convention People's Party (CPP), the National Democratic Congress (NDC), the New Patriotic Party (NPP), the People's National Convention (PNC), and the Progressive People's Party (PPP). As the political parties have unequal strengths in terms of resources and membership, it was decided to fix the minimum and maximum number of samples to collect from each party as twenty-five and seventy-five, respectively. Given the specific nature of respondents required for this research and the parties involved, a randomized selection was not feasible; therefore, an attempt was made to undo any biases in the data collection. Consequently, respondents from the seven constituencies were grouped into clusters of polling stations using the Electoral Commission of Ghana's code book. Each of the seven constituencies was allotted five and six polling stations based on the sample size, which ranged from thirty-seven (Ablekuma South) to fifty-one (Bantama), as per table 5.3. Finally, the selection criteria were that in each cluster, at least one party official and at least one card-bearing member of each of the five political parties was sampled.

## Dependent Variable

What this research sought to address is why a party elite or a card-bearing member of a political party will vote skirt and blouse (split-ticket). To establish this, respondents were asked, *"Have you ever voted skirt and blouse (that is to vote for presidential and parliamentary candidates in the same election from different political parties) before?"* Thus, the dependent variable is skirt and blouse voting which is a dichotomous variable; a respondent voted skirt and blouse or not. I generated the dependent variable by coding respondents who answered "Yes" as "1" and "No" responses were coded as "0."

## Independent Variables

The focus of this chapter is to empirically ascertain why Ghanaian party elites and party card-bearing members will vote skirt and blouse or advocate for skirt and blouse voting (split-ticket voting), a phenomenon which is uncommon in political science discourse/literature. This seems to show that Ghanaian voters behave in a manner inconsistent with ticket-splitters in other parts of the globe as far as the conventional political science literature is concerned. Two models of logit regression were run using two coding rules to assess how the different coding affected skirt and blouse voting (ticket-splitting). Details of the coding are provided in the appendix (table 5.8).

*Contentious Primaries*: I compute contentious primaries using Question 5, *"Please select the statement that most closely matches your view: "In general, the recent parliamentary primaries of your political party were successful."* For Model 1, respondents who answered "Strongly Agree" or "Moderately Agree" were coded as "0," those who responded "Strongly Disagree" or "Moderately Disagree" were coded as "1," while those who selected "Neutral" were coded as "2."[8] In Model 2, respondents who answered "Strongly Agree" or "Moderately Agree" were coded as "0"; those who responded "Strongly Disagree" or "Moderately Disagree" were coded as "1," because those who disagree that the party primaries were successful are potential skirt and blouse voters.

*Threaten to Leave Party*: I measured the variable "Threaten to Leave Party" using Question 6, *"Did any defeated candidate of your party threaten to leave the political party?"* Respondents who selected "Yes" were coded as "1," "No" coded as "0," and "Don't Know" coded as "2." In Model 2, respondents who answered, "Strongly Agree" or "Moderately Agree" were coded as "0," those who responded, "Strongly Disagree" or "Moderately Disagree" were coded as "1."

*Go Independent*: I generated the variable, "Go Independent" using Question 9, *"Did some losing parliamentary contestants go independent?"* Respondents who answered "Yes" were coded as "1," "No" coded as "0," and

"Don't Know" coded as "2" for Model 1. While in Model 2, respondents who answered "Strongly Agree" or "Moderately Agree" were coded as "0"; those who responded, "Strongly Disagree" or "Moderately Disagree" were coded as "1."

*Common Pool*: The variable "Common Pool" was measured using Question 17, "*Leading to the elections did your party maintain a common pool of resources for both presidential and parliamentary campaigns?*" In both Models 1 and 2, respondents who answered "Yes" were coded as "1," while those who selected "No" were coded as "0"

*Endorsement*: In Model 1, the variable "Endorsement" was generated using Question 21, "*Did your party endorse another candidate for either the presidential or parliamentary slot?*" Respondents who answered "Yes" were coded as "1," "No" were coded as "0," and "Don't Know" were coded as "2." While in Model 2, respondents who answered "Strongly Agree" or "Moderately Agree" were coded as "0"; those who responded "Strongly Disagree" or "Moderately Disagree" were coded as "1."

*Candidate Quality*: The variable "Candidate Quality" was generated regarding reasons given by respondents' decision for voting skirt and blouse. In both models, respondents who chose candidate quality (which was the most popular response) were coded as "1"; otherwise, they were coded as "0."

## Control Variables

*Restricted Choice*: I control for "Restricted Choice" using Question 24, "*Did your party contest in both presidential and parliamentary seats in all constituencies?*" In Model 1, respondents who selected "Yes" were coded as "1," "No" were coded as "0," and "Don't Know" were coded as "2." In Model 2, respondents who answered "Strongly Agree" or "Moderately Agree" were coded as "0"; those who responded, "Strongly Disagree" or "Moderately Disagree" were coded as "1."

*Party ID*: The control variable "Party Identification" (Party ID) was generated using Question 3, "*If you answered Yes, on Question 2, which political party is that?*" Respondent's party affiliation was coded as per their responses; CPP 41, NDC 87, NPP 86, PNC 38, and PPP 44.

*Education*: I control for education using the educational qualification of respondents. In both models, education is on an eight-point scale from "0" to "8" ranging from "Some Primary Schooling" to "University Completed and Beyond."

# MODELING INTRAPARTY/INTERPARTY
# COORDINATION THEORY

To understand the behavior of Ghanaian politicians and party elites in respect to their role in the facilitation of skirt and blouse voting, two factors need to be taken into account. The first is the instances where the parties' nomination process is characterized by irregularities, especially within the two dominant ones, NDC and NPP. The political parties in Ghana have ensured that, as much as possible, they promote free, fair, and transparent internal competition. Against this backdrop, the NDC and the NPP have allowed the nation's Electoral Commission (EC) to supervise the elections of officials and candidates of their parties at all levels (Daddieh & Bob-Milliar, 2012; Debrah, 2014). Additionally, the parties have done their best to come out with single winners to contest the election on their respective party's ticket. They have also ensured that there is proper linkage between the presidential and the parliamentary candidates by resorting to the use of the party structures to conduct their campaigns (Debrah, 2014; Osei, 2012). The NDC and the NPP have always ensured that, as much as possible, they prevent disappointed nomination seekers from contesting the elections as independent candidates even after acrimonious party primaries (Daddieh & Bob-Milliar, 2012; Osei, 2012). In most cases, these acts of intraparty coordination successes often ensure that the party wins both seats in a constituency. This notwithstanding, the parties have experienced serious setbacks in their intraparty coordination, which is characterized by defections and inability of party elites to persuade some disappointed nomination seekers from entering the elections as independent candidates (Boafo-Arthur, 2008; Daddieh & Bob-Milliar, 2012; Debrah, 2014; Frempong, 2017; Osei, 2012). Good examples of how disappointed nomination seekers going independent can cause split-ticket voting and consequently split outcome is the 2000 elections. In the 2000 general elections, there were four independent winners who unseated incumbent parliamentarians who were seeking third term in the NDC. Each of the independent winners (Boniface Abubakar Saddique of Salaga constituency, Joseph Akudibillah of Garu-Tempane constituency, Rashid Bawa of Akan constituency, and James Victor Gbeho of Anlo constituency) contested the election as independent candidates after unsuccessful primaries (Frempong, 2017). Aside from the four independent winners, other candidates who went independent indeed caused the defeat of the NDC in six constituencies: Abetifi, Akropong, Akwatia, Ashaiman, Asutifi North, and Techiman South (Frempong, 2017).

The second factor is what I will refer to as the acts of "revisionist politicians" who will like to alter the political status quo in their parties by rocking the political boat or stirring controversy within the party, or who will take advantage of a controversy and, amid that controversy, leave the party to contest as independents (Ichino & Nathan, 2013, 2017). The revisionist politicians are those who harbor presidential and parliamentary ambitions but know that if they were to play by the rules as prescribed by the status quo, they may not achieve their goals and therefore must adopt unconventional strategies. Unlike a president who has a two-term limit, there is no term limit for a parliamentary candidate. So, an in-party competitor who wants to get to Parliament but has a senior colleague in the same constituency who has been in Parliament for more than two terms will begin to work against that member of Parliament by either disputing the parliamentary primaries (Ichino & Nathan 2013, 2017) as undemocratic or advocating for skirt and blouse voting. The reason is that if the more senior parliamentarian from his party loses, it will create an opportunity for him to achieve his goal. Again, those who harbor presidential ambitions also often use the party's structures to sabotage their presidential candidate. Though the president has a two-term limit, apart from former presidents Rawlings and Mahama, all the other presidents in Ghana's Fourth Republic made three attempts before winning. When they win, they can seek reelection, giving an individual about twenty years (three attempts at the presidency plus two possible terms making five multiplied by four years), in-party competitors who cannot wait will advocate skirt and blouse voting and at times openly campaign against their party members which their out-party opponents will use against them (their party).

Between 1992 and 2008, it was not possible for Ghanaian political parties to win the elections by counting on their individual strengths. For instance, in the 1992 elections, the NDC and other two political parties formed an alliance and made Mr. Rawlings, the NDC candidate, their presidential candidate. Mr. K. N. Arkaah of NCP, a junior partner, was made the running mate while the alliance supported the parliamentary candidates of the other parties. In 1996, again, the NDC and two other parties formed the Progressive Alliance and helped the parliamentary slots of its junior partners. The NPP and PCP also formed the Great Alliance which made the PCP candidate its running mate and deferred some of the parliamentary seats for its alliance partner. In all instances, the junior parties deferred their presidential race to their senior partners, got the running mate, and had their senior partners defer some of the parliamentary contests to them. Thus, the relationship between and among Ghanaian parties in alliance is such that the junior parties defer the presidential race to their senior partners and endorse their senior partners' presidential candidates and in return, their senior partners defer some of the parliamentary races, as well as endorse and support their junior partners. Therefore, the interparty relations between and among Ghanaian parties in alliance is shaped to produce a certain type of voting behavior among their supporters. It is worth pointing out, however, that not all the party supporters were in favor of the kind of arrangements that their parties entered into with their alliance partners (Frempong, 2017) because such arrangements required strategic withdrawals that denied their members the opportunity to contest in certain constituencies. Such persons in opposition to their party's arrangement with another party at times call on their supporters to boycott the elections or vote against their parties.

Therefore, understanding the nuances and intricacies of Ghanaian ticket-splitting requires unraveling the contextual peculiarities and hurdles that the Ghanaian political elites and candidates face within their parties and in negotiating with other parties for electoral purposes. Internally, the politician is faced with an in-party competitor whose presidential career requires a prospective presidential candidate to wait about twenty years while a parliamentary hopeful must wait in "perpetuity."[9] The best possible means to overcome such hurdles is for the prospective candidate to adopt a revisionist approach by disputing the nomination process or calling on his supporters to vote skirt and blouse. When it comes to relations between and among parties in alliance, some candidates will have to withdraw and endorse their candidature of their alliance partners. In such instances some people must abandon their political dreams of winning elections at least for a period. In all these instances, aggrieved members who are unable to control their emotions or do not receive an assurance as an appropriate payoff for what they will have to forgo will trigger certain indications of intraparty and interparty coordination failures that are likely to facilitate ticket-splitting and eventual defeat of their in-party competitors. The intuition behind voter choice of party elites and aggrieved members under the strategic coordination theory operates on the assumption that they (the aggrieved members) will themselves vote against their parties and persuade their supporters to vote against at least one office of their party in a given constituency if the party fails to negotiate acceptable payoff. This payoff is often a promise of position in the new government if the party wins power.

## RESULTS

Two models were run using the same survey datasets under different coding rules to ensure that the results were robust and not based on the coding. Furthermore, to ensure that the results are not influenced by missing data, multiple imputation technique was employed to deal with missing data (StataCorp, 2017).

It appears most of the coefficients were in their expected directions as per table 5.5. Consistent with the theoretical expectations of the chapter, the results provide strong empirical evidence in support of the strategic coordination induced ticket-splitting especially with respect to interparty coordination. For instance, H2A and H2B; endorsement and strategic withdrawal were both significant in terms of direction and magnitude in Model 1. In

Model 2 however, while H2A was significant, H2B strategic withdrawals was not but both have their signs in the expected direction. Among the intraparty coordination variables, only H1A and H1C—contentious primaries and "go independent" (aggrieved nomination seeker contesting the election as independent candidate)—were significant with the signs in the expected direction in Model 1. In Model 2, however, only "contentious primaries" was significant while "go independent" was not but both have the signs in the expected direction. Interestingly, the other intraparty coordination variables, H1B and H1D—threaten to leave party and common pool—were not significant in both models, though common pool had the signs at the expected direction in both models. Candidate quality was highly significant both in terms of magnitude and direction in Models 1 and 2. Interestingly, the control variables were not that significant as per table 5.5.

It can be said that, largely, the different coding rule was not responsible for the significance level of the following variables: contentious primaries, endorsement, and candidate quality since the different coding rules used did not markedly affect their significance level nor their expected direction. The same thing, however, cannot be said about strategic withdrawal and go independent because they lost their significant level when the coding rule was changed as shown in Model 2 per table 5.5, though their expected direction was retained. Interestingly, among the control variables, only party identification (ID) was significant in Model 2, while the rest, restricted choice and education, were not significant, and their signs were not that consistent. Party ID, however, has its signs in the expected direction in both models but not significant in Model 1. In fact, given that most of the strategic coordination variables were significant in both models but the control variables were not provide support for some consideration of their explanation of ticket-splitting.

Finally, to ensure that missing data was not responsible for the results in Models 1 and 2 in table 5.5, multiple imputation was employed to replace missing data and the same binary logit regression used initially for Models 1 and 2 was used to run Models 3 and 4. The results as shown in table 5.6 are not different from those in table 5.5. In fact, H2A and H2B—endorsement and strategic withdrawal—had the same significant levels in terms of magnitude and in the same expected direction. As H2A—endorsement—was significant in both models as in table 5.5, H2A was in table 5.6. Again, in the same way that H2B—strategic withdrawal—was not significant in Model 2 in table 5.5, it was not significant in Model 4 in table 5.6. Furthermore, contentious primaries, go independent, and party ID remained the same in terms of magnitude and direction. Also, education maintained its signs in table 5.6 as in table 5.5, though it was not significant in all the four models. The only difference between the results from the models with missing values and those run with multiple imputation was in respect to two variables:

**Table 5.5.  Logit analysis of "ticket-splitting" using survey data (with missing data).**

| Variables | With Missing Data (Model 1) | With Missing Data (Model 2) |
|---|---|---|
| Contentious Primaries | 0.8045** | 1.1228* |
| | (0.3124) | (0.6658) |
| Threaten to Leave Party | -0.6668 | 0.0256 |
| | (0.4505) | (0.6940) |
| Go Independent | 1.0094* | 0.4125 |
| | (0.5305) | (0.6478) |
| Common Pool | -0.6243 | -0.3305 |
| | (0.5599) | (0.6379) |
| Endorsement | 1.1265*** | 2.1346*** |
| | (0.4047) | (0.7611) |
| Strategic Withdrawal | 1.1002*** | 0.7370 |
| | (0.4083) | (0.7235) |
| Restricted Choice | 0.3825 | -0.3727 |
| | (0.4940) | (0.6658) |
| Party ID | 0.2954 | 0.5056** |
| | (0.1917) | (0.2555) |
| Candidate Quality | 3.0806*** | 2.8185*** |
| | (0.4534) | (0.4955) |
| Education | 0.0384 | -0.1151 |
| | (0.1047) | (0.1197) |
| Constant | -7.2376*** | -8.7285*** |
| | (1.5572) | (2.2770) |
| Observations | 247 | 192 |

Standard errors in parentheses; *** $p < 0.01$, ** $p < 0.05$, * $p < 0.1$

threaten to leave party and restricted choice. Whereas restricted choice has its signs in the expected direction in all but Model 2—threaten to leave party—has its signs right in only Model 2.

## DISCUSSION

Per the results from the fitted logit regression above, many of the variables are significant and in the expected direction consistent with findings from

*Samuel Darkwa*

**Table 5.6. Logit analysis of "ticket-splitting" using survey data (with multiple imputation).**

|  | With Imputation (Model 3) | With Imputation (Model 4) |
|---|---|---|
| Contentious Primaries | 0.7102** | 1.0149 * |
|  | (0.2934) | (0.5913) |
| Threaten to Leave Party | -0.4430 | -0.4250 |
|  | (0. 4117) | (0.5915) |
| Go Independent | 0.8049* | 0.1317 |
|  | (0.4502) | (0.5433) |
| Common Pool | -0.4686 | -0.1316 |
|  | (0.5262) | (0.5633) |
| Endorsement | 1.0678*** | 1.6912** |
|  | (0.3717) | (0.6431) |
| Strategic Withdrawal | 0.8447** | 0.5114 |
|  | (0.3765) | (0.6367) |
| Restricted Choice | 0.7501 | 0.3155 |
|  | (0.4622) | (0. 5797) |
| Party ID | 0.2063 | 0.3862** |
|  | (0.1784) | (0.2070) |
| Candidate Quality | 2.9756*** | 2.4299*** |
|  | (0.4441) | (0.4670) |
| Education | 0.0120 | -0.0797 |
|  | (0.0973) | (0.1039) |
| Constant | -6.8038*** | -7.7437 *** |
|  | (1.4594) | (1.8568) |
| Observations | 303 | 303 |

Standard errors in parentheses; *** $p < 0.01$, ** $p < 0.05$, * $p < 0.1$.

similar studies on coordination. A couple of them, however, were surprisingly different from expectation. In fact, research on coordination and voter behavior has found that coordination can be elite-driven through strategic entry (Arriola & Arriola, 2013; Benoit, 2001; Cox, 1999) or voter-driven through strategic voting (Conroy-Krutz, 2013; Cox, 1999). Therefore, coordination variables that were significant, such as contentious primaries, endorsement, and strategic withdrawal (which were elite driven) are not surprising. For instance, as of 1999, Cox had found that the decline in vote share suffered by Japan's LDP was the result of its inability to overcome coordination problems it confronted in the 1960s (Cox, 1999). The fate of the Japan LDP is not different from the many smaller parties in Ghana that align with the first president of Ghana, Dr. Kwame Nkrumah. Those parties are not able to overcome the coordination problems that have led their parties to be reduced to a pale shadow of the original CPP, which had won all the elections in Ghana from the 1950s up to the mid-1960s. Sure, apart from parties that belong to the CPP who have been swept with the currents of coordination, in Ghana the low and high tides of coordination can be seen when one considers the performance of the three main party traditions in Ghana today: the Nkrumahists (represented by the many fragmented parties that trace their origin to Nkrumah's principles), Danquah-Busia-Domo tradition (represented by the NPP), and the Akatamansonia tradition (represented by the NDC) (Amponsah, 2006; Jonah, 1998; Osei, 2012). It could be said, however, that the NDC and the NPP have benefited from coordination to the extent that they command over 97 percent of the presidential vote share and together have 100 percent of the parliamentary seats (Agyeman-Duah, 2005; Frempong, 2017). Therefore, the Nkrumahist groups must lift their coordination game because they are suffocating under coordination problems.

In the early 1990s, despite Rawlings being very popular, the NDC formed an alliance with its coalition members to help secure two successive electoral victories for the party and facilitate the winning of parliamentary seats for its alliance members. Due to how the alliance was shaped, it led to ticket-splitting because of how the NDC endorsed and supported the parliamentary candidates of its junior partners (in the same constituency, an NDC member was likely to vote NDC at the presidential race and for its alliance partner at the parliamentary race). The same was the case with the NPP and its alliance members. In fact, in the 1996 elections, the NPP and People's Convention Party (PCP) entered an alliance and the CPP deferred its presidential slot to the NPP, endorsed and supported the NPP presidential candidate, and in return the NPP deferred some of the parliamentary races to the PCP. In the end, all the five seats the PCP won were in constituencies where the NPP deferred to, endorsed, and supported the PCP (Agyeman-Duah, 2005; Frempong, 2017; Osei, 2012). In all these instances, the results were a skirt and blouse outcome (split outcome) which is a strong indication that there was significant skirt and blouse voting. Again, in these instances, party elites and candidates openly encouraged skirt and blouse voting. These instances of skirt and blouse voting represent the high tides of interparty coordination in Ghana and it indeed promoted skirt and blouse voting.

Coordination has also adversely affected the political parties in situations where there was evidence of a skirt and blouse outcome, which points to possible skirt and blouse voting. For instance, when Rawlings was completing his second term, he handpicked his vice president Professor John Atta-

Mills in 1998 at the party's congress as his successor (Debrah, 2004; Frempong, 2017; Osei, 2012). This infuriated other party members who had presidential ambitions. As a result of this undemocratic act, a splinter group, the National Reform Party, broke away from the NDC and campaigned against the NDC. Meanwhile, Mr. Kow Nkensen Arkaah, who was Rawlings's vice president between 1993 and 1997, broke ties with Rawlings and the NDC and led part of the Nkrumahist tradition (the National Convention Party-NCP of which he was the leader) to join the NPP, the largest opposition party to form the Great Alliance (Agyeman-Duah, 2005; Frempong, 2017; Osei, 2012). These are some instances that Ghanaian political elites and candidates will openly advocate ticket-splitting. Political elites' penchant of advocating ticket-splitting is not unique to Ghana because in the United States, for instance, during the 1996 elections, it was said that some Republican congressional candidates campaigned to be elected alongside President Clinton so that they could check him (Burden & Kimball, 2009). Ghana's own ticket-splitting is widespread. Though the Republicans by their acts were endorsing President Clinton ahead of their own presidential candidate, the tendency of the American electorate buying into such calls is likely to be ineffective compared with Ghana where leaders' opinions are almost sacrosanct. It is also interesting to note that party elites and candidates are supposed to campaign for the electorates to support all their candidates and if they rather select to advocate skirt and blouse, the effects can be huge.

## CONCLUSIONS

In sum, this chapter tried to address unusual questions in split-ticket voting by trying to find out why party elites advocate ticket-splitting or which candidate will split their ballot and advocate same instead of the conventional question: Why do some voters split the ballot and others do not? Again, it has also tried to understand how this elite behavior has affected the current distribution of votes and seat share of parties in Ghana. In addressing these questions, I carried out an elite survey in Ghana in 2017, sampling 296 party elites and card-bearing members of seven Ghanaian political parties. Also interviewed were seven members drawn from academia, the media, and civil society. Though the sample was not randomly selected, it was selected to be representative of party officials from constituencies that have experienced skirt and blouse outcomes and those that have not. It also sampled persons at the center of the main determinants of party officials advocating ticket-splitting and those who were not.

As evidenced by the results from the fitted binary logit regressions, all the interparty coordination variables (endorsement and strategic withdrawal) were significant. Also significant were some of the intraparty coordination variables (contentious primaries and a member going independent) and candidate quality. The intraparty coordination variables have made us aware that party elites are likely to split their ticket and advocate for the same where the party's nomination process is undemocratic. That is to say, in normal times, as long as the party's nomination process is transparent and democratic, we do not expect Ghanaian politicians and party elite to engage in ticket-splitting or to advocate it. However, in non-normal times where a politician calculates and finds that adhering to the status quo would mean that they wait in "perpetuity," they would like to accuse others of irregularities in the nomination process (Ichino & Nathan, 2013, 2017) and use that excuse to get party officials to take decisions in their favor or to leave with other supporters to contest as independent. Others who have parliamentary and presidential ambitions can sabotage their party candidates to lose the elections so that they can win a candidate that has lost on the party's ticket (Frempong, 2017). In all these instances, these persons advocate skirt and blouse voting. In fact, leaving one's party and contesting as independent is not peculiar to Ghana. In the 2000 U.S. election, former Republican Senator James Jeffords of Vermont defected and contested as independent (Burden & Kimball, 2009). It is likely that his defection caused ticket-splitting. It would be interesting to find out how he and his family and friends voted especially where after his defection he started fraternizing with Democrats.

At the interparty sphere, opinions are divided about the effects of the coordination between bigger and smaller parties in Ghana, which invariably have contributed to ticket-splitting, as in most instances, the smaller parties support the bigger parties in the presidential race and the bigger ones defer some parliamentary seats to the smaller parties. In fact, some respondents are of the view that it was largely because of interparty coordination that the smaller parties could pick the few seats in Parliament in the past. However, situations where the members of big parties have refused to coordinate with the smaller parties have led to what Mr. Kwesi Jonah refers to as "the withering away of the smaller parties" (field interview, March 13, 2017). To him, the country has lost the voice of the smaller parties. In sharp contrast to this view, Dr. Ofori Mensah is of the view that the smaller parties have not articulated their own view since the inception of the Fourth Republican Parliament. To him, the smaller parties have always supported the bigger parties who supported them and as such have not presented their own platform (field interview, March 24, 2017). Thus, others think that though skirt and blouse voting, and subsequently skirt and blouse outcome, have helped the smaller parties to have representation in Parliament (because in the few occasions that the smaller parties have gone into Parliament it was due to interparty coordination), the relationship worked against the smaller parties. The reality is that in many instances, the bigger parties poach the viable candidates of the smaller parties and independent candidates by giving them ministerial appointments and other governmental appointments. These candidates have supported the policies of the government of the day and have not had their own voice. The resultant effect is that they incur the anger of their own parties and that of the public.

In sum, it is critical to carry out empirical research on how coordination problems affect parties, elites, and candidates. Such research will help party elites to identify and guard against intraparty coordination problems such as linkage problems which happen where there is no harmony between the parliamentary and presidential candidates' campaigns. Again, such research will help political parties to take steps to improve internal democracy if they know that imposition of a candidate on a constituency, for instance, will cause skirt and blouse voting. We also observe that young politicians who have legislative ambition but are not able to realize such ambition because their seniors who are already on the legislature have no term limit adopt strategic coordination that may hurt their own party's chance of winning an election. My field research shows that although politicians do not often overtly advocate ticket-splitting, many do so when they see it to be in their interest and do so more at the grassroots level. Such conduct takes place largely due to coordination problems that parties are unable to identify and address in the first place. Such a revelation will help politicians and crafters of constitutions to have a second look at ways of reviewing existing laws and policies to limit internal conflicts.

Ghana currently does not have a third party. The Nkrumahists who won independence for Ghana and formed the governments under the First and Third Republican Constitutions have now run out of steam due to the existence of several splinter groups that together attract less than 2 percent of the voter share. In fact, the 2016 elections results show that the two leading political parties pulled about 98 percent of the presidential votes cast and 100 percent of the legislative seats (Electoral Commission, 2016; Frempong, 2017). This is due to coordination problems faced by the Nkrumahist elites. By such research, they can identify their coordination problems and craft proactive solutions for them, as well work out preelection coalitions ahead of the 2020 elections. They can also figure out how to position themselves given that the Akatamansonia and the Danquah-Busia-Domo traditions occupy center-left and center-right, respectively, and the Nkrumahist, who are the original leftist party, can draw some votes from the left when they come together. Their coordination problem does not affect that tradition alone, but it does affect Ghana's democracy given that there is policy vacuum at the far left and far right.

It is hereby suggested that further research into the phenomenon of ticket-splitting should also consider instances where party elites will strategically encourage split-ticket voting. Thus, questions such as why would parties, elites, and candidates encourage ticket-splitting can advance our knowledge of the phenomenon. Another thing I chanced upon in my fieldwork was how the financing of opposition election campaigns contributes to the phenomenon. It was alleged that some politicians finance the campaigns of their opponents with the view that the recipients of such funds will find fault with their party's nomination process and create confusion that will trigger observable indicators of the intraparty coordination failures discussed above. Such acts often divide the votes of the opponent's party and, consequently, enhance the chances of the financier to win the election. This invariably promotes ticket-splitting in the recipient's part. It would, therefore, be great to research such acts in the future.

## APPENDIX

Table 5.7.    Details of respondents interviewed/surveyed.

| Description | Number | Percentage |
|---|---|---|
| Member | 25 | 8.25 |
| Chair | 24 | 7.92 |
| Secretary | 23 | 7.59 |
| Youth leadership | 25 | 8.25 |
| Campaign Coordinator | 21 | 6.93 |
| Treasurer | 12 | 3.96 |
| Director of Elections | 8 | 2.64 |
| Women Organizer | 24 | 7.92 |
| Grassroots/Cadres | 30 | 9.9 |
| Member of Parliament | 8 | 2.64 |
| Research | 12 | 3.96 |
| Results Analyst | 15 | 4.95 |
| Polling Agent | 28 | 9.24 |
| Communication team member | 30 | 9.9 |
| Civil Society | 5 | 1.65 |
| National Commission for Civic Education | 1 | 0.33 |
| Academia | 3 | 0.99 |
| Media | 9 | 2.97 |
| Total | 303 | 100 |

**Table 5.8.   Coding at the elite level of analysis.**

| Variable | Description of the Variable (questions in 2017 field survey) | Model 1 Coding Rule | Model 2 Coding Rule |
|---|---|---|---|
| Split (DV) | To measure the DV, respondents were asked in Q5 "Have you ever voted skirt and blouse (that is to vote for presidential and parliamentary candidates in the same election from different political parties) before?" | Respondents who answered "Yes" were coded as "1" and "No" coded as "0" | Respondents who answered "Yes" were coded as "1" and "No" coded as "0" |

**Independent and Control Variables**

| | | | |
|---|---|---|---|
| Successful/ Contentious Primaries | I compute successful primaries using Q5, "Please select the statement that most closely matches your view. In general, the recent parliamentary primaries of your political party were successful." | Respondents who answered Strongly Agree & Moderately Agree were coded as "0," those who responded Strongly Disagree & Moderately Disagree were coded as "1," and those who selected "Neutral" were coded as "2" | Respondents who answered Strongly Agree & Moderately Agree were coded as "0," those who responded Strongly Disagree & Moderately Disagree were coded as "1," and those who selected "Neutral" were coded as a missing value |
| Threaten to Leave Party | Threaten to Leave Party was measured using Q6, "Did any defeated candidate of your party threaten to leave the political party?" | Respondents who selected "Yes" were coded as "1," "No" coded as "0," and "Don't Know" coded as "2" | Respondents who selected "Yes" were coded as "1," "No" coded as "0," and "Don't Know" coded as missing value |
| Go Independent | I generated the variable 'Go Independent' using Q9, "Did some losing parliamentary contestants go independent?" | Respondents who answered "Yes" were coded as "1," "No" coded as "0," and "Don't Know" coded as "2" | Respondents who answered "Yes" were coded as "1," "No" coded as "0," and "Don't Know" coded as missing value |
| Common Pool | The variable "Common Pool" was measured using Q17, | Respondents who answered "Yes" were coded as "1" | Respondents who answered "Yes" were coded as "1" and |

| | | | |
|---|---|---|---|
| | "Leading to the elections did your party maintain a common pool of resources for both presidential and parliamentary campaigns?" | and those who selected "No" coded as "0" | those who selected "No" coded as "0" |
| Endorsement | The variable "Endorsement" was generated using Q21, "Did your party endorse another candidate for either the presidential or parliamentary slot?" | Respondents who answered "Yes" were coded as "1," "No" coded as "0," and "Don't Know" coded as "2" | Respondents who answered "Yes" were coded as "1," "No" coded as "0," and "Don't Know" coded as missing value |
| Strategic Withdrawal | I generate the variable, "Strategic Withdrawal" using Q23, "Did your party decide to leave out any constituency or withdraw a candidate from a particular constituency to help another party win that seat?" | Respondents who selected "Yes" were coded as "1," "No" coded as "0," and "Don't Know" coded as "2" | Respondents who selected "Yes" were coded as "1," "No" coded as "0," and "Don't Know" coded as missing value |
| Restricted Choice | The variable "Contest both Offices" was generated using Q24, "Did your party contest in both presidential and parliamentary seats in all constituencies?" | Respondents who selected "Yes" were coded as "1," "No" coded as "0," and "Don't Know" coded as "2." | Respondents who selected "Yes" were coded as "1," "No" coded as "0," and "Don't Know" coded as "missing value |
| Party ID | It was generated using Q3, "If you answered Yes on Question 2, which political party is that?" | Respondent's party affiliation was coded as per their responses: CPP 41, NDC 87, NPP 86, PNC 38, and PPP 44. | Respondent's party affiliation was coded as per their responses: CPP 41, NDC 87, NPP 86, PNC 38, and PPP 44. |
| Candidate Quality | The variable "Candidate Quality" was generated using Q27 in respect to the reasons given by | Respondents who chose candidate quality (which was the most popular response) were | Respondents who chose candidate quality (which was the most popular response) were |

| | respondents' decision for voting skirt and blouse. | coded as "1" and otherwise as "0." | coded as "1" and otherwise as "0." |
|---|---|---|---|
| Education | I control for education using the educational qualification of respondents. | Education is on an eight rater-scale from "0" to "8," from "I don't know" to "University completed and beyond" | Education is on an eight rater-scale from "0" to "8" from "I don't know" to "University completed and beyond" |

# NOTES

1. https://www.ghanaweb.com/GhanaHomePage/features/Let-s-vote-skirt-and-blouse-154036.

2. A situation where one concept has more than one meaning creates conceptual ambiguity; as a result, I reclassified *skirt and blouse voting* into *skirt and blouse voting* (split-ticket voting) and *skirt and blouse outcome* (split-district outcome) to harmonize it with similar conventional political science concepts for comparability.

3. I use the term "interparty coordination" to characterize any form of pre-electoral interactions and/or arrangement between parties and candidates, as well as individual deals capable of affecting their electoral performance. It also encompasses their negotiations for policy and office prior to the elections.

4. The swing constituencies are erratic in their voting patterns and any political party that wins the swing regions wins the national elections since 1992.

5. Constituency with more than 60,000 registered voters is considered large because it exceeds the national average of about 56,000 registered voters and about 39,000 valid votes cast as per the 2016 electoral statistics.

6. Klottey Korle constituency is at times written Korle Klottey or Osu Klottey.

7. One of the faculty from the Department of Political Science in the University of Ghana interviewed is the author of *Elections in Ghana 1951–2016*. The next has also written extensively on elections. He was a former head of the department and has headed the governance centers of two think tanks. He is currently the head of the governance center of the Institute for Democratic Governance (IDEG) in Ghana. The third wanted to remain anonymous. I also received a great deal of support from the immediate head of the political science department who is now the deputy commissioner at the EC (Electoral Commission). He introduced me to the president of the political science students at the University of Ghana.

8. I did not drop respondents who selected "Don't Know" and "Neutral" but coded them with the value "2," because Ghanaian party elites/candidates often have diplomatic ways of not selecting responses that reflect their true behavior when they have options for "Don't Know" and "Neutral." However, in the second coding those were dropped and treated as missing data for comparison purposes.

9. This situation is not unique to Ghana; however, it has become an issue such that if an MP spends more than two terms in Parliament, that member becomes a target within his or her party. In fact, one of the MPs I interviewed during my fieldwork (Hon. Alhassan Fuseini Inusah), who had been threatened with skirt and blouse voting in the 2016 election on his fourth attempt, hinted he was not going to stand for reelection. I am not surprised he has confirmed that decision. https://www.myjoyonline.com/politics/2018/July-3rd/inusah-fuseini-bows-out-of-2020-parliamentary-race.php.

# REFERENCES

Agyeman-Duah, Baffour. (2005). *Elections and Electoral Politics in Ghana's Fourth Republic.* No. 18. Ghana Center for Democratic Development.

Amponsah, Nicholas. (2006). "Political Traditions and Electoral Politics in Kintampo North and South, Sissala West and Wa Central." In Boafo-Arthur, Kwame (ed.), *Voting for Democracy in Ghana: The 2004 Elections in Perspective. Vols. 1 & 2.* Accra: Freedom Publications, 287–307.

Arriola, Leonardo R., and Leonardo Rafael Arriola. (2013). *Multi-ethnic Coalitions in Africa: Business Financing of Opposition Election Campaigns.* Cambridge: Cambridge University Press.

Asunka, Joseph. (2016). "Partisanship and Political Accountability in New Democracies: Explaining Compliance with Formal Rules and Procedures in Ghana." *Research & Politics* 3(1).

Beck, Paul Allen, et al. (1992). "Patterns and Sources of Ticket-Splitting in Subpresidential Voting." *American Political Science Review* 86(4): 916–928.

Bennett, Andrew. (2004). "Case Study Methods: Design, Use, and Comparative Advantages." In D. F. Sprinz and Y. Wolinsky-Nahmias (eds.), *Models, Numbers, and Cases: Methods for Studying International Relations,* 19–55. Ann Arbor: University of Michigan.

Benoit, Kenneth. (2001). "Two Step Forward, One Steps Back: Electoral Coordination in the Hungarian Elections of 1998." Typescript. Trinity College, Dublin.

Benoit, Kenneth, Daniela Giannetti, and Michael Laver. (2006). "Voter Strategies with Restricted Choice Menus." *British Journal of Political Science* 36(3): 459–485.

Boafo-Arthur, K. (2006). "The 2004 General Elections: An Overview," In Boafo-Arthur (ed.), *Voting for Democracy in Ghana: The 2004 Elections in Perspective, Vol. 1,* 33–58. Accra: Freedom Publications.

Boafo-Arthur, Kwame. (2008). *Democracy and Stability in West Africa: The Ghanaian Experience.* Nordiska Afrikainstitutet; Department of Peace and Conflict Research, Uppsala University.

Born, Richard. (1994). "Split-Ticket Voters, Divided Government, and Fiorina's Policy-Balancing Model." *Legislative Studies Quarterly* 19(1): 95–115.

Boucek, Françoise. (2009) "Rethinking Factionalism: Typologies, Intra-Party Dynamics and Three Faces of Factionalism." *Party Politics* 15(4): 455–485.

Box-Steffensmeier, Janet M. (1996). "A Dynamic Analysis of the Role of War Chests in Campaign Strategy." *American Journal of Political Science* 40(2): 352–371.

Burden, Barry C. (2009). "Candidate-Driven Ticket-Splitting in the 2000 Japanese Elections." *Electoral Studies* 28(1): 33–40.

Burden, Barry C., and David C. Kimball. (1998). "A New Approach to the Study of Ticket-Splitting." *American Political Science Review* 92(3): 533–544.

Burden, Barry C., and David C. Kimball. (2009). *Why Americans Split Their Tickets: Campaigns, Competition, and Divided Government.* Ann Arbor: University of Michigan Press.

Campbell, Angus, Philip E. Converse, Warren E. Miller, and E. Donald. (1960). *The American Voter.* Chicago: University of Chicago Press.

Campbell, Angus, and Warren E. Miller. (1957). "The Motivational Basis of Straight and Split-Ticket Voting." *American Political Science Review* 51(2): 293–312.

Conroy-Krutz, Jeffrey. (2013). "Information and Ethnic Politics in Africa." *British Journal of Political Science* 43(2): 345–373.

Cox, Gary W. (1997). *Making Votes Count: Strategic Coordination in the World's Electoral Systems.* Cambridge: Cambridge University Press.

Cox, Gary. (1999). "Electoral Rules and Electoral Coordination." *Annual Review of Political Science* 2(1): 145–161.

Crutzen, Benoit S. Y., Micael Castanheira, and Nicolas Sahuguet. (2009). "Party Organization and Electoral Competition." *Journal of Law, Economics, & Organization* 26(2): 212–242.

Daddieh, Cyril. (2009). "Democratic Consolidation without a Second Turnover: Ghana's Remarkable 2004 Elections." *Elections and Democratization in West Africa* 2: 43–74.

Daddieh, Cyril K., and George M. Bob-Milliar. (2012). "In Search of 'Honorable' Membership: Parliamentary Primaries and Candidate Selection in Ghana." *Journal of Asian and African Studies* 47(2): 204–220.

Dalton, Russell J. (2013). *The Apartisan American: Dealignment and Changing Electoral Politics.* Los Angeles: Sage.

De Vries, Walter, and V. Lance Tarrance. (1972). *The Ticket-Splitter: A New Force in American Politics.* Grand Rapids: Eerdmans.

Debrah, Emmanuel. (2004). "The Politics of Elections: Opposition and Incumbency in Ghana's 2000 Elections." *Africa Insight* 34(2–3): 3–15.

Debrah, Emmanuel. (2014). "Intra-Party Democracy in Ghana's Fourth Republic: The Case of the New Patriotic Party and National Democratic Congress." *Journal of Power, Politics & Governance* 2(3): 57–75.

Debrah, Emmanuel, and Ransford Edward Van Gyampo. (2013). "The Youth and Party Manifestos in Ghanaian Politics—The Case of the 2012 General Elections." *Journal of African Elections* 12(2): 96–114.

Electoral Commission. (2016). "The 2016 Presidential Results." Electoral Commission Ghana. http://www.thumbsapp.com.gh/. Retrieved September 20, 2018.

Frempong, Alexander Kaakyire Duku. (2017). *Elections in Ghana: 1951–2016.* Tema, Ghana: Digibooks Ghana Ltd.

Frymer, Paul. (1994). "Ideological Consensus within Divided Party Government." *Political Science Quarterly* 109(2): 287–311.

Golder, Sona Nadenichek. (2006). *The Logic of Pre-Electoral Coalition Formation.* Columbus: Ohio State University Press.

Ichino, Nahomi, and Noah L. Nathan. (2013). "Do Primaries Improve Electoral Performance? Clientelism and Intra-Party Conflict in Ghana." *American Journal of Political Science* 57(2): 428–441.

Ichino, Nahomi, and Noah L. Nathan. (2017). "Primary Elections in New Democracies: The Evolution of Candidate Selection Methods in Ghana." Working paper. Ann Arbor: University of Michigan.

Jervis, Robert. (2017). *Perception and Misperception in International Politics: New Edition.* Princeton: Princeton University Press.

Jonah, Kwesi. (1998). "Political Parties and the Transition to Multi-Party Politics in Ghana." In K. A. Ninsin (ed.), *Ghana: Transition to Democracy*, 72–94. Accra: Freedom Publications.

Kadima, Denis, and Cassam Uteem. (2006). *The Politics of Party Coalitions in Africa.* EISA, 2006.

Key, Valdimer Orlando, and Milton Curtis Cummings. (1966). *The Responsible Electorate: Rationality in Presidential Voting, 1936–1960.* Foreword by Arthur Maass. Cambridge: Harvard University Press.

Lartey-Adjei, Festus. (December 7, 2012). https://www.ghanaweb.com/GhanaHomePage/NewsArchive/Be-Bold-vote-skirt-and-blouse-Sakara-258747.

Lindberg, Staffan I. (2013). "Have the Cake and Eat It: The Rational Voter in Africa." *Party Politics* 19(6): 945–961.

Maddox, William S., and Dan Nimmo. (1981). "In Search of the Ticket Splitter." *Social Science Quarterly* 62(3): 401.

Malone, Thomas W. (1988). *What Is Coordination Theory?* Cambridge: Massachusetts Institute of Technology.

Moravcsik, Andrew. (2001). *Liberal International Relations Theory: A Social Scientific Assessment.* Nos. 1–2. Cambridge: Weatherhead Center for International Affairs, Harvard University.

Navia, Patricio, and José Luis Saldaña. (2015). "Mis-coordination and Political Misalignments in Ticket-Splitting: The Case of Chile, 2005–2009." *Contemporary Politics* 21(4): 485–503.

Osei, Anja. (2012). *Party-Voter Linkage in Africa: Ghana and Senegal in Comparative Perspective.* Wiesbaden, Germany: Springer Science & Business Media.

Petrocik, John R., and Joseph Doherty. (1996). "The Road to Divided Government: Paved without Intention." In Peter F. Galderisi (ed.), *Divided Government: Change, Uncertainty, and the Constitutional Order.* Lanham, MD: Rowman & Littlefield.

Roscoe, Douglas D. (2003). "The Choosers or the Choices? Voter Characteristics and the Structure of Electoral Competition as Explanations for Ticket-Splitting." *Journal of Politics* 65(4): 1147–1164.

Scheiner, Ethan. (2005). *Democracy without Competition in Japan: Opposition Failure in a One-Party Dominant State*. Cambridge: Cambridge University Press.

StataCorp, L. P. (2017). *Stata Multiple-Imputation Reference Manual Release 15*. College Station, TX: Stata Press.

Volden, Craig. (2002). "The Politics of Competitive Federalism: A Race to the Bottom in Welfare Benefits." *American Journal of Political Science* 46(2): 352–363.

Weghorst, Keith R., and Staffan I. Lindberg. (2013). "What Drives the Swing Voter in Africa?" *American Journal of Political Science* 57(3): 717–734.

*Chapter Six*

# Are Members of Parliament (MPs) in Ghana Responsive to Their Constituents in Policy Making?

*Evidence from the National Health Insurance Scheme*

## Hassan Wahab

Is democracy about responsiveness of the elected officials to voters? This question has preoccupied political theorists for a long time (Urbinati & Warren, 2008; Mansbridge, 2011; Rehfeld, 2009). Do elected representatives in Ghana care about their constituents or not? Do elected officials owe the electorate a duty to act to reflect their perspectives in policy decisions? According to one school of thought, elected officials are trustees of the people in a democracy (Burke, 1790/1960). They are obliged to act in the interests of those who are governed even though the representative is expected to exercise his independent judgment (Burke, 1790/1960). The Burkean conception of representation gives elected officials the latitude to pursue the interests of the totality of the population rather the interests of their constituents. On the other hand, the delegate model postulates that elected representatives are chosen to act on behalf of their constituents by conveying their views in policies; thus, elected officials are conduits for channeling the popular views of constituents for solutions (McCrone & Kuklinski, 1979). This is because elected officials draw their mandate from the electorate who voted them into power through the ballot box (Aryee, 2017; Debrah, 2008/ 2009; Gyimah-Boadi, 2009).

Despite the importance of the concept of responsiveness in a democracy, the literature on Ghana's democratization has tended to focus more on patronage, ethnicity, and neo-patrimonial politics (Bates, 1989, 2008; Bratton &

van de Walle, 1994; van de Walle, 2001; Fridy, 2007); popular perceptions
of government's performance (Aryee, 2011; Bawumia, 1998; Jeffries, 1998;
Lindberg & Morrison, 2005, 2008; Nugent 2001a, 2001b; Whitfield, 2009;
Youde, 2005; Osei, 2013); and nonperforming representatives who were
punished by the voters at the polls (Myjoyonline, June 13, 2015; Kokutse,
October 29, 2012; Kelly & Benning, 2013; Boafo-Arthur, 2008; Frempong,
2017). This study examines how MPs "carried" the health care concerns of
constituents into policy action and contributes to the burgeoning literature on
Ghanaian democratization and public policy. This study departs from the
conventional election studies by examining how elected officials translated
the will of voters into policy decision. This insight is especially important
when viewed from results of a 2005 Afrobarometer survey which found that
while 90 percent of Ghanaians expected their elected representatives to listen
to their views, 56 percent of MPs neither visited their constituencies nor
listened to them (Afrobarometer, November 2005). Moreover, a growing
number of media reports indicate that Ghanaian MPs, particularly when they
are in opposition, do not care to work together with MPs from the ruling
party to solve problems that matter to their constituents, and that on the few
occasions that they did work together, the issues involved their own emolu-
ments—selfish interests (Kasapafmonline.com, November 2, 2015).

Analyzing data from official Ghanaian parliamentary records in the form
of floor speeches, I argue that, at least on the salient issue of health care,
elected officials showed they cared about their constituents. A salient issue is
one that citizens demand action on, and elected officials and political parties
promise to act on. Not only did citizens and civil society demand action
(Brande, January 5, 1997; Kusi-Ampofo et al., 2014), it featured prominently
in the 2000 election campaigns of politicians and political parties (New Patriotic Party, 2000; National Democratic Congress, 2000). The remainder of
this paper is organized into three sections. The first section examines the
historical trajectories of the policy landscape in relation to health care in
Ghana. The second analyzes how MPs responded to popular needs by passing national health insurance legislation, which was a hotly debated campaign issue in the 2000 election. The final section is devoted to conclusions
and lessons.

## THE STATE OF HEALTH CARE DELIVERY
## IN GHANA BEFORE 2000

Prior to Ghana's independence in 1957, relatively few citizens outside the
traditional safety net of the extended family in the village had access to
public health care in what was then the Gold Coast (Anyinam, 1989; Mac-
Lean, 2010; Senah, 2001; Waddington & Enyimayew, 1990). User fees,

though minimal, were charged at the few hospitals and clinics available at the time and were only waived for indigenes. Following independence in 1957, the government under Prime Minister Kwame Nkrumah instituted a policy that extended health care to all residents of Ghana, as a concrete manifestation of the benefits of independence. Under the policy, all Ghanaians could seek medical attention in any government hospital or health center and pharmacy at no financial cost to them, and whatever user fees existed under the colonial period were removed. State spending on social programs, including health care, was dramatically increased (Agyepong & Adjei, 2008; Carbone, 2011; Senah, 2001). Furthermore, the government made health education services more available and accessible, which emphasized preventive and community-based health care services rather than a hospital-based curative system (Carbone, 2011). Public health workers (colloquially known as Tankas) were sent to private homes, businesses, market centers, offices, and the like to conduct cleanliness inspections, and those found not to have met the required cleanliness standards were ticketed and fined.

In the mid-1960s, the Ghanaian economy began to tumble, partly due to the fall in the price of cash crops, such as cocoa, in the world market (Agyepong & Adjei, 2008; Arhinful, 2003). Citizens' dissatisfaction with government increased as the economy worsened and political tension between the government and the opposition heightened. Eventually, the Nkrumah government was overthrown in a coup d'état believed to have been sponsored by the United States' CIA in 1966 (Apter, 1968; Afrifa, 1966). Meanwhile, Ghana's population was growing at a pace faster than anticipated. In recognition of the lack of revenue to support the free health care program, the military regime, which formed the National Liberation Council (NLC), issued the Hospital Fees Decree (NLC 360) to reintroduce fees for services in 1969. Later in 1969, the military handed over power to a constitutionally elected government the Progress Party (PP), led by Kofi A. Busia as prime minister.

In 1970, the Busia administration amended NLC 360 to become the Hospital Fees Act (Act 387). Act 387 maintained payment of some minimum fees for services, ostensibly to discourage their abuse (Agyepong & Adjei, 2008; Seddoh & Akor, 2012; Waddington & Enyimahew, 1990). On January 13, 1972, the Busia government was also overthrown in a military coup d'état. Subsequently, Ghana experienced two successive coups d'états (July 5, 1978–June 4, 1979; June 4, 1979–September 24, 1979), a brief democratically elected government interregnum (September 24, 1979–December 31, 1981), and a long military rule (December 31, 1981–January 7, 1993), before the beginning of the current constitutional democratic dispensation.

By December 31, 1981, when President Hilla Limann was overthrown by the Provisional National Defense Council (PNDC), health care delivery and services in Ghana had deteriorated so much that in some public hospitals, patients provided their own bedding, medicine, food, and even stationery for their medical records (Senah, 2001; Seddoh & Akor, 2012). The country's hospitals and clinics lacked basic and essential medical supplies and medical professionals left the country in droves (Anyinam, 1989; Ghanaweb.com, September 26, 2003, January 24, 2001, July 8, 1999); patients were detained at health care centers until they paid the bills for their care (Ghanaweb.com, July 15, 2003, January 28, 1999), and high prescription costs forced many Ghanaians to self-medicate instead of seeking proper health care (Asenso-Okyere et al., 1998; Boafo-Arthur, 1999; Van De Boom, Nsowah-Nuamah, & Overbosch, 2008).

In 1983, the PNDC government adopted the International Monetary Fund (IMF) and the World Bank–promoted Structural Adjustment Program (SAP). As part of SAP, the government instituted the Hospital Fees Regulation (HFR) in 1985. The HFR sought to recover 15 percent of recurrent health costs by substantially raising fees for diagnostic procedures, consultations, surgery, hospital accommodation, and the like (Carbone, 2011; Nyonator & Kutzin, 1999; Agyepong & Adjei, 2008). This resulted in patients picking up most of the cost for health care, which effectively placed health care services outside of the reach of many, if not most, Ghanaians (Asante & Aikins, 2008; Hutchful, 2002; Konadu-Agyemang, 2000; Waddington & Enyimayew, 1990; Anyinam, 1989; Seddoh, Adjei, & Nazzar, 2011; Seddoh & Akor, 2012). Government expenditure on health care, which was 10 percent of the national budget in 1982, dropped to 1.3 percent by 1997 (Konadu-Agye-mang, 2000). By 2000, the per capita outpatient department (OPD) attendance had dropped to 0.3 from 1.9 in 1970 (Seddoh & Akor, 2012); the cost of medicine alone accounted for over 60 percent of treating malaria, one of the commonest illnesses in Ghana (Asenso-Okyere & Dzator, 1997; McIntyre et al., 2006).

Notwithstanding the successive governments' attempts at providing affordable and sustainable health care to Ghanaians, the idea of establishing a national health insurance program in the country's recent history was first introduced at the highest levels of government in 1992 by then head of state Flight Lieutenant Rawlings six months before the country's return to constitutional rule in January 1993 (Rawlings, 1993). Affordable health care became a salient issue during the 2000 election campaigns (Brande, January 5, 1997; Kusi-Ampofo et al., 2014; New Patriotic Party, 2000; National Democratic Congress, 2000; Rajkotia, 2009). Prior to the 2000 general elections, the National Democratic Congress (NDC) government had begun a pilot of a national health insurance scheme project in the Dangme West and Nkoranza districts of the Greater Accra Region and Brong Ahafo Regions respectively—several mutual health organizations had sprung up across the country, sometimes with the support of agencies like the United States Agency for International Development (USAID) and the Danish International Development Agency (DANIDA) with the aim of exploring ways of providing affordable and accessible health care. These pilot projects introduced exemptions for the elderly, children under five, and pregnant women from paying user fees (Sulzbach, Garshong, & Banahene, 2005; Atim et al., 2001; Gobah & Liang, 2011).

Notwithstanding these efforts, the cash-and-carry system remained. For instance, Nyonator and Kutzin (1999) observed that of the 1,895 recorded patient contacts with health care providers in the Volta Region in 1995, less than 1 percent received exemptions because according to the minister of health, there was no clear guidance on how to identify the various persons to be exempted. The lingering problem with access to and the funding of health care added to the economic woes of the people, thereby fueling popular discontent (Carbone, 2011; Rajkotia, 2007, 2009). The concerns raised about problems associated with the cash-and-carry system became a political issue that engaged the attention of the politicians to the extent that the National Health Insurance solution was proposed as the solution. For instance, the NPP referred to the cash-and-carry system as "callous and inhuman" (NPP Manifesto, 1996, pp. 36–37). It declared further, "the NPP Government shall abolish the iniquitous 'cash and carry' system of (P)NDC. Under NPP administration, nobody in Ghana will be denied medical attention because of his or her inability to pay" (New Patriotic Party, 2000, p. 31) On its part, the NDC assured Ghanaians of the following:

> Health insurance will be a major strategy for mobilizing additional resources and for ensuring financial access in time of need. The pilot work already carried out will form the basis for a mix of insurance schemes, both public and private, national and local, to cater for salaried employees, the self-employed as well as both urban and rural communities. The National Health Endowment Fund whose Coordinating Committee was inaugurated in July 1999 and whose Board of Trustees has already been established will be made operational. We will review the "cash-and-carry" system in order to improve on its efficiency and ensure increased access to basic health services. The exemptions policy will also be reviewed in terms of coverage as well as disease spread, and more funds will be provided to support the needy. (National Democratic Congress, 2000, p. 24)

## DID MPS RESPOND TO THE POPULAR HEALTH CARE CONCERNS?

After receiving a mandate from the people to govern, the next political action that engaged the attention of the politicians was the initiation of processes for the enactment of the National Health Insurance Scheme (NHIS). The passage of the NHIS commenced protracted political debates by MPs regarding the funding and access to quality health care in the country. The debates, which were reduced to an NPP and NDC affair, examined the nature, shape, and form of the health care reform proposal. The National Health Insurance Bill (NHIB) was laid before Parliament on July 11, 2003, by the minister for health, Dr. Kwaku Afriyie, and was immediately referred to the Health and Finance Committees for speedy action (Hansard, July 11, 2003, pp. 2409–2410). In order to enable the opposition NDC to prepare for the debate on the NHISB, the minority chief whip and NDC member of Parliament for Avenor Constituency E. K. Doe Adjaho asked for copies of the bill:

> Mr. Speaker, this is a very important Bill and I just want to find out when the Bills would be available for distribution. It is a very important Bill and we would want to have a look at it as early as possible. (Hansard, July 11, 2003, p. 2410)

The submission of the report to the House by the Joint Committee on Health and Finance in five weeks is suggestive of the importance MPs attached to the health care. The remarks made by the cochairman of the joint committee and MP for Afigya-Sekyere East, K. A. Kyeremateng, attests to this fact (the other cochairman of the committee was the NPP NP for Abetifi, E. A. Agye-pong):

> As the success of our kindled efforts at instituting a National Health Insurance Scheme is dependent on the general acceptance of majority of Ghanaians, the Committee took due cognizance and devised fruitful means of reaching out to the people. Indeed, in addition to the traditional norm of advertising for comments on the Bill from stakeholders and the general public, the Committee toured six regional capitals and solicited views on the Bill (Hansard, August 19, 2003, pp. 76–77)

Following a meeting of the joint committee on Health and Finance, which included members of the NPP and NDC to discuss modalities of the health care reform legislation on July 29, 2003, a decision was reached for committee members to tour six of the ten regional capitals of the country (Bolgatanga, Kumasi, Tamale, Ho, Sunyani, and Accra) and hold consultations with stakeholders before the passage of the legislation.

Notwithstanding the initial enthusiasm shown by the NDC MPs to debate the NHIB, they withdrew from the debate. The majority leader of Parliament, Felix Owusu-Adjapong, communicated the NDC's decision not to participate in the debate to the House:

> The Minority in Parliament has decided to boycott further proceedings on the discussion of the National Health Insurance Bill which commenced on Tuesday, 29th July 2003. The decision is to ensure that interests of the people of Ghana are defended and protected. (Hansard, August 18, 2003, p. 64)

Despite the boycott of the proceedings at the committee level and in the chamber over the NHIB, the minority NDC MPs issued a press statement on August 1, 2003, supporting the Kufuor administration's willingness to pursue the path of consultation with stakeholders on the proposed health care reform bill (Hansard, August 18, 2003, pp. 64–65). Hence, while sustaining their boycott, NDC MPs on the joint committee continued their participation in all proceedings pertaining to the bill, touring to interact with stakeholders. For instance, the NPP MP for Nsuta/Kwaman, Kwame Osei-Prempeh observed,

> I am very sad that our friends on the opposite side have decided to boycott this very important Bill. Mr. Speaker, I am a member of your Joint-Committee which went around the country to solicit views on the Health Insurance Bill. Mr. Speaker, during our rounds, the Hon. Ranking Member for Finance, Moses Asaga, and Hon. Dr. Mustapha Ahmed, who was the acting Ranking Member on Health, made very invaluable contributions at the various stages of the tour. . . . In fact, in Kumasi, Hon. Moses Asaga had the longest applause that we ever received during the tour because of the contributions he made to the Bill. (Hansard, August 19, 2003, p. 150)

Since the NDC had withdrawn its participation in all parliamentary activities, it would, and should, have been a prime opportunity for the NPP to push through its health care reform agenda—there was no opposition in Parliament to resist them. But no. The floor speeches of MPs—only NPP MPs—during the debate suggested how much of their attention was focused on their constituents. A sampling would be appropriate here. The MP for Ahafo Ano South S. K. B. Manu, a rural constituency, said,

> Mr. Speaker, coming from a rural setting and having lived in a rural area almost throughout my life, I want to [pass this Bill]. Mr. Speaker, if you go to my district, Ahafo Ano South, for example, we have got only one district health facility which is now being upgraded to become a district hospital with only one doctor. Mr. Speaker, we are talking about a district with a population of over 10,000 people having to be served by this hospital with one doctor. (Hansard, August 19, 2003, p. 104)

The MP for Jaman South constituency and deputy minister for food and agriculture, Anna Nyamekye, stated,

> Mr. Speaker, those who complain about the scheme being rushed, I do not know what they mean by that. We are talking about people's health and others are saying that we must wait. Can people's health wait? This is the question I would want to pose to those who say that it is being rushed. . . . This committee initially visited Tamale, Koforidua, Takoradi, Kumasi, Bolgatanga, Ho, and Kumasi. The committee also visited Elmina, all in the interest of health insurance. They always made it clear that people could come up and bring up whatever contributions they had and whatever problems they had to present.

So, if we meet today and people are saying that we are rushing it, I do not agree with them. And that is why, Mr. Speaker, I would want to ask all of us in this House to help bring up this scheme because people's lives cannot wait. (Hansard, August 19, 2003, pp. 125–126)

Kwame Osei-Prempeh, MP for Nsuta/Kwamang, struck a similar tone when he stated,

Mr. Speaker, as other . . . members have said, the lives of our people cannot wait. . . . Last three weeks, I went to my constituency and my uncle was ill; he was down, and I asked them why they had not sent him to the hospital and they said there was no money. I left my driver behind to carry him to the Mampong Hospital the following morning. The following morning when I got there, on my feet, I spent two million Cedis buying drugs. I left Mampong on Tuesday and got to Accra. On Thursday, I was called that my uncle was dead. I called the doctor and he said that he spent too long a time at home and therefore there was no alternative. Mr. Speaker, are they saying that people's lives should wait? I believe that if there was a health insurance scheme, my uncle would have been alive by now. He would not have spent three weeks at home until I went there to carry him to the hospital. Mr. Speaker, this is the reality of the situation and those people who are saying that we have to wait and wait and wait are doing a great disservice to this nation. (Hansard, August 19, 2003, pp. 151–152)

The MP for Tarkwa Nsuaem constituency Gifty Eugenia Kusi appealed to workers thus:

Mr. Speaker, I would want to appeal to workers of this nation to really be happy with me and support the Government in its efforts to bring this National Health Insurance Scheme into being. Especially, workers should be mindful of the fact that very soon, we would all be on pension if we do not die before our pensionable age. Mr. Speaker, if you go on pension or if you are retrenched, and I am speaking from experience as an MP for Tarkwa where retrenchment has been the order of the day—Most of the mining companies had retrenched their workers and people are forced to go on pension at a very young age. Recently, I had a meeting with the Pensioners Association of the Wassa West district and Mr. Speaker, majority of them . . . never enjoyed any exemptions when they reported at the hospitals. They are made to buy their own drugs and most of them cannot afford. (Hansard, August 19, 2003, pp. 129–130)

Yaw Osafo-Maafo, minister for finance and economic planning and MP for Akim Oda constituency stated,

It is the responsibility of any government—and we consider it an obligation on this Government that we make sure that Ghanaians, no matter the age, are not anxious about their health, hence the National Health Insurance Scheme. We need it and we would not allow anybody to stampede us in doing something

which we been voted for to do. We have been voted for to make sure that the
quality of life of our nationals, Ghanaians is improved upon. That is what we
have been voted for. (Hansard, August 19, 2003, p. 158)

The point is that nearly all MPs who spoke in Parliament linked their support
for the legislation to how it would help their constituents have better/easier
access to affordable health care. There was robust and at times contentious
debate about certain provisions of the proposed bill during the consideration
stage, even though all the members in the chamber were from the NPP
because the NDC had suspended its activities in Parliament. One such contentious discussion was about a proposal by Kwame Osei-Prempeh, the MP
for Nsuta-Kwamang Beposo, to include a clause to section 79 of the bill that
dealt with sources of funds for the health insurance program thus, "Any
worker who contributes two and half percent of his social security contribution shall have that as his contribution or part thereof on the premium pay-
able to his district mutual health insurance organization." He added the following reason:

> Mr. Speaker, part of workers' contributions to SSNIT [Social Security and
> National Insurance Trust] is going to be used to support the health insurance
> scheme. Most of them [i.e., workers] have been asking what benefit they
> would be getting. It is appropriate to compensate them in a way; and therefore,
> I believe that this amendment would go a long way to assure them that they
> would be catered for in their time of retirement. They are going to have
> medical care even when they do not have money and therefore it is proper to
> capture this to assure them. (Hansard, August 21, 2003, p. 316)

The proposed amendment was to address vehement opposition from labor
unions that contributors to the SSNIT fund would pay the health insurance
premium as well. The proposal created an impression that workers in the
formal sector, who typically contribute to the SSNIT fund, were reluctant to
support citizens in the informal sector, particularly farmers, who do not typically contribute to the SSNIT fund. Thus, the proposed amendment did not
sit well with many members in the chamber. Here is how S. K. B. Manu
reacted to the proposed amendment to exclude SSNIT from paying the premium:

> Mr. Speaker, I rise to oppose the amendment in the sense that it is a very
> dangerous one. Mr. Speaker, if he is thinking about those in the formal sector
> going to pay so much so that they have to be reimbursed in a form that he is
> proposing, what are we saying about cocoa farmers, for example, who over the
> years have offered their monies to build this nation? Mr. Speaker, how many
> of those farmers today even have the capacity to send their children to the
> universities that their toils and sweat helped to build? So, if today, those in the
> formal sector are also to contribute something that would benefit those in the

informal sector, I do not see the place of the amendment. I therefore vehement-
ly oppose it. (Hansard, August 21, 2003, p. 319)

The MP for Berekum constituency, Nkrabea Effah Dartey, passionately
argued against the proposed amendment thus:

> Let us think for just one second and remember how farmers in this country
> have virtually bankrolled this nation's development throughout all the re-
> gimes, from Dr. Kwame Nkrumah's time up till today. Moneys meant for
> farmers are always taken off by Central Government to finance all national
> development programs. How many children of farmers all over the country get
> access to Prempeh College or get access to Achimota School or get access to
> Mfantsipim Secondary School? It is the children of the rich, the children of
> lawyers, children of doctors who ironically get access to Cocoa Marketing
> Board (CMB) scholarships. Farmers' children are left in the bush even today
> as I speak. And look at the sacrifices they make. Mr. Speaker, in Dormaa
> Ahenkro, a woman in the farm was asleep in the bush in the cocoa farm when
> she felt somebody sucking her breast. It turned out to be a snake, a puff adder
> and she died. Farmers are making all these sacrifices and yet nobody—It is the
> child of a farmer who, when he or she goes to the hospital, enjoys no subsidy.
> No doctor says, "because you are the child of a cocoa farmer, get this treat-
> ment and go free." Meanwhile, workers all over the country, those in the
> formal sector, in the Ghana National Petroleum Corporation (GNPC)—I
> worked at GNPC for ten years. Whenever I went to the hospital, they paid my
> fees for me. When I was an army officer, I went to the 37 Military Hospital
> and they paid my bills for me. But if you are the child of a farmer, you go to
> the hospital and you pay and if you do not pay, you die. . . . Mr. Speaker, I am
> opposed to the amendment and I think every Ghanaian who is patriotic and
> appreciates the dynamics of the argument should oppose the amendment. I am
> even surprised that the Hon. Member [Kwame Osei-Prempeh, the MP for
> Nsuta-Kwamang Beposo], who is from a cocoa growing area, even moving
> such an amendment. (Hansard August 21, 2003, pp. 321–322)

Similarly, the MP for Tema West, Abraham Osei-Aidooh, proposed that
contributors to the SSNIT fund whose contributions equal the money required for a beneficiary under a district mutual scheme should be exempted
from making any additional payment to receive health care (Hansard, August
26, 2003, pp. 505–506). In supporting the proposal, the MP for Abetifi constituency, Eugene Atta Agyepong, suggested that allowing additional payment by such SSNIT contributors would amount to double payment (Hansard, August 26, 2003, p. 509). Hearing this line of argument, the MP for
Amenfi East constituency Joseph Boahen Aidoo stated,

> Mr. Speaker, my Hon. friend is misleading [my emphasis] the House. It is not
> double payment because it is just like going to deposit your money at the
> bank. . . . If you put your money at the bank and then somebody decides to go
> for that money and use it, you cannot go to the bank to ask: "why have I put

my money there and you are giving to Mr. So, and So to use? He should not be allowed to use that money." Mr. Speaker, the two and a half percent which the Government intends to take is money that had been lodged with SSNIT and the organization has come out, the institution has come out clearly to state that it is not going to affect the individual entitlements of members contributing to the SSNIT fund. So, he is misleading the House. It is not double payment. (Hansard, August 26, 2003, pp. 509–510)

Clearly irritated by the suggestion that he was misleading the House, the Abetifi constituency MP said, "Mr. Speaker, it is interesting, a non-banker teaching a banker how deposits and other moneys are put at the bank. . . . I am telling you, I have had at least twenty years" (Hansard, August 26, 2003, p. 510). The Speaker then interjected:

Order! Order! Hon. Members in this House are equal in all respects and they are entitled to air their views on whatever subject, whatever the field. The fact that he is dealing with banking is no reason that bankers' view alone should prevail. You will need the votes of other Hon. Members to be able to carry your views, your provisions through and therefore they are entitled to their view also. (Hansard, August 26, 2003, p. 510)

The point requires reiteration: even with only NPP MPs debating the proposed legislation, representatives—all claiming constituency or national interests—strongly contested, disagreed, and agreed on some provisions. In the end, the NPP-controlled Parliament passed the National Health Insurance Bill on August 26, 2003 and it received presidential assent on September 5, 2003, as Act 650.

## CONCLUSION

This paper has shown that members of Parliament in Ghana pay particular attention to crucial national issues that bother the minds of citizens. The MPs prioritized issues emanating from the electorate and channeled their concerns into policy decisions. They recognized that a core function they (MPs) perform in Parliament is the promotion of the interests of the electorate in policy making. Given that the issue of health care delivery became a crucial national concern in the 2000 election campaign, the MPs felt obliged to pursue the interests of the citizens by passing the National Health Insurance Act, which was thought to be the antidote to the prevailing cash-and-carry system of health care delivery. The response given to the health care concerns of the electorate in the form of the NHIS signaled the extent to which the MPs prioritized the interests of the electorate. While the boycott by the NDC MPs suggests they were less responsive to the concerns of the people, their comments outside Parliament helped straighten the rough edges of the bills, which no doubt improved the quality of the health care legislation. The active commitment to the passage of the National Health Insurance Bill into a national health insurance law by the NPP MPs is a testament to the deep interest they have toward issues that affect the lives of their electorates. If democracy is about how elected members meet the needs of their electorate, then there is significant evidence of how elected officials worked zealously to translate the overwhelming concerns of the people into policies.

## REFERENCES

Afrifa, Akwasi Amankwaa. (1966). *The Ghana Coup: 24th February 1966*: [London]: F. Cass.
Afrobarometer. (November 2005). "Parliament of the Fourth Republic of Ghana—Views From the Grassroots." CDD-Ghana, accessed February 23, http://www.afrobarometer.org/files/documents/briefing_papers/AfrobriefNo20.pdf.
Agyepong, Irene Akua, and Sam Adjei. (2008). "Public Social Policy Development and implementation: A Case Study of the Ghana National Health Insurance Scheme." *Health Policy and Planning* 23(2): 150–160.
Anyinam, Charles A. (1989). "The Social Cost of the IMF's Adjustment Programs for Poverty: The Case of Health Care in Ghana." *International Journal of Health Services* 19(3): 541–547.
Apter, David E. (1968). "Nkrumah, Charisma, and the Coup." *Daedalus* 97(3): 757–792.
Arhinful, Kojo Daniel. (2003). *The Solidarity of Self-Interest: Social and Cultural Feasibility of Rural Health Insurance in Ghana*. Leiden, NL: African Studies Center.
Aryee, Joseph R. A. (2011). "Manifestos and Elections in Ghana's Fourth Republic." *South African Journal of International Affairs* 18(3): 367–384.
Aryee, Joseph R. A. (2017). "Ghana's Elections of 7 December 2016: A Postmortem." *South African Journal of International Affairs*. Accessed November 7.
Asante, F., and Moses Aikins. (2008). "Does the NHIS Cover the Poor?" Accra, Ghana: Institute of Statistical Social and Economics Research (ISSER) and School of Public Health, University of Ghana, Legon, Accra.
Asenso-Okyere, W. Kwadwo, and Janet A. Dzator. (1997). "Household Cost of Seeking Malaria Care: A Retrospective Study of Two Districts in Ghana." *Social Science & Medicine* 45(5): 659–667.
Asenso-Okyere, W. K., Adote Anum, Isaac Osei-Akoto, and Augustina Adukonu. (1998). "Cost Recovery in Ghana: Are There Any Changes in Health Care Seeking Behaviour?" *Health Policy and Planning* 13(2): 181–188. doi: 10.1093/heapol/13.2.181.
Atim, Cris, Steven Grey, Patrick Apoya, Sylvia J. Anie, and Moses Aikins. (2001). "A Survey of Health Financing Schemes in Ghana." *Bethesda: Abt Associate*. doi:10.1080/10220461.2017.1378124
Bates, Robert H. (1989). *Beyond the Miracle of the Market: The Political Economy of Agrarian Development in Kenya*. New York: Cambridge University Press.
Bates, Robert H. (2008). *When Things Fell Apart: State Failure in Late-Century Africa. New York: Cambridge University Press*. New York: Cambridge University Press.
Bawumia, Mahamudu. (1998). "Understanding the Rural–Urban Voting Patterns in the 1992 Ghanaian Presidential Election. A Closer Look at the Distributional Impact of Ghana's Structural Adjustment Programme." *The Journal of Modern African Studies* 36(1): 47–70.
Boafo-Arthur, Kwame. (1999). "Ghana: Structural adjustment, Democratization, and the Politics of Continuity." *African Studies Review* 42(2): 41–72.
Boafo-Arthur, Kwame. (2008). "Democracy and Stability in West Africa: The Ghanaian Experience." Uppsala: Department of Peace and Conflict Research, Uppsala University.
Brande, Daniel Mensah. (January 5, 1997). "Letter from Ghana: Kill or Cure." Accessed March 24, 2015. http://newint.org/features/1997/01/05/ghana/.

Bratton, Michael, and Nicolas van de Walle. (1994). "Neopatrimonial Regimes and Political Transitions in Africa." *World Politics* 46(4): 453–489.

Burke, Edmund. (1790 [1960]). *Reflections on the Revolution in France*. London: Penguin Books.

Carbone, Giovanni. (2011). "Democratic Demands and Social Policies: The Politics of Health Reform in Ghana." *The Journal of Modern African Studies* 49(3): 381–408.

Debrah, Emmanuel. (2008/2009). "The Economy and Regime Change in Ghana, 1992–2004." *Ghana Social Science Journal* 5&6(1&2): 84–113.

Frempong, Alex Kaakyire Duku. (2017). *Elections in Ghana: 1951–2016*. Tema, Ghana: Digi-Books.

Fridy, Kevin S. (2007). "The Elephant, Umbrella, and Quarrelling Cocks: Disaggregating Partisanship in Ghana's Fourth Republic." *African Affairs* 106(423): 281–305.

Ghanaweb.com. (January 24, 2001). "Shortage of Nurses Hits Where They Are Needed the Most." accessed June 28, 2018. https://www.ghanaweb.com/GhanaHomePage/News-Archive/Shortage-of-Nurses-Hits-Where-They-Are-Needed-the-Most-13232.

Ghanaweb.com. (January 28, 1999). "Upper East hospitals Offer Free Medicare for Paupers/ Aged" Accessed June 28, 2018. https://www.ghanaweb.com/GhanaHomePage/News-Archive/artikel.php?ID=4889.

Ghanaweb.com. (July 8, 1999). "Korle Bu Children's Ward Cries for Help." Accessed June 28, 2018. https://www.ghanaweb.com/GhanaHomePage/NewsArchive/artikel.php?ID=7580.

Ghanaweb.com. (July 15, 2003). "Detained Old Lady at Korle Bu Rescued by Philanthropist." Accessed June 28, 2018. https://www.ghanaweb.com/GhanaHomePage/NewsArchive/artikel.php?ID=39300.

Ghanaweb.com. (September 26, 2003). "More Local Doctors Abandon the Country." Accessed June 28, 2018. https://www.ghanaweb.com/GhanaHomePage/NewsArchive/More-Local-Doctors-Abandon-The-Country-43657.

Gobah, Freeman Kobla, and Zhang Liang. 2011. "The National Health Insurance Scheme in Ghana: Prospects and Challenges: A Cross-Sectional Evidence." *Global Journal of Health Science* 3(2): 90.

Gyimah-Boadi, Emmanuel. (2009). "Another Step Forward for Ghana." *Journal of Democracy* 20(2): 138–152.

Hansard. (August 18, 2003: 64). Parliamentary Debates. Accra, Ghana: Republic of Ghana.

Hansard. (August 18, 2003: 64–65). Parliamentary Debates. Accra, Ghana: Republic of Ghana.

Hansard. (August 19, 2003: 76–77). Parliamentary Debates. Accra, Ghana: Republic of Ghana.

Hansard. (August 19, 2003: 104). Parliamentary Debates. Accra, Ghana: Republic of Ghana.

Hansard. (August 19, 2003: 125–126). Parliamentary Debates. Accra, Ghana: Republic of Ghana.

Hansard. (August 19, 2003: 129–130). Parliamentary Debates. Accra, Ghana: Republic of Ghana.

Hansard. (August 19, 2003: 150). Parliamentary Debates. Accra, Ghana: Republic of Ghana.

Hansard. (August 19, 2003: 151–152). Parliamentary Debates. Accra, Ghana: Republic of Ghana.

Hansard. (August 19, 2003: 158). Parliamentary Debates. Accra, Ghana: Republic of Ghana.

Hansard. (August 21, 2003: 316). Parliamentary Debates. Accra, Ghana: Republic of Ghana.

Hansard. (August 21, 2003: 319). Parliamentary Debates. Accra, Ghana: Republic of Ghana.

Hansard. (August 21, 2003: 321–322). Parliamentary Debates. Accra, Ghana: Republic of Ghana.

Hansard. (August 26, 2003: 509). Parliamentary Debates. Accra, Ghana: Republic of Ghana.

Hansard. (August 26, 2003: 509–510). Parliamentary Debates. Accra, Ghana: Republic of Ghana.

Hansard. (August 26, 2003: 510). Parliamentary Debates. Accra, Ghana: Republic of Ghana.

Hansard. (July 11, 2003: 2409–2410). Parliamentary Debates. Accra, Ghana: Republic of Ghana.

Hansard. (July 11, 2003: 2410). Parliamentary Debates. Accra, Ghana: Republic of Ghana.

Hutchful, Eboe. (2002). *Ghana's Adjustment Experience: The Paradox of Reform*. Oxford, UK: James Currey Ltd.

Jeffries, Richard. (1998). "The Ghanaian Elections of 1996: Towards the Consolidation of Democracy?" *African Affairs* 97(387): 189–208.

Kasapafmonline.com. (November 2, 2015). "Prez Mahama on Public Perception: MPs Are Rubble Rousers." Accessed September 1, 2018. http://kasapafmonline.com/2015/11/02/prez-mahama-on-public-perception-mps-are-rubble-rousers/.

Kelly, Bob, and R. B. Benning. (2013). "The Ghanaian Elections of 2012." *Review of African Political Economy* 40(137): 475–484.

Kokutse, Francis. (October 29, 2012). "'Skirt and Blouse' Politics Stalk Ghana Presidential Election." Accessed June 28, 2018. http://www.africareview.com/News/Ghana-presidential-election-intrigues/-/979180/1606128/-/1stspt/-/index.html.

Konadu-Agyemang, Kwadwo. (2000). "The Best of Times and the Worst of Times: Structural Adjustment Programs and Uneven Development in Africa: The Case of Ghana." *Professional Geographer* 52(3): 469–483. doi: doi:10.1111/0033–0124.00239.

Kusi-Ampofo, Owuraku, John Church, Charles Conteh, and Timothy B. Heinmiller. (2014). "Resistance and Change: A Multiple Streams Approach to Understanding Health Policy Making in Ghana." *Journal of Health Politics, Policy and Law* 40(1): 195–219.

Lindberg, Staffan I., and Minion K. C. Morrison. (2005). "Exploring Voter Alignments in Africa: Core and Swing Voters in Ghana." *The Journal of Modern African Studies* 43(4): 565–586.

Lindberg, Staffan I., and Minion K. C. Morrison. (2008). "Are African Voters Really Ethnic or Clientelistic? Survey Evidence from Ghana." *Political Science Quarterly* 123(1): 95–122.

MacLean, Lauren M. 2010. *Informal Institutions and Citizenship in Rural Africa: Risk and Reciprocity in Ghana and Cote d'Ivoire*: Cambridge University Press.

Mansbridge, Jane. (2011). "Clarifying the Concept of Representation." *American Political Science Review* 105(3): 621–630.

McCrone, Donald J., and James H. Kuklinski. (1979). "The Delegate Theory of Representation." *American Journal of Political Science* 23(2): 278–300.

McIntyre, Diane, Michael Thiede, Göran Dahlgren, and Margaret Whitehead. (2006). "What Are the Economic Consequences for Households of Illness and of Paying for Health Care in Low- and Middle-Income Country Contexts?" *Social Science & Medicine* 62(4): 858–865.

Myjoyonline. (June 13, 2015). "Fallen MPs: Dr. Anane, Gifty Klenam, Isaac Osei, Addai Nimo et al. Out of Parliament." Accessed June 28, 2018. http://m.myjoyonline.com/marticles/politics/fallen-mps-dr-anane-gifty-klenam-isaac-osei-addai-nimo-et-al-out-of-parliament.

National Democratic Congress. (2000). "2000 Manifesto: Spreading the Benefits of Development." Accessed December 18, 2014. http://www.ghanareview.com/NDC.html.

New Patriotic Party. (1996). Manifesto of the New Patriotic Party: Development in Freedom Change, and Agenda for Change. Accra, Ghana: The New Patriotic Party.

New Patriotic Party. (2000). *Manifesto—Development in Freedom: Agenda for Positive Change*. Accra, Ghana: The New Patriotic Party. Accessed December 18. http://www.ghanareview.com/NPP.html.

Nugent, Paul. (2001a). "Ethnicity as an Explanatory Factor in the Ghana 2000 Elections." *African Issues*: 2–7.

Nugent, Paul. (2001b). "Winners, Losers and Also Rans: Money, Moral Authority and Voting Patterns in the Ghana 2000 Election." *African Affairs* 100(400): 405–428.

Nyonator, Frank, and Joseph Kutzin. (1999). "Health for Some? The Effects of User Fees in the Volta Region of Ghana." *Health Policy and Planning* 14(4): 329–341. doi: 10.1093/heapol/14.4.329.

Osei, Anja. (2013). "Political Parties in Ghana: Agents of Democracy?" *Journal of Contemporary African Studies* 31(4): 543–563.

Rajkotia, Yogesh. (2007). *The Political Development of the Ghanaian National Health Insurance System: Lessons in Health Governance*. Bethesda, MD: Health Systems Project 20/20, Abt Associate Inc.

Rajkotia, Yogesh. (2009). *National Health Insurance in Ghana: Politics, Adverse Selection, and the Use of Child Health Services*. Thesis/dissertation.

Rawlings, Jerry J. (1993). Selected Speeches of Flight Lieutenant J. J. Rawlings, Chairman of the P.N.D.C. Accra, Ghana: Information Services Department.

Rehfeld, Andrew. (2009). "Representation Rethought: On Trustees, Delegates, and Gyroscopes in the Study of Political Representation and Democracy." *American Political Science Review* 103(2): 214–230.

Seddoh, Anthony, Sam Adjei, and Alex Nazzar. (2011). "Ghana's National Health Insurance Scheme: Views on Progress, Observations, and Commentary." *Accra, Ghana: Centre for Health and Social Services* 20.

Seddoh, Anthony, and Samuel A. Akor. (2012). "Policy Initiation and Political Levers in Health Policy: Lessons from Ghana's Health Insurance." *BMC Public Health* 12 (Supplement 1): S10.

Senah, Kojo. 2001. "In Sickness and in Health: Globalization and Healthcare Delivery in Ghana." *Research Review* 17(1): 83–89.

Sulzbach, Sara, Bertha Garshong, and Getrude Banahene. (2005). "Evaluating the Effects of the National Health Insurance Act in Ghana: Baseline Report." Bethesda, MD: Abt Associates Inc.

Urbinati, Nadia, and Mark E Warren. (2008). "The Concept of Representation in Contemporary Democratic Theory." *Annual Review of Political Science* 11(1): 387–412.

Van De Boom, G. J. M., N. N. N. Nsowah-Nuamah, and G. B. Overbosch. (2008). "Health-Care Provision and self-Medication in Ghana." In *The Economy of Ghana: Analytical Perspectives on Stability, Growth and Poverty*, edited by Ernest Aryeetey and Ravi Kanbur, 392–416. Woodbridge, UK: James Currey.

van de Walle, Nicholas. (2001). *African Economies and the Politics of Permanent Crisis, 1979–1999*. New York: Cambridge University Press.

Waddington, Catriona J., and K. A. Enyimayew. (1990). "A Price to Pay, Part 2: The Impact of User Charges in the Volta Region of Ghana." *International Journal of Health Planning and Management* 5(4): 287–312.

Whitfield, Lindsay. (2009). "'Change for a Better Ghana': Party Competition, Institutionalization and Alternation in Ghana's 2008 Elections." *African Affairs* 108(433): 621–641.

Youde, Jeremy. (2005). "Economics and Government Popularity in Ghana." *Electoral Studies* 24(1): 1–16.

*Chapter Seven*

# When Government Is Unaware It Is Incommunicado

## Margaret I. Amoakohene and Kwasi Ansu-Kyeremeh

Government-citizen engagement is considered an important indicator of democratic governance (Beetham, 1994; Munck, 2009). Akanlig-Pare (2001, p. 422) sees it as "the diffusion of democratic values;" while McKwartin (2001, p. 18) claimed that "the state-owned media" were contributing to "the shaping of electorate choices through the dissemination of political information." In all these government-citizen communication regimes, citizens may not have heard government, as the Watson Commission found; or, they may have heard it loudly, but not clearly (Amoakohene, 1996). Yet still they may not have heard because the message lacked clarity (Fosu, 2016). In all these instances, government would be incommunicado; that is, not be in any real communication, and hence, being out of touch, with the citizenry.

This study of political communication in Ghana attempts a review of government-citizen communication. It focuses on a phenomenon of government in power being incommunicado in an environment of presumed "chaotic" communication. First, the government tends to rely on the English language to communicate with citizens who predominantly use local languages in their day-to-day transactions. Second, the government or party in power communicates through media outlets whose attributes is incongruent to the characteristics of the audience. Those outlets tend to be unidirectional, impersonal, and mass-targeted, whereas Ghanaian audiences are largely communal and interactive in their communication and media habits (Amoakohene, 2004). Furthermore, governments traditionally tend to communicate through the state-owned media. However, the Ghanaian audience seems more interested in the programs of the privately owned media. Finally, the state-owned media usually presents one viewpoint, effectively that of the government, whereas privately owned media, in their varied positions, allow for dissenting views.

The Ministry of Information (MoI), which organizes government communication, aims at "a two-way communication channel between the people and government" in its messaging (MoI, 2018). However, Halliday and Matthiessen (2004, p. 178) note that the milieu combines with the "actors" and the messaging "process" to produce the communicative act. Analysis of the sociopolitical and cultural context ought, therefore, to have always been a consideration in government communication with citizens. Incidentally, both language and media are deeply embedded in the social setting. Without the appropriate channel, the message is unlikely to reach its audience. Indeed, for audience members who do not communicate in the language selected for communication, or do not patronize the chosen medium, or both, the government would be incommunicado and limited in its effort to interactively relate to the governed. This study highlights language and channel limits in Ghana government-citizen communication.

The government communicates in English, which is not understood by a majority of the citizens. It also previously owned and controlled the mass media as instruments of political communication. Relishing radio's one-way format, which excluded public participation, for example, was celebrated by Governor Hodson (Ansu-Kyeremeh, 2001) while Gyasi (2011) discussed that context's adversarial journalism. It was a period of rife censorship (Anokwa, 1996). Today, government (state) media competes with private media for readers, listeners, and viewers in a plural media environment which is widely accessible and of limitless content, even "cacophonous" (Duodu, 2018). Somehow, the operating political communication model projects a public that is denied critical information by state-owned media or is overloaded with government criticism by private media; neither of which contributes to an understanding of, and appreciation for, service by the government to the governed.

It is important because in Ghana it is a rarity to find an in-between adversarial broadcasting content that is balanced in its criticism of government for the public good, as anticipated by the 1992 Constitution of Ghana. Thus, ownership, diversity, and inclusiveness, rather than enhancing quality, have tended to devalue content, which then lacks in truth, fairness, accuracy, and balance. Tietaah's (2014, 2017) Media Foundation for West Africa (MFWA)–sponsored studies have detected lapses in language use. In response to earlier, similar concerns, the National Media Commission (NMC; 2009), constitutionally mandated to monitor standards, had published guidelines on accepted language use. Its attempt to criminalize content was, however, struck down by the Supreme Court for having "no legally accepted justification and no need for that regulation as it amounted to censorship"

(GBC, March 16, 2017). This picture of media overregulation followed by underregulation emerges from Amoakohene's (2012) analysis.

Meanwhile, researchers have been preoccupied with "positivist interpretation" of the phenomenon (Ansu-Kyeremeh, 2014, p. 224), often uncritically casting the mass media as made-to-benefit without cost. Any lapses in the performance of a medium would be blamed on the environment failing to respond to fit that medium's characteristics. That is, the context should necessarily adjust to fit the medium's communication format for communication efficiency. So constantly, researchers are in search of that kind of fulfilling structural context adjustment to suit the medium's nature and thereby creating an incongruence of medium needing no adaptation to suit the context. Virtually all research on Ghanaian political communication (Karikari, Essuman-Johnson, Ansu-Kyeremeh & Koomson, 1995; Akanlig-Pare, 2001; Amoakohene, 2012; Fosu 2016; Hasty, 2005; Liu & Horsley, 2007; Rich, 2013; Smith & Temin, 2001; Tietaah, 2014, 2017) has been about government media-use, which is only part of government communication.

Research results usually find radio, for instance, to be the most popular media and the one with the greatest audience penetration and access.[1] The extent to which radio may not fit its context is hardly discussed (Ansu-Kyeremeh, 1992), despite the unrealistic demand for "massification and individuation of the community-oriented African social system" (Ansu-Kyeremeh, 2014, p. 225). The radio efficacy debate, like with media in general, has essentially almost always been about the form of communication, and less so the hosting context.

## THE PROBLEM

Before westernization, local leaders found ways to communicate with the people through indigenous communication systems (Ansu-Kyeremeh, 2005). The British colonial government introduced and employed the cinema (1927), the newspaper (1822), and especially the radio (1935). Later, post-independence governments added the television (1965) as their main means of communication (Ansu-Kyeremeh & Karikari, 1997). Over the years, there has been some level of government dissatisfaction, a recent exemplifier being President Kufuor's lamentation that his "Ministers [were] not telling government's success story" (Ansu-Kyeremeh, 2007). It appears the massive communication infrastructure at the government's disposal deceives it into a state of complacency. From that perspective, research cannot continue to concentrate on the medium while its discursive and communicative contexts are downplayed. Thus, this study's focus is on the language medium by which the politically communicating actor engages for effective communication.

## FRAMEWORK AND LITERATURE

Te Molder's (1995) analysis of government communicators' talk is an empiricist research approach that leaves room for eclectic interpretation from various theoretical and analytical perspectives. It may demand agenda-setting probes (whether the government was succeeding in setting an agenda through its public communication). Or, it may attract media richness of interpretation (whether the government was engaging the citizenry through the realistic and result-yielding channels). From the public relations function viewpoint of Liu and Horsley (2007), who adopt the terms "macroenvironment" and "microenvironment" of media, it may simply be an inventory of public relations, or stock-of-government communication tools.

Liu and Horsley's (2007) study treated government communication as a public relations function. However, this study is along the "mundane" research of Te Molder (1995) on the topic. It called for factual information. However, whereas that study was a discourse analysis that dwelt on "the planner," how PR may approach the talk, this one focused on beyond "talk" context analysis.

Amoakohene's (2012) government-media relations research identified a number of issues that relate to this study. Among her discoveries were methods used by governments to muzzle the press and mediation characterized by partisan political considerations. An example would be the exclusion of disliked press from covering the seat of government. The government would also resort to intimidation by using the courts to jail editors whose mode and content of communication were viewed as hostile. Ansu-Kyeremeh (1999–2001) catalogues various oppressive actions against media people including imprisonment during the era of the "culture of silence." Another is censorship attempts, something prohibited by Ghana's 1992 Constitution. In addition, governments have been seen to use their huge advertising budgets to prop up friendly media while starving the critical media to extinction. A government imposed "culture of silence" between 1982 and 2000 by the Rawlings military-cum-civilian administrations has been a widely discussed topic (Ansu-Kyeremeh, 2001; Amoakohene, 2012).

Ansu-Kyeremeh (2001), for example, wondered why government thought that the more it succeeded in preventing others, but itself, from informing the public, the more it would succeed with its own communication. The idea was that, the government would be conscious of "the extent to which messages are understandable" to the audience as Fosu (2016, p. 3) recommended after studying message clarity. It is anticipated that further concrete philosophical or theoretical issues could emerge from the current study's methodology.

DATA COLLECTION AND ANALYSIS

An existentialist empirical inquiry, this study involved examining policy documents and other official publications by state institutions of communication relevance. The institutions were the National Communications Authority (NCA) and the National Media Commission (NMC). Their regulatory, monitoring, and training roles demand that they assemble data and information on the nature and operations of communication and media systems. Thus, their organizational websites were particularly useful for policy information and statistical data. The publications and web content of an independent media monitoring and training organization, the Media Foundation for West Africa (MFWA; www.mfwa.org), were also reviewed. MFWA engages in research into media performance and identifies lapses in practice to provide reason and knowledge to play its advocacy role. Its research results are published as reports, policy briefs, and baseline studies in book or article format. Attention was also paid to the websites of former leaders Jerry John Rawlings, John Agyekum Kufuor, and John Dramani Mahama.

Also, ephemeral literature, including the 1992 Constitution of the Republic of Ghana and other legislative instruments, among them those establishing the NCA and the NMC as well as some online news portals, were sourced. Stories published in newspapers or online on government communication activities and events were gleaned to help enrich the data. From all these sources, facts were sought on the language by which the government communicated and the channels through which its messages were passed. At the backdrop were known government communication practices, such as nationwide presidential live (radio and television) broadcasts as well as addresses to Parliament. Additionally, the media appearances by political party communication team members, who acted as knowing everything about every topic, an everyday occurrence, were monitored. It was all a matter of paying attention to government communication acts. For the analysis of the information and data gathered, tables were constructed to summarize the findings. The summaries included communication channels available to government, radio and television audience statistics, and the direction of flow of government communication.

FINDINGS

The data gathered provide insights into communication outlets available to the government and the language used to communicate with the citizenry, to partly show how these were enabling or disenabling to effective government communication. It was observed that communication was not limited to central government members (such as ministers of state and other presidential appointees or functionaries at the grassroots, the Metropolitan, Municipal and District Chief Executives (MMDCEs) playing their constitutional and local government legislation roles as the president's appointed representatives. The president may also expect traditional leaders to voice his (the president's) concerns. For these and other surrogates, the low technology community information centres (CICs) would be a tool. Information officers (from the Ministry of Information) were also posted to all district headquarters to improve the flow of information. Much of government communication with the governed was, however, through the technologically mediated mass media.

## COMMUNICATION OUTLETS

Over the years, leaders and governments have acquired and relied on various means by which they have been communicating with citizens. This study sought information about these as a prelude to determining the public availability of and citizen accessibility to these outlets. Table 7.1 summarizes the findings on the main technologically mediated modes of communication employed by the government, namely, radio, television, and newspaper.

## INCIDENCE OF INCOMMUNICADO

State ownership grants the government wide-range legal access to print, electronic, and online outlets. A Ministry of Information website post lists state-owned media (*Daily Graphic, Ghanaian Times, Mirror, Spectator,* and Ghana News Agency) as its "agencies," government access to which is guaranteed by the Constitution. All these notwithstanding, the government's state of incommunicado was observed particularly regarding the newspaper (table 7.1). But for the amplification of newspaper contents by radio and television per their "newspaper review" programming, the print media may be of negligible or of not much consequence as instruments of effective communication by the president and his government. Readership of their online versions, like the hard copy, was restricted to the literate and internet savvy. Moreover, all newspapers were published in English with not a single local-language newspaper.

One notes paltry newspaper patronage across the ten regions (table 7.1). All the eleven dailies, sixty-seven weeklies, twenty-three biweeklies, and five triweeklies are published in the English language. The national capital, Accra, surpasses all nine other regions put together in terms of place-of-newspaper production. Actually, the readability issues, such as understanding the language in which the message is presented (English), as raised by Fosu (2016), worsen the patronage figures and therefore may further dimin-

**Table 7.1.    Communication outlets.**

| Radio 471 | Television 128* | Newspaper (% Coverage)+ |
|---|---|---|
| Campus 21 | Analogue Terrestrial 21 | Ashanti (5661728) 7 |
| Commercial 340 | Digi Terrestrial Pay TV 1 | Brong Ahafo (2786400) 4 |
| Community 74 | Digi Terrestrial Pay TV 5 | Central (2521118) 7 |
| Public 31 # | Digi Terrestrial F-To-A TV 23 | Eastern (3171743) 5 |
| Public (Foreign) 5 | Digi Terrestrial F-To-A TV 4 | Greater Accra (4811710) 59 |
| — | Satellite TV (Pay Direct) 8 | Northern (2993554) 8 |
| — | Satellite TV (F-To-A, 10 | Upper East (1244983) 2 |
| — | Satellite TV (F-To-A)1 | Upper West (829984) 3 |
| — | Digital Cable Television 55 | Volta (2549256) 3 |
| — | | Western (3023529) 3 |

\* = A total of fifty-three TV stations were on air as at the end of September 30, 2017 (source: NCA 2018), https://nca.org.gh/licensing-authorisation/broadcasting-authorisation/radio/ (viewed June 3, 2018); + = Figures in parentheses represent population sourced from http://statsghana.gov.gh/, population projection by districts 2015–2020 (viewed June 14, 2018); # = The Ministry of Information (MoI) claims these stations as its agencies.

ish the impact of the presidential print media messaging. Fosu's (2016) grammatical and readability (textual) analysis of newspapers suggested that grammatical mistakes affect reader understanding of the newspaper contents, even among the literate.

Table 7.2 has important implications for the government being incommunicado. The top two most popular radio stations broadcast in the local language (Akan) only, so did the top two television stations. No programs were broadcast in English. With radio- and television-mediated government communication virtually always in English, the government was certainly incommunicado as far as the non-English speaking grassroots audience was concerned. The question of understanding content raised within Fosu's (2016) readability study relates to the appropriateness of the language of broadcast.

Indeed, the president, as head of government, is incommunicado by virtue of station ownership and language of broadcast. A president's constitutionally privileged access to the state-owned media does exclude the top ten radio stations and the top four television stations, many of which, in both cases, broadcast in the local languages, mainly Akan-Twi. It is almost beyond comprehension, then, that the government would not use its massive media arsenal to counter whatever emanates from the private media but would rather complain against them (the private media) in the manner the attorney general did (Bannerman, 2016).

**Table 7.2.    Top ten radio and TV audience share (%).**

| Radio | Audience Share | Television | Audience Share |
|---|---|---|---|
| PEACE FM | 9.7 | UTV | 19.2 |
| *Adom FM* | 9.0 | *Adom TV* | 17.1 |
| City FM | 5.2 | TV3 | 14.8 |
| *Joy FM* | 4.9 | *Joy Prime* | 11.2 |
| HELLO FM | 3.3 | GTV | 8.5 |
| Kessben FM | 3.1 | *Joy News* | 8.3 |
| *Nhyira FM* | 3.0 | GhOne | 7.7 |
| OKAY FM | 2.6 | Metro TV | 5.8 |
| Radio Gold | 2.5 | Viasat One | 5.3 |
| Oman FM | 2,3 | Max | 0.3 |
| Other | 54.5 | Other | 1,8 |

Source:   https://www.businessghana.com/site/news/Entertainment/140306/Ghana%20Q4
%202016%20Radio%20%26%20TV%20Audience%20Ratings%20  Report,   June   3,
2018),  Multimedia  Group  Adom,  Asempa,  Hitz,  Joy,  Luv,  and  Nhyira  (in  italics)  and
Despite Group HELLO, NEAT, OKAY, and PEACE (in caps).

## GOVERNMENT'S COMMUNICATION OPPORTUNITIES

Both tables 7.1 and 7.2 present an array of communication outlets available
to the government as constituted in all of its forms and personified in the
president as its head. To become president, Article 55 (12 and 11) of the
Constitution (Republic of Ghana, 1992) provides the presidential candidate
and political party "time and space on the state-owned media to present their
programmes to the people." Once president, one

> shall at all times have access to sound or television broadcasting, the Press and
> other media of mass communications or information which are financed from
> public funds for the purpose of broadcast, announcement or publication of any
> matter which appears to the President to be in the public interest. (Section 19,
> National Media Commission Act, 1993, Act 449)

In table 7.3, we present the activity (programs), the kind of language used in
presenting such programs, the direction of information flow and the feedback
received from the audience.

However, in five out of seven opportunities for the president to communicate directly with the people, he does so in the English language (table 7.3). It
is only when the president, as head of government, is on durbar (political
rallies or meetings of the president and party members with the general

**Table 7.3.   Language and direction of communication flow.**

| Activity | Language | Direct flow | Two-step* | Feedback |
|---|---|---|---|---|
| Meet the Press | English | X | — | X |
| Press Conference | English | X | — | X |
| People's Assembly | English/Local | X | — | X |
| Press Statement | English | — | X | — |
| Interview | English | — | X | — |
| Tour Durbar | Local/English | X | — | X |
| State of Nation Address | English | X | — | — |

* Indirect through surrogate

public and traditional leaders) tours that he sometimes communicates in the local language. He may intersperse English with some local language in the "People's Assembly" format, which is a town-hall-style forum where the president answers questions directly from members of the public. Even that still remains an English-language exercise. In the interpretation of "presidentialism" by Tiffen (1989, p. 137), heads of government, even when they are not "president," project the image of the person as the government, thus rating their communication key in civic engagement. All or much of political communication centers on the leader/president.

Even President Kufuor's innovative "People's Assembly," recycled as President Atta Mills's "Town Hall Meeting," both designed to bring the government closer to the grassroots in interactive communication, were conducted mainly in English. However, Jerry John Rawlings, as a national leader, is known to have made capital out of "broken" Twi, which readily endeared and connected him to ordinary citizens. Incidentally, the profit-making private media had found money in the right choice of language. TV3, for instance, began dubbing Mexican telenovelas in English in October 1997. However, it was Peace FM's decision to broadcast exclusively in Twi (a local language) that became a rating lightning rod. The audience base of its television UTV spiked when it decided to dub the Indian telenovela *Kum Kum Bagya* in Twi. In table 7.4, we present the current and past presidents of Ghana, the types of governments they served in and their press activities.

From table 7.4, we learn that every leader, president, head of state, prime minister, head of a constitutional or military government has had the opportunity of direct communication with the citizenry through live broadcasts and speeches during tour durbars. In the case of the durbars, though, the directness has been restricted to only the audience assembled at one durbar at a

**Table 7.4. Which leader, which activity?**

| Leader | Gov't Type | MtP | Press Conf | Ppl's Assem | Press Stat | Interview | Tour Durb | Sess Addr | Live Bcast |
|---|---|---|---|---|---|---|---|---|---|
| Nkrumah | Const | | X | — | X | X | X | X | X |
| Ankrah + | Military | X* | X | — | X | X | X | — | X |
| Busia | Const | | X | — | X | X | X | — | X |
| Acheampong | Military | | X | — | X | X | X | — | X |
| Rawlings | Military | | X | — | X | X | X | — | X |
| Limann | Const | | X | — | X | X | X | X | X |
| Rawlings | Military | | X | — | X | X | X | — | X |
| Rawlings | Const | | X | — | X | X | X | X | X |
| Kufuor | Const | X | X | X | X | X | X | X | X |
| Mills | Const | X | X | — | X | X | X | X | X |
| Mahama | Const | | X | — | X | X | X | X | X |
| Akufo—Addo | Const | X | X | X | X | X | X | X | X |

+ Citing Asante (1996), Amoakohene (2012, p. 21) said the military-police junta led by Ankrah "institutionalized regular weekly meetings with editors of national media organizations as a boost to government-media relations although such meetings were said to be used to instruct the media on what to do." * Ankrah is quoted as saying, "[O]ne who pays the piper will have to call the tune" (Asante, 1996, p. 41). Legend: MtP—Meet the press; Press Conf—Press Conference; Ppl's Assem—People's Assembly; Press Stat—Press Statement; TourDurb—Tour Durbar; Sess Addr—Sessional Address; Live Bcast—Live Radio & Television Broadcasts.

time. Beyond that audience, others can have access when the speech is reproduced (and possibly multiplied) by the media, a mode that invites all the implications of intermediation gatekeeping.

Table 7.5 has, as headings, the names of Ghana's presidents/heads of state, their governments, periods of rule, and various means by which they communicated, no longer as in the person president but on behalf or in the name of the president.

An important facet of table 7.5 is the seat of government, the nerve center from where communication on behalf of the president/head of state may be initiated and executed by his personal (press) secretary or a director of communication. Jerry John Rawlings's Provisional National Defence Council (PNDC) administrations had what was referred to as the Castle Information Bureau, which was known for its convivial, cozy, and incestuous relations with the state-owned media. It would develop stories and plant them in the state-owned media. It is on record that Elvis Aryeh "once doubled as the President's personal Press Secretary" (Boadu-Ayeboafo, 2018, p. 13) from where he assumed editorship of the largest circulating and most influential state-owned newspaper, the *Daily Graphic*.

While Rawlings and Limann had press secretaries, Kufuor had a spokesperson, Mills and Akufo-Addo have had directors of communication, and Mahama more often used the Ministry of Communications (formerly, Ministry of Information, a unit that was reinstated by Akufo-Addo).[2] The constant reorganization of a ministry in charge of government communication and information could be an indication of the government feeling an incommunicado effect. As Ansu-Kyeremeh (1995, 2007) has noted, some streamlining might be needed to trim personnel, reduce bureaucracy, and keep focus. The president may resort to in-presidency surrogacy; but surrogacy functioned beyond the Castle/Jubilee House. There has been the Ministry of Information (MoI) and its agency the Information Services Department (ISD), which deploys staff to handle PR at the other MDAs. Surrogacy-implementing agencies often organized programs and activities in the English language, which excluded at least a quarter of the population from participation.

## PRESIDENTIAL COMMUNICATION PLATFORMS

This study found (tables 7.4 and 7.5) certain avenues open to the president to communicate with the public at various times in the nation's history, directly or indirectly. Among these are the Castle Information Bureau (CIB; English), where government propaganda stories were developed and planted in the state-owned media. During certain periods, such as the Mills administration, there has been the directorate of communications (DoC) at the presidency. The Ministry of Information and Information Services Department, which

**Table 7.5. Surrogates.**

| Pres/HoS | Gov't | PERI | PCT | MoI | ISD | CIB | Per Sec | MDAPR | ParOff | Minist | MMDCEs | PAssem |
|---|---|---|---|---|---|---|---|---|---|---|---|---|
| Nkrumah | CPP | 1951–1966 | — | X | X | — | X | X | X | X | X | — |
| Ankrah | NLC | 1966–1969 | — | X | X | — | — | X | X | X | X | — |
| Busia | PP | 1969–1972 | — | X | X | — | X | X | X | X | X | — |
| Acheampong | NRC–SMC | 1972–1979 | — | X | X | — | X | X | X | X | X | — |
| Rawlings | AFRC | 1979 | — | X | X | — | — | X | — | X | X | — |
| Limann | PNP | 1979–1981 | — | X | X | — | X | X | X | X | X | — |
| Rawlings | PNDC | 1982–1993 | — | X | X | X | X | X | — | X | X | — |
| Rawlings | NDC | 1993–2000 | — | — | X | X | X | X | X. | X | X | X |
| Kufuor | NPP | 2001–2008 | X | X | X | — | — | X | X | X | X* | X |
| Mills | NDC | 2009–2012 | X | — | X | — | — | X | X | X | X | X |
| Mahama | NDC | 2012–2016 | X | — | X | X | — | X | X | X | X | — |
| Akufo–Addo | NPP | 2017– | X | X | X | — | — | X | X | X | X | X |

Pres/HoS—President/Head of State; Gov't—Government; CPP—Convention People's Party; NLC—National Liberation Council; PP—Progress Party; NRC—National Redemption Council; SMC—Supreme Military Council; AFRC—Armed Forces Revolutionary Council; PNP—People's National Party; PNDC—Provisional National Defence Council; NDC—National Democratic Congress; NPP—New Patriotic Party; PERI—Period of rule; PCT—Party Communication Team; MoI—Ministry of Information; ISD—Information Services Department; CIB—Castle Information Bureau; Per Sec—Personal Secretary; MDAPR—Ministries, Departments, Agencies PRs; ParOff—Party Officers; Minist—Ministers; MMDCEs—Metropolitan, Municipal & District Assemblies; PAssem—People's Assembly.

deployed its experts as public relation officials (PROs) to units within ministries, departments, and agencies (MDAs), communicated messages to citizens in English.

There have been the institutionalized Meet the Press (MtP) series, press conferences, as well as the occasional issuance of press statements by the press secretary to the president or the director of communications (DoC) at the presidency. Interviews get granted from time to time and they are usually to the foreign press. Then, there have been the *Tour Durbar* speeches (few and far between though), which are the exception in local-language use. Above all is the constitutionally mandated sessional/state of the nation addresses delivered to Parliament in English. Many of the presidential communication platforms are classified as belonging to the surrogacy (table 7.5). There are also the various social media platforms used especially under Mahama and Akufo-Addo. All, except the durbar address, are conducted in the English language.

The political party communication team (PCT) concept needs some elaboration. Asamoah-Boateng (2018) quotes former president Rawlings as saying, "Some little ones are so vicious with their mouth and use insults as their weapons to discredit others," apparently in "newspaper review" contributions.[3] The PCT is less, and indeed hardly studied as a phenomenon of political communication. The phenomenon has its roots in the Twi program *Obiara Nka Bi*, which had a phone-in segment that was broadcast by the University of Ghana radio station *Voice of Legon* (now *Radio Universe*). Later, the program was adapted as a newspaper review segment of *The Breakfast Show* morning program by GTV, the state-owned broadcaster. Initially, representatives of the two largest political parties the National Democratic Congress (NDC) and the New Patriotic Party (NPP) would be invited for in-studio participation as panelists.

Usually, the party representatives would make their contribution on a topical issue selected by the host and would react to audience phoned-in contributions or answer audience questions. The format of participating political party representatives has endured to become a "newspaper review" program genre. It has dominated survey after survey (such as those by geopoll.com) as the most popular program among the radio listening public. Political party representation is now extended to others, such as the Convention People's Party (CPP), the People's National Convention (PNC), and the Progressive People's Party (PPP) besides the NDC and NPP. However, the quality (a major source of the Cameron Duodu [2018] cacophony characterization) and content of the "newspaper review" programming is challenged in two basic ways. One is the caliber of the party representatives. The other is the unfulfillable requirement that a panelist be all-knowing with expertise in every topic discussed.

In table 7.5 are indicated surrogates used by the president or head of government, besides party communication team members in the second stage of the two-step flow of his messages. In almost all his direct messaging, the president communicates in English; so do his surrogates. It is usually only the party communication team members who, in their indirectly communicating surrogate role, would often use the local language in which the program is conducted. A rare case of a president communicating directly in a local language would be when he addresses local communities during tour durbars.[4]

As indicated earlier, Jerry Rawlings may be accused by a section of the media of playing to the gallery with his broken Twi. He nevertheless made communication capital out of television soundbites or radio actualities, perhaps cynically selected by suspicious media, especially in the era of the culture of silence (Ansu-Kyeremeh, 1999–2001) to mock him. But as noted, it served as a positive resonation–heightening device for him. Akufo-Addo is much endowed with multilingual proficiency. Apart from his 2018 sessional address Ewe quip, he is fluent in Ga and Hausa in addition to his mother tongue Twi. Regrettably, he does not seem to be taking full advantage of this linguistic capital, thereby dissipating a major language and communicative advantage he could exploit.

## DISCUSSION

Patterns of government communication emerge from data in the tables. In table 7.1, one finds thirty-one publicly owned radio stations and one television station, all operated by the Ghana Broadcasting Corporation (GBC) as a state broadcaster. This affords the government extensive nationwide coverage of its activities. The wide reach, though, seems to mislead the government into some kind of complacency. Distance reach of signal does not translate into easy access, which is constrained by the use of English as the language medium. Furthermore, the president or the government, communicates in English and by so doing excludes a quarter of the population who do not understand that language. They are often illiterate in an environment in which only the schooled have English language capacity. The literacy rate in 2015 was 76.58 percent. To the illiterate then, the government is incommunicado by language medium of communication. It is interesting that an *Illiterates Protection Ordinance* (1912, No. 4) had sought to prevent exploitation of citizens unable to read and write in English. Elsewhere, such as in the United States, presidents crave direct communication.[5]

However, even when the message is communicated in the local language to extend its reach and enhance its understanding, the government may fudge its own message into incommunicado with unplanned approaches. Message inconsistency arising out of poor coordination between source and surrogacy (or various surrogacies) could make that happen (Amoakohene, 2011). Ansu-Kyeremeh (2007) cites the example of the hazard of surrogated communication when at a project commissioning ceremony, the vice president, the regional minister, and the district chief executive each stated a different cost of a project that was being commissioned.

Based on the data, the government was somehow incommunicado in the language by which it was communicating and its false belief in ready access (because of available space in the state-owned media) when the evidence indicated less-than-likely enthusiastic patronage of those media (tables 7.1 and 7.2). That is to say, the competition spurned by freedom of expression and media pluralism was not translating into quality of content which was rather "cacophonous" (Duodo, 2018).

Things are not that much different within today's media digisphere. The websites of the MoI and state-owned media seem to carry less comprehensive information and are lagging in recency compared to the online portals of the private media. Obiorah (2018) notes that Graphiconline, placed fourth as the most visited site, is the only state-owned site among the ten most visited websites in Ghana. Private media online portals correct mistakes they are susceptible to in their aggressive pursuance of the scoop. GBC, for example, seems to be haunted by an early mistake of incorrectly sourcing the Internet. Ratings, such as the one by geopoll.com, tend to show less-than-enthusiastic patronage. Although social media cross-sourcing is a challenge to both media systems, private media seem to be managing, driven by the principle of getting it accurate first (with the risk of later retraction and other hazardous consequences). Their state-owned counterparts want to get it whenever (even if late) and right than first and wrong. In that sense, the 1992 Constitution's expectation of adversarial relations between the president/government and the press seems far from realization with the state-owned media.

In the pluralist environment, the audience is no longer captive. One does not have to read the state-owned newspaper (*Daily Graphic* or *Ghanaian Times*), listen to the state-owned radio (Radio Ghana), nor watch the state-owned television (Ghana Television). There are alternatives: over one hundred newspapers (NMC), by NCA more than two hundred radio stations, and at least eighty television stations. Availability of or easy access to the medium, thus, does not necessarily translate into patronage.

The president and his surrogates are challenged by the presence, at the seat of government, of the presidential press corps. Indeed, this is obvious from the pluralism indicator whereby since "President Kufuor, things have changed dramatically. Private news organizations have been invited to post permanent representatives to the Castle and Kufuor invites both state and private journalists to accompany him on official visits both nationally and internationally" (Hasty, n.d.). Amoakohene (2012, p. 118) made a similar observation comparing the Rawlings administration's exclusionist treatment of private media journalists to Kufuor's inclusiveness. She noted, "The situation, however, changed under President Kufuor, to allow journalists from the private media to accompany the President and his appointees on official trips."

Nonetheless, to those who do not speak and understand English, the government is officially and effectively incommunicado. The president hardly ever officially, directly communicates to that minority, since all his official communication is in English. Meanwhile, no law imposes that restriction. The fact that no law restricts the president's use of language leaves room for a paradigm shift by governments; yet, so far none has attempted any change. They hold on to the practice, hoping for everyone to be able to understand English. An NPP campaign (iterated by communication team members) seems to suggest the latter with claims that its free Senior High School (SHS) education policy would produce the schooled, who by implication would become English speaking.

It is striking how the characterization of state-owned broadcast frequencies by the NCA has evolved from "government-owned" at the beginning of the pluralism debate to the current "public-owned." In the American regulation model, which Ghana has confusedly tried to copy despite its broadcasting being rooted in British tradition, the American Federal Communication Commission (FCC) oversees all communication, while Ghana has split the function of oversight between the constitutional NMC and an Act established NCA. The data above appears to be pointing at enhanced means, such as the appropriate language and an audience whose characteristics are understood in order to take advantage of media attributes and audience attitudes.

The study also raises questions about the notion of adversarial relations between the government and the media. It is a matter that focuses on praise-singing or incessant criticism of government by the media. Whereas praise-singers are likely to self-censor even when there is no pressure from the government to censor, the critical press may succumb to irresponsibility. Adversarial practice cannot be the perpetual condemnation of everything the government says and does.

Effectively, though, by Tiffen's (1989) "presidentialism," the government is the president. So, whether said by the president himself or by others on his behalf, acts of governance are attributable to the president. Thus, if the government is not communicating well, it is the president not communicating well. Therefore, one ought to forget about surrogacy, cognizant of the fact that all the party communication teams, Ministry of Information, Information Services Department, Castle Information Bureau, press secretaries to the president, MDAs, PROs, party officers, ministers, and MMDCEs not communicating effectively points to a president who is not communicating effectively. A combination of mostly indirect communication, complacency over media access, and exclusionist language of communication denies government communication of audience reach and resonance.

With massive media resources at the disposal of the government, it could be complacently self-sufficient in its approach. Attributes of the selected language (English) and platforms or the array of tools and avenues do not match audience characteristics. The language restriction does not allow adequate exploitation of the nationwide reach of government media. Perhaps, it is about time the government learned about the medium by choosing the language of the people, as the success of Peace FM and UTV have shown and not insisting on the people learning the language of the medium. This study may have set out as an inventory of communication tools but has, somehow, turned out to be a search for embedded risk factors in government-to-citizen communication.

## RECOMMENDATIONS

It is about time researchers probed the limitations of a leader's direct communication with the citizenry. Presidentialism has reduced the possibilities of direct communication. The language in which a president communicates could be a factor because it limits reach. Presidents may use social media to boost their direct communication strategies, cognizant however of the fact that it may come with language constraints. Within the Ghanaian context, it would be interesting to establish which leader takes to social media to enhance direct communication with the audience for what acceptance impact. Furthermore, detailed examination of the websites of MDAs should throw more light on government-citizen information sharing.

Then there is the case for means inclusiveness. Ordinarily, there are many indigenous communication systems (ICS) the government may choose to use. They include those identified for health communication by Ansu-Kyeremeh, Richter, Vallianatos, and Aniteye (2016). It would be useful to know the extent to which these are employed, especially by the president's messaging surrogates. This is important because the literature encountered during this study was all about modern media and therefore not representing the total picture of government-citizen communication. Thus, holistic studies that include literature on the ICS would lead to a fuller understanding of the existence of a government that is in a state of incommunicado. Since the ICS are mainly interactive, their inclusion would assist in assessing that dimension of government communication. It could help verify the Ministry of Information website's two-way communication claim.

The findings of such research would throw more light on how the language medium of a communication act, direct or indirect, may factor into enhanced or diminished understanding between communicator and audience.

The results of this research reveal overreliance on the English language, a practice that seems to alienate one quarter of the audience base, who would not understand the communicating president/leader. Any such realization could help in redesigning and fashioning government communication with the citizenry to include the excluded. Greater insights from the voices of the strategists, message designers, actors, and policy implementers on incommunicado should be helpful. Thus, a study that goes beyond documents to interview people and seek views would provide more enriching data on the phenomenon.

If there was any doubt as to whether government is ever in incommunicado with some segment of the citizenry over some time, its answer does not seem to be in doubt from the results of this study. Citizens who do not understand the English language and those who would choose not to patronize state-owned media are typical examples. The unanswered questions arising out of the study include the extent of exclusion, what and how much time of the exclusion of sections of the general public in government's communication, and who precisely are excluded. Future research would need to tackle these unresolved issues to throw greater light on why the government becomes incommunicado.

## SUMMARY

It is surprising that no government seems to have diagnosed incommunicado as a governance communication challenge created by less access to the media that matter most; a less direct and more indirect communication approach; and excessive use of the English language almost to the exclusion of local languages. This chapter has identified elements of a state of incommunicado. The realization would call for action to break down the barriers to effective communication in order to enhance flow and deepen comprehension. Direct communication could then be organized to have greater resonating feed. In fact, the indirect intermediated multiplier potentially has higher risks and is less effective. It is fraught with the danger of the exaggerations of spin and misinformation and it is more difficult to coordinate with other government outlets than direct communication.

The fact that there is no sign of a paradigm shift indicates the government does not realize it is incommunicado at all with the people. The people's assembly and the town hall meeting concepts are few and far between. Incommunicado, as defined by the audience or communicator, is unlikely to completely disappear. Presidents and governments everywhere complain about the dearth of effective government-citizenry communication. The issue is for the president and governments of Ghana to examine any role language(s) selected to communicate with their citizenry or audiences play.

Also to be examined are the channels through which such communications are done, in order to detect clues to the incidence of incommunicado. That way, they will be able to develop strategies to reduce the effect of incommunicado.

## NOTES

1. It is usually the mainstream media (newspaper, radio, and television) that get measured in spread, penetration, reach, and other indicators of democratic access and use.

2. Governments have been organizing for greater communication success. Changed from Ministry of Information to the Ministry of Communications in Rawlings's time, changed back to Information by Kufuor, reverted to Communications over the Mills and Mahama periods and back to Information in the Akufo-Addo era. A typical challenge, however, are the inconsistencies that sometimes occur in official communications as a result of surrogated communications thereby creating noise with government communication.

3. Initially, the Party Communication Team (PCT) syndrome was the NPP countering the (unconstitutional) NDC Propaganda Secretary position that preceded it. The PCT appears to be the NPP's response to the former when it assumed office in 2001. The PCT had existed in various forms other than media panelists such as the NLC/Busia Centre for Civic Education, Limann's Vigilante and Rawlings' People's Defence Committees/Cadres.

4. To familiarize himself with conditions across the country, the president tours various parts of the country. He addresses the public durbars that are organized to welcome and listen to him.

5. Even in the media-saturated United States, presidents still exploit the advantage of direct "Weekly (Radio) Address" or "Your Weekly Radio Address" to directly reach citizens. Franklin D. Roosevelt found avenue in early 1930s "fireside chats"; George W. Bush used audio podcasts; and Barack Obama, YouTube. Despite his Twitter obsession, Donald Trump is continuing with the weekly video address model.

## REFERENCES

Akanlig-Pare, George. (2001). "The 2000 Presidential and Parliamentary Elections in Ghana: Wa Central and Sissala Constituencies." In Joseph R. A. Aryee (ed.), *Deepening Democracy in Ghana: Politics of the 2000 Elections, Vol Two*, 417–432. Accra: Freedom Publications.

Amoakohene, Margaret I. (July–September 1996). "Kufuor Heard Loud But Not Clear." *Media Monitor* 4(9–10).

Amoakohene, Margaret I. (2004). "Researching Radio Audiences in an Emerging Pluralistic Media Environment: A Case for the Focus Group Discussion (FGD) Method." *African Media Review* 12(2): 25–40.

Amoakohene, Margaret I. (2011). "Information Management: The Nemesis of Ghanaian Governments." *Ghana Social Science Journal* 8(1&2): 150–173.

Amoakohene, Margaret I. (2012). *Political Communication in Ghana's Emerging Democracy*. Saarbrucken: Lap Lambert Academic Publishing.

Anokwa, K. (1996). "Press Performance under Civilian and Military Regimes in Ghana: A Reassessment of Past and Present Knowledge. In F. Eribo and W. Jong-Ebot (eds.), *Press Freedom and Communication in Africa*, 9–10. Asmara: Africa World Press.

Ansu-Kyeremeh, K. (1992). "Cultural Aspects of Constraints on Village Education by Radio." *Media, Culture and Society* 14(1): 111–128.

Ansu-Kyeremeh, K. (November 25, 1995). "The State of the Art: Prospects for the Future of Information "Delivery" in the 21st Century." Presentation at Annual Review Conference of Information Officers, Christian Village, Santasi, Kumasi, Ghana (Mimeo).

Ansu-Kyeremeh, K. (2001). "Culture of Silence: Change without Continuity in an African Communication Framework." *Legon Journal of Humanities* 12: 31–52.

Ansu-Kyeremeh, K. (2005). "Indigenous Communication in Africa: A Conceptual Framework." In K. Ansu-Kyeremeh (ed.), *Indigenous Communication in Africa: Concepts, Applications and Prospects*, 15–25. Accra: Ghana Universities Press.

Ansu-Kyeremeh, K. (2007). *Ka Nea Woahu: An African Communication Paradigm*. Accra: Adwinsa Publications.

Ansu-Kyeremeh, K. (2008). *Ka Nea Woahu (Publish Only the Verified)*. Inaugural Lecture, University of Ghana. Accra: University of Ghana.

Ansu-Kyeremeh, K. (2014). "Critically 'Trending' Approaches to Communication Theory and Methods of Inquiry in Ghana." In S. Agyei-Mensah, Joseph Atsu Aryee, and Abena D. Oduro (eds.), *Changing Perspectives on the Social Sciences in Ghana*, 221–238. New York: Springer.

Ansu-Kyeremeh, K., A. Gadzekpo, and M. Amoakohene. (2015). Introduction. In K. Ansu-Kyeremeh, A. Gadzekpo, and M. Amoakohene (eds.), *Communication Research and Practice in Ghana*, xi–xiv. Accra: Digibooks Ghana.

Ansu-Kyeremeh, K., and K. Karikari. (1997). Media Ghana: Ghanaian Media Overview, Practitioners and Institutions. Accra: School of Communication Studies.

Ansu-Kyeremeh, K., Magdalena Richter, Helen Vallianatos, and Patience Aniteye. (2016). "Rural Women's Exposure to Health Messages and Understandings." *Journal of Healthcare Communications* 1(3): 18. http://healthcare-communications.imedpub.com/exposure-to-the-health-message-and-rural-womens-understanding-of-health.pdf (viewed June 18, 2018).

Asamoah-Boateng, Kwame. (2018). "NDC Lies Too Much—Rawlings." http://dailyguideafrica.com/ndc-lies-too-much-rawlings/ (viewed June 6, 2018).

Asante, Clement. (1996). *The Press in Ghana: Problems and Prospects*. New York, London: University Press of America, Inc.

Bannerman, Alexander. (July 18, 2016). "NMC Rules on Attorney General's Complaint against Joy FM's Kojo Yankson." https://www.myjoyonline.com/news/2016/july-18th/nmc-rules-on-attorney-generals-complaint-against-joy-fms-kojo-yankson.php (viewed May 29, 2018).

BBC World Service Trust (n.d.). "African Media Development Initiative: Ghana Context." http://downloads.bbc.co.uk/worldservice/trust/pdf/AMDI/ghana/amdi_ghana7_newspapers.pdf (viewed June 3, 2018).

Beetham, David. (1994). *Defining and Measuring Democracy*: London: Sage.

Boadu-Ayeboafo, Yaw. (January 18, 2018). "Countdown Begins iii Encounters with the Military." https://www.graphic.com.gh/features/thinking-aloud/countdown-begins-iii-encounters-with-the-military.html (viewed June 3, 2018).

Duodu, Cameron (columnist). (2018). "Politics in the Era of Cacophony." *Daily Guide*. http://dailyguideafrica.com/politics-in-an-era-of-cacophony/ (viewed June 2, 2018).

Ekwelieh, Sylvanus. (1978). "The Genesis of Press Control in Ghana." *Gazette* 24: 196–206.

Fosu, Modestus. (2016). "A Linguistic Description of the Language of Ghanaian Newspapers: Implications for the Readability, Comprehensibility and Information Function of the Ghanaian Press." *Ghana Journal of Linguistics* 5(1): 1–36.

Geopoll.com. (January 19, 2017). "Ghana Q4 2016 Radio and TV Audience Ratings Report." BusinessGhana. https://www.businessghana.com/site/news/Entertainment/140306/Ghana%20Q4%202016%20Radio%20%26%20TV%20Audience%20Ratings%20Report (viewed June 3, 2018).

Ghana Broadcasting Corporation (GBC). (March 16, 2017). "Supreme Court Declares NMC's Media Content Regulation Law Unconstitutional." http://www.gbcghana.com/1.10294716 (viewed August 8, 2018).

Ghana News Agency. (2018). "President Nana Addo-Dankwa Akufo-Addo Believes His Free Senior High School Education Programme Is "Antidote to Illiteracy in Africa." http://www.ghananewsagency.org/print/123071 (viewed July 7, 2018).

Ghana Statistical Service (GSS) (n.d.). "Population Projection by Region 2015–2020." http://statsghana.gov.gh/ (viewed June 14, 2018).

Gyasi, Ibrahim Kwaku. (March 14, 2011). "Governments and the Media: Partners or Adversaries?" *Ghanaian Chronicle*.

Halliday, M. A. K., and C. M. I. M. Matthiessen. (2004). *An Introduction to Functional Grammar* (3rd ed.). London: Hodder Education.

Hasty, Jennifer. (n.d.). Ghana Press, Media, TV, Radio, Newspapers, Press Reference. http://www.pressreference.com/Fa-Gu/Ghana.html (viewed June 3, 2018).

Hasty, Jennifer. (2005). *The Press and Political Culture in Ghana*. Bloomington: Indiana University Press.

Karikari, K., A. Essuman-Johnson, K. Ansu-Kyeremeh, and A. K. Bonnah Koomson. (1995). *Democratic Governance in Ghana under the 1992 Constitution*. Accra: Institute of Economic Affairs.

Liu, Brooke Fisher, and J. Suzanne Horsley. (2007). "The Government Communication Decision Wheel: Toward a Public Relations Model for the Public Sector." *Journal of Public Relations Research* 19(4): 377–393, https://www.tandfonline.com/doi/abs/10.1080/10627260701402473 (viewed June 15, 2018).

McKwartin, Dan. (2001). "Institutions, Electoral Process, Value Preferences and Democratic Practice in Ghana." In Joseph R. A. Aryee (ed.), *Deepening Democracy in Ghana: Politics of the 2000 Elections, Vol Two*, 12–33. Accra: Freedom Publications.

Media Foundation for West Africa (MFWA). (2018). http://www.mfwa.org/publication-type/reports/ (viewed June 27, 2018).

Ministry of Information (MoI). (2018). What we do. http://moi.gov.gh/index.php/about-us/the-ministry (viewed July 7, 2018).

Munck, Geraldo L. (2009). *Measuring Democracy: A Bridge between Scholarship and Politics*. Baltimore, MD: Johns Hopkins University Press.

National Communications Authority (NCA). (n.d.). https://nca.org.gh/licensing-authorisation/broadcasting-authorisation/radio/ (viewed June 3, 2018).

National Communications Authority (NCA). (n.d.). "Authorised FM Radio Stations as at Third Quarter of 2017." https://nca.org.gh/industry-data-2/authorisations-2/fm-authorisation-2/ (viewed June 3, 2018).

National Communications Authority (NCA). (n.d.). "List of Authorised TV Broadcasting Stations in Ghana as at Third Quarter of 2017." https://nca.org.gh/industry-data-2/authorisations-2/fm-authorisation-2/ (viewed June 3, 2018).

National Media Commission (NMC). (n.d.). "Regional Coverage, Accra," https://www.facebook.com/national.media.commission.ghana/photos/rpp.188544357846219/1311339535566690/?type=3&theater (viewed June 3, 2018).

National Media Commission Act 1993 (Act 449). Accra: Assembly Press.

National Media Commission. (2009). *Guidelines for Local Language Broadcasting*. Accra.

National Redemption Council (NRC). (1973). *A Guide to the Study of the Charter of Redemption Specially Prepared for Committees of the Revolution*. Accra: Information Services Department.

Obiorah, Chukah. (2018). "10 Most Visited Websites in Ghana." https://buzzghana.com/visited-popular-websites-ghana/ (viewed July 27, 2018).

Republic of Ghana. (1992). *Constitution of the Republic of Ghana, 1992*. Accra: Assembly Press.

Rich, Sarah. (2013). "How to Improve Government-to-Citizen Communication." http://www.govtech.com/e-government/How-to-Improve-Government-to-Citizen-Communication.html (viewed June 15, 2018).

Smith, D. A., and J. Temin. (2001). "The Media and Ghana's 2000 Elections." In Joseph R. A. Aryee (ed.), *Deepening Democracy in Ghana: Politics of the 2000 Elections* 1: 160–178. Accra: Freedom Publications.

Te Molder, Hedwig. (1995). "Discourse of Dilemmas: An Analysis of Government Communicators' Talk." PhD thesis, Landbouwuniversiteit te Wageningen.

Tietaah, Gilbert (ed.). (2014). *Watching the Watchdog: Spotlighting Indecent Election Campaign Language on Radio*. Accra: Media Foundation for West Africa.

Tietaah, Gilbert (ed.). (2017). *Watching the Watchdog: Indecent Campaign Language Use on Radio During Ghana's 2016 Elections*. Accra: Media Foundation for West Africa.

Tiffen, Rodney. (1989). *News and Power*. Wellington: Allen & Unwin.

*Chapter Eight*

# Pragmatic Analysis of First-Person Pronoun Deixes in President Nana Akuffo-Addo's 2018 State of the Nation Address (SONA)

## Kofi Agyekum

During the last two decades there has been great interest in research on language and politics. Many scholars in West Africa (especially Nigeria and Ghana), East Africa, and Southern Africa have researched into Political Discourse Analysis (PDA). Among such scholars from Nigeria are Adegoju (2014), Adetunji (2006), Alo (2012), Ayeomoni and Akinkuolere (2012), Bello (2013), and Taiwo (2009). In Ghana, linguists who have worked on the interface between language and politics include Agyekum (2017, 2015, 2013, 2004), Dadugblor (2016), and Obeng (2018a, 2018b, 2012, 2002a, 2002b, 1997). This paper is a recapitulation and an extension of the previous papers I published on language and politics using the framework of political discourse. In Agyekum (2017, 2015, 2013, 2004), I examined the interface of language and politics, especially in victory and inaugural speeches, political apology, campaign promises, and political invectives. The focus of this current paper is to follow up on political speeches with a focus on examining personal deixes in the 2018 state of the nation address (SONA) by the president of the republic of Ghana, Nana Addo Dankwa Akuffo-Addo. The topic of deixes has not been popularly researched using data from political speeches in Ghana.

Taiwo (2009) observes that language is the conveyer belt of power; it moves people to vote, debate, or revolt and is therefore a central explanation of political stability and polarization. For their part, Ayeomoni and Akinkuolere (2012) assert that

[n]o matter how good a candidate's manifesto is; no matter how superior
political thoughts and ideologies of a political party may be, these can only be
expressed and further translated into social actions for social change and social
continuity through the facilities provided by language. (p. 462)

The strong synergy and symbiotic relationship between language and politics
is such that no political activity can exist without the use and manipulation of
language (Agyekum 2017, 2013; Chilton 2004, 1998).

Wilson (2001, p. 398) describes political discourse as "language used in
formal and informal political context with political actors, such as politicians,
political institutions, government, political media and political supporters
operating in political environments with political goals." In Agyekum (2017,
p. 103), I asserted that "a successful politician is an orator who uses political
language with varied and elaborate persuasive and rhetorical skills meant to
paint a clear picture of the nation for the citizenry to see him as a competent
ruler and to lure potential voters." The state of the nation's address (SONA),
where the president gives a positive image of his administration, is also full
of oratory, politeness, speech acts, deixes, persuasion, and diplomacy (see
Duranti, 2006, p. 469).

On political speeches, Reisigl (2010, p. 243) noted, "A speech is a structured verbal chain of coherent speech acts uttered on a special social occasion for specific purpose by a single person and addressed to a more or less
specific audience." In this definition, we see speech as a form of mass communication since it emanates from one person to more people. Every speech
involves some "delivery" so as to achieve its aims and purposes. Political
speeches are meant to fulfill political intentions that relate to power. Any
speech event involves speech acts, which implies that certain words in the
speech are accompanied by actions and one cannot separate the verbal from
the nonverbal communication.

## CRITICAL DISCOURSE ANALYSIS (CDA) AND POLITICAL
## DISCOURSE ANALYSIS (PDA)

The SONA used for this study is analyzed within the framework of Critical
Discourse Analysis (CDA). In some of my earlier studies (Agyekum, 2017,
2015, 2013, 2004), I used CDA and found it very useful and theoretically
appropriate for analyzing different political discourse categories.

On the literature on CDA, the seminal works of Fairclough (1998, 1989)
and Van Dijk (1998, 1997) stand out. Fowler (1991, p. 5) asserts that "Critical linguistics simply means an inquiry into the relations between signs,
meanings and social and historical conditions which govern the semiotic
structure of discourse, using a particular kind of linguistic analysis." (See
also Agyekum, 2017, p. 104.) Wodak et al. (1999, p. 8) opine that "Critical

Discourse Analysis (CDA) centres on authentic everyday communication in institutional, media, political or other locations rather than on sample sentences or sample texts constructed in linguists' minds. [It] regards both written and spoken 'discourse' as a form of social practice."

In this paper, I elucidate the *microstructures* focusing on the pronoun deixes especially the first person (*I*, *me*, *my*, *we*, *us*, *our*), and relate them to the *macrostructures* focusing on such themes as economy, health, education, agriculture, security, transport, energy, and so on. In examining the macrostructures, we will also pay attention to extra-linguistic social variables, participants, the ethnographic settings, the goals of the speech, and the political gains of the government.

Regarding the concept of political discourse, it is true to note that there are different categories of speeches that qualify as *political*. Such speeches differ from each other in terms of content, length, setting (time and space), situation, topic, theme, and political domain. Speeches, in general, may differ in terms of their functions, the speaker and the addressees, the degree of the speaker's preparedness, the form of presentation, the style, and structure (Jucker, 1997).

Conventionally, speeches are normally "texts" and hard copies so that people, especially journalists, can lay hands on copies for their reports. Political speeches therefore tend to be prepared in writing. There are, however, variations between prepared speeches and their oral versions that are presented before the people. Very few political speakers go strictly according to their written texts. Indeed, delivering a political speech is like a performer in an *oral literature* setting who enacts the performance before an audience. The type of audience, the venue, the situation, the political season, and the time the speaker has at his disposal to deliver and finish the speech all affect the presentation.

There are many categories of political speeches with different purposes; however, one of the core issues in political speeches is that they all aim to advertise one's political position and to gain or maintain power. The politician wants to assert himself against his political opponents so as to execute a specific political policy or ideology. One clear example of political speech that serves this purpose is the election or campaign speech. Reisigl (2010, p. 247) notes that a "politolinguistic differentiation of political speeches is based on 'field of political action' which refers to places of social forms of practice." There are political speeches by executive and administrative personnel including the president, cabinet ministers, chancellors, mayors, metropolitan chief executives (MCEs), and district chief executives (DCEs). The content of such speeches includes welcome and farewell speeches, appointment speeches, state of the nation addresses (SONA), and inaugural speeches.

## OBJECT OF STUDY

The object of this study is to examine President Akuffo-Addo's SONA by relating the speech's *microstructures* to its macrostructures. In pursuing this objective, we will focus on first person pronoun deixes and relate them to such themes as agriculture, economy, energy, education, health, security, and transport, among others mentioned in the speech. Also discussed is how interconnecting the micro- and macrostructures help anchor and amplify the president's political achievements and projected goals.

## METHODOLOGY

The SONA was given around 10 a.m. at the Ghanaian Parliament House on February 8, 2018. The data for this paper was taken from four online portals: Ghanaweb, Peacefmonline, Myjoyonline, and Staronline. The speech was also reported by almost all of the Ghanaian newspapers including the *Daily Graphic* and the *Ghanaian Times*; the two most important newspapers in Ghana. Various TV and radio stations captured the speech live. I employed the same methodology used for his victory and inaugural speech in Agyekum (2017). I compared the original audio and the written texts and found that both synchronized. I analyzed the text by identifying the deixis (pronominals), their semantic and pragmatic functions, the speech acts they correlate with, and their roles in political discourse. I studied previous works on pronominal choices in political speeches in Australia, America, Nigeria, and so forth.

I will analyze the sentences and other linguistic units in the texts and draw general conclusions from them. I will also look at the text as a product of a sociopolitically determined context (see Agyekum, 2017, p. 105). I will establish that the president's choices of linguistic elements, especially pronoun deixes, indicate the purposes, goals, and achievements made after his first year in office based on the political ideology of his party the New Patriotic Party. To analyze the personal deixes, especially the *personal pronouns* in the speech, I used the "Word Tips" tool for generating a count of word occurrences guidelines in Microsoft to check the frequency of the personal pronouns. This tool helped to determine the accuracy of statistics of the paper (see tables 8.1 and 8.2).

## STATE OF THE NATION'S ADDRESS (SONA)

Historically, the state of the nation's address (SONA) emerged from the British practice of opening Parliament with a speech from the Throne. This phenomenon was later adopted by the United States when President George

**Table 8.1.   Frequency of the uses of person pronouns.**

|    | Pronoun | Frequency | Cumulative Total | % |
|----|---------|-----------|------------------|---|
| 1  | I       | 96        | 96               | 22.12 |
| 2  | me      | 4         | 100              | 0.92 |
| 3  | my      | 27        | 127              | 6.22 |
| 4  | we      | 125       | 252              | 28.80 |
| 5  | us      | 21        | 273              | 4.84 |
| 6  | our     | 117       | 390              | 26.96 |
| 7  | you     | 13        | 403              | 3.0 |
| 8  | your    | 2         | 405              | 0.46 |
| 9  | yours   | 0         | 405              | 0 |
| 10 | they    | 7         | 412              | 1.61 |
| 11 | them    | 7         | 419              | 1.61 |
| 12 | their   | 15        | 434              | 3.46 |
|    | Total   | 434       | 434              | 100% |

Washington delivered the first such message before a joint session of Congress in New York on January 8, 1790 (see Gerhard, 2006). Many countries, including Ghana, have since adopted this "State of the Nation Address" and have actually enshrined it in their respective constitutions as a presidential requirement (Bayram, 2009).

The state of the nation address is the account or evaluation of the condition of a country and the future program for said country. Campbell and Jamieson (2008, p. 164) posit that the SONA is "central to the maintenance of the presidency" itself as it enables the president to act as a "national historian, keeper of the national identity, and voice of national values." In Ghana, Article (67) of the 1992 Constitution, the supreme law of this country, states, "the President shall, at the beginning of each session of Parliament and before a dissolution of Parliament, deliver to Parliament a message on the state of the nation."

## DEIXES

Cruse (2006, p. 44) states that "[d]eictic expressions form a subtype of definite referring expressions. They can be loosely thought of as expressions which 'point to' their referents." He continues that "deixis" "most typically designates referring expressions which indicate the location of referents

**Table 8.2.  Frequency of the use of first-person pronouns.**

|   | Pronoun | Frequency | Cumulative Total | % |
|---|---------|-----------|------------------|---|
| 1 | I | 96 | 96 | 24. 62 |
| 2 | me | 4 | 100 | 1. 03 |
| 3 | my | 27 | 127 | 6.92 |
| 4 | we | 125 | 252 | 32.05 |
| 5 | us | 21 | 273 | 5.38 |
| 6 | our | 117 | 390 | 30.00 |
|   | Total | 390 | 390 | 100 |

along certain dimensions, using the speaker (and time and place of speaking) as a reference point or 'deictic center.'"

Deixes have been termed "shifters" since they shift their meanings from context to context. Levinson (1983, p. 54) avers that "[d]eixis concerns the ways in which languages encode . . . features of the context of utterance . . . and thus also concerns ways in which the interpretation of utterances depends on the analysis of that context of utterance." Deixis is often described as "verbal pointing" by means of language. Other terms for deixes include deictic expressions, deictic markers, deictic words, or indexicals. They thus help to decode the context of meaning of an utterance and the relationship between the structure of languages and the contexts of usage (see Levinson, 1983, p. 55).

Deixis is key to the understanding of the various situations and circumstances surrounding an utterance. It denotes when, who, and where, as well as the circumstances and the overall sociocultural and pragmatic background of an utterance. One could therefore understand an utterance very well when the deictic background and puzzles have been unfolded. In discussing deixes, Marmaridou (2000, p. 99) opines that deixis is "a grammatical category which reveals our conceptualization of human beings as objects in space and of human language as an object in time with the speaker as the center of this conceptualization." Fillmore (1966) aptly captures the nature and functions of deixes and states that

> [d]eixis is the name given to those aspects of language whose interpretation is relative to the occasion of utterance; to the time of utterance, and to times before and after the time of utterance; to the location of the speaker at the time of the utterance; and to the identity of the speaker and the intended audience. (p. 220)

Deixes can cover some of the component parts of a speech encounter and give it the importance and understanding it deserves. Fillmore's statement captures *personal, temporal, spatial,* and *social* deixis. Cruse (2004) added a fifth category called *discourse deixis.*

## Personal Deixis

Personal deixis is the focus of this paper and the rest of the discussion will be on personal deixes, especially first-person pronouns. Personal deixis encodes the role assumed by the participants in the speech interaction. Personal deixis refers to the speaker and addressee's point of reference. Politicians use personal pronoun deixis to express multiple identities of and for themselves and others for various reasons (see Allen, 2007, p. 2).[1] Deictic reference is tied to the speaker's context, which is the deictic center. Personal deixis operates on triadic parameters that are represented by personal pronouns *"I/me," "you," "he or she,"* and their respective plurals *"we," "you,"* and *"they."* Other personal deixis includes impersonal pronouns (e.g., *somebody, someone,* and *this/that person*).

Pennycook (1994) discussed the politics and power and stressed that pronouns are deeply embedded in naming people and groups, and are thus, always political because they always imply relations of power. Politicians use pronouns as tools of reinforcement of political inclusion, ideologies and programs, misrepresentation of the political realities, dominance and showing of power, manipulation of facts and the people, deception, and propaganda (see also Maalej, 2013, p. 657).

Bull and Fetzer (2006, p. 5) emphasize that "politicians use personal pronouns to good effect: for example, to accept, deny, or distance themselves from responsibility for political action; to encourage solidarity; to designate and identify both supporters and enemies. Their choice of pronouns may also reflect their own personal and political ideologies." (See also Proctor & I-Wen Su, 2011, p. 3252.) Let us look at the tables below that capture the frequency of the use of personal pronouns in the 2018 SONA.

Table 8.1 presents the different pronouns, their frequency of usage, cumulative totals, and associated percentages. A total of 434 personal pronouns were recorded in the text. Out of these, a significant total of 390 representing 89.86 percent were first-person pronoun deixes, singular and plural. Only 44 (10.14 percent) of these belonged to the second- and third-person singular and plural. It is based on this statistical information that I have decided to concentrate our discussion on the first-person pronoun deixes. My focus now is on the analysis of the data in table 8.2.

In table 8.2, we can see clearly that the emphasis was on the first-person plural; it scored higher in all the derivations than the first-person singular (1SG) The highest score on table 8.2 is the subject (nominative) *we*, scoring 125 (32.05 percent), its genitive form *our* was second, scoring 117 (30 percent). The 1SG subject *I* (nominative) placed third with 96 (24.62 percent) and its genitive *my* was forth, accounting for 27 (6.92 percent). It is evident from the table that the accusative forms *me* and *us* did not feature prominently in the SONA 2018.

We could posit that since it was an address from the president and his team, government, and party, we should expect more of the nominative (agentive, *I* and *we*) pronouns to indicate their collective actions, policy assertives, commitment, directives, and declaratives. The agentives were followed by the genitives to indicate possessions in terms of their policies, achievements, resources, national properties, the people, infrastructure, and so on. The reason why the 1PL is higher than the 1SG is also based on the fact that the 1SG refers only to the president, whereas the 1PL refers to a collective multi-varied entity including the president and his vice president, his cabinet ministers, his government, his party, and (in most cases) the entire population of Ghana. I will elaborate on this point in subsequent sections.

## The First-Person Singular Pronoun—*I*/*me*/*my*

In Agyekum (2017, p. 112), I remarked that in most political speeches, the pronoun *I* is used when the speaker wants to speak as an individual rather than as a representative of a group. The pronoun *I* and its variants indicate personal intellectual capabilities, credibility, and integrity. The pronoun *I* is used in situations where the speaker wants to be self-centered and use *I* as an ego-boosting strategy. The pronoun *I* has been used in positive light in different contexts to refer to the individual's personal involvement, positive achievements (and rarely his failures), and his institutional identities or those of his government, party, pledges, policies, or nation. In his summary, on personal pronouns in political discourse, Bello (2013, p. 94) notes that "[p]ronouns used to index self, like "I" and "me," simply show alignments with positive realities of achievements, humility and personal integrity all as commodities to be used in exchange for political acceptance."

## Analysis of First-Person Singular Pronoun in SONA 2018

The president used various verbs where the words are backed by actions, whether covert or overt, to indicate things that he personally considered very important in his address and therefore used the 1SG *I*. These include assertives, directives, commissives, expressives, and declaratives. In addition, he employed perception, cognitive, and desiderative verbs. The president started the speech by using the first-person pronoun *I* (1SG) to refer to himself in the first two paragraphs. In the next subsections, I discuss the examples of the use of the 1SG and the accompanying speech act verbs.

## Expressive Speech Acts in SONA

Expressives are representatives and interpretations of the psychological inner state of the speaker either to himself or to the addressee. A speaker expresses an inner feeling toward something that he or she deems to be true in the world, and to which he or she is sincerely giving his or her state of mind (see Agyekum 2017, p. 106). Expressives denote statements of pleasure, pain, likes/dislikes, joy, sorrow, love, or hatred. Expressive verbs include *apologize, thank, condole, congratulate, complain, lament, protest, deplore, compliment, praise, welcome,* and *greet* (see Duranti, 1997; Mey, 2001, p. 121; Yule, 2000, p. 53). Below are excerpts from the SONA 2018 where the pronoun *I* is used with expressives (see bolded terms).

1. I am **happy** to be here again in this august House. (b) I am **happy** to announce that Ecobank Ghana Ltd has already offered to engage all 3,000 young people, after the training programme. (c) We are beginning to address the problems of our Armed Forces. I am **happy** to report that work has started on the Barracks Regeneration Programme.

2. I am **glad** to state that our good relations with Cote d'Ivoire have not been affected any way by the resolution of the dispute. (b) I am also **pleased** to report that the 3-year IMF-supported Extended Credit Facility Programme, begun in 2015, comes to an end this year.

3. I would like to start by expressing my **sincere gratitude** to the House. (b) I am equally **grateful** to those chiefs, who have supported the fight against galamsey.

4. I **fear** that one of these days one more car will join the madness on the roads in Accra, and our city will be completely gridlocked.

5. Mr. Speaker, I have an **apology** to make to the House.

6. I have **experienced** some of the most memorable moments of my political career.

The expressive adjectives used are *happy, glad, pleased, gratified, grateful, apologize, afraid,* and finally *experience.* All these show the inner psychological feeling of the president toward issues revolving around him, his government, and the nation.

## Assertives

Assertives are speech acts that commit the speaker to the truth of the expressed proposition. Weigand (2010, p. 162) avers that "assertives express a claim to truth which is not immediately evident and has to be proved if the interlocutor asks." They include verbs like *state, suggest, boast, complain, claim, report,* and *warn* (see Cruse, 2004, p. 356). Below are statements in the SONA 2018 that employ assertives:

7. (a) I can **state** that, since November, there has been no report of premix diversion, a marked improvement from the past. (b) I am glad to **state** that our good relations with Cote d'Ivoire have not been affected any way by the resolution of the dispute.

8. Mr. Speaker, I do not **suggest** in any way, that these headline-grabbing figures mean we are anywhere near resolving our economic problems.

9. Last year, I made a brave **assertion** in this House by stating that the Takoradi to Paga railway would be initiated in the year 2017.

10. (a) I am **sure** the House will want to join me, in paying tribute to the members of our forces in the Operation Vanguard that are protecting our environment. (b) We shall promote and enthusiastically encourage investment and use of renewable energy. I am **sure** that the House shares my relief that DUMSOR[2] is no longer part of our everyday lexicon. (c) A look at the national budget would tell you we are spending a lot of money on education, and I am **certain** that it is a worthwhile investment. (d) I am **certain** that the interventions we are introducing will boost morale in the service. (e) I am **convinced** that there is enough goodwill in the country to propel the first occupant of the position as prosecutor. (f) I am **confident** that, by the time I come back next year, God willing, an appreciable improvement would have been made in the sanitation situation in the country.

11. (a) I am **glad** to report that the Black Star is shining. . . . It explains also the warmth with which I am greeted wherever I go in the world. (b) I am **happy** to report that we have now recognized the need to go further than our reputation for being hospitable. We are building a Ghana, where tourists will feel at home, and we shall feel proud when they say, "I was in Ghana."

## Commissives

Commissives are speech acts that bind the speaker to the truth of the proposition of his utterance to perform some posterior action or event (see Agyekum, 2013, 2017; Cruse, 2006). Commissive verbs include *promise, vow, swear, offer, volunteer, pledge, contract, bid, bet, accept*, and *assure* (see Duranti, 1997, p. 224). A promise is a declaration or an assurance made to another person and a commitment and obligation to an act. The excerpts below exemplify the above-mentioned assertion.

12. (a) As I **promised**, our economists have found imaginative ways to deal with the oppressive debt situation. (b) I **promise** that there will be no hiding place for criminals. (c) Mr. Speaker, I have an apology to make to the House. I **promised** last year that we would pass into law the Affirmative Action Bill. This did not happen. (d) My **commitment** to the promotion of the advancement of women is without question. (e) Mr. Speaker, in line with **our commitment** to building a fair and inclusive society, we **promised** last year, to increase the share of the District Assemblies Common Fund.

We can argue that unlike inaugural, victory, or campaign speeches, which are full of promises and other commissives, SONA has fewer commissives hence the abundance of expressives and assertives.

## Declaratives

Declaratives are speech acts that effect immediate changes in the current state of affairs. Typical examples of verbs that come under these are to *name*, *declare*, *bid*, *resign*, and so on. (see Cruse, 2004, p. 357). In the view of Weigand (2010, p. 145), "declaratives are unique by their coincidence of making and fulfilling the claim to create a specific state of affairs by declaring its existence." Examples of declaratives from this speech are cited below:

13. I **propose** that the constitutional processes for a Referendum should be initiated.

14. I have **signed** into law, the Office of Special Prosecutor Act, an essential step in our overall strategy to combat corruption . . .

15. I have **made** it publicly known that anyone, who has information about acts of corruption by any of my appointees, should bring it forward.

16. In the meantime, I have **thrown** my full weight behind the "*He-forShe*" campaign, and the Gender and Development Initiative for Africa (GADIA), an initiative stemming from my position as the African Union's Gender Champion.

## Directives

In directives, the speaker asks for an action to be performed by the hearer, the speaker, or a third person. They express the wish or the desire of the speaker for the hearer to do something or put up certain behavior or direct the person toward cognitive or linguistic action(s) in the future. The verbs under these include *order*, *request*, *command*, *advise*, *warn*, *demand*, *ask*, and *beg*. Excerpts 17 to 19 exemplify instances of directives in the SONA.

17. Last year, I **directed** our state-owned oil development company, the Ghana National Petroleum Corporation (GNPC), to pay particular attention to our onshore deposits.

18. (a) I **urge** the House and all citizens to support the police to deliver the service we deserve. (b) I **urge** all Ghanaian males to join together in giving Ghanaian females the dignity they deserve.

19. I further **entreat** all of us, male and female, to support the 2030 United Nations Sustainable Development Goals.

Directives were used in connection with onshore deposits, the police and security, gender, UN sustainable development goals, and so forth.

## PERCEPTION, COGNITION, AND DESIDERATION VERBS

These are verbs that involve mental processing. Downing and Locke (2006, p. 139) aver that "we organise our mental contact with the world by means of mental processes. Mental processing involves *cognition, perception, affectivity* and *desideration.*" They remark that the verbs that fall under these four main types are as follows: cognition (*know, understand, believe, doubt, remember,* and *forget*); perception (*see, notice, hear, feel,* and *taste*); affectivity (*like, love, admire, miss,* and *hate*); and desideration (*hope, want, desire,* and *wish*). We will concentrate only on cognition and desideration since they featured more prominently in SONA 2018 than perception and affectivity verbs. Excerpts 20a to 20d exemplify instances of cognition whereas excerpts 21a to 21c exemplify those of desideration.

### Cognition

20. (a) Mr. Speaker, I **believe** that last year, when I came to the House, I conveyed my dismay at the full extent of the economic mess, in which our nation was mired. (b) Mr. Speaker, I **believe** that the future lies in the promotion of aquaculture. (c) I **know** that when it comes to the economy many of us have very low tolerance for what we consider as boring figures, and we do not see that they affect the reality of our everyday lives [see also example 25]. (d) Mr. Speaker, I **know** I am not saying anything new exactly; every government has said it.

### Desideration

21. (a) I **hope** that our efforts at improving the conditions of work for health workers would be appreciated. (b) I **hope** that, eventually, there will be something big for us to cheer about. (c) I do not **need** to repeat that crime wears no political colours.

## THE PRONOUN *WE*

The pronoun *we* and its variants are used to invoke a sense of collectivity and shared responsibility. The pronoun *we* can be used to indicate a collective action by a political actor's (the president's) government, party, and the nation. It is a tactical means of assimilating other participants into the subject matter in a speech so that the speaker's single voice now represents a multiple voice. Agyekum (2017, p. 112) states as follows: "The pronoun *we* can refer to the president and just another person, e.g., he and his vice-president elect, the president and his group, such as his party, his government or an expanded group such as the nation Ghana and the people, and even extended to African leaders assembled."

In the literature, a distinction is made between exclusive and inclusive *we*. Pennycook (1994, p. 175) discusses the use of the pronoun *we* and argues that *we* is always simultaneously inclusive and exclusive, a pronoun of solidarity and of rejection, of inclusion and exclusion. Pennycook (1994, p. 176), further avers that "if '*we*' claims authority and communality, it also constructs a 'we/you' or a 'we/they' dichotomy" (see also Maalej, 2013, p. 639). Whether *we* would be used as an exclusive or inclusive marker depends on the speaker and what his intentions are; it could be used as a solidarity and persuasive device to convince the speakers, but more especially the addresses to share and side with him on his policies, ideologies, and programs (see Adetunji, 2006, p. 188; Íñigo-Mora, 2004).

The use of *we* also implies that the politician has the authority to speak on behalf of the group with a unanimous voice even though he has not had a previous deliberation with them. Allen (2007) states that *we* is used when politicians are talking about a shared characteristic and specific political belief. The hearers have to determine whether they share these commonalties or not; whether they are included or excluded in the scope of reference. In the view of Bello (2013, p. 94), "the use of ' *we* ' and ' *us* ' creates multi-faceted dimensions and groupings all serving different political purposes."

Adetunji (2006, p. 188) further asserts that President Obasanjo's use of deixis reflects politicians' way of associating and dissociating from actions taken by them or their officers and conscripting their audience into accepting views and positions on controversial issues (cited in Quinto, 2014, p. 1). The pronoun *we* serves to frame politicians and individuals in terms of sociopolitical solidarity and closeness. If it is used as an exclusive *we*, then the politician wants to shield himself and pass on the burdens, direct attacks, and political responsibilities to other members of the society, especially to political opponents and past governments.

The president in his SONA 2018, started by referring to the previous year and said "a year ago, I came as our newly elected President into a House, where everybody was trying to get used to new positions. There was a large number of fresh entrants, trying to find their feet as the new honourable members."

22. A year later, **we** can safely say that none of **us** now turns round in surprise, when addressed by **our new titles. We** are all used to the reality.

In the above passage, the collective *we* refers to the president himself and members of Parliament (that is, the majority and the minority political actors. The new titles could be looked at from (1) the positions in Parliament such as the Speaker and his deputies, majority and minority leaders and their deputies, chief whips, holders of parliamentary positions serving the ministries, and so on; (2) the MPs who have been appointed as ministers or deputy ministers, hence the reference to new titles. In the excerpt below, we observe other uses of *we*.

23. (a) You would recall, Mr. Speaker, that I said "**we** would have to implement some tough, prudent and innovative policies to get us out of the financial cul de sac **we** were in." (b) **We** have reduced taxes, **we** are bringing down inflation and interest rates, economic growth is increasing, from the alarming 3.6 percent at December 2016, to 7.9 percent in our first year. (c) **We** have increased our international reserves and maintained relative exchange rate stability. (d) **We** have paid almost half of arrears inherited, and, crucially, **we** are current on obligations to statutory funds.

The above passage is on the state of the economy and the president uses the collective *we* in example 23a, to refer to the nation. The nation had to be ready for the tough measures and this general *we* is further supported by the expression "*to get us out of the financial cul de sac we were in.*" The subsequent *we* in 23b, 23c, and 23d can refer to the other executive branch, that is the ministers and other government appointees, as well as to the NPP as a whole, which has been able to reduce taxes and bring down inflation. The president further commented on financial issues relating to education, pension, and job creation as seen in the following excerpts:

24. (a) Mr. Speaker, **we** have restored teacher and nursing training allowances. **We** have doubled the capitation grant, and, to confound the skeptics and professional naysayers, **we** have implemented Free Senior High School education. (b) **We** have been able to transfer some GH¢3.1 billion of Tier 2 pension funds into the custodial accounts of the pension schemes of the labour unions. (c) Mr. Speaker, **we** are, therefore, able to say with confidence that **we** are creating the atmosphere needed for the creation of jobs.

The *we* used in all the above examples (24a–c) refers to his government and party but just after those statements he shifted to what I will refer to as the *national* "*we*," where it refers to the nation and the people. The areas touched under these included the economy and transportation, especially railway, as seen below.

25. (a) I know that, when it comes to the economy, many of us have very low tolerance for what **we** consider as boring figures, and **we** do not see that they affect the reality of our everyday lives. But, as I said earlier in the year, this current set of boring figures happens to spell good news for our economy. (b) Again, we are nowhere near the levels **we** would all like, but, when you are starting from inside a deep hole, it takes a while to make an impression on the ground, and the good thing is that **we** are pointing in the right direction. (c) Mr. Speaker, if **we** are to open up our country, **we** have to build a fast, safe and reliable railway network. . . . **we** are making progress. **We** are in the final stages of agreeing with a significant investor.

In example 25c above, the first part encodes a national *we* but the last two instances of *we* are shifted to the government to indicate the efforts being made by the president and his government on reliable railway network. There is another swift to the *governmental "we,"* as found in the excerpts below.

26. **We** are currently engaged in the very big exercise of creating new regions. It is a long and rather-complicated process. **We** are in unchartered territory, but all the indications are that it is going well.

27. **We** have taken the clear and unambiguous mandate given to this government by the people of Ghana as a spur to take some of these long-promised actions, indeed, to open up our country and transform our economy. This year **we** are determined to take the decisions that would change the destiny of our country.

28. (a) **We** are asking that everybody is guided by the priorities set up in the NPP Manifesto, on which **we** fought and won the mandate of the Ghanaian people. **We** expect, for example, the provision of water and toilets to feature prominently on the agenda of the Development Authorities. (b) Mr. Speaker, **we** are determined to find the needed resources to complete the Eastern Corridor roads. **We** are determined to bring our road network to a befitting status, and this year **we** shall witness much more activity on the roads.

There are certain portions of the SONA 2018 where we meet a mixture of national and partisan/governmental *we*. The style here is to paint a negative picture that has been caused by *we* as a people (i.e., the nation), which could be attributed to past governments. The second *we*, which is governmental, indicates that despite the mess created by all of us, there is now a government headed by me (the president) that has the positive policies to solve the national problems. Let us look at the following excerpts. Those in the bracket are part of my analysis: "(1)" refers to nation; and "(2)" refers to government.

29. (a) Mr. Speaker, I know I am not saying anything new exactly; every government has said it, and it has been in every plan **we (1)** (as a nation) have drawn up in this country since independence. But the difference this time is that **we (2)** (as a government) have started, and there is dream of a modern railway network in our country. (b) Mr. Speaker, **we (1)** need an educated and skilled workforce to be able to operate the modern economy **we (1)** are creating. The Free SHS is a start towards this goal. It is a policy that has come to stay. **We (2)** (as a government) are reforming the schools' curricula to deal with the weaknesses in our education system. (c) In much the same way, **we (1)** dare not compromise on the health of the population. **We (2)** (as a government) have cleared a substantial part of the debts and arrears that were choking the National Health Insurance Scheme. (d) For generations, **we (1)** have bemoaned Ghana's reliance solely on rain-fed agriculture. **We (1)** have had to depend more and more on imported fish. **We (2)** have started work to these problems. **We (2)** have also instituted measures to avert premix diversions, and strict auditing of landing beaches are in place. **We (2)** have set about it with a lot of enthusiasm. **We (2)** have identified 100 dams in five

regions across the country. (e) **We (1)** still have problems with the cost of power, and **we (2)** are working to put Ghana at a competitive advantage. **We (2)** intend to find private sector operators to buy into the state-owned thermal plants, and inject the capital needed to bring power tariffs down.

The dual meanings of *we* were used for commenting on highly important national issues confronting the people, including education, health, infra-structure, agriculture, and power. In all the above examples "*we* (1)" refers to the nation, and "*we* (2)" refers to the government, the cabinet or the party. The instances of "*we* (1)" are followed by verbs of complaint, bemoaning, negligence, and problems. The instances of "*we* (2)" are then employed and followed by verbs of actions, pro-activeness, solutions, creativity, reforma-tion, transformation, and good intentions. All these are brought in to show the achievements and proper management of the president and his govern-ment, and also to raise them above those of the opponents and previous governments.

## USE OF THE FIRST-PERSON POSSESSIVE PRONOUNS *MY* AND *OUR*

The text is full of the singular and plural first-person possessive pronouns, *my* and *our*. This is elucidated and exemplified below:

### Use of the First-Person Singular Possessive Pronoun *My*

In the use of *my*, there is an individual denotation referring to the president as an individual office holder.

30. (a) Mr. Speaker, the subject of job creation has to be at the top of **my agenda**. Every major policy that **my government** has implemented in the past year has been essentially about the youth. We will equip the youth with the skills that will enable them to be productive. (b) Moreover, as we work to open up the country, **my government** will continue to reach out to our traditional rulers, so that, together, we can address pressing issues facing our nation, and its peace and stability. (c) One of the most ambitious of **my presidency**, is to make Accra the cleanest city in Africa, by the end of **my term**. (d) In 2017, **my first year in office,** 394 Sole Sourcing Requests were made. (e) Further, **my discussions** with the nation's political leaders, includ-ing the former Presidents of the Republic, convince me that it is a step we must take to ensure the judicious use of the country's resources. (f) It is, in **my view** that the reform of our schools' curricula should instill in our youth respect for the traditional values of discipline.

We will notice that the noun phrases (NPs) that are heads of these posses-sive constructions are abstract notions, ideas, and intangibles (e.g., *govern-ment, first year of office, discussions,* and *view*). These mean that the president can have these ideas as the inputs to create tangible things like roads, infrastructure, and agriculture that will belong to the people. We will see in the next section that the domains of the possessed items are mostly concrete items.

## The First-Person Plural Possessive Pronoun *Our*

In the case of the genitive of the plural *we*, which is *our*, we observed that it referred to the nation, the party, the government, or the ministers, the president, and his vice president. The pronoun *our* is normally used to express collectivity and patriotism, especially when the possessed entity is marked by country as in *our country*. Sometimes a politician may use this to create the impression that he loves the country and has the interest of the country and the people at heart more than others, especially his opponents. If this is overused, it will flout the Gricean maxim of quantity and therefore indicate deception. Adegoju (2014) therefore avers that

> [i]n fact, it is ritualistic in political discourses that no matter how desperately a leader is pursuing a self or group interest, the moment they use *our* to show a collective sense of belonging, it takes the discerning audience to figure out traces of deceit in such a linguistic manipulation. In this sense, meaning becomes slippery, as it is difficult to differentiate personal interest or group interest from the much-touted "national interests." (p. 54)

Let us look at the excerpts where the president used *our* and the possessed nouns that come after it.

31. (a) The number of young people, who cannot find work, is staggering, and a threat to **our national security**. I am determined to work to guarantee and secure the future of the young men and women of **our country**. (b) The law enforcement agencies will crack down very hard on all those who would disturb the peace of **our nation**. We will give the Police the resources they need to do their job. (c) Mr. Speaker, we shall not allow miscreants of any sort to terrorize **our population**. We know that it is in all **our interests** that those charged with ensuring **our security** are able to concentrate on their jobs without distractions like inadequate and inappropriate housing. It is vital that all of us give maximum support to the noble and brave men and women of **our security services**. We are aimed at guaranteeing the safety of **our people**, the integrity of **our environment**, and the **peace of our nation**. (d) Mr. Speaker, **our nation** is on the right path. We will build a Ghana Beyond Aid. (e) I thank you very much for your attention. May God bless us all, **our Parliament**, and **our nation** Ghana, and make her great and strong.

32. (a) There is a crying need for work to be done on all **our roads**. We are determined to bring **our road network** to a befitting status, and this year we shall witness much more activity on the roads. (b) The eastern corridor is

a strategic road that would provide a much shorter and cheaper link between the southern and northern parts of **our country**, and a suitable, alternative route for **our land-locked neighbours**. (c) The start of the digital address system, the introduction of paperless transactions at **our ports**, the rapid and continuing spread of broadband services are all helping to formalise and modernise **our economy** and raise funds. (d) It also fits in with our determination to open up **our country** and make jobs and facilities available in all parts of the country. Mr. Speaker, problems associated with **our environment** and the galamsey phenomenon have taken up a lot of the time and energy of this government. (e) Mr. Speaker, the state of sanitation in **our cities** is wholly unacceptable. **Our cities** have been engulfed by filth.

33. (a) Agriculture forms the backbone of **our flagship 1–District-1–Factory programme**. (b) Mr. Speaker, fishing in **our country**, an industry that provides a living for ten percent of the population, has been bedeviled by many problems in the past. (c) We cannot look on, as **our very existence** as a country is put in jeopardy and **our water bodies, forests and land mass** are destroyed. But this generation of Ghanaians dares not preside over the destruction of **our lands**. The state of **our rivers and forests** remains a great cause for worry, and it is **our sacred** duty to protect them. I hope I can count on the total support of the House to help nurse **our degraded lands** and rivers back to health. (d) The most reliable, and, ultimately, cheapest answer to our **power needs**, lies with renewable energy sources. (e) I think it is equally critical for us not to ignore the possibilities of **our onshore** deposits, especially in the Voltaian Basin.

34. (a) Government will tackle the major challenge on sanitation with strategies that are intended to effect a change in **our attitudes** towards waste generation, as well as to improve dramatically **our methods** of waste management. (b) Mr. Speaker, in line with **our commitment** to building a fair and inclusive society, we promised, last year, to increase the share of the District Assemblies Common Fund. (c) In **our current economic circumstances**, we are turning **our attention** to private sector participation.

35. (a) We will ensure that **our young technologically savvy people** would keep Ghana firmly in the exciting IT economy and its many opportunities. (b) The health needs of **our people** are being better served. (c) The slightest change in the rainfall pattern exposed **our farmers** to the loss of a season's harvest. The construction of dams will make a big difference to all **our lives** and the livelihoods of **our farmers**. (d) In my view, the reform of **our schools' curricula** should instill in **our youth** respect for the traditional values of discipline.

The 1SG plural genitive *our* is prominently used to refer to individuals and to an array of things considered important by the political actor (the president). Among the referents are *our people, farmers, youth, security, country, nation, traditional rulers, onshore deposits, power needs, parlia-*

*ment, economy, agriculture, education and curricula, land and forestry, environment, sanitation,* and *good relations.* There are other abstract domains that relate to values, attitudes, methods, commitment, attention, interests, and circumstances.

## SUMMARY AND CONCLUSION

This paper has thrown light on the use of personal pronouns in political discourse. In such discourse, the manner in which pronouns are employed in political contexts gives us an indication of the sociopolitical relations between the politician, the citizens, and the relations of power. We further saw that personal pronouns can be used to indicate the politicians' actions, responsibilities, achievements, solidarity, collectivism, individualism, political ideologies, and political identifications, as well as to paint the negativities and quantum of negligence of political opponents. Politicians will normally select pronouns that will boost their egos and place their political groups into higher and positive levels.

In his summary on personal pronouns in political discourse, I side with Bello (2013) who noted that, among other things, that personal pronouns like *I* and *me* are used to indicate positive realities of achievements, humility, and personal integrity that will allow politicians to be accepted. The use of *we* and *us* creates multifaceted dimensions and groupings for different political purposes.

The pronoun *we* and its genitive *our* top the table with 125 and 117 tokens respectively and this is not surprising because *we* gives an impression of the inclusiveness of the people who are ideologically manipulated into the side of the speaker. The use of ambiguous and multiple identified pronouns like *we* and *our* assist politicians to broaden their scope and persuade most people into their political camps. The use of the 1SG *I* and its genitive *my* were placed third and fourth in tables 8.1 and 8.2 because they captured the activities, work, policies, and reports coming directly from the president.

This paper has contributed to the pragmatics, discourse, and semantics of personal pronoun deixes in the political discourse analysis of Ghana. It has also opened avenues for future researchers in Ghanaian political discourse analysis.

## NOTES

1. Proctor and I-Wen Su (2011, p. 3253), assert that "[w]e cannot ascertain a personal pronoun's meaning within a single sentence; the meaning of a pronoun is established above the syntactical level. Extralinguistic information also aids the analyses. It becomes important to know the topic and venue of the conversation because both variables influence personal pro-

noun choice. We argue that pronominal choice in part reveals with whom a politician is identifying himself/herself. Many crucial decisions are made based on this information."

2. Dumsor is a term that was coined by the FM stations to refer to power outages in Ghana in 2013–2014. See Obeng (2015).

# REFERENCES

Adegoju, A. (2014). "Person Deixis as Discursive Practice in Nigeria's 'June 12' Conflict Rhetoric." *Ghana Journal of Linguistics* 3(1): 45–64.
Adetunji, A. (2006). "Inclusion and Exclusion in Political Discourse: Deixis in Olusegun Obasanjo's Speeches." *Journal of Language and Linguistics* 5(2): 177–191.
Agyekum, K. (2004). "Invective Language in Contemporary Ghanaian Politics." *Journal of Language and Politics* 3(2): 345–375.
Agyekum, K. (2013). "The Pragmatics of Campaign Promises in Ghana's 2008 Elections." *Legon Journal of Humanities* 24: 37–63.
Agyekum, K. (2015). "The Pragmatics of Political Apology in Ghana's Contemporary Politics." *Legon Journal of Humanities* 26(1): 58–79.
Agyekum, K. (2017). "The Pragmatics of Nana Akuffo Addo's Victory and Inaugural Speeches." *Issues in Political Discourse Analysis* 5(2): 1–24.
Allen, W. (2007). "Australian Political Discourse: Pronominal Choice in Campaign Speeches." In M. Laughren and I. Mushin (eds.), *Selected Papers from the 2006 Conference of the Australian Linguistic Society*, 1–13.
Alo, M. A. (2012). "A Rhetorical Analysis of Selected Political Speeches of Prominent African Leaders." *British Journal of Arts and Social Sciences* 10(1): 87–100.
Ayeomoni, O. M., and O. S. Akinkuolere. (2012). "A Pragmatic Analysis of Victory and Inaugural Speeches of President Umaru Musa Yar'Adua." *Theory and Practice in Language Studies* 2(3): 461–468.
Bayram, F. (2009). *Ideology and Political Discourse: A Critical Discourse Analysis of Erdogan's Political Speech.* Newcastle: Longman Publishers.
Bello, U. (2013). "If I Could Make It, You Too Can Make It! Personal Pronouns in Political Discourse: A CDA of President Jonathan's Presidential Declaration Speech." *International Journal of English Linguistics* 3(6): 84–96.
Bull, P., and A. Fetzer. (2006). "Who Are We and Who Are You? The Strategic Use of Forms of Address in Political Interviews." *Text & Talk* 26(1): 3–37.
Campbell, K. K., and K. H. Jamieson. (2008). *Presidents Creating the Presidency: Deeds Done in Words.* Chicago: University of Chicago Press.
Chilton, P. A. (1998). "Politics and Language." In L. J. Mey (ed.)., *The Concise Encyclopedia of Pragmatics*, 668–695. Amsterdam: Elsevier.
Chilton, P. A. (2004). *Analysing Political Discourse: Theory and Practice.* London: Routledge.
Cruse, A. (2004). *Meaning in Language: An Introduction to Semantics and Pragmatics* (2nd ed.). Oxford: Oxford University Press.
Cruse, A. (2006). *A Glossary of Semantics and Pragmatics.* Edinburgh: Edinburgh University Press.
Dadugblor, S. K. (2016). *Clusivity in Presidential Discourse: A Rhetorical Discourse Analysis of State-of-the-Nation Addresses in Ghana and the United States. Open Access Master's Thesis.* Michigan Technological University.
Downing, A., and P. Locke. (2006). *English Grammar: A University Course* (2nd ed.). London: Routledge.
Duranti, A. (1997). *Linguistic Anthropology.* Cambridge: Cambridge University Press.
Duranti, A. (2006). "Narrating the Political Self in a Campaign for U.S. Congress." *Language in Society* 35(4): 467–497.
Fairclough, N. (1989). *Language and Power.* London: Longman.
Fairclough, N. (1998). "Political Discourse in the Media: An Analytical Framework." In A. Bell and P. Garrett (eds.), *Approaches to Media Discourse*, 142–162. Oxford: Blackwell Publishers.

Fillmore, C. J. (1966). "Deictic Categories in Semantics of 'Come.'" *Foundations of Language* 2: 219–227.

Fowler, R. (1991). *Language in the News: Discourse and Ideology in the Press.* London: Routledge.

Gerhard, P. (2006). *State of the Union Messages*: New York: USA Presidency Project.

Gu, Y. (1990). "Politeness Phenomena in Modern Chinese." *Journal of Pragmatics* 14(2): 237–257.

Íñigo-Mora, I. (2004). "On the Use of the Personal Pronoun We in Communities." *Journal of Language and Politics* 3(1): 27–52.

Jucker, A. H. (1997). "Persuasion by Inference: An Analysis of a Party Political Broadcast." In J. Blommaert and C. Bulcaen (eds.), *Political Linguistics: Belgian Journal of Linguistics* 11(1): 121–137.

Levinson, S. C. (1983). *Pragmatics.* Cambridge: Cambridge University Press.

Maalej, Z. A. (2013). "Framing and Manipulation of Person Deixis in Hosni Mubarak's Last Three Speeches: A Cognitive-Pragmatic Approach." *Pragmatics* 23(4): 633–659.

Marmaridou, S. S. A. (2000). *Pragmatic Meaning and Cognition.* Amsterdam: John Benjamins Publishing Company.

Mey, J. L. (2001). *Pragmatics: An Introduction* (2nd ed). Oxford. Blackwell Publishers.

Obeng, S. G. (1997). "Language and Politics: Indirectness in Political Discourse." *Discourse and Society* 8(1): 49–83.

Obeng, S. G. (2002a). "Metaphors in Ghanaian Political Communication." In S. G. Obeng and B. Hartford (eds.), *Surviving through Obliqueness: Language of Politics in Emerging Democracies*, 83–112. New York: Nova Science Publishers.

Obeng, S. G. (2002b). "The Language of Politics." In S. G. Obeng and B. Hartford (eds.), *Surviving through Obliqueness: Language of Politics in Emerging Democracies*, 1–18. New York: Nova Science Publishers.

Obeng, S. G. (2012). "The Peace Corps as a Successful United States Foreign Policy: A Phenomenological Account of My Experiences with American Peace Corps Volunteers Who Served in Ghana between 1971 and 1978." *War and Peace Journal* 4: 30–46.

Obeng, S. G. (2015). "Grammatical Pragmatics: On the Contributions Made by Akan to Ghanaian English Political and Social Interaction with Particular Reference to 'Dumsor.'" Plenary Speaker at the conference on *Multilingualism in the African Context: Resource or Challenge?* 1st School of Languages Conference. Organized by the School of Languages, the Language.

Obeng, S. G. (2018a). *Conflict Resolution in Africa: Language, Law and Politeness in Ghanaian (Akan) Jurisprudence.* Durham, NC: Carolina Academic Press.

Obeng, S. G. (2018b). "Language and Liberty in Ghanaian Political Communication: A Critical Discourse Perspective." *Ghana Journal of Linguistics* 7(2): 199–224.

Pennycook, A. (1994). "The Politics of Pronouns." *ELT Journal* 48(2): 13–18.

Proctor, K., and L. I-Wen Su. (2011). "The 1st Person Plural in Political Discourse-American Politicians in Interviews and in a Debate." *Journal of Pragmatics* 43(13): 3251–3266.

Quinto, E. J. M. (2014). "Stylistic Analysis of Deictic Expressions in President Benigno Aquino III's October 30th Speech." *The Southeast Asian Journal of English Language Studies* 20(2): 1–18.

Reisigl, M. (2010). "Rhetoric of Political Speeches." In R. Wodak and V. Koller (eds.), *Handbook of Communication in Public Sphere*, 243–270. Berlin: De Gruyter Mouton.

Taiwo, R. (2009). "Legitimization and Coercion in Political Discourse: A Case Study of Olusegun Obasanjo Address to the PDP Elders and Stakeholder's Forum." *Issues in Political Discourse Analysis* 2(2): 191–205.

Van Dijk, T. A. (1997). "What Is Political Discourse Analysis?" In J. Blommaert and C. Bulcaen (eds.), *Political Linguistics: Belgian Journal of Linguistics* 11: 11–41.

Van Dijk, T. A. (1998). *Ideology: A Multidisciplinary Approach.* London: Saga Publications.

Weigand, E. (2010). *Dialogue: The Mixed Game.* Amsterdam: John Benjamins Publishing Company.

Wilson, J. (2001). "Political Discourse." In D. Schiffrin, D. Tannen, and H. E. Hamilton (eds.), *The Handbook of Discourse Analysis*, 398–415. Oxford: Blackwell Publishers Ltd.

Wodak, R., et al. (1999). *The Discursive Construction of National Identity.* Edinburgh: Edinburgh University Press.

Wodak, R., and P. Chilton, eds. (2005). *A New Agenda in Critical Discourse Analysis Theory: Methodological and Interdisciplinarity.* Philadelphia: John Benjamins.

Yule, G. (2000). *Pragmatics.* Oxford: Oxford University Press.

*Chapter Nine*

# Discursive Construction of the Representative Claim in UK and Ghanaian Parliamentary Discourse

Kwabena Sarfo Sarfo-Kantankah

An essential characteristic of democratic governance is representation, whose core feature is claim-making, that is, the claim that one stands for and knows the interests of others (Saward, 2006). Based on the concept of representation, this paper investigates how the United Kingdom (UK) and Ghanaian parliamentarians construct their claims of representation. The paper seeks to answer this question: *How do UK and Ghanaian parliamentarians express their claims of representation?* In attempting to answer the above-mentioned question, the paper examines two forms of representative claim-making, namely, *direct* and *indirect* forms. Direct claims are investigated through transitivity (Halliday, 1978; Halliday & Matthiessen, 2004), which allows for the analysis of grammar as experience, and how social actors are represented (van Leeuwen, 2008). Indirect claims are explored through deictics/indexicals by drawing on the principle of referencing, "an act by which a speaker (or writer) uses language to enable a listener (or reader) to identify something" (Yule, 2010, p. 131). The paper argues that deictics/indexicals are used to indirectly construct representative claims. It offers some insights into how MPs create and exploit relationships with their constituents for political purposes. The paper is organized into five sections: section 1 is the introduction and is followed by section 2, which is a discussion of the concept of representation that theoretically contextualizes the paper. Section 3 deals with a description of the data used in the study and the methods of analysis employed in the synthesis and analysis of the data. In section 4, the actual analysis and discussion of the data are done, and this is followed by section 5, where I provide a brief conclusion of the study.

## REPRESENTATION

In his *Representative Government*, Mill (1861) argues that the best form of government is representative government, a system of government in which "the whole people, or some numerous portions of them, exercise through deputies periodically elected by themselves the ultimate controlling power" (pp. 31, 57). The fundamental principle is that the elected representative represents the interests of the electorate. But to what extent, in practical terms, does the representative represent the interests of the people? In Mill's (1861) own terms, should a parliamentarian "be bound by the instructions of his constituents? Should he be the organ of their sentiments, or of his own; their ambassador to a congress, or their professional agent, empowered not only to act for them, but to judge for them what ought to be done?" (p. 138).

While the underlying principle is the representation of the interests of the people, there is no doubt that the representative will represent his own interest as well. These two ways of representation have been called *delegate representation* and *trustee representation*. "Delegate" representatives are required "to follow their constituents' preferences," while "trustee" representatives are expected "to follow their own judgment about the proper course of action" (Dovi, 2017, n.p). Dovi (2017) states that every form of political representation exhibits the following features:

1. some party that is representing (the representative, an organization, movement, state agency, and so forth, in our case, parliamentarians);
2. some party that is being represented (the constituents, the clients, etc.);
3. something that is being represented (opinions, perspectives, interests, discourses, etc.);
4. a setting within which the activity of representation takes place (the political context, in our case, parliament or a parliamentary context); and
5. something that is being left out (the opinions, interests, and perspectives not voiced).

For Pitkin (1967), representation means acting on behalf of and for "the interest of the represented, in a manner responsive to them," a kind of "principal-agent relationship" (pp. 8 and 209). Thus, Urbinati (2000) sees representation as "advocacy" with "two components: the representative's 'passionate' link to the electors' cause and the representative's relative autonomy of judgment" (p. 773). The first component can be observed in Alcoff's (1991, p. 9) explication that "[i]n both the practice of speaking for as well as the practice of speaking about others, I am engaging in the act of representing the other's needs, goals, situation, and in fact, who they are." This encapsulates the concept of representative democracy, where representatives are elected to represent the interests of the electorate. However, there has been a long-standing general view "that citizens do not trust politicians and political parties, since they project on to them [politicians/political parties] instrumental motives" (Hay, 2007, p. 37). People feel that politicians represent their own interests rather than the collective. This often makes people question the necessity of representative democracy. But Dobson (1996, pp. 126–127) argues in favor of democratic representation thus:

1. interests are subjectively perceived, for only the "shoe-wearer" knows where the shoe pinches (Graham, 1986, as cited in Dobson, 1996, p. 126);
2. it recognizes human autonomy, an "in principle" autonomous decision making, where "the choice of representative is . . . autonomously made"; and
3. "elected representatives will in principle represent the interests of their constituents more effectively than appointees because of the need to resubmit themselves to re-election."

The concept of representation has been studied from various perspectives, including *the citizen-candidate model* developed by Osborne and Slivinski (1993) and Besley and Coate (1997). The model is based on costs and benefits associated with electoral competition, "where the number of candidates is an endogenous feature of equilibrium outcomes" (Cadigan, 2005, p. 197). Examining representative governance from an economic perspective, *the citizen-candidate model* operates on the assumption that "any citizen may become a candidate for office, that a winner is chosen from among the candidates by voting with ties broken by the flip of a coin, that all voters have preferences among a set of policies and that the office-holder adopts his preferred policy" (Usher, 2003, p. 1). For Rasch (2011), "[m]odern representative democracies can be seen as deliberative" (p. 2), which is "more public-orientated" (Bächtiger, 2014, p. 147) and directed "towards mobilizing an outside audience—voters, citizens, as well as partisan rank and file" (Bächtiger, 2014, p. 148), combining "accountability to the people with reflection and reason giving" (Sunstein, 2006, p. 49).

The discussion so far indicates that the essence of representative democracies is the representation of the people's interests. For Saward (2006), the representative can express his or her concern for the people's interests through the "representative claim," that is, "a claim to represent or to know what represents the interests of someone or something" (p. 305). Saward (2006) states features of the representative claim, that is, the "axes along which representative claims vary" (pp. 306–309), namely,

1. Singular-multiple: one claim can imply multiple variations.

2. Particular-general: representative claims have different levels of generality, ranging from specific to general backgrounds/contexts.
3. Implicit-explicit: representative claims can be either indirect or direct.
4. Internal-external: representative claims can be either private or public.

The literature on representation suggests that there is more theoretical explication of representation (and/or representative claim), but less empirical exploration of it, especially among parliamentarians generally, and UK and Ghanaian parliamentarians specifically. This is what makes this paper original: it contributes to and expands the frontiers of research on the concept of representation. The paper explores representative claim-making through transitivity and deictics/indexical/referencing.

Transitivity is the grammar of experience; it represents the modeling of experience. It is that aspect of systemic functional linguistics that involves "the grammar of processes . . . and the participants in these processes, and the attendant circumstances" (Halliday, 1978, p. 30). It indicates how people "account for their experience of the world around them" (Simpson, 1993, p. 88). The paper looks at direct claim-making through relational, verbal, and material processes. Relational processes generally concern things "of being," with the "central meaning . . . that something is" (Halliday, 1994, p. 112) and are "typically realized by the verb *be* or some verb of the same class (known as *copular verbs*)" (Bloor & Bloor, 2013, p. 122). A material process encodes a "process of 'doing'" and happening, which expresses the "notion that some entity 'does' something" (Halliday, 1978, p. 102; Halliday & Matthiessen, 2004, p. 207; Bloor & Bloor, 2013, p. 112). Verbal processes refer to the process of saying (Halliday & Matthiessen, 2004) and "relate to the transfer of messages through language" (Thompson, 2014, p. 106).

The paper also argues that the construction of the representative claim is largely implicit/indirect, including the use of deictics/indexicals. As Chilton (2004) puts it "[t]he deictic centre is constructed as a relation between speaker and hearers inside a political entity, and personal proximity seems to be a possible inference" (p. 139). The construction of representation by parliamentarians is often implied through deictic expressions "act[ing] as pointers" (Duranti & Goodwin, 1992, p. 43), such as to "designate" and "specify the identity or placement in space or time of individuated objects [in this case, the represented] relative to the participants [MPs]" (Hanks, 1990, p. 5). According to Chilton (2004, pp. 57–58), "in processing any discourse people 'position' other entities in their 'world' by 'positioning' these entities in relation to themselves along (at least) three axes, space, time and modality." The above-mentioned principles, excluding modality, inform our analysis of the data under discussion.

# DATA AND METHODS

The data for this paper are Hansards of the UK Queen's Address debates (UK QADs) and Ghanaian State of the Nation Address debates (GH SON-ADs). The UK QADs are formal debates on the Queen's Speech, which is written by the government but delivered by the Queen and "marks the formal start of the parliamentary year [and] sets out the government's agenda for the coming session, outlining proposed policies and legislation" (UK Parliament, 2015, n.p). When the Queen delivers the address, both the House of Lords and the House of Commons debate "the Government's legislative program as presented in the Queen's Speech" for about five or six days (Priddy, 2014). This paper focuses on the House of Commons debates in 2006, 2009, and 2013, respectively representing the periods of prime ministers Tony Blair, Gordon Brown, and David Cameron. The data were obtained from the UK parliamentary website (www.parliament.uk) and form a little over one million tokens/running words.

The GH SONADs are debates on the Ghanaian State of the Nation Address obtained from the Hansards department of the Parliament of Ghana. Article 67 of the Ghanaian Constitution enjoins the president of Ghana to, "at the beginning of each session of Parliament and before a dissolution of Parliament, deliver to Parliament a message on the state of the nation." Thus, the president of the Republic of Ghana every year gives an address to the Parliament of Ghana, and by extension the people of Ghana, on the economic, social, and political state of the country. The address highlights achievements and challenges of the previous year and outlines key policy objectives. Following the president's address, members of Parliament (MPs) debate its content in terms of whether or not it was the true reflection of the state of the nation. The GH SONADs data are debates from 2005 to 2015 (excluding 2007 and 2014, which were unavailable). The data span the administrations of three presidents: J. A. Kufuor (2005–2008), J. E. A. Mills (2008–2012), and J. D. Mahama (2012–2015). The data size is about 616,000 tokens or running words. The imbalance between the two corpora is the result of differences in time allocation for the debates. Whereas the UK QADs lasted for six days of about eight hours each, the GH SONADs of 2005–2010 lasted for three days each and those of 2011–2013 lasted for six days of about three hours each. Also, the difference is somehow proportional to the sizes of the two parliaments: while the House of Commons has 650 MPs, the number of Ghanaian MPs has changed from 200 in 1993–2004 and 230 from 2005 to 2012 to 275 between 2013 and the present. Again, the difference does not affect the analysis because we employ normalized frequency (NF) calculations in order to make the two sets of corpora comparable (see section 4.1).

This paper employs a corpus-assisted discourse studies (CADs) approach: it uses a discourse analytical approach but utilizes corpus-linguistic techniques and tools as and when necessary (Partington, 2010). Specifically, it uses concordances through *Wordsmith Tools* (Scott, 2012) to examine in context some identifiable linguistic indicators of claim-making. A concordance refers to "a list of a given word or word cluster with its co-text on either side" (Gabrielatos & Baker, 2008, p. 15) or "a collection of the occurrences of a word-form, each in its own textual environment" (Sinclair, 1991, p. 33), which allows for the examination of patterns of meaning associated with the word under investigation. For example, figure 9.1 offers a sample of concordance lines for the word "represent." The words to the left of "represent" indicate its context, which allows us to interpret "represent" co-textually.

As noted earlier, a key feature of this paper is the empirical exploration of representative claim-making. And, arguably, there is no context that better represents representative democracy than parliaments, hence the choice of the parliamentary data for this study.

## ANALYSIS AND DISCUSSION

This section constitutes an analysis and a discussion of explicit/direct claims and how they are constructed using transitivity. Also examined are the implicit/indirect ways of constructing a representative claim, including the use of deictics/indexicals.

### Explicit/Direct Constructions of the Representative Claim

There are instances in the parliamentary debates where MPs directly state that they "represent" their constituents and their constituents' interests; they "speak for" or "on behalf of" the constituents, "stand for" them or "champion" their cause. The most obvious way of claiming representation is the use of the word "represent" (as in *I represent . . .*). Therefore, the first step toward the analysis was to identify synonyms of "represent" (including "stand/speak/act for," "stand/speak/act on behalf of," and "champion the cause of"). I then used *concordancing* to search for instances of the uses of

|   N   | Concordance |
|-------|-------------|
| 1 | former fisheries Minister—which is slightly bizarre, as I represent one of the most inland constituencies in the |
| 2 | in the Queen's Speech. I want to enter another plea. I represent a part of the country where a significant |
| 3 | those on the Conservative Benches. Those of us who represent less prosperous areas of the country know a |
| 4 | have been absolutely catastrophic for the people we represent. Mr. Redwood: Why then did the Government |
| 5 | it will infuriate the British people whom we are here to represent. The Prime Minister said-hon. Members will |
| 6 | the viewpoint of the part of south-west England that I represent, there seems to be little in the speech that |

**Figure 9.1.   Sample concordance lines of represent from UK QADs.**

these expressions in the data, in order to examine them in context (tables 9.2, 9.3, and 9.4) and count their frequencies (see table 9.1).

A normalized frequency (NF) analysis indicates that these expressions were statistically more frequent in the UK than the Ghanaian data. NF statistically allows for the standardization of two corpora of different sizes in order to make them comparable. It is based on the equation $x/100,000 = raw$ occurrence/corpus size, where $x$ represents the normalized frequency for each corpus (see Lorenz, 1999, p. 19). The result indicates that the abovementioned expressions occurred 4.35/100,000 words in the UK data and 2.6/100,000 words in the Ghanaian data. This implies that the UK MPs made more direct representative claims than their Ghanaian counterparts. These statistics do not reveal the discursive constructions of the representative claim. Thus, through transitivity, we explore how MPs discursively construct direct claims of representation.

From a transitivity perspective, representation is construed as covering different kinds of experience: it is defined by specifying the mandate of the parliamentarian (relational clauses) (table 9.2); it is verbalized (verbal clauses; table 9.3), and it is acted out (material clauses; table 9.4). The mandate of the parliamentarian is given by his/her constituents. Thus, when an MP identifies him- or herself via a relational process (I-Token), through the constituents (Value), he or she affirms his or her mandate as a representation of the constituents. The MP establishes a direct link between him- or herself and the constituents / the people, thereby defining him- or herself through them. In other words, MPs see themselves as the embodiment (Token) of their constituents (Value) (Thompson, 2014). The relational processes also allow MPs to see representation as a purpose or a reason (see examples 8 and 9).

These verbal processes portray the MPs as "advocates" (Urbinati, 2000, p. 773) of their constituents, where they speak for/on behalf of the represented, including their parties (table 9.3). The assumption is that MPs are the

**Table 9.1.   Explicit claim markers and their frequencies.**

| | Frequency | |
|---|---|---|
| **Marker** | **UK** | **GH** |
| Represent | 20 | 11 |
| On behalf of | 20 | 3 |
| Speak for | 4 | 1 |
| Stand for | 0 | 1 |
| Champion | 0 | 1 |
| Total | 44 | 16 |

*Kwabena Sarfo Sarfo-Kantankah*

**Table 9.2.   Relational processes in direct claims.**

| Token | Process: Relational | Value | |
|---|---|---|---|
| 1. I | represent | a constituency . . . where we have high unemployment . . . | |
| 2. I | represent | more Muslim voters than any other member of Parliament . . . | |
| 3. I | represent | the people of Juapong | |
| 4. I | represent | one of the constituencies . . . | |
| 5. We | represent | the people | |
| 6. We | stand | for the Ghanaian people | |
| | | **Value** | **Circumstance: Behalf** |
| 7. I | would stand | here | on behalf of the Akan youth |
| | | **Value** | **Circumstance: Purpose** |
| 8. We | are | here | to represent our constituents and to put the country first |
| **Carrier** | **Process: Relational** | **Attribute** | **Circumstance: Reason** |
| 9. I | am | proud | represent my fellow Yorkshireman Alan Bennett |

mouthpiece of their constituents, as in example 12. Apart from speaking for them, the MPs are also expected to act on behalf of their constituents as exemplified in table 9.4. MPs carry the mandate of their constituents to express their concerns for the government to act on their needs.

These material processes construe representation from two angles. First, it is construed as the purpose/outcome of the democratic action of the constituents/the people (see examples 16, 17, 18). The represented are seen as Actors whose act of electing representatives makes it possible for MPs to become representatives. Therefore, when MPs remind their fellow MPs that they are elected to represent the people (see 17–18), they are being reminded of the mandate bestowed on them—to serve the interest of the people. Second, the

**Table 9.3.  Verbal processes in direct claims.**

| Sayer | Process: Verbal | Circumstance: Behalf |
| --- | --- | --- |
| 1. I | speak | for my constituents |
| 2. I | speak | for many business people |
| 3. I | can speak | for my constituents, who do not want their schools shut |
| 4. I | wish to respond | on behalf of my party |
| 5. I | am speaking | for all the good people from the North |

material processes indicate that representation is not only about recognizing oneself as a representative or speaking for the interests of others, but also performing/acting out the role. The MP (Actor) must do something for the benefit of the represented, as in example 15.

Whether representation is relationally, verbally, or materially construed, the underlying issue is that MPs claim to represent the interest of the people. For an MP to say that he or she represents a certain group of people, be it individuals, constituent(s), or community(ies) is to claim that he or she knows the interests, needs, desires, wants, preferences, problems, and so on of those people (Saward, 2006). It reflects Stasavage's (2007) view that when representatives make decisions in public, for example, during debates on the floor of Parliament, they are motivated to use their actions to signal a sense of loyalty to their constituents. In representative democracies where the mandate to represent emanates from the people, such claim-making is essential, given that "levels of trust and confidence in politicians and political institutions are low" (Hay, 2007, p. 36; see also Leonard, 2015; and BBC, 2014). It is a way of holding themselves accountable to the people and letting them know that MPs are fighting for the people's interests. It should, however, be recognized that representative claim-making by MPs on the floor of Parliament does not necessarily translate into practical attendance to the needs of the people. It may be mere conceptualization or indicative of a desire to capture the attention of constituents for political gains, which makes representation a claim, rather than a fact or the given outcome of an electoral process or other (Saward, 2006).

Parliamentarians' claim of representing different kinds of "constituents"—their electoral areas, social groups, and the general public—are mostly expressed in two ways, which I call *I-represent* and *we-represent* constructions. When MPs use *I-represent* constructions, they express themselves as single individuals representing specific constituents/constituencies with specific interests, as in examples 1–4. The represented can also be a single individual (example 9), an ethnic (example 7) or a social group (example 11). This kind of representation invokes what is referred to as "tribalism theory" or the "Latin view" (Cova & Cova, 2002, p. 595), which "proposes that

**Table 9.4.  Material processes in direct claims.**

| Actor | Process: Material | Goal | Circumstance: Behalf |
|---|---|---|---|
| 1. I | have set out | my concerns | on behalf of my constituents . . . |

| Actor | Process: Material | Goal | Circumstance: Purpose |
|---|---|---|---|
| 2. The people of Holborn and St. Pancras | have elected | me | to represent them |

| Goal | Process: Material (+Actor) | Circumstance: Purpose |
|---|---|---|
| 3. We | were voted | to represent the people of this country |
| 4. We | are elected | to represent the people who put us here and their interests |

micro-groups are created through shared tastes and lifestyles" and "who are linked by a shared passion or emotion" (Krishen et al., 2014, p. 744). For instance, the *Akan youth* (example 7) may not only be a "Tribe," but also "advocates" who are "capable of collective action" (Cova & Cova, 2002, p. 602). Generally, MPs employ the *I*-constructions to frame their messages to suit particular targets of interest (Krishen et al., 2014).

On the other hand, *we*-constructions often present national interests, as in examples 5, 6, 8, 17, and 18. They largely construe representation as an institutional phenomenon. For instance, in example 8, MPs ("we" – Token) are defined through Parliament ("here" – Value), and Parliament is projected as representing the people (Purpose). MPs admonish their colleagues to recognize themselves as representatives of the people in general, a kind of national interest advocacy (examples 17, 18). This suggests that whereas *I*-constructions of the representative claim emphasize individual gains, *we*-constructions emphasize the collective within which the individual is also situated but in which the *I-ness* is either not emphasized or is de-emphasized, even though it still exists. More importantly, both constructions portray MPs as having the interests of the people at heart. But to what extent do such claims correspond to actual performance of political responsibility such as providing for the physical and material needs and wants of the people? The question is necessary, considering that "[i]n politics, portrayals of constituencies or the nation or voters' interests are just that: portrayals. . . . There is no self-presenting subject whose essential character and desires and interests are transparent, beyond representation" (Saward, 2006, p. 312).

There is also an indication of a party's representative claim (example 13), which is rare in both datasets. Only two such instances were found in the UK data, and none from the Ghanaian data. During debates, every MP speaks as either a majority or minority party member, which makes party representation a given. Claims of party representation appear to be more implicit/ indirect, especially through personal, spatial, and temporal deictics.

## IMPLICIT/INDIRECT CONSTRUCTION OF THE REPRESENTATIVE CLAIM

This section explores how MPs position the represented in relation to themselves through the use of deictic/indexical expressions. Deictics have substantial significance in political discourse, since "[p]olitical actors are . . . always situated with respect to a particular time, place and social group" (Chilton, 2004, p. 57), and "deixis is basic to language in its capacity to constitute both subjects and objects" (Hanks, 2005, p. 191). The use of deictics by MPs allows them to "localize" the people, the general public, or their constituents in relation to MPs' position as parliamentary representatives. The assumption is that the way MPs position the represented in relation to themselves suggests a representative claim. This section looks at person/ social, place/spatial, and time/temporal references in order to demonstrate how they constitute representative claim-making.

### Signaling Closeness and Loyalty to the People through Personal/Social Deictics

Personal deictics such as *I*, *we*, *us*, *our*, *you*, *he*, *she*, *they*, and *them* allow a speaker to construct relationships between him- or herself, addressees, and third parties. Consider example 19.

*Example 19: UK QADs 10 May 13/Col. 337*

> **Mr. Duncan Smith (Con):** Let *me* remind *Labour Members* that, for all *their* crocodile tears, long-term unemployment nearly doubled in *two years* under the previous Government. . . . That was a failure on *their* part. *They* gerrymandered the figures on youth unemployment, but when *we* take the gerrymandering out, *we* find that youth unemployment is now lower than when the Labour Government left office.

In example 19, the personal deictics *[t]hey* and *we* are contrastive. *They* and *their . . .* , which refer to *Labour Members* and their behavior, construct Labour as an out-group and create antagonism between them and the Conser-

vatives, *we*. While the statement views Labour MPs as insincere, it portrays
the Conservatives as honest. The *we-they* reference implies "*We* stand for the
interest of the people, *they* do not." These pronouns can be used to "include"
and "exclude" political actors (Adetunji, 2006, p. 189), establish "solidarity"
with audience or "antagonism" with political opponents (Kuo, 2002, p. 29),
and/or ideologically "signal in-group and out-group membership, as in *Us* vs.
*Them*," leading to "positive self-presentation and negative other-presenta-
tion" (van Dijk, 2011, pp. 397, 398). Chilton (2004) points out that in political discourse the first-person plural pronouns, *we*, *us*, and *our* "can be used to
induce interpreters to conceptualize group identity, coalitions, parties, and
the like either as insiders or outsiders" (p. 56).

MPs display a considerable level of attachment to the people through the
use of person references (see figures 9.2 and 9.3). Expressions such as *our
country*, *our nation*, and *our people* indicate inclusiveness and the idea of
sharing in the plight and needs of the citizenry, as well as an emotional
bonding with the people—all these suggest that MPs claim to represent the
interests of the people.

The *our*-expressions "establish an extra-textual relationship between
speaker [MPs] and hearers [the citizenry] such that the hearers are postulated
as present in the same (political) space and as proximate to the speaker"
(Chilton, 2004, p. 139). The use of *our* makes MPs "sound like the collective
voice of' the people" (Heinrichs, 2010, p. 46), expressing "collective good"
as against "self-interest" (Krishen et al., 2014, p. 742), "signal[ling] closeness" to people (van Dijk, 2011, p. 398) and "establish[ing] empathy by
demonstrating that" the MPs share "the same values as the audience [the
citizenry]" (Charteris-Black, 2014, p. 17). Being proximal references, their
use is attitudinal (Glover, 2000, p. 915); it humanizes the conditions MPs
describe and seeks to establish goodwill and trust with the people, which
implies a representation of the interests of the people.

**Figure 9.2.**

| N | Concordance |
|---|---|
| 1 | the work that they are doing. What matters now is that, with our allies, we take the right actions to maximise the |
| 2 | , yet hospitals have closed; more laws on immigration, yet our borders are still completely out of control. Every year, |
| 3 | [...] Our thoughts are with their families. They died serving our country and we honour their memory. I also pay tribute |
| 4 | matched by failure on crime. After nine years, every part of our criminal justice system is in a shambles. The chairman |
| 5 | has been a privilege. The Queen's Speech shows that our determination to continue improving the lives of people |
| 6 | ; Vol. 250, c.14-15.] What better description could there be of our Government today? The tragedy of this Prime Minister is |
| 7 | to link the basic state pension to earnings; we had that in our last manifesto. The Treasury has finally been forced to |
| 8 | men and women who were killed in Basra on Sunday [...] Our thoughts are with their families. They died serving our |
| 9 | , I have seen for myself the extraordinary work that our troops are doing as part of a NATO operation—now |

**Figure 9.3.**

## Claiming Concern for Communities and Constituencies through Place/Spatial Deictics

Place/spatial deictics designate geographical location vis-à-vis the location of the speaker. They are used to locate referents as either near/proximal (e.g., *here, this, these*) or far/distal (*there, that, those*) (van Dijk, 2011; Adetunji, 2006). Chilton (2004) sums up the significance of spatial referencing in political discourse thus: "[s]patial representations, including metaphorical ones, take on an important aspect in political discourse. If politics is about cooperation and conflict over allocation of resources, such resources are frequently of a spatial, that is, geographical or territorial, kind" (p. 57). Arguably, there is no political arena where cooperation and conflict over allocation of resources occur more than Parliament, where parliamentarians negotiate for and facilitate the allocation of resources and developmental projects to their constituencies. Thus, closely related to person references in parliamentary debates are place/spatial references. The close relationship between the two manifests in the fact that oftentimes a reference to a constituency (or a town in a constituency) implies reference to the constituents. Parliamentarians represent constituencies and their core responsibility is to represent the interests of their constituents. As Alun Michaels (MP) puts it, "[a]ny legislature must look like the people whom it represents" (UK QADs 15 Nov 2006/Col. 12). Consider example 20.

*Example 20: UK QADs 9 May 13/Col. 207*

> **Helen Jones (Lab):** The first priority is to build a prosperous economy *throughout the regions and nations of this country*. This Government has systematically taken money out of many of *our regions*, which have already been hit by unemployment. They have transferred £1 billion out of the north of England in *their local government settlement alone*. They have hit *those big cities* suffering most from unemployment through *their welfare reforms*; for example, *Birmingham* will lose £10 million on council tax changes alone, and *Liverpool* is losing more than £7 million in bedroom tax.

*[T]his country*, and *those big cities* are spatial expressions, with *Birmingham* and *Liverpool* being examples of the spatial referents of *those big cities*. During debates, MPs make place/spatial references to show their concerns for the needs of such places. Spatial references in the debates indicate the extent to which government policies affect such places, as in *welfare reforms* making *Birmingham* and *Liverpool* lose millions of pounds. Consider also Example 21.

*Example 21: GH SONADs 8 Feb 06/Col. 557*

> **Mr. Iddrisu [NDC]:** Mr. Speaker . . . over the last few months we have all been witnesses to the clashes between mining communities and mining com-panies operating in *those areas*, but that did not attract a comment by His excellency, the President. Mr. Speaker, also about security and the state of *our country*, there have been some disturbances *in Bimbilla*, the Nanumba area. . . . There have been some disturbances *in Wa in the Upper West Region*, the Dagbon tragedy remains unresolved, but no comment whatsoever came from the President about that. What he chose to do was to describe the state of the nation as good.

When Mr. Iddrisu says that *there have been disturbances* in *Bimbilla, the Nanumba area, Wa*, and *Dagbon*, the underlying reference is *people*, for it is people who cause disturbances and it is people who suffer from them. His concern is, therefore, for the people. His point that the president did not comment on these disturbances suggests that the president did not care about the people of those areas. Mr. Iddrisu implies that while he stands for the interest of those people, the president does not; just as Helen Jones constructs herself as representing the interests of the people of *those big cities* (example 20), whereas the government appears to be uninterested in their welfare. Reference to specific geographical entities such as *Birmingham, Liverpool, Bimbilla*, and *Wa* designates them as spatially distinct, with distinctive con-cerns relative to other places. It is a way of specifying and spatially locating the effects of government policies. Such references imply concerns for the needs of the people.

## Accounting for the Period of Governance through Time/Temporal Deictics

Time/temporal deictics (e.g., *after 2001*, below) indicate the time of an utter-ance, which has three dimensions: past (before the moment of the utterance), present (the moment of the utterance), and future (after the moment of the utterance) (Adetunji, 2006). Time/temporal references are a major resource for comparing one government's performance against another government's performance over a period of time. Different governments assume the reigns of governance at different times and periods, and therefore, to consider which government offered the right policies and interventions and met people's needs and aspirations is to compare such periods. It is a way of expressing accountability to the people. For instance, in example 22, Nana Akomea (NPP, government MP) compares the *period after 2001* to periods from 1983 through 2000, saying that his government has achieved the longest . . . consecutive *growth in our GDP since 1983.*

*Example 22: GH SONADs: 8 Feb 06/Col. 543–4*

> **Nana Akomea (NPP):** Mr. Speaker, the period *after 2001* has seen the longest periods where we have had continuous consecutive growth in our GDP *since 1983.* Mr. Speaker, if you look at the figures in 1993 this country grew, Gross Domestic Product (GDP), by five (5) per cent; *in 1994* it fell to 3.8, in 1995 it rose slightly to four (4) per cent; in 1996 it rose to 4.6 per cent; in 1997 it dropped to 4.2, *in 1998* it rose to 4.7 *in 1999* it dropped to 4.4 and *in the year 2000* it dropped 3.7 per cent. But if you look at the figures after 2001, Mr. Speaker, they were 4.2 per cent *in 2001*, 4.5 per cent *in 2002*, 5.2 per cent *in 2003*, 5.8 per cent.

This "historical periodization" (Chilton, 2004, p. 56) allows Nana Akomea to comparatively assess and give the audience a picture of what various governments achieved in terms of Gross Domestic Product (GDP) growth. The figures mentioned are significant in relation to the time references employed. It is these time references which indicate whether or not a certain achievement is substantial, making temporal referencing an important aspect of the parliamentary debates and parliamentary representation.

In the UK QADs (example 23), Alun Michael (government MP) does a similar comparison of periods.

*Example 23: UK QADs 15 Nov 2006/Col. 7*

> **Alun Michael (Lab/Co-op, government MP):** *Since 1997, we have had a golden age of radical domestic legislation: the minimum wage delivered after 100 years of campaigning* – laws promoting social inclusion, education, enterprise, justice, child welfare and much, much more (lines 9–13). . . . The Queen's Speech promises to protect victims, and I hope that the courts are listening, because *since 2003* the Attorney-General has referred 341 lenient sentences to the Court of Appeal (lines 20–22).

Alun Michael is speaking in 2006, and therefore *since 1997* is a period of nine years. In the light of *100 years of campaigning*, a nine-year period of achieving *a golden age of radical legislation* leading to *minimum wage* delivery and the several social services appears enormous. It projects the government as more responsible than previous governments. However, David Cameron disagrees (example 24).

*Example 24: UK 15 Nov 06/Col 13–17*

> **Mr. David Cameron (Con, leader of the opposition):** . . . when he was Leader of the Opposition, he said: "Millions of people are desperate for changes in the Child Support Agency," yet *today*, under his Government, that situation is more chaotic than ever. *Twelve years ago*, as Leader of the Opposition, he said that the pension system was a scandal, yet it is his Government who has taken from every pension fund in the country. *Twelve years ago* . . . he said that the Government "are so riven by faction . . . that they cannot address the interests of the country." . . . What better description could there be of our Government *today*? . . . The paradox of new Labour is that, *12 years on*, the Prime Minister is still desperately looking for his legacy. . . . *Nine years ago*, the Prime Minister claimed that there were 24 hours to save the NHS, yet *today*, 20,000 jobs are being cut in the health service.

Consider Cameron's references to the following periods: *Twelve years ago/ on [n]ine years ago*, and *today*. As Cameron is speaking in 2006, *today* refers to a twelve-year period. Thus, *today* emphasizes *twelve years*, which is repeated several times across the speech. His repetition of *twelve* and *nine years* can be said to be in direct reaction to Alun Michael's reference to a nine-year achievement record. If after twelve years, a prime minister, in Cameron's terms, *is still desperately looking for his legacy*, then it is a mark of failure. If the prime minister cannot *save the NHS* after nine years in office and *20,000 jobs are being cut in health services*, then it is a failure to represent and act in the interests of the people.

MPs' ability to periodize and compare different government's performance suggests that one government is better at managing the affairs of the country and representing the interests of the people than the other. This is important because, "[f]or political discourse in general subjectively "positioned" time periods can be of considerable importance—history, and which parts of it are "close" to the "us" is central to national ideologies and to justifying present and future policy" (Chilton, 2004, p. 59). Without measuring performance relative to time, it would be difficult to see which political party has more credibility and should be voted for in the "next" elections. As noted by DePauw (2007), "[V]oters support the platform that best matches their individual preferences and interests of the moment—at the same time judging that party's past record in terms of veracity, probity, economic competence, and cohesion" (p. 3). Thus, temporal references in parliamentary debates could be said to be a way of being held accountable to the people, indicating MPs' trustworthiness as representatives of the citizenry.

As mentioned earlier, parliamentary debates are deliberative. They are about persuading people (especially, the electorate) to make choices between policies that will (presumably) determine their future. For Heinrichs (2010), it is "the audience's own beliefs, values, and naked self-interest" that determine the outcome of deliberative discourse and "[t]o persuade them, you offer a prize . . . which is the promise that your choice will give the judges [audience] what they value" (p. 107). MPs' comparison of periods of time between governments creates an oppositional construct of "desirables" and "undesirable" (Fairclough, 2003, p. 177). For example, Alun Michael's nine-year period is compared with a hundred-year period, while Nana Akomea compares a six-year to a seventeen-year period. These comparisons create a contrast, whose effect is a polarization along government-opposition lines. Each group of MPs attempts to show that their policies are more desirable and are more people-focused than the other. The state of people's well-being is expressed as the direct result of government policies and actions. The next section examines how MPs construct the represented and their concerns.

### People Are Getting Better but People Are Worse Off: Constructing the Represented and Contesting the Claims

Thompson (2012, p. 1) has suggested that representative claim makers construct "the objects of their claims in the process of representing them," in which "rival accounts" are possible; and that "elected politicians may seek to represent their constituents by portraying them in a particular way." Portraying the represented in particular ways allows the representative to legitimize his or her claims and political action. For instance, Krishen et al. (2007, pp. 745, 752) have said that in political policy marketing, "negative information attracts more attention from the recipient than positive information." So, how do MPs construct the represented as objects of their claims?

One of the underlying reasons for delivering the GH SONAD and the UK QAD is to demonstrate how governments have managed, are managing, or will manage the socioeconomic affairs of the country for the benefit of the people. The addresses and MPs' debates, thus, show a considerable level of people-focusing. Fore-fronting people's concerns is crucial, for in parliamentary debates, MPs "are in fact out to gain the support of a broader . . . usually non-interactive and heterogeneous audience . . . supporters, opponents and neutral bystanders . . . [who are] their primary addressee[s]" (van Eemeren & Garssen, 2009, p. 6). Apart from demonstrating, among other things, how responsible governments are, the addresses have some bearing on the government's fortunes in the next elections as well as MPs' chances of getting reelected. Governments and MPs are aware that to be (re)elected, they have to be able to persuade the electorate that they are capable of doing relevant and "vital things" which not everybody is capable of. They have to perform and construct themselves discursively in ways that inspire confidence in their ability to implement policies responsibly, to establish and retain order, protect the citizens from danger, keep the economy going, be competitive on the world stage and so forth. (Wodak, 2011, p. 202)

This is the image each group of MPs tries to project, resulting in arguments and counter-arguments about whether or not the government's policy interventions will help (or have helped) improve the lives of the people, as illustrated in figure 9.4. Whereas government MPs construct the represented in positive frames, opposition MPs use negative frames.

These arguments and counterarguments are a feature of representative claim-making, as "there is no representative claim without its being open to a counter-claim" (Saward, 2006, p. 304). The contention leads to contrastive constructions of the represented, such as *people are getting better; people are worse off*. Table 9.5 illustrates these contestry constructions (note: even though there are other hyponyms of *people* such as *men/women, youth, elderly, Ghana(ians)*, and *Britain*, I use only *people* for illustration purposes). For instance, while Ghanaian government MPs say *people are getting better* (table 9.4, lines 3, 7), opposition MPs say *everyday people are struggling . . .* (lines 17, 18), *seriously, people . . . are hurting* (line 26). Similarly, whereas UK government MPs say *[w]e have cut taxes for people . . .* (line 33), *people can take home free of income tax* (line 41), *to continue improving the lives of the people . . .* (line 37); opposition MPs claim *people are worse off . . .* (line 51), *people are not better off* (line 52), *people are desperate for changes* (line 53). These are syntactic parallel structures that emphasize the contrast of

**Concordance 1: government MPs - GH SONAD**
1 the President mentioned investment in people and investment in jobs as a major
2 cess – to make sure that movement of people and goods around and on the
3 quadrupled and you can see clearly that people are getting better. Madam Speak
4 economy was still managed prudently; people did not give in to excesses. Mr.
5 for this gap, this loophole that young people have been falling through. It pro
6 resources are used for the benefit of the people. His Excellency, having realiz
7 have four, clearly indicating that the people in this country are getting better
8 deliver so much on the needs of our people. [Interruptions.] 21 Feb 2012/Col
9 achieving this optimum investment in people is through the new educational re
10 look at physiological needs of the people, it is talking about food and wat
11 n salt and natural gas – I believe the people of Ada might be smiling by now
12 iry given to this Government by the people of this country, so much has been
13 ted and this has brought relief to the people of Kasoa, Awutu, Senya Bereku,
14 you come to the safety needs of the people, there cannot be better safety than
15 talking about the health needs of our people. This was extensively discussed
16 and security and protecting the people will remain the cornerstone

**Concordance 2: opposition MPs - GH SONAD**
17 put food on the table; everyday no people are struggling to pay school fees
18 rural level. Mr. Speaker, everyday no people are struggling to put food on
19 has not been appealed against and now people are in prison for that case –
20 e consuming and cumbersome. Ordinary people cannot access justice.
21 Madam Speaker, people have sacrificed. People continue to sacrifice. The
22 body says, yenno adie, it is because the people do not have money to buy the
23 divide us politically. Madam Speaker, people have sacrificed. People contin
24 jobs. I am talking about very ordinary people in B.U. (Butinabutu) in Esika
25 bridging the gap, be further divided the people of this country. His Ashanti
26 ent. But Madam Speaker, seriously, the people of this country are hurting.
27 But the President should answer to the people of Ghana. But what about the
28 President must come and report to the people of Ghana through the House
29 tell us the conditions in which the people of this country find themselves.
30 stability is important only insofar as the people see that the quality of their lives
51 hospitals that I know, the people who went there were given codeine and APC
32 ker, if you raise taxes and inflict the people with national reconstruction I

**Concordance 3: government MPs - UK QAD**
33 ted completely. We have cut taxes for people in work and we are also cutting
34 businesses, to build a society in which people who work hard are properly re
35 We also share a belief in giving the people of Wales and Scotland a greater
36 success in inspiring progress for the people of Wales. However, the greatest
37 tion to continue improving the lives of people in this country is undiminished.
38 ecent, hard-working families. It is the people and their sense of community
39 engineering skills. Not enough young people in the UK understand the range
40 d those statistics are individual young people standing tall, able to use their
41 this tax year the amount that people can take home free of income tax
42 rove the quality of education for young people, to support those who have us
43 ined Kingdom today. I believe that most people have no problem with saying
44 on policy priorities, and not just the people developing, manufacturing and s
45 red. Any legislature must look like the people whom it represents. That was
46 nce and reforming child care to enable people to enter or stay in employment.
47 he Conservatives a generation of young people were denied hope and opportu
48 remarkable job for local children and young people. We also have the headqua

**Concordance 4: opposition MPs - UK QAD**
49 Gracious Speech offer to those young people? Absolutely nothing – no change.
50 look at what is happening to our young people and our businesses, and the squeeze
51 no action on private pension charges. People are worse off under the Tories.
52 ple that they are better off. However, people are not better off; they are worst
53 the Opposition, he said: "Millions of people are desperate for changes in the
54 There are now four times more young people claiming benefits for more than
55 nt. It is so repetitive and hollow that people feel they have heard it all before
56 On living standards, we all met many people in this campaign who are struggling
57 is the job guarantee for Britain's young people? It is not there. Where are the
58 unemployment, with one in five young people not getting a job, and turned
59 nt understand the difficulties that the people of Britain face? I have to say, t
60 scrap benefits on which millions of elderly people rely-attendance allowance
61 jobs and pay, which are at the heart of people's concerns. The problem is the
62 e problem. There is no point in telling people that they are better off when his
63 anger and as hundreds of thousands of people took to the streets, he was ma
64 ting worse, not better; 1 million young people without work, low growth, fall

**Figure 9.4. Concordance shot of people in GH SONADs and UK QADs.**

views. There is a validation-denial juxtaposition. Both groups express concern for the well-being of the people, but in different ways: they argue from "a gain [positive] versus a loss [negative] perspective" (Krishen et al., 2014, p. 745). According to Stasavage (2007), "modern political representation implies that representatives should act according to the expressed interests of their constituents" (p. 62), but to be able to act in the interests of constituents, MPs should be able to determine what those interests are. MPs' ability to indicate those interests suggests that they are "concerned . . . with the construction and, ideally, the realization of a sense of the collective good" (Hay, 2007, p. 2), which underlies the value system of democratic governance. Portraying themselves as the embodiment of people's interests, the MPs presume that they know the needs and concerns of the people: *education for young people* (table 9.4, lines 42, 17), employment (line 48, 58), *jobs and pay* (line 61), *work* (line 64), *health* (line 15), *justice* (line 20), *security and protecting* . . . (line 16), *quality of their lives* (line 30), and so on. What the MPs disagree on is the means to achieving these.

I refer to the attributive expression of a good–bad quality of life to people as *people-are* constructions. These constructions are a "moral evaluation legitimation" (van Leeuwen, 2008, p. 110), which MPs use to establish "goodwill" and "trust" with the people (Charteris-Black, 2014, p. 9). The term embodies all expressions that convey a sense of concern for the people. The attributive evaluation of people's concern is made through attributive relational processes such as *people are/feel* . . . , with adjectives/adjectival phrases, nouns/noun phrases as complements (Fairclough, 2003, p. 172; Thompson & Hunston, 1999, pp. 4, 13–14). Table 9.5 provides examples of *people-are* constructions.

The attributive relational processes describe people as carriers of certain attributes: good or bad conditions of life. What MPs do is to compare these attributes. The comparative adjectives indicate that MPs are comparing the living conditions of people across governments and periods. Such comparisons are a way for MPs to justify their own government's performance or to condemn other governments' performance, since "comparisons in discourse almost always have a legitimating or delegitimating function" (van Leeuwen, 2008, p. 111). (Note: even though "desperate" is not comparative, the com-

**Table 9.5.** *People-are* constructions.

| Carrier | Linking Verb | Attribute (Adjective) | Reference in Table 9.4 |
| --- | --- | --- | --- |
| People | are getting | better | line 3 |
| | are | worse off | line 51 |
| | are | not better off | line 52 |
| | are | desperate for changes | line 53 |

plement "for changes" implies a comparison.) The contestations between the MPs demonstrate the polarized stance between government and opposition MPs on people's concerns during parliamentary deliberation, where making claims of representing and working for the interests of the people is essential.

## CONCLUSION

This paper sought to explore the ways in which UK and Ghanaian parliamentarians as representatives of the people constructed their claims of representation. The paper has demonstrated that parliamentarians construct their representative claims in two main ways: explicit/direct and implicit/indirect ways. An examination of direct claim-making, through transitivity, indicates that MPs construe representation as comprising different kinds of experience: it is defined by specifying the mandate of parliamentarians (relational processes); representation is verbalized (verbal processes), and it is acted out (material processes). These explicit constructions employ two main expressions: *I*-represent and *we*-represent constructions.

The indirect construction of the representative claim appears to be quite more complex. It is achieved through deictic/indexical referencing—personal, temporal, and spatial referencing. To the extent that the GH SONADs and the UK QADs are debates about policies of political parties as government and opposition with far-reaching implications for the well-being of the masses, group and social identity creation during such debates is crucial. MPs construct representation by using personal deictics to create trustworthiness, goodwill, and closeness to the people, which implies empathy and working in the interest of the people. Time/temporal deictics are important for the reason that "the location and/or extent of social activities are timed in relation to other social activities . . . [which] allows for measurement and for time spans of different levels of magnitude" (van Leeuwen, 2008, pp. 77–78). During debates, MPs construct various kinds of "historical periodization" (Chilton, 2004, p. 56). This allows them to create a situational picture of where we have come from, where we are, and what the future looks like; which creates the opportunity for them to evaluatively compare the performance and achievements of past and present governments in order to demonstrate whose accomplishments are better. This is a form of accountability for political stewardship. Place/spatial deictics allow MPs to make references to specific geographical or territorial areas (e.g., constituencies), which they believe need some attention. The paper has argued that such references imply reference to the people. Another indirect way of constructing a representative claim is constructing the represented in a manner that portrays the conditions in which the people find themselves. However, such constructions generate contestations between government and opposition

MPs. Whereas government MPs construct the represented in a positive frame, which justifies the government's political action and/or policy as valid; opposition MPs do so negatively, in order to delegitimize the government's policy decisions and action. In each case, government and opposition MPs imply that they represent the interests of the people.

## REFERENCES

Adetunji, A. (2006). "Inclusion and Exclusion in Political Discourse: Deixis in Olusegun Obasanjo's Speeches." *Journal of Language and Politics* 5(2): 177–191.

Alcoff, L. (1991, Winter). "The Problem of Speaking for Others." *Cultural Critique* 20: 5–32. http://www.jstor.org/stable/1354221. Retrieved July 16, 2018.

Bächtiger, A. (2014). "Debate and Deliberation in Legislatures." In S. Martin, T. Saalfeld, & K. Strøm (eds.), *The Oxford Handbook of Legislative Studies*, 145–166. Oxford: Oxford University Press.

BBC. (2014). "Put Misbehaving MPs in 'Sin Bin,' Think Tank Recommends." http://www.bbc.co.uk/news/uk-politics-26133375. Retrieved March 11, 2015.

Besley, T., & S. Coate. (1997). "An Economic Model of Representative Democracy." *Quarterly Journal of Economics* 112(1): 85–114.

Bloor, M., & T. Bloor. (2013). *The Practice of Critical Discourse Analysis: An Introduction.* London and New York: Routledge.

Cadigan, J. (2005). "The Citizen Candidate Model: An Experimental Analysis." *Public Choice* 123: 197–216. doi: 10.1007/s11127–005–0262–4.

Charteris-Black, J. (2014). *Analysing Political Speeches: Rhetoric, Discourse and Metaphor.* UK: Palgrave Macmillan.

Chilton, P. (2004). *Analysing Political Discourse: Theory and Practice.* London: Routledge.

Cova, B., & V. Cova. (2002). "Tribal Marketing: The Tribalisation of Society and Its Impact on the Conduct of Marketing." *European Journal of Marketing* 36(5/6): 595–620.

DePauw, S. (2007, May 7–12). "Deliberation and Reason-Giving in Parliament: A Preface to Analysis." Paper presented at the ECPR Joint Sessions Helsinki. https://ecpr.eu/Filestore/PaperProposal/c93497e3-05e5-4522-9f56a4ce8990652f.pdf. Retrieved March 9, 2017.

Dobson, A. (1996). "Representative Democracy and the Environment." In W. M. Lafferty & J. Meadowcroft (eds.), *Democracy and the Environment*, 124–239. UK: Edward Elgar.

Dovi, S. (2017). "Political Representation." In E. N. Zalta (ed.), *The Stanford Encyclopedia of Philosophy* (Spring 2017 Edition). https://plato.stanford.edu/archives/spr2017/entries/political-representation/. Retrieved February 18, 2017.

Duranti, A., & C. Goodwin (eds.). (1992). *Rethinking Context: Language as an Interactive Phenomenon.* Cambridge: Cambridge University Press.

Fairclough, N. (2003). *Analysing Discourse: Textual Analysis for Social Research.* London: Routledge.

Gabrielatos, C., & P. Baker. (2008). "Fleeing, Sneaking, Flooding: A Corpus Analysis of Discursive Constructions of Refugees and Asylum Seekers in the UK Press 1996–2005." *Journal of English Linguistics* 36(5): 5–38.

Glover, K. D. (2000). "Proximal and Distal Deixis in Negotiation Talk." *Journal of Pragmatics* 32(7): 915–926.

Halliday, M. A. K. (1978). *Language as Social Semiotic: The Social Interpretation of Language and Meaning.* Baltimore, MD: University Park Press.

Halliday, M. A. K., & C. M. I. M. Matthiessen. (2004). An Introduction to Functional Grammar (3rd ed.). UK: Arnold.

Hanks, W. F. (1990). *Referential Practice: Language and Lived Space among the Maya.* Chicago, IL: University of Chicago Press.

Hanks, W. F. (2005). "Explorations in the Deictic Field." *Current Anthropology* 46(2): 191–220.

Hay, C. (2007). *Why We Hate Politics*. Cambridge: Polity Press.

Heinrichs, J. (2010). *Winning Arguments*. England: Penguin.

Krishen, A. S., R. Raschke, P. Kachroo, M. LaTour, & P. Verna. (2014). "Promote Me or Protect Us? The Framing of Policy for Collective Good." *European Journal of Marketing* 48(3/4): 742–760.

Kuo, S-H. (2002). "From Solidarity to Antagonism: The Uses of the Second-Person Singular Pronoun in Chinese Political Discourse." *Text* 22(1): 29–55.

Leonard, A. (2015). "NCCE Survey: 62% Ghanaians Don't Trust MPs." http://www.ghanalive.tv/2015/04/23/ncce-survey-62–ghanaians-dont-trust-mps/. Retrieved March 8, 2015.

Lorenz, G. R. (1999). *Adjective Intensification: Learners vs Native Speakers. A Corpus Study of Argumentative Writing*. Amsterdam-Atlanta, GA: Rodopi B.V.

Mill, J. S. (1861). *Representative Government*. Kitchener, ON: Batoche Books.

Partington, A. (2010). "Modern Diachronic Corpus-Assisted Discourse Studies (MD-CADS) on UK Newspapers: An Overview of the Project." *Corpora* 5(2): 83–108.

Pitkin, H. F. (1967). *The Concept of Representation*. Berkeley and Los Angeles: University of California Press.

Priddy, S. (2014). "Queen's Speech—Proposers and Seconders of the Loyal Address since 1900." *Commons Library Standard Note*. http://www.parliament.uk/briefing-papers/ SN04064/. Retrieved April 14, 2015.

Rasch, B. E. (2011, October 20–22). "Legislative Debates and Democratic Deliberation in Parliamentary Systems." Paper presented at the Oslo-Yale International Workshop on *Epistemic Democracy in Practice*. New Haven: Yale University.

Saward, M. (2006). "The Representative Claim." *Contemporary Political Theory* 5(3): 297–318.

Scott, M. (2012). *Wordsmith Tools Version 6*. Liverpool: Lexical Analysis Software.

Simpson, P. (1993). *Language, Ideology and Point of View*. London: Routledge.

Sinclair, J. (1991). *Corpus, Concordance, Collocation*. Oxford: Oxford University Press.

Stasavage, D. (2007). "Polarization and Publicity: Rethinking the Benefits of Deliberative Democracy." *The Journal of Politics* 69(1): 59–72.

Sunstein, C. R. (2006). *Infotopia: How Many Minds Produce Knowledge*. Oxford: Oxford University Press.

The Constitution of the Republic of Ghana. (1992). Ghana Publishing Corporation: Assembly Press.

Thompson, G. (2014). *Introducing Functional Grammar* (3rd ed.). London and New York: Routledge.

Thompson, G., & S. Hunston. (1999). "Evaluation: An Introduction." In S. Hunston & G. Thompson (eds.), *Evaluation in Text: Authorial Stance and the Construction of Discourse*, 1–27. Oxford: Oxford University Press.

Thompson, S. ( 2012). "Making Representations: Comments on Michael Saward's 'the Representative Claim.'" *Contemporary Political Theory* 11(1): 111–114. http://eprints.uwe.ac.uk/ 17860. Retrieved March 7, 2017.

UK Parliament. (2015). *State Opening of Parliament*. http://www.parliament.uk/about/how/ occasions/stateopening/. Retrieved April 27, 2015.

Urbinati, N. (2000). "Representation as Advocacy: A Study of Democratic Deliberation." *Political Theory* 28(6): 758–786.

Usher, D. (2003). "Testing the Candidate-Citizen Model." *Queen's Economic Department Working Papers No. 1013*. Department of Economics, Queen's University.

van Dijk, T. A. (2011). "Discourse and Ideology." In T. A. van Dijk (ed.), *Discourse Studies: A Multidisciplinary Approach*, 379–407. London: Sage.

van Eemeren, F. H., & B. Garssen. (2009). "In varietate condordia—United in Diversity: European Parliamentary Debate as an Argumentative Activity Type." In J. Ritola (ed.), *Argument Cultures: Proceedings of OSSA 09*, CD-ROM, 1–15. Windsor, ON: OSSA.

van Leeuwen, T. (2008). *Discourse and Practice: New Tools for Critical Discourse Analysis*. Oxford: Oxford University Press.

Wodak, R. (2011). *The Discourse of Politics in Action*. UK: Palgrave Macmillan.

Yule, G. (2010). *The Study of Language* (4th ed.). Cambridge: Cambridge University Press.

*Chapter Ten*

# How Much Communication Is in Ghanaian Presidents' State of the Nation Addresses?

## Margaret I. Amoakohene

The state of the nation address or sessional address (as it is sometimes referred to) is a major policy directional statement or a statement containing policy proposals (Shogan, 2015) of a government that spells out areas of government concentration of action. In Ghana, as elsewhere, the state of the nation address covers all major sectors of the economy, is widely publicized and scrutinized by the media, and is debated by Parliament. The Constitution of the Fourth Republic of Ghana in article 67 of chapter 8 requires and indeed prescribes that the president of the Republic at the beginning of each session of Parliament deliver "a message on the state of the nation." Article 67 specifically states under "Presidential Messages" that "[t]he President shall, at the beginning of each session of Parliament and before a dissolution of Parliament, deliver to Parliament a message on the state of the nation." Before this, article 34 (2) of chapter 6 under "The Directive Principles of State Policy" and "Implementation of Directive Principles" states,

> The President shall report to Parliament, at least, once a year all the steps taken to ensure the realization of the policy objectives contained in this Chapter; and, in particular, the realization of basic human rights, a healthy economy, the right to work, the right to good health care and the right to education.

It is difficult to understand how these expectations of the speech or "report to Parliament" can be achieved without clear and effective communication. Thus, the extent to which "all the steps taken to ensure the realization of the policy objectives" have been communicated to citizens outside of Parliament might only be explored through the amount of attention paid to communication in a document or speech form/event such as the state of the nation address. Democratic governance requires that governments engage with their citizens and this is affected through communication, which is important to achieving harmony and citizen participation.

Gbensuglo (2015) sees article 34 as perhaps requiring an address in addition to the state of the nation and/or sessional address delivered by the president to Parliament as provided for under article 67 of the 1992 Constitution. Additional or not, it serves to provide a template containing essential content categories to be included by presidents in crafting their state of the nation addresses. According to Attafuah (2009), the address must include discussions on basic human rights, what makes a healthy economy, the right to work, the right to good health care, and the right to education, which he describes as fundamental conditions of liberty and human welfare for Ghanaians. He believes creating these conditions of human rights, freedoms, and welfare is the foremost responsibility or job description of the state and the president. This constitutional requirement has been respected by each of the five presidents Ghana has so far had in its Fourth Republic, which commenced in January 1993. Each president has unfailingly delivered a message on the state of the nation to Parliament every year he has been in office detailing his governments' priority areas for the allocation of funds and other resources. The study on which this chapter was based examined each of those addresses for their mentions and expectations as the media of mass communication.

## COMMUNICATION AND THE MEDIA

Communication and the media are important to the flow of news and information and to building and sustaining democracy. Many studies have explored how the media—especially television, the Internet, and social media—have changed the political landscape (Dahlgren, 2009; Dahlgren, 2013; Gurevitch et al., 2009; Hallin & Mancini, 2004) of their studied countries and/or worldwide. The media, as channels of political communication, have the capacity to stifle or amplify the voices of politicians and their political parties as well as the issues concerning them. Dahlgren (2009), for instance, made a veritable connection between the media and political engagement, indicating that there was a strong thread linking citizens with communication and democracy. One way of establishing a democratic government's attitude or posture toward this connection is through the state of the nation address. The address intersects politics and communication mediated and shaped by several factors and various kinds of relations involving the state, media, economy, sociocultural, and political factors (Benson, 2004; Schudson, 1994, 2000).

Since the First Republic of Dr. Kwame Nkrumah (1957–1966), all political regimes in Ghana have used the media to advance their causes. Dr. Nkrumah's socialist government, for example, used national newspapers, radio, and television to inform the people about the government's policies, programs, and achievements (Amoakohene, 2012). Similarly, the National Liberation Council (NLC) military government, which succeeded Dr. Nkrumah, used the media to propagate its ideas of free enterprise and other political and ideological objectives mainly as its publicity and propaganda tool. Both constitutional democratic governments of the Second and Third Republics of Dr. Kofi Abrefa Busia (1967–1972) and Dr. Hilla Limann (1979–1981) also used the cordial democratic atmosphere they created for media work to their advantage.

The 1970s and 1980s were considered "the doldrums of the press in Ghana" with a "culture of silence" (Ansu-Kyeremeh & Karikari, 1998, p. 3) during which the Acheampong and Rawlings regimes suppressed and controlled the media in order to use them to serve their purposes. Indeed, the tension and repression that characterized the media environment under General Ignatius Kutu Acheampong's and Flight-Lieutenant Jerry John Rawlings's regimes ensured that their programs and activities received the needed media attention. Such considerations of the political use of the media underscored Ghana's long tradition of state ownership (and control) of mass media, dating back to pre-independence times (Amoakohene, 2012).

Therefore, if repressive and unconstitutional regimes, which came to power on their own accord and without public legitimacy, found the media to be an important tool for publicizing their activities and for seeking support, it is even more critical for constitutionally elected governments to appreciate the role of the media in democratic governance. Such governments include all those in the Fourth Republic headed sequentially by Jerry John Rawlings (1993–2001), John Agyekum Kufuor (2001–2009), John Evans Atta Mills (2009–2012), John Dramani Mahama (2012–2017), and Nana Addo Dankwa Akufo-Addo (since January 2017). These governments have needed to build the consensus and support of the electorate both to advance their programs and to ensure victory in the next election in the four-year cycle.

## FOCUS OF THE ISSUE

The operating manual of the Fourth Republic of Ghana, the 1992 Constitution, among other things, recognizes the importance of free and unfettered communication by devoting chapter 12 to guarantee the "Freedom and Independence of the Media." Amoakohene (2012) indicates that chapter 12 contains some of the main principles of the Constitution, which seek to enhance democracy, freedoms, and rights, not only of the media but also of all citizens. The chapter also "details the structure of a National Media Commission charged with overseeing the press and appointing the board members of state-owned media" (Plattner, 2012, p. 68). The Constitution thus places some emphasis on communication, the mass media, and its watchdog role in society.

The impact of communication, particularly using the new media, on politics and democracy has been well documented (Dahlgren, 2013; Plattner, 2012; Hallin & Mancini, 2004; McNair, 2003; Blumler & Kavanagh, 1999). Indeed, in a communications revolution, one cannot help but communicate, and do so with clarity and purpose. Governments are required to build cohesion and oneness with the citizenry through communication, which is described as "an interaction that allows individuals, groups, and institutions to share ideas" (Hanson, 2011, p. 7) and as the glue that binds different levels/sectors of society together (Maneerat et al., 2005). The goal of communication is to make meaning and to achieve understanding through the use of words (language) or action (symbols and signs), as Gamble and Gamble (2013) point out.

Blumler and Kavanagh (1999) note the central role of media coverage in the political success of modern democratic and information societies. For their part, Deacon et al. (1999) explain that "[m]odern democracies depend on a media system that delivers accurate information and informed analysis and gives space to the broadest possible range of voices, opinions and perspectives" (p. 34). The state of the nation address has the potential to enable the media to do exactly that if they are properly recognized in such addresses. This is important because in modern democracies, governments, like all organizations, survive ultimately only by public consent; and this consent does not exist in a communication vacuum (Tymson & Lazar, 2002). Dahlgren (2013), for instance, points out that many forms of crises have led to people's apathy and estrangement from governments and from the political processes of their countries. Such crises include corruption and sometimes scandals of the political elite, which ultimately serve to alienate the citizenry from the government. Corruption, whether real or perceived is a burning issue in Ghanaian governance especially in the face of recent revelations implicating some in the public service, judiciary, and football administrations. The level of corruption is of such significant proportion to have attracted the appointment of a special prosecutor to investigate and deal with such cases.

In order to combat distrust and civic apathy, as well as to build assurances of probity and accountability, the onus falls on those in positions of responsibility to communicate transparency both through deed and through verbal communication. An important question needing attention is whether the governments of Ghana in the Fourth Republic have seen communication as having a role in the social and economic development of the country. Each of those five presidents has had an opportunity to deliver a state of the nation address to Parliament each year they have been in office. Although democratic participation involves more than access to the media, the free flow of information from the government to the citizenry and vice versa in a symmetric communication environment oils the wheels of democracy. The sessional address perhaps satisfies Saward's (1994) belief that "[t]here must be a constant and formal process of public notification of decisions, options, arguments, issues and outcomes" (p. 17) by governments. There are two important questions for which answers are sought, synthesized, and analyzed:

1. To what extent has a state of the nation address integrated or incorporated the media (and communication)?
2. To what extent did communication (or the media) constitute an important sector in those addresses?

## MODERN DEMOCRACIES, SESSIONAL ADDRESSES, AND COMMUNICATION

The concept of a modern democracy is based on the principle of representation where those elected by the people represent them in the legislature (Plattner, 2012). This idea of representation enables the governed to participate, or at least have a "share" and a say, in the government. Much of this is achieved through two-way communication between politicians and the electorate, subdivided into the trio of political parties, the mass media, and civil society, all of which have "profound effects upon the quality and sustainability of democracy" (Plattner, 2012, p. 66). The form of communication that ensues could be described as polyadic with the media often acting as pseudo-epicenters for the trio without which modern democracies cannot function. In Plattner's estimation, these "provide the channels through which the opinions of the people are formed and transmitted" (Plattner, 2012, p. 66). He sees the trio as constituting "the intermediate realms" which are "informal" and "interlinked" such that "changes in one of them usually affect the other two" (p. 67). In Ghana's politically liberalized system and deregulated media, multiple public spheres emerge to situate the media's agency in the political process within the political ecology. Although elsewhere, especially in the United States of America and much of the western world, political actors are increasingly "experimenting with new ways of circumventing the major media outlets and more directly reaching the voters" (Plattner, 2012, p. 70) via new media platforms such as Facebook, Twitter, and Instagram, many constraints in Ghana and other parts of Africa slow down any such usage. Constraints such as low education, poor economies, and limited access to technology, among other factors, make the mass media interface between politicians and the electorate necessary to provide reasonably reliable sources of news and information. Since the electorate ought to be *citizens* and not spectators, they need to be brought together as "part of a common enterprise" (Plattner, 2012, p. 71) through media agency that fosters a platform for public discourse involving a cross-section of the populace. This makes the media an important part of the sessional address which is one main platform for interaction between the government represented by the president, and the citizenry. It signals a media-friendly approach that indicates openness of governance and demonstrates that the government is providing more information to satisfy the publicity demand of democracy (Amoakohene, 2012).

## RELATED STUDIES

Among the studies that have looked at the state of the nation address, there is general agreement on its functionality as a communication tool geared towards articulating an intentional path to the development of the nation in a way that gives attention to the various sectors of the economy. Shogan (2015), for instance, found that the state of the union address of the United States was a communication between the president and congress in which the former would report on the state of the country and provide policy proposals for the ensuing legislative year. Klinogo (2016), though, believes presidents of many African countries present the state of the nation address to citizens yearly in order to communicate to them specific goals set for each sector. His analysis of President John Mahama's sixty-four-page state of the nation address delivered to Parliament on Thursday, February 25, 2016, aimed to discover how much developmental value, and per which sectors such value could be discerned.

The state of the nation address sets government priorities and provides updates on previous years' achievements. For state of the nation addresses to be successful, it is believed that while recounting past achievements, they ought to be visionary, paint a clear picture of future expectations, and demonstrate how to achieve them in ways that are reassuring (Sikanku & Boadi, 2018; Shogan, 2015). Shogan (2015) identified recurring thematic elements in U.S. sessional addresses as rhetoric about the past and future, bipartisanship, and optimism. Recounting past accomplishments and future goals, the address paid homage to historical achievements of the nation and its recurring national values. In the case of President Mahama's 2016 address, Klinogo (2016) identified priority areas as infrastructure, education, material supply to the health sector, and provision for the aged, the disabled, and head porters (kayaye).

Others included youth development, training programs, financial support and employment for the youth, as well as technological advancements in communication. In arriving at these priority areas, Klinogo (2016) considered the textual space allocated to each sector in terms of pages allotted: the more textual space given to a sector, the more important it was deemed to be. The highest textual space was devoted to infrastructural development while decentralization and security agencies got the least, perhaps because development of infrastructure directly or indirectly impacted other sectors. Between the highest and least covered were sectors such as good governance; health, agriculture, and the general economy; education and the electricity power crisis ("dumsɔ"); social protection (the aged, the marginalized, and the vulnerable); foreign relations; and youth and sports. It must be noted that although using textual space to judge the importance attached to issues covered in an address may yield insightful results, examining content and language or vocabulary used may be an even more important yardstick for measuring salience or significance. One may also combine both approaches in a single study.

In Shogan's (2015) view, the state of the nation address has the potential to strengthen a president's position as chief executive, using the address to convey policy priorities and also to publicize past achievements. In presidencies that have four-year terms with opportunity for reelection for a second term of office as pertains to Ghana, Kenya, and the United States, the year of an address defines and determines the mode and tone of delivery and communication. It is customary, according to Shogan (2015), that in the inaugural or first state of the nation address, presidents attempt to set the tone and tenor for their new administrations. So, most of the rhetoric contained in early term addresses tends to be forward-looking, as presidents discuss their positions on many policy issues in an attempt to direct the legislative agenda for the next four years. In the second and third years (midterm addresses), presidents tend to use a greater proportion of the address to claim credit by highlighting their policy achievements. These claims heighten in an election year to demonstrate preparedness to continue governing with an active and clear agenda if elected to a second term. However, discussion of elections is only done indirectly and with a non-partisan tone despite electoral considerations in the final year address (Shogan, 2015), essentially to establish a level playing field as constitutionally required without taking undue advantage of the opportunity granted by the sessional address.

Ways of ascertaining the veracity of claims made in addresses include parliamentary or congressional debates, the media (reporters, journalists), and researchers who regularly examine both the content and delivery styles of specific governments' state of the nation addresses (Sikanku & Boadi, 2018; Klinogo, 2016; Shogan, 2015; Attafuah, 2009). Websites like https://africacheck.org/ constantly verify reports and debates for key claims made in the yearly state of the nation addresses of various countries in Africa. Sikan-ku and Boadi (2018), for instance, found job creation, sanitation, and water, among other contents, and observed an appeal to national unity as a priority concern in President Akufo-Addo's 2018 state of the nation address.

Sometimes, presidents might miss an opportunity for specific content areas in their addresses. However, Sikanku and Boadi's (2018) suggestion that President Akufo-Addo missed an opportunity to play up national values and sentiments, to honor historical figures and to appeal to the nation's sense of patriotism is problematic because an "appeal to national unity" is about national values and patriotism. Besides, the address is meant to cover more tangible areas of governmental focus or emphasis, as evident in all twenty-six addresses studied for this chapter. Similarly, the authors' inability to identify any broad themes of the president's worldview or the framework guiding his presidency in their assessment of the 2018 address's stylistic and communicative elements is debatable. Indeed, important sectors such as sani-tation, the economy (economic performance), education, transportation (roads and railway), agriculture, the environment, security, housing, sports, gender, and Information and Communications Technologies (ICTs) were contained in the address.

Amoakohene (2012) noted two approaches to the media between the National Democratic Congress (NDC) and the New Patriotic Party (NPP), the two political parties that have so far formed governments in Ghana's Fourth Republic. Specifically, in relation to sessional addresses of 1993, 1994, 2001, and 2002, she found minimal emphasis on the media as both 1993 and 2002 addresses did not specifically mention the media. In 1993, President Rawlings talked about "the need to broaden the composition of the National Media Commission to make it a truly democratic framework for regulating the activities of the media" (p. 16). Although he said, "an environ-ment of free exchange of views" (p. 38) was necessary for democracy, his address did not specifically mention the media. That of 1994 was rather more threatening: "Destructive, distorted and often outright untrue stories continue to fill some sections of the media with obvious political bias. . . .We need the media to contribute to the creation of a positive national democratic culture, propped by truth, objectivity and decency" (p. 2). Conversely, President Kufuor's address of 2001 provided the impetus for increased media activity, freedoms, and involvement in political discourse by noting,

> Set free, I have no doubt our media will play their honourable role with a heightened sense of responsibility. We shall expand the boundaries of freedom by repealing the laws that criminalize speech and expression. Mr. Speaker, the Criminal Libel Law will be repealed as a mark of confidence in a responsible media.

However, that of 2002 discussed good governance from various perspectives but excluded any mention of the media. It talked about security, public services, local government, judiciary, legal services, and many more sectors, focusing on activities aimed at economic recovery without assigning any role for the media. So, the question worth pondering over or answering is this: How much media or communication is contained in various state of the nation addresses and for what purpose?

## METHOD

The study that informed this chapter examined texts of all twenty-six state of the nation addresses delivered to parliament by five presidents of Ghana. It noted areas or sectors covered in each address and examined text extracts that specifically focused on communication, media, and any of the twelve search words considered reasonably similar in meaning, as well as the extent of their coverage. A qualitative study using both content and textual analyses examined the contents of the twenty-six state of the nation addresses from 1993 to 2018 for the importance each address attached to communication and the media. It used the following search words: "communication," "information," "mass media," "broadcasting," "radio," "television," "newspaper," "journalist," "journalism," "news," "digital," and "telecommunication" to detect the presence of communication or any of its related words in the address. These words were believed to be either synonymous with or similar in meaning to "communication" and "media," the two words that formed the thrust of the study. For each mention of the above-listed words, the whole paragraph was extracted and studied in-depth to assess the place of communication and/or media in each address, and for that matter in government priority or emphasis.

In the twenty-six-years' state of the nation addresses, five presidents from the National Democratic Congress (NDC) and the New Patriotic Party (NPP) were studied. Political power in Ghana changed hands four times, alternating between the NDC and the NPP during the period. Flight-Lieutenant Jerry John Rawlings (NDC) and Mr. John Agyekum Kufuor (NPP) each served two terms of office totaling eight years and gave eight addresses each. For their part, Professor John Evans Atta Mills and Mr. John Dramani Mahama (both NDC) served one term of office each and so met this constitutional requirement four times apiece. At the time of this study, the president, Nana Addo Dankwa Akufo-Addo (NPP), had only been in office for nineteen months and had delivered two addresses so far to Parliament. In all, the NDC gave sixteen addresses while the NPP gave ten. All these state of the nation addresses were examined for their mention and import of communication and the media.

## FINDINGS

Whereas communication and the media never constituted stand-alone sectors on which any president focused attention, certain sectors, including telecommunications/ICTs, pervaded all sessional addresses. These sectors included the economy, health, education, water (and sometimes sanitation), agriculture/food security, employment (unemployment and labor), the private sector, the public sector, roads (and transport), and governance and foreign relations (policy). Added to these were concerns about mining, energy, power, housing, trade, industry, and investments. Any mention of the media or communication was in relation to telecommunications and ICTs, which appeared to engage the attention of all presidents in nearly all state of the nation addresses and under which media/communication was sometimes mentioned. Other mentions of the media were situated within the remit or mandate of the National Media Commission (NMC), a constitutional body set up to, among other functions, (a) promote and ensure the freedom and independence of the media; (b) ensure . . . the highest journalistic standards in the mass media; and (c) insulate the state-owned media from governmental control (article 167 of 1992 Constitution of the Republic of Ghana). Findings have not only separated the two political parties (NDC and NPP) that have formed governments in the Fourth Republic, they have also examined sessional addresses delivered by each president per year to determine any similarities and differences over time.

## PRESIDENT JERRY JOHN RAWLINGS (NDC): 1993–2000

The "media" was only mentioned in the 1993 sessional address of President Rawlings in the context of an expanded composition of the NMC for the purposes of its regulatory responsibility. Other concerns raised were about telecommunications; telecommunication networks; telecommunication infrastructure; and a desire to "review the existing telecommunication and broadcasting framework including existing legislation with the view of creating the enabling environment for the accelerated provision of reliable and efficient services. In 1994, the address highlighted the media's agency in creating a positive national democratic culture, propped by truth, objectivity and decency" as a result of which "[D]estructive, distorted and often outright untrue stories . . . with obvious political bias could not be allowed to persist." This veiled threat appeared ominous enough to define President Rawlings's media relations. Although his 1995 address did not specifically mention the media, it did say something about information and communication in reference to broadcasting guidelines and bills expected to be introduced or passed by Parliament aimed at enhancing communication between the government and the citizenry. He recalled his government's policy on private broadcasting which had already been outlined before the House and noted the need for specific guidelines:

> While the National Communication Authority Bill will address some of the regulatory issues, it is the considered view that there is the need for a well-defined set of guidelines for independent broadcast services. The government will introduce a Bill to this effect once a consensus is arrived at by the relevant bodies. . . . Similarly, a Bill designed to create a more efficient information service machinery to enhance the channels of communication between government and the people will be laid before Parliament for consideration. (President Rawlings's 1995 State of the Nation Address)

The 1995 address also talked about the separation of Ghana Postal Services Corporation from Telecommunications Services of the former Posts and Telecommunication Corporation (P & T) meant "for greater efficiency and cost-effectiveness while increasing the availability of telecommunication facilities throughout the country." Expectedly, therefore, the 1996 address referred to the doubling of telecommunication capacity in the previous year and a new telecommunications policy designed to involve private participation "to ensure competition, efficiency, and rapid expansion of services throughout the country." Expectations of expanded services usually came with concerns of misuse and abuse due to insecurity arising out of a general apprehension of their exploitation and the need to protect data and people's privacy. This was to be dealt with by an "Authority" and the address did not lose sight of the regulation of the sector. He noted that it was expected that a number of outstanding issues that related to the National Communication Authority Bill would be resolved in order to make it possible for the establishment of the "Authority" that will regulate the development of the sector.

With specific regard to the media, President Rawlings indicated that his government's pledge to the independence and freedom of the media had been adequately demonstrated. He however noted that that like sections of the public, he was deeply troubled about incongruous material and lack of decorum that was beginning to harm consumers. He noted,

> Whilst the government acknowledges the contribution of those media which have kept us on our toes with constructive and productive criticism, we hope that those practitioners who find it hard to distinguish between freedom and license will show more social responsibility in the year ahead.
>
> With the opening-up of broadcasting to the private sector, we are already witnessing healthy competition and greater creativity in our airwaves. At the same time, some public concern has already been expressed about some of the material entering our homes.

> A broadcasting policy framework designed to address this and other con-
> cerns for now and the future will be made public in the course of the year.
> (President Rawlings's 1996 State of the Nation Address)

In the second term of Rawlings's presidency (1997–2000), there was a shift
in focus from the euphoria surrounding issues about independent broadcasting and increases in the number of radio stations (1997–1998) to the result of
implemented policies regarding the telecommunications industry
(1999–2000). In spite of references to the new telecommunications policy,
and the "rapid expansion, variety and improved quality of telecommunication services," the announcement of a strategic investor and regulation by the
National Communications Authority, the thrust of the 1997 address, insofar
as it related to communication, was on the NMC, broadcasting and privately
owned/commercial independent radio stations. He indicated that "one of the
most remarkable features of our new democracy has been the emergence of a
free and vibrant broadcast system," a fact that has been widely acknowledged
(Amoakohene, 2012; Ayee, 2001; Ansu-Kyeremeh & Karikari, 1998). He
added that in "two years, we have seen the transformation of our airwaves
through a network of independent radio stations, providing a mix of information, entertainment and education not only in the nation's capital but at a
number of regional centres."

The president could not "lose sight of the need for a well-defined regulatory framework" and so turned his attention to the National Media Commission:

> We are all anxious to enhance the freedom of the press as one of the pillars of
> our democracy. The framers of our constitution gave us an institution, the
> National Media Commission to take on the dual function of protecting the
> freedom of the press and protecting the people from infringement of their
> freedom arising from abuses of press freedom. Such a task requires a high
> sense of responsibility, sound grounding in the ethics of the media, an even-
> handed disposition and a commitment to justice and fairness.

The following statements in the address provide some proof of the president's contentious (even caustic) relations with the first commission chaired
by Professor Kofi Kumado:

> There is the tendency to yield to the temptation to play to the gallery by
> creating the impression that we can best discharge our duties if we are seen to
> be in conflict with government. That tendency undermines our credibility and
> inevitably affects our capacity to perform our duties satisfactorily. It may have
> caused the Commission to lose the opportunity to establish the moral authority
> that would have enabled both media practitioners and the public to crave its
> adjudication and subsequently accept to be bound or influenced by them. As a

result, people have preferred to resort to the established courts of law in the search for the protection of their reputations and freedoms.

It is my hope that the new Media Commission will take a cue from the past and establish a new moral authority that will enable it to fulfil its functions. It will have to show the courage to call for respect for truth and the highest professional ethics. This is the way to ensure that the expansion of the frontiers of press freedom will not mean the contraction of the liberty of the individual.

The 1998 address provided details of achievements already recorded as a result of wise "communication and information policies" that stressed "the best modern information technology as well as information dissemination." The president reported "19 radio and 3 TV stations" as well as "136,600 telephone lines with 88,515 subscribers" up from "only 70,000 lines just under a year ago before the P&T Corporation was partly divested" with "plans to provide an additional 50,000 lines and 1,500 pay-phones by the end of 1998." The president, however, raised concerns about lack of regulation and indicated his government's desire to fix it:

But as we acknowledge the emergence of a new broadcasting industry which has in turn given great stimulus to the advertising industry, we cannot lose sight of the need for a well-defined regulatory framework. Accordingly, we will put before parliament, comprehensive proposals for the regulation of the broadcasting industry as is done worldwide. We shall also undertake the review of outmoded legislations including the Cinematography Act. (President Rawlings's 1997 State of the Nation Address)

The 1998 address also reported the introduction, during the year, of a National Communications Policy to "take account of the liberalized communication environment as well as the technological developments in the sector." Furthermore, the "Ministry of Communications plans to ensure accessibility to and application of information technologies" in addition to "promoting the use of communication technology in public offices."

President Rawlings's apprehension of media freedom was clear in these addresses, particularly that of 1997. Not only did he fear possible media irresponsibility, something he was anxious about, he was also concerned about commissioners of the National Media Commission (NMC) abusing their positions for political gains and personal aggrandizement. Rawlings's preoccupation with media irresponsibility should be placed within the context of weakened governmental controls and some media excesses of the 1990s with newly introduced freedoms after over a decade of suppression. Ansu-Kyeremeh and Karikari (1998) noted that the state stranglehold on the media ceased to exist after the repeal of the newspaper licensing law (PNDCL 211) in 1992, as well as liberalization of the airwaves and media pluralism in the first half of that decade. In Amoakohene's (2012) estimation, the ability of both the state and the market to control or limit free expression was thereby substantially reduced in the newly liberated media environment. However, media offenses were either reported to the NMC or the law courts for prosecution making the early years of media pluralism and liberalization some of the most difficult, according to Amoakohene (2012).

Documents Amoakohene (2012) reviewed showed the 1990s as the period during which the most cases were brought against the media both before the NMC and the law courts with some court cases ending in the imprisonment of some editors and journalists. It is within this media environment that Rawlings's concerns find some legitimacy. "We are all anxious to enhance the freedom of the press as one of the pillars of our democracy," he indicated and noted the duality of the National Media Commission's function of protecting both the press and the people from infringement of their freedom arising out of abuses of press freedom. President Rawlings added, "Such a task requires high sense of responsibility, sound grounding in the ethics of media, an even-handed disposition and a commitment to justice and fairness." To him, the "worst thing that can happen" to the NMC was for "those who are privileged to serve on it to see it as another vehicle in the pursuit of some grand political design, an instrument of political warfare, in combat with government and other interests, and some self-serving medium for the upliftment of individual egos." Regulation, to him, was therefore the way to go.

In 1999 and 2000, the focus of the address was principally on the telecommunication sector with the president reporting in 1999 that a "National Communication Policy developed during 1998" was awaiting the approval of cabinet. Improvements in Ghana Telecom's performance since its privatization had resulted in targets being exceeded. The president hoped improved telecommunication facilities would be used "to enhance the image of Ghana as an investment destination while at the same time, safeguarding against the criminal misuse of these technological innovations."

Therefore, while touting rapid developments in the telecommunications industry, especially increases in the number and spread of telephone lines and the Internet, the 2000 address also expressed concern about abuse of broadcasting facilities. The president was concerned that "the prerogatives of the market and thereby profit" had become "a defining factor in the broadcast industry" such that "very little circumspection" was exercised in what was broadcast to listeners which did not "measure up to their responsibility" and "our cultural values." He observed that the media owed "a responsibility to use the medium to promote unity, stability and social cohesion" rather than "gratuitous insult to other Ghanaians." Guidelines put in place to regulate the broadcasting industry were expected to reflect and address such concerns.

# PRESIDENT JOHN AGYEKUM KUFUOR (NPP): 2001–2008

All of President Kufuor's state of the nation addresses were very lean on media and communication. Only sporadic references were made to the telecommunications industry and ICTs with expanded space for the use of technology such as the mobile phone and e-commerce via the Internet as "the elements that can and must play a role in our arsenal of economic rejuvenation." The pronouncement in the 2001 address of the repeal of the criminal libel law was, however, canonical; a most significant achievement on the media front.

Even though concerned about economic recovery, Kufuor's 2002 address found no overt role for the media but focused on telecommunications and expansion of the ICT sector to allow for greater participation and competition to "accelerate access to telephones, Internet and information technology throughout the country." The same issues occupied his addresses of 2003 to 2008 without any mention of the media. He talked about "a communication infrastructure company," the "communication industry," and "communication service providers" (2003); the commissioning of a "Multi-Media Centre . . . to serve as an incubator wherein private companies in the ICT industry can be nurtured" (2004); and plans advanced "to rapidly improve the telecom infrastructure" (2005). Given the contexts of their use, all these references to "communication" appear to relate to "telecommunications."

In 2006, President Kufuor indicated an extension of a "[f]ibre optic backbone to cover the entire nation" and "enable the citizenry to access affordable broadband connectivity." In 2007, he disclosed that his government had secured a concessionary loan facility to "ensure that every District has access to high speed Internet connection and promote a wider penetration of ICT services throughout the country." The last (2008) address stated, "[G]overnment is endeavoring to make information and communication technology available to large sections of the society." In fact, this theme of *access to* and *expansion of* ICTs for job creation permeated all of Kufuor's addresses during his two terms of office.

# PRESIDENT JOHN EVANS ATTA MILLS (NDC): 2009–2012

President Mills's four addresses (2009–2012) returned the focus to the media without any mention of ICTs, although in 2010 his very brief mention of communication focused on infrastructure stating, "[W]e will facilitate the development of a reliable, cost-effective and world-class communications infrastructure." His 2009 address provided the most comprehensive coverage of the media and also the most reassuring except for Kufuor's 2001 address announcing the repeal of the criminal libel law.

We will continue to respect the diversity and independence of the media and in shaping opinion in our democracy. A credible media is reflected in the quality of information they process for the consumption of the public and as a Government, we recognize our responsibility to be accessible to the media in order to bridge the information gap. In the course of the year, I will begin a monthly radio broadcast to the nation as part of measures to enhance communication with the citizenry.

The media's shortfalls were not lost on the president in 2009 as he encouraged them to deal with their own weaknesses while holding governments to account as expected by the Constitution:

In as much as we all value accountability of government and free expression, we expect the media to look at its own inadequacies and endeavor to reconnect with the mass of citizens and to live by the tenets such as its own ethical code and the constitutional obligations enshrined in the 1992 Constitution.

President Mills also announced other media-friendly measures designed to "address transparency through a three-dimensional approach." These were "[e]nsuring the passage of the Freedom of Information Act," "[e]xpediting the passing of a National Broadcasting Law," and "[e]laboration of a Code of Conduct in Government that includes key information disclosure, ethics and anti-corruption measures." Together, the president believed "these measures will enable both citizens and statutory Constitutional bodies to access the needed information to demand accountability from office-holders in the public and private sectors."

In 2011 and 2012, President Mills returned to the subject of media responsibility, though the 2012 address also gave an update on progress made in ICTs and the telecommunications industry. In 2011, the president made the following observation:

[A]ll of us subscribe to the rule of law and free speech. It is however, not enough to believe or proclaim, but rather to practice one's belief in an acceptable and peaceful manner. Political stability is a gift of political discipline by all actors. Those of us in leadership positions bear the heaviest burden in ensuring that our actions and utterances do not incite lawlessness and damage our sense of community.

The media has a huge responsibility in the effort we must all make to encourage rational exchanges among reasonable people with different views. Let us all keep one thing in mind; just because you have the right to say something does not mean you should. Exercising good judgment is important. We must not always find fault with each other; sometimes it also helps to tell stories about Ghanaians rising to the occasion. The draft Broadcasting Bill has been too long on the drawing board. It is time to consider seriously its enactment to help control the excesses that sometimes characterize exchanges in the electronic media.

The concerns raised in President Mills's last sessional address in 2012, in addition to media responsibility as indicated above, was on technology, that is, digital broadcasting along with information and communication technologies. The president mentioned the media as among "four critical matters that should engage our attention in this Election Year." After the judiciary's role in the expeditious settlement of election disputes as the first, the second was "the role of the media in the elections." He stated,

> Polarized or not; aligned or not; biased or not; the Ghanaian media has a responsibility to work to preserve Ghana's democracy. Speaking for myself, I have confidence in the ability of my brothers and sisters in the media to rise to the occasion. On the perception of polarization, alignment and bias, however, the media has to speak for itself through its deeds.

## PRESIDENT JOHN DRAMANI MAHAMA (NDC): 2013–2016

President John Mahama, who took over from President John Atta Mills, also served one term of office and gave four state of the nation addresses from 2013 to 2016. In 2013, although the address focused on progress made in the telecommunications sector, it found space for the media, its standards and regulatory framework.

> Mr. Speaker, the Broadcasting Bill has been on the drawing board for a long time. We must hasten to pass the Bill so that national standards for the electronic media can be established. The newly established Media Development Fund aimed at improving capacity within the media will be operationalized this year.
>
>   We shall also support the National Media Commission to enact the needed Regulations that will establish an organizational framework and standards to ensure balance, fairness, access, opportunity and objectivity in the media.

President Mahama also announced that access to "[c]ommunity radio will be improved to allow millions more to benefit from the unique attributes of this medium" and indicated, "I will implement the Freedom of Information Act as soon as it is passed by Parliament." In 2014, however, the media were left out of the sessional address while emphasis was placed on the expansion of and access to ICTs with such phrases as "infrastructural expansion"; "mobile telephony"; "to further expand access to broadband infrastructure for increased Internet access in the country"; and "the construction of the Eastern Corridor Fibre Optic network."

   The 2015 address continued in the same "ICT and Telecommunication sector" vein with the additional introduction of phrases like "fibre optic project"; "information superhighway"; "digital economy"; "a growing telecommunications industry"; and "a dynamic regulatory framework." It also reported the introduction of four policies in the ICT sector: "The Mobile Virtual Network Operating License"; "The Interconnect Clearing House License"; "The International Wholesale Carrier License"; and "the Unified Telecom License." These policies were also reported in the 2016 address. There was also the construction of "Community Information Centres"; all in an attempt "to use the medium of ICT to promote an all-inclusive information and knowledge society to benefit underserved and un-served communities."

President Mahama's last sessional address (2016), while continuing with the same telecommunication and ICT theme "as foundations for a strong digital ICT market," also discussed the importance of the media to Ghana's democracy. The president spoke about the establishment of a "Government Online Portal—the e-Services portal—to provide Government services online. He envisioned "paperless" parliamentary and cabinet sessions; an "expansion in mobile and fixed broadband including 4G LTE"; "the establishment of the National Data Centre among others"; the blossoming of "Ghana's digital economy" and the reality that "more digital jobs are being created with every click of the button." In order "to ensure digital inclusion," his government was training more girls in ICT. Finally, as relates to this sector, the president went back to the NDC government's pet subject of regulation stating, "A growing telecommunications industry requires a dynamic regulatory framework."

President Mahama subsequently reported on bills still being considered including "the Right to Information Bill . . . still in Parliament." On this bill, he commented, "Indeed, I think the Right to Information Bill by the time it is passed, will go down in the history of this country as the longest bill ever under Parliamentary consideration." With this, the president turned his attention to the media raising concerns about "concocted allegations and other salacious fabrications anonymously circulated on social media under the masthead of fake newspapers," which hinder the fight against corruption by "making it difficult to differentiate what is truth, and what is political propaganda." He further admonished, "Similarly, sweeping and generalized conclusions drawn on the basis of scanty and often misleading information ought to be guarded against." Again, the president warned against the use of insults and inappropriate language in the media: "I wish to ask the media to be circumspect in the use of language, and to avoid insults." In spite of these concerns, there was praise for the media's boundary-spanning role and performance as conveyor of messages from politicians to the electorate.

> Mr. Speaker, I want, on behalf of all Ghanaians, to salute the media for the good work they have been doing in communicating our voices to the electorate. I believe that as they have done in the last elections, this year, again, they

will be a useful conduit for sending the messages of political parties to the electorate.

## PRESIDENT NANA ADDO DANKWA AKUFO-ADDO (NPP): 2017–2018

In Nana Akufo-Addo's inaugural state of the nation address in 2017, there was no mention of either the media or telecommunications. His 2018 address, however, found space for ICTs and telecommunications. It mentioned "the advance of technology"; "[t]he cyber population, that is busy on Facebook, Twitter, Instagram, WhatsApp and other social media outlets"; and "the virtual world." President Akufo-Addo was excited that "[m]ore and more of us are banking, and paying our bills, online" and that "[a] wealth of knowledge and information is now available on the net to make teaching and learning easier." He recounted other benefits of technological innovations to the country: "The start of the digital address system, the introduction of paperless transactions at our ports, the rapid and continuing spread of broadband services are all helping to formalize and modernize our economy." There was also "the development of a technology park" to make all these services readily available and accessible. "In their own way, these modern communication tools are opening up our country and the world to us all," President Akufo-Addo indicated. In spite of these many benefits, however, the president did not lose sight of the hazards of technology. He expressed these downsides and his government's attempts at confronting them as follows:

> Unfortunately, and predictably, a whole new set of dangers of cyber insecurity and fraud have emerged with these modern tools. We are working to strengthen cyber security to build confidence and protect the use of electronic communications in national development and ensure that our young technologically savvy people would keep Ghana firmly in the exciting IT economy and its many opportunities.

## DISCUSSION

President Rawlings's first-term state of the nation addresses (1993–1996) could be described as the experimental stages of the implementation of the Constitution and its provisions and requirements and Amoakohene's (2012) observation of President Rawlings's (1993) reference to broadening the composition of the National Media Commission (NMC) for the purposes of making the commission truly democratic for regulating the media should be seen in/from this perspective. Similarly, the president's 1994, 1995, and 1996 concerns and direction to and about the media should be placed in this context. The period coincided with radical changes in communication on the international stage and President Rawlings's review of the existing telecommunications and broadcasting framework was done to reflect those international concerns for free speech and expression, media liberalization, and expanded access. Nonetheless, it is noteworthy that he refused to sign the original National Communications Authority (NCA) bill because the NMC was mentioned in it but signed a later version with NMC removed.

President Rawlings disagreed with the suggestion that the NMC, rather than the NCA, should manage and allocate broadcasting frequencies as proposed and submitted by some media institutions, including the then School of Communication Studies at the University of Ghana. Among other things, this was to enable the NMC to effectively monitor media and sanction noncompliance using frequency allocation in the performance of its functions as prescribed by the Constitution. The president was uncomfortable with and averse to the level of independence exercised by the commission, which would not yield to his control. In fact, President Rawlings and the first NMC had a tension-filled relationship as could be gleaned from his references to the commission in his 1993 and 1997 state of the nation addresses. In 1993, he hinted at amending the Constitution to expand the membership of the NMC saying , "[W]e may need to consider revisions to the Constitution in accordance with the Constitution itself" and actually succeeded in doing so to bring the membership of the NMC from fifteen to eighteen with a broadened composition. The 1997 address was even more explicit on the president's dissatisfaction with the Commission, as observed from his expectations of the new commission as compared to the performance of the previous one.

Media regulation, whether in terms of broadcasting or telecommunications, appeared to be President Rawlings's pet subject concerning communication, and justifiably so given the media's important role in Ghana's Fourth Republic. Amoakohene (2012) recounted studies that indicated the mass media's central role in Ghana's transition to democracy and transformation. She noted that they served as catalysts for speedy dissemination of information as well as platforms for discussion of national and international issues thanks to media pluralism and liberalization of the airwaves. The media were instrumental in safeguarding Ghana's democracy through playing their watchdog role, thereby ensuring political accountability, promoting active and empowered citizens through the provision of information and fora for discussion, as well as by providing a voice for the voiceless, especially at those early stages. They were even credited with a change of government through the ballot box in the 2000 elections: "The mass media have been touted as the institution which largely contributed to the defeat of the NDC" (Ayee, 2001, p. 6).

In spite of its importance, the media, as a sector, did not appear to be a policy priority of NPP governments, as their ten sessional addresses (eight by President Kufuor and two by President Akufo-Addo) showed. The party's initial media-friendly approach through the repeal of the criminal libel law in its maiden state of the nation address in 2001 was not followed by any such commitments in subsequent addresses. Nonetheless, Amoakohene (2012) reported on the Kufuor government's media-friendliness in many other ways, including traveling with Ghanaian journalists and without being biased toward them. Note that the NDC excluded what they deemed unfriendly media houses, whereas the Kufuor government opened the seat of government to Ghanaian media practitioners. Reading through the sessional addresses, it was obvious that the media's importance to NDC governments was more in terms of regulation, ostensibly to rein the media in, than it was in terms of attempts at developing the sector or engendering a rapprochement.

Shogan's (2015) observation that in fourth-year addresses (which also constitute the election year in many democracies including Ghana and the United States (where Shogan's study was based)), if election issues are mentioned and discussed at all, they are done in a non-partisan manner using a bipartisan tone. Shogan's observation was obvious in all but two such addresses as related to the media. In this regard, we recall Presidents Rawlings, Mills, and Mahama's confidence in, and appeals to the media in their 1996, 2000, 2012, and 2016 addresses. President Rawlings's election year addresses of 1996 and 2000, for instance, showed concerns about the media in ways that reflected the general mood of all political parties in the country. In the 1996 address, insofar as it related to communication, it was all-encompassing, focusing on both telecommunication and the media with references to the "National Communications Authority Bill"; "communication technology"; "broadcasting"; and "commitment to the independence of the media." In 2000, while stating commitment to "modernizing the facilities of the Ghana Broadcasting Corporation (GBC) to enable it to fulfil its mission not only as a public service broadcaster but also as a standard-bearer in our world of broadcasting," he bemoaned the lack of "circumspection in what is broadcast" to listeners.

Similarly, sentiments expressed by Presidents Mills and Mahama (both of the NDC), regarding the media in their election year addresses, were shared with many in the country. President Mills in 2012, for example, considered the media as one of "four critical matters that should engage our attention in this election year." The other three were the judiciary, "the state of industrial relations in an election year," and "chieftaincy disputes and ethnic conflict." He had confidence in the media's ability "to work to preserve Ghana's democracy." For his part, President Mahama's acknowledgement of the contributions of the media to democratic participation and appeal to their sense of judgement and decorum in his 2016 address was strikingly similar to those made earlier by President Rawlings in 1996.

It must be stated, though, that the import of President Mills' acknowledgement of the media was similar to both his predecessor (President Rawlings) and successor (President Mahama) although expressed in consonance with his calm demeanor. On the other hand, neither of President Kufuor's election year addresses of 2004 and 2008 acknowledged the media or appealed to their sense of responsibility. They did not even mention the media but only reported on progress made in the ICT sector. In fact, apart from the 2001 address, no other one of the eight that President Kufuor delivered made the media an important sector to report on. Similarly, neither of the two sessional addresses delivered so far by President Akufo-Addo has mentioned the media. However, because functional democratic governance requires an informed citizenry and an empowered media, communication (not just telecommunications or ICTs, which are only ways of making communication faster) must be central to ensuring popular participation in political processes and policy making.

As Gbensuglo (2015) noted, it is essential to ensure that the governing processes are open, transparent, and inclusive of all legitimate interests and that the state is responsive to the different needs of society. Communication is required to improve relations between citizens and the government to enable the two sides work together for the general good. The state requires the support of its citizens to solve society's problems and to provide remedies for the deficits of democracy (Gbensuglo, 2015). Not acknowledging the importance of the media or communication to be reflected in sessional addresses is potentially harmful to democratic governance, particularly to the fortunes of political actors.

Shogan's (2015) observation that, while inaugural addresses have sought to set the tone for the ensuing years of the term of office, mid-term addresses have focused on past achievements, may be partially true given that the examination of the twenty-six sessional addresses in Ghana relating to communication and to the NDC and NPP governments proved Shogan's observation to be true. President Rawlings's maiden state of the nation address (1993) established his preoccupation with the media and its regulation. From telecommunications (networks, infrastructure, and facilities) to broadcasting (framework), to the media and the National Media Commission (NMC), nothing about communication escaped his attention. His first address in his second term (1997) simply expounded on these earlier concerns in the communications sector with greater emphasis on broadcasting (system, industry, and regulation), radio stations, ethics of the media, and the NMC than on telecommunications and the new telecommunications policy.

However, President Kufuor's announcement of the repeal of the criminal libel law in his inaugural state of the nation address (2001) was not followed by any attention to the media in subsequent addresses. As Amoakohene (2012) indicated, Kufuor's 2002 address did not make any mention of the media although it discussed good governance from various perspectives including security, public services, local government, and judiciary and legal services. Nonetheless, the president's excitement about technology and the use of ICTs for various purposes was reflected in an elaboration of his government's attention to developments and expansion of the sector in his 2005 and all other addresses.

On his part, President Mills's initial (2009) promise "to respect the diversity and independence of the media" appeared to be a theme that kept recurring in all his four addresses. Each of his addresses, except that of 2010, mentioned the media, radio, and broadcasting. In 2010, the address briefly indicated an attempt to "facilitate the development of a reliable, cost-effective and world-class communications infrastructure."

President Mahama's unique attribute as a professional communicator somewhat impacted his focus on the media and communication. His maiden state of the nation address focused on both the media (community radio) and telecommunications (ICT infrastructure and expansion) with mentions of the Freedom of Information Bill, Broadcasting Bill, Media Development Fund, and the National Media Commission. However, the theme of communication/media only resurfaced in his last address in 2016, whereas ICTs and telecommunications constituted the main thrust of his focus on communication in both the 2014 and 2015 addresses. As regards President Akufo-Addo's inaugural address (2017), as already indicated, there was no mention of communication (whether media or ICTs), although like the others, it touched on all other sectors, especially those relating to finance, security, energy, and power supply.

## CONCLUSIONS AND RECOMMENDATIONS

The NDC governments' sixteen state of the nation addresses paid greater attention to the media than the NPP's ten addresses (because NDC has been in political office longer than the NPP), only one of which (Kufuor's 2001 address) focused on the media's freedom from criminal prosecution for publications. Generally, however, compared to other sectors covered in those addresses, the media and communication did not appear to occupy much significant space. It could be surmised that the NPP presidents' very scanty mentions of the media were the result of *a laissez-faire* attitude or posture, while the NDC presidents' preoccupation with media responsibility/irresponsibility and regulation could be interpreted as a fear of the power of the media, particularly of radio broadcasting.

Be that as it may, presidents of the NDC, in general, addressed the media much more directly and concretely than the NPP, indicating how they expected them to contribute to advancing the national cause. Thus, the NDC focused more on media control than did the NPP. The NDC governments used more words to refer to media responsibility, irresponsibility, and their pet subject of regulation, which appeared more times in their addresses than in those of the NPP governments. Considering the often-menacing manner of such media references, especially under President Rawlings, however, it is doubtful what impact his appeals to the media yielded. To ascertain this, it might require another study that interviews media practitioners and/or analyzes media content in the weeks and months following the sessional address as well as examines the contents of the address as they relate to the media and communication.

Given its annual ritual and the wide publicity and discussions it engenders, it may be useful to consciously approach the state of the nation address as a communication space where audiences of all types converge to discuss what is essential to all citizens and thus to impact public opinion. Presidents should give equal attention to all sectors of the economy in their state of the nation addresses to avoid marginalizing any sector. With specific reference to the communication sector, it is important to understand that ICTs or advances in technology are but one of three influencers of the media. The other two are economic development and alterations in the shape of society (Plattner, 2012).

Unduly emphasizing technology or telecommunications/ICTs to the near exclusion of the media thus misaligns the cardinal role of communications in society and its place in the sessional address. As journalism tilts more towards infotainment, increasing cynicism (especially of the political elite), and more-episodic-than-thematic coverage (Schudson, 2005), politicians need to engage more rather than disengage from the media. It is important to note that the media legitimizes events, sources, listeners, readers, and viewers essentially through positive reportage and repeated coverage; has the capacity to add to information presented; and does not only organize news and information but also organizes audiences (Schudson, 2011) who may largely be the electorates that presidents indirectly try to reach through their sessional addresses.

Official government sources, such as the state of the nation address, provide what Gandy (1982) referred to as information subsidies, which in Schudson's (2011) view constitute the largest amount of news for reporters and thus dominate what is fed to audiences as news, which is a product of transactions between journalists/reporters and their sources. Presidents must capitalize on this to take advantage of the central and indispensable role of the media in modern democracies to promote active and empowered citizens. Regularly featuring the media as a necessary sector in sessional addresses would enable the Ghanaian media to take advantage of the importance of official sources of information as opposed to what Amoakohene (2012) described as "traditionally uncooperative and hostile officialdom."

Increased rapprochement between politicians and the media has the capability of reducing skepticism of and about politicians and official information, mutual mistrust and suspicion, access restrictions, and subsequently help to increase dependence on sources for news (both political and non-political). A broadened definition of the media to encompass mainstream practitioners, citizen journalists, bloggers, and other new media operatives is needed by presidents and their governments to publicize their plans, activities, and actions. Furthermore, they need the media to combat "fake news," lies and allegations of corruption, join hands to fight illegal activities such as illegal mining (popularly referred to as "galamsey," an intractable problem in Ghana), and to make the government look more attractive.

## REFERENCES

Amoakohene, M. I. (2012). *Political Communication in Ghana's Emerging Democracy.* Saarbrücken, Germany: LAP LAMBERT Academic Publishing.
Ansu-Kyeremeh, K., & Kwame Karikari. (1998). *Media Ghana: Ghanaian Media Overview, Practitioners and Institutions.* Legon, Accra: School of Communication Studies Press.
Attafueh, Kenneth Agyemang. (October 16, 2009). "Ethnic Diversity, Democratization, and Nation-Building in Ghana." *The Future of Africa.*
Ayee, J. R. A. (2001). Introduction. In J. R. A. Ayee (ed.), *Deepening Democracy in Ghana: Politics of the 2000 Elections,* Vol. One. Accra: Freedom Publication Ltd.
Benson, Rodney. (2004). "Bringing the Sociology of Media Back in." *Political Communication* 21: 275–292.
Blumler, Jay G., & Dennis Kavanagh. (1999). "The Third Age of Political Communication: Influences and Features." *Political Communication* 16(3): 209–230.
Dahlgren, Peter. (2009). *Media and Political Engagement: Citizens, Communication, and Democracy.* Cambridge: University Press.
Dahlgren, Peter. (2013). *The Political Web: Media, Participation and Alternative Democracy.* Basingstoke: Palgrave Macmillan.
Deacon, D., M. Pickering, P. Golding, & G. Murdock. (1999). *Researching Communications: A Practical Guide to Methods in Media and Cultural Analysis.* London: Arnold.
Gamble, T. K., & M. Gamble. (2013). *Communication Works.* New York: McGraw-Hill.
Gandy, Oscar H., Jr. (1982). *Beyond Agenda Setting: Information Subsidies and Public Policy.* Norwood, New Jersey: Ablex Publishing Company.
Gbensuglo, A. B. (2015, June). "Governance and Socio-Economic Development Debate in Sub-Saharan Africa: Issues and Perspectives in Ghana." *Journal of Social Science Review* 1(1).
Gurevitch, M., S. Coleman, & J. G. Blumler. (September 2009). "Political Communication—Old and New Media Relationships." *The Annals of the American Academy of Political and Social Sciences* 625(1): 164–181.
Hallin, Daniel C., and Paolo Mancini. (2004). *Comparing Media Systems: Three Models of Media and Politics.* Cambridge: Cambridge University Press.
Hanson, Ralph E. (2011). *Mass Communication: Living in a Media World.* Washington, DC: CQ Press.

Klinogo, G. R. (2016). "Development Discourse Analysis of the 2016 State of the Nation's Address." *Social Science and Law Journal of Policy Review and Development Strategies*, 2315-8387.

Maneerat, N., C. L. Hale, & A. Singhal. (2005). "Organization Identification in Two Thai Organizations." *Asian Journal of Communication* 15(2): 188–214.

McNair, Brian. (2003). *An Introduction to Political Communication* (3rd ed.). London: Routledge.

Plattner, Marc F. (2012). "Media and Democracy: The Long View." *Journal of Democracy* 23(4): 62–73. National Endowment for Democracy and The Johns Hopkins University Press.

Saward, Michael. (1994). "Democratic Theory and Indices of Democratization." In David Beetham (ed.), *Defining and Measuring Democracy*, 6–24. London: Sage.

Schudson, Michael. (1994). "The 'Public Sphere' and Its Problems: Bringing the State [Back]." In *Notre Dame Journal of Law, Ethics & Public Policy* 8: 529–546.

Schudson, Michael. (2000). "The Sociology of News Production Revisited (Again)." In James Curran & Michael Gurevitch (eds.). *Mass Media and Society* (3rd ed.), 175–200. London: Arnold.

Schudson, Michael. (2004). "The Place of Sociology in the Study of Political Communication." *Political Communication* 21(3): 271–273.

Schudson, Michael. (2005). "Four Approaches to the Sociology of News." In James Curran & Michael Gurevitch (eds.), *Mass Media and Society* (4th ed.), 172–197. London: Hodder Arnold.

Schudson, Michael. (2011). *The Sociology of News* (2nd ed.). Norton Publishers.

Shogan, C. J. (2015). "The President's State of the Union Address: Tradition, Function, and Policy Implications." *Congressional Research Service*, 7–5700.

Sikanku, E., & F. K. Boadi. (2018). "SONA 2018: An Assessment of Akufo-Addo's Style and Communication." https://www.ghanaweb.com/GhanaHomePage/features/SONA-2018-An-assessment-of-Akufo-Addo-s-style-and-communication-625283.

Tymson, C., P. Lazar, & R. Lazar. (2002). "What Do Public Relations Practitioners Do?" In C. Tymson, P. Lazar, & R. Lazar (eds.), *The New Australian and New Zealand Public Relations Manual*. Australia: Tymson Communications.

Tymson, C., P. Lazar, & R. Lazar (eds.). (2002). *The New Australian and New Zealand Public Relations Manual* (Millennium Edition), 42–57. NSW, Sydney: Tymson Communications.

*Chapter Eleven*

# Power, Domination, and Manipulation in Students' Parliamentary Discourse in a Ghanaian University

Dora F. Edu-Buandoh and
Nancy Boahemaa Nkansah

Political discourse refers to the discursive properties in the political domain as well as the relevant systems, organizations, actors, cognition, and other related spaces that inform politics (van Dijk, 1997). Some research has been done on parliamentary discourse from different perspectives: intertextuality (Gadavanij, 2002); knowledge (van Dijk, 2003); stance-taking (Vasilescu, 2010); linguistic features (Tsakona, 2012); politeness (Murphy, 2014); gender (Bijeikiene & Utka, 2006; Atanga, 2012); showing and telling (Shenhav, 2008); identity construction (Illie, 2010); and rhythm and prominence (Appartaim, 2012). These studies have been relevant to general research in political discourse. Van Dijk (1997) opines that political discourse analysis is critical since it deals with political power, abuse, and various forms of resistance; an assertion corroborated by Chilton (2004), Wodak (2009), and Fairclough and Fairclough (2013). All these studies on parliamentary discourse have had national parliaments as their focus. However, the present study looks at pseudo-political discourse in the University of Cape Coast (UCC) Students' Parliament by critically analyzing the discursive and contextual levels of language use that are employed to enact power, domination, and manipulation.

It is important for this pseudo-political discourse to be studied because it inadvertently finds itself in the main national politics considering that the tertiary institutions in Ghana have become grooming grounds for national political participation and for future political actors. The UCC Students'

Parliament engages in political discourse that can be described as a mimic of national parliamentary discourse because of its close resemblance to national political discourse, although the decisions and bills passed do not directly bind students. The resemblance of students' parliament to national parliament is in terms of the proceedings they follow, the standing orders, the two benches, and the leadership style. The students' parliaments have gained some recognition from national parliament. Students' parliaments in Ghana are under the Public Affairs Directorate of Ghana's House of Parliament. In view of this relationship, the national parliament invites student parliamentarians for programs such as constituency fora and Commonwealth debates. The constituency fora are held by Ghana's Parliament in various constituencies to educate the public on governance and parliament. In the same way, Ghana's Parliament organizes Commonwealth debates with support from the British Council for students' parliaments in Ghana to mark Commonwealth Day celebrations. On the other hand, the UCC Students' Parliament, sometimes, hosts members of Ghana's House of Parliament, and even political aspirants of some political parties. These are done for mentorship purposes, to get invitees to contribute/speak on relevant national issues, and for aspirants to also engage the students on what they intend to do when given the nod to make informed decisions.

## DISCURSIVE FEATURES IN PARLIAMENTARY DISCOURSE

Discursive features of different genres contribute extensively to differential power relations that may exist in given social, cultural, and political contexts. These genres determine the participants in the discourse and also provide the systems that should inform the discourse orders. Parliamentary discourse is generically interactional in nature. In particular, it is constructed with participants taking turns to engage in the interaction centers on policies, legislative instruments, and the constitution of order. The hierarchical relationship that exists among parliamentarians provides a tenor for the discourse. Topics for debates in a particular parliamentary discourse can trigger unique discursive features that may not be present in another parliamentary debate on another topic. Some studies discussed below show that different genres in political discourse in different contexts yield different projections of linguistic as well as discursive features.

Gadavanij (2002) claims that intertextuality as a discourse strategy is dominant in no-confidence debates of Thailand. He explains that intertextuality in no-confidence debates in Thai parliament occurs at two levels: the combination of genres and of voices. The first level displays three types of intertextuality: intertextuality within a single clause, which he refers to as mixed intertextuality; intertextuality where there is sequential intertextuality of different stages of discourse; and the type where one genre is embedded in another. The other level of intertextuality in no-confidence debate of Thai parliamentary discourse is the use of reported speech both as narrative tool and to make negative comments and accusations. These discursive features identified by Gadavanij (2002) may not be present in the parliamentary debates of other countries because discursive features are culturally tied to the beliefs and practices of the people who use them.

Van Dijk's (2003, 2006a) studies on speeches by Tony Blair in the British House of Commons reveal the discursive features of another parliamentary discourse in a different context. He portrays the knowledge used—explicit, implicit, and contextual—as more important than other features in the discourse. Explicitly, there is the use of shared knowledge in making plausible inferences, promises, facts, agreements, and evidentials, and it is usually expressed through lexical choices and phrases. Implicit knowledge is realized through implications and presuppositions of events and knowledge, whereas contextual knowledge deals with knowledge about the communicative events or situations that relate to the setting, participants, and the ongoing event. He also found the use of pronouns and adverbs to demonstrate the contextual knowledge to be paramount. Again, it is important to note that these discursive features identified by van Dijk (2003) may be peculiar to the culture and genre of British Parliamentary discourse.

With reference to manipulation in parliamentary discourse, van Dijk's (2006a) analysis of Tony Blair's address that gave legitimacy to the war against Iraq maintains that the address emphasizes ideological polarization by positive self-presentation, projection of self-power, discrediting of opponents, and emotionalizing the argument. The MPs, in that context, were therefore manipulated to accept the reasons legitimizing the war.

Romanian parliamentarians adopt both indirect and direct strategies in taking metastance in their parliament. The indirect metastance, which is considered objective by Vasilescu (2010), is marked on the verb phrase and the use of both positive and negative politeness strategies. However, the direct metastance, which is usually subjective in nature, is realized through the use of personal credentials, evaluations, and emotions that are peculiar to the speaker. Grammatically, this type of metastance is marked on noun phrases and hedged assertions. There is also a *self*-praise and blame of the *other* which is relationship centered (Vasilescu, 2010).

Appartaim (2012) studied the sociophonetics of Ghanaian parliamentary discourse. Considering that speech is the primary mode of communication in parliament, analyzing prominence and rhythm in parliamentary discourse becomes crucial. Appartaim found that Ghanaian parliamentarians achieve prominence in their interactions in Parliament and these include the use of pitch and intensity, pitch and duration, and intensity and pitch to mark strong syllables. On the other hand, weak syllables are marked with the use of weak pitch, low intensity, and short duration. These phonetic realizations have implications as discursive features for the realization of power, dominance, and inequality in the discourse. For example, a raised pitch may indicate dominance in a context where a member is on the floor contributing and another member raises his or her voice to drown the earlier speaker's voice, thereby interrupting the earlier speaker's turn.

In a more related context (with this paper), Attuahene Mensah's 2012 study on register analysis of the UCC Students' Parliament shows that while parliamentarians refer to the Speaker with title only, the Speaker and the other members of Parliament refer to one another with varied address forms. He points out that the register serves the discoursal functions of giving information, directives, and advice as well as asking questions. The address terms, as well as complex and simple noun phrases, are the dominant linguistic features used by the participants while the use of contractions, repetitions, pause fillers, and incomplete sentences marked the discourse as spoken. Atuahehene Mensah also discovered the use of specialized vocabulary in the discourse of the parliamentarians. As Atuahehene Mensah looks at the linguistic forms that inform the register of the students' parliamentary discourse that he studied, our paper identifies the linguistic forms that inform the manipulative and dominance discourse in the data. Furthermore, both papers use data collected from the UCC Students' Parliament.

The studies mentioned show parliamentary discourse as not only about debate but as a site for different discourses for different pragmatic functions, identity constructions, and power manifestations, an area this paper shows interest in.

## THE CONCEPTUAL FRAMEWORK OF DISCOURSE, POWER, AND MANIPULATION

Foucault's (1972) definition of discourse as "systems of thoughts composed of ideas, attitudes, and courses of action, beliefs and practices that systematically construct the subjects and the worlds of which they speak" has been cited in much of the research on discourse. Discourse is a tool for social organization through the use of linguistic forms that communicate meanings inherent in them and also that have the potential to communicate situated meanings and mediate ideological justifications for changing or maintaining the status quo. When discourse becomes a medium for power, it becomes critical for analysts to determine who stands to gain from the discourse and who is left out in the discourse for whatever reason.

Power, therefore, can be gleaned from the way individuals are governed by the discourses they engage in. From a social viewpoint, discourse is embedded in social institutions, and as such embodies language, documents, conventions, objects, and even buildings and architecture (Gee, 1996). Social institutions as portrayed in the use of language have power embedded in their discursive features and orders of discourse as Foucault has suggested. Linking discourse to power, Fairclough (1989, 2014) asserts that there is no language use without power and that language enacts power and is influenced by power. This paper looks at pseudo-parliamentary discourse used in the UCC Students' Parliament as a way of establishing any power and ideological relationships at play.

Van Dijk (2006a) identifies social power and individual power as two main areas of power distribution. Social power, he explains, is drawn from group or society's identity and power, and that when individuals draw from such power, it is because they belong to the group but not because they are powerful in their own entities. He continues that power is usually expressed through differential recognition and access to discoursal genres, content, and styles. This means that power can be enacted in how language is used to mark specific ways of speaking and enacting activities. It stands to reason that when groups of people use language in specific ways, they may enact activities that show discursive features of power and inequality, especially in political discourse. The domain of politics gives room for individuals to draw from collective group identity and power to engage in discourses that will portray them as members of the group against those who do not belong to the same group. Van Dijk adds that though powerful groups are able to control, they can be resisted by the less powerful through ambiguity or ambivalence and silence. Fairclough (1989) maintains that power is recognized in contexts where powerful participants control and constrain the contributions of non-powerful participants. These constraints can be on the contents, the relations, or on the subjects. In parliamentary discourse, there is a likelihood that there will be group discourses because there is always the group(s) in power and the group(s) in opposition. The discourse analyzed in this paper draws from these group discourses and subsequent sections examine how group power is enacted and expressed in individual discourses to show related ideologies such as manipulation. The distribution of social and individual power in the UCC Students' Parliament is evident in the discourse of the Majority and Minority Benches as well as in that of their leaders.

Manipulation, according to van Dijk (2006a), refers to the control of people against their will or their best interests, and it is done at two levels of discourses: cognitive and discursive. He asserts that manipulation in group discourses has the tendency of ideologically positioning the *self* against the *other*; so, the *self* emphasizes its own positive representation and the negative representation of the *other*. This assertion is important for our analysis considering that we examine the discourse of the two opposing benches in the UCC Students' Parliament to determine how the discourses manipulate each other. Discourse, power, and manipulation are conceptualizations of the social processes that evolve from communicative events. The following sections present the data used for this study, which is then analyzed using Fairclough's (1989) three-tier model of Critical Discourse Analysis (CDA).

## DATA

The data analyzed for this paper is an eighty-seven-minute recording of proceedings of one parliamentary sitting of the UCC Students' Parliament. We took an informed consent from the Speaker but in order for us to get a naturally occurring data, we did not make the date for recording known to the Speaker and the parliamentarians.

The University of Cape Coast (UCC) Students' Parliament was established in December 2003 as the first students' parliament in Ghanaian tertiary institutions. It is not a statutory body; however, it enjoys recognition among students and also from the UCC Management. It is considered a student organization and is required to register with the office of the Dean of Students' Affairs annually. Membership is open to all students who have no disciplinary issues (records) in the institution. The parliament admits students without any discrimination on the basis of sex, religion, political affiliation, or ethnic background. The current membership has a numerical strength of fifty student parliamentarians. The parliament seeks to inculcate in its members the rudiments of parliamentary debates and to provide a platform for UCC students to address campus and national issues, especially those affecting students and the youth, in order to make informed contributions towards the issues. The parliament is also meant to enable students to appreciate the system of governance among university students and to ensure the understanding of the culture of democracy, civic education, and matters relating to their constitution (Awotunde, personal communication, July 5, 2016).

## DATA ANALYSIS: FAIRCLOUGH'S THREE-TIER FRAMEWORK

Fairclough's (1989) three-tier CDA analytical framework—made up of *description, interpretation,* and *explanation*—was applied to the data to bring out the discursive features present in the discourse and how they draw from and inform sources of power. The description stage of the framework—the first tier—presents the discursive features of the text by showing linguistic forms used in the discourse ecology. The second tier of Fairclough's (1989) CDA model is about interpreting the text that has been described. The interpretation process focuses on how the reader or listener interacts with the text mentally to bring out the relationship between the text, intertextual contexts, and situational context in order to unravel power and ideological meanings embedded in the discourse. The third tier, explanation, projects the relationship that exists between an interaction and the social context in which the interaction takes place. The three tiers form a tri-method that is used to unravel covert instances of power, dominance, and manipulation in the data. Clause types, modality, topic formulation, turn-taking, and graphological setting are the sites in the discourse for analysis. The recorded data was transcribed and coded for analysis using these.

There were three major participants in the data used: the Speaker of Parliament, the Majority Bench, and the Minority Bench. Each bench had leaders, whips, ministers, ranking members, and members. The participants knew the orders of discourse to follow and each was expected to use the appropriate discursive features to engage in the discourse. The Speaker, who directed the communicative event, had the duty to propose the debate and moderate the proceedings that followed.

## TEXT ANALYSIS AND DISCUSSION

Clause types, modality, turn-taking, topic-control, and formulation are the key areas that marked ideological implications in the data. These are linguistic as well as discourse forms that could be explained in the contexts, they occur in line with the concept that language enacts power. Fairclough states that whereas an interaction covers a transitory space, the social context is more structured and durable (Fairclough, 2001, p. 22). The context of a students' parliament is structured and tends to yield to forms of covert and/or overt power sources.

## DESCRIPTION OF USE OF CLAUSE TYPES

It was observed that out of the four main traditional clause types—declaratives, imperatives, interrogatives, interjections—three were used in the recorded data. Interjections were not present. The clause types used by the Speaker, the Majority and the Minority Benches in the UCC Students' Parliament are presented below in simple percentages to show the distribution of use, and further discussed to bring out the focus of the paper.

Table 11.1 shows that the Speaker and the members of parliament used more declaratives than the other clause forms. The Speaker's utterances in declaratives were mainly for debate formulations, setting the agenda for discussion, introducing the topic and directing the debate. The Speaker also used declaratives to call people to order, to control the topic, to grant permission, to ask questions, to interrupt, and to emphasize an issue on the floor. The excerpts below illustrate instances where declaratives were used:

**Table 11.1.   Distribution of clauses type usage.**

|  | Declarative | | Imperative | | Interrogative | |
|---|---|---|---|---|---|---|
|  | No. | % | No. | % | No. | % |
| Speaker | 159 | 14 | 26 | 54 | 33 | 41 |
| Majority Bench | 314 | 30 | 0 | 0 | 22 | 7 |
| Minority Bench | 611 | 56 | 22 | 46 | 42 | 52 |
| Total | 1084 | 100% | 48 | 100% | 97 | 100% |

*Source:* From data collected.

### Excerpt 1

[133]**Speaker:** Quickly honourable members (.) I just want to remind us that the [134]motions tabled before this august house this morning substantively are the [135]SRC and its so far (.) That means (.) we're going to try and do an objective [136]assessment of the programmes and projects of the SRC (.) as they have been [137]duly elected into office some time now (.) and then on the subsidiary (.) we're [138]going to discuss the water crisis that has hit the university community (.) That [139]is (.) the University of Cape Coast and the entire membership (.) We're going [140]to look at the nitty-gritties of that (.) Those are the motions tabled this morning (.)

In excerpt 1, the Speaker uses declaratives throughout, as expected, to engage in the orders of discourse of parliament. From line 133 to 140, he sets the agenda for the debate. He gives the context as *we're going to try and do an objective assessment of the programmes and projects of the SRC*. He also identifies a related topic for discussion as *the water crisis that has hit the university community*. By giving these two topics as the tabled motions for the day, it is expected that members of the parliament will debate on only these two issues. Excerpt 2 shows the use of declaratives by the Speaker:

### Excerpt 2

[141]**Speaker:** Honourable members (.) I duly implore your high (.) your [142]honourableness this morning (.) to debate these motions devoid of your [143]personal sentiments and various personal effects in the motion (.) Let us be as [144]objective as possible and then look at issues as they are (.) but not as they may [145]be (.) Quickly honourable members, I want to move to the majority bench to [146]give us an opening statement . . . [Majority member stands] Honourable A2, [147]you have the floor.

In excerpt 2, lines 141–144 are syntactically structured as declaratives; however, the pragmatic functions are imperative in nature. The use of *I duly implore* brings an indirectness that mitigates the force of speech act of imperative in that utterance, specifically the conventional indirectness strategy. In a similar fashion, the expression *Let us* is a discourse marker that marks politeness and mitigates the effect of the utterance. The next move in excerpt 2 is the use of a declarative by the Speaker to indicate who takes the floor after his opening. It also grants permission to the Majority member (A2) to take the floor.

## Excerpt 3

[472]**Speaker:** However, (.) Honourable B1 (.) I plead with you that some of the words [473]you use, not to compromise (.) you should be very much more flexible in the [474]kind of words you use (.) I mean your diction (.) because some of the words [475]are not very parliamentary (.)

In excerpt 3, the Speaker employs declarative sentences to call a member of the Minority Bench to order. Members of parliament are expected to use appropriate forms of language during debates on the floor of the house. The use of certain expressions other than what is expected is therefore a breach of parliamentary procedure, and in the case of excerpt 3, the Speaker had to remind the parliament that appropriacy of language use is expected of members.

The Majority Bench used declaratives to give directives, suggestions, and commands, as well as to place a point of order and to control the topic either from their perspective or that of the opponent. Though, technically, it is the Speaker who holds the institutional authority to direct the discourse, the data showed that the Majority Bench, sometimes, "arrogated" to itself the power of controlling the topic in order to force its opinions on the discussion. The following excerpts show how the Majority Bench used declaratives to do that in the discourse.

## Excerpt 4

[21]**Acting Majority Leader:** Erh Mr. Speaker (.) we have so many issues to [22]discuss but before we move on to that, I've been alerted that uhm there was [23]some by-election held and then we have a new MP elect(.) He is in our midst [24]here and I (.) want to propose that Mr. Speaker (.) please swear him in so that he [25]becomes part of the house(.) as the law demands so Mr. Speaker (.) I want to [26]implore on the minority leader so that he seconds this motion (.) so that you [27]swear him in (.) Thank you . . .

**Excerpt 5**

[302]**Acting Majority Leader:** So Mr. Speaker (.) I believe that even if the reservoir [303]another one is created (.) I believe it will be of much importance than the [304]borehole that is being drilled because for all you know the conclusion that will [305]come will lead to no avail (.) So (.) I am suggesting that (.) more of these [306]storage mediums should be created in order to collect water when there is [307]water available and supply them when the need arises (.) Mr. Speaker, I will [308]not hijack the floor (.) I will like to resume my seat for honourable members [309]to also take part in this debate (.) Thank you . . .

The declaratives used by the Acting Majority Leader in excerpt 4 were to give suggestions to the Speaker and to redirect the Speaker before the start of the debate for the day. The Acting Majority Leader used declaratives in excerpt 5 to contribute to the debate on the floor of the house. In excerpt 5, the declarative is used to perform its discourse function of giving information. The Minority Bench is marked as the unit that uses more declaratives than any other group. The Bench uses declaratives to threaten the opposition Majority, to express their willingness on an issue, to give directives, to inform, to ask for permission, and also to control the topic. It is interesting that the Minority, which in a real sense does not have power, was able to gain more talk time than the Majority. This has implications for the discussions of power and resistance in subsequent sections. The following excerpts illustrate:

**Excerpt 6**

[31]**Minority Leader:** Mr. Speaker (.) I wouldn't be very charitable today if the [32]majority leader begins proposing (.) the moment he begins proposing (.) I will [33]be opposing Mr. Speaker (.) he should better start following our procedures [34]accordingly

In lines 31–24, the Minority Leader issues a threat using declaratives.

**Excerpt 7**

[90]**Minority Leader:** Mr. Speaker (.) this is a wrongly-tabled motion and this [91]Bench is not going to second such a lousy motion Mr. Speaker (.) so for him to [92]Mr. Speaker (.) for there to be smooth debate in this house Mr. Speaker (.) he [93]should regroup and organise himself and table the motion again Mr. Speaker (.) [94]I am not the chairman of the business committee and for that matter I was not [95]called by the Speaker accordingly to even advise the house (.) so Mr. Speaker [96](.) the mandate as befallen the honourable member to

advise this house should [97]be turned back to him again Mr. Speaker he (.) he should prepare and rise and [98]come back again(.)

The Minority Leader in the first sentence of excerpt 7 makes a point of order to correct a parliamentary procedure. He then goes on to direct the Majority Leader to do the right thing by observing parliamentary procedures.

In excerpt 8 below, the Minority Member uses declaratives to call for a point of order to correct an impression that the inability of the university to dig boreholes to improve the water situation in the community is due to the geographical location of the university.

## Excerpt 8

[269]**Minority Member 1:** Thank you Mr. Speaker (.) Mr. Speaker (.) I am on my [270]feet for a point of order and information seeking (.) Mr. Speaker, on the [271]Majority Bench, we have a water and sanitation expert . . . and a member of the [272]majority bench telling *US* (emphasized) that the entire university community [273](.) cannot work on the water project just because the water was salty? If the [274]water is salty (.) it is different from the school not being in the correct [275]geographical area. The water can be muddy, but I know that the water and [276]sanitation expert there knows that there could be some transformation (.) The [277]fact is that the leadership is not ready to put in money to do that (.) [Cheers of [278]hear, hear, from the minority side].

The other two clause types—interrogatives and imperatives—are not used in the discourse as much as declaratives. The data showed that the Majority Bench did not use imperatives at all. Furthermore, the difference between the use of imperatives by the Speaker and the Minority Bench is so small (refer to table 11.1) that it creates the impression the Speaker had no hold on the Minority in the discourse.

## Excerpt 9

[630]**Speaker:** Honourable member (.) may u wind up?

## Excerpt 10

[192] **Speaker:** Order in the house! Honourable members (.) observe order! . . . [193]Honourable B2 (.) address the chair (.)

The Speaker, in the two excerpts above, used imperatives to control the house. Excerpt 9 has an interrogative form, but the function is imperative while excerpt 10 is an imperative both in form and function.

## Excerpt 11

[366]**Minority Member 1:** Mr. Speaker, is this happening? Mr. Speaker (.) let's go to [367]one (.) ATL (.) is the internet service there working? The answer is no (.) [368]Adehye (.) is it working? No (.) Oguaa Hall has now become dumsor (.) [369]I don't know whether they have now joined ECG (.) Mr. Speaker (.) Casely [370]Hayford Hall (.) is the internet service there working? No (.)The industrial [371]city, a whole industrial city, VALCO, is it working? No (.) and the new born [372]baby (.) the last baby (.) Kwame Nkrumah Hall (.) the hall of excellence (.) is [373]it working? No (.) Mr. Speaker (.) what has happened to this? . . . Let's look at our [374]own house of parliament. Let's all try to turn our attention to . . .

## Excerpt 12

[467] **Minority Leader:** Mr. Speaker (.) else (.) Mr. Speaker, allow him to sit down (.)

A Minority Member asks series of questions in excerpt 11 to stress his point on poor internet and electricity facilities in Students Halls of residence as his contribution to the debate. The questions are structured as rhetorical questions, but he also provides the answers to draw attention to his concerns. In excerpt 12, the Minority Leader issued an imperative to get the Speaker to perform his duties as the one who controls the discourse of the house. The background to that excerpt was the request from the Minority Bench that the Speaker asks the Deputy Majority Leader not to contribute to the proceedings of the day because he was not properly dressed for parliament.

### INTERPRETATION OF USE OF CLAUSE TYPES

The use of different clause types points to systems of meanings that go beyond the grammatical functions of the clause but also directly or indirectly serve communicative and pragmatic functions. From the description of the data, it could be seen that many power issues were at play in the discourse. The use of linguistic forms was not as neutral as they seemed to be.

In lines 141 and 143, the Speaker could have used direct imperatives to give bald-on-record directives. Using a declarative as an imperative states the desire of the Speaker indirectly and makes it seem as if the Speaker is only making a request; but in fact, the Speaker is imposing his desires on the addressee. The Speaker, in pretending not to impose his authority on the other participants, is trying to fit into the orders of discourse of parliamentary debates, where democratic structure requires of members not to impose their views but to argue their views logically to persuade others. The pretense points to manipulation of the addressee to believe that the addressor (Speaker) is only making a request. If the addressee does not recognize the veiled threat in the imperative and treats the utterance as a harmless directive, he or she fails to understand the underlying power and the Speaker stands to gain from this ignorance on the part of the addressee. As van Dijk (1989) observes, "direct control of action is achieved through discourses that have directive pragmatic function (elocutionary force), such as commands, threats, laws, regulations, instructions, and more indirectly by recommendations and advice" (p. 27). In effect, when declaratives are used to pragmatically function as directives, they invariably directly control the actions of the addressee. The data also shows the Minority Bench using declaratives as imperatives to control the Majority, thus showing that it also wields power.

Declaratives, according to Greenbaum (1996) and Hurford, Heasley, and Smith (2007), are used to make propositions or statements and to convey information. Interrogatives serve to ask questions and imperatives give commands, orders, or directives. But according to Downing and Locke (2006), these meanings are used by speakers to influence and control others and to commit themselves to certain courses of action. In the excerpts discussed, it could be deduced that the participants were using the clause types in line with Downing and Locke's assertion.

In addition to clause types, other linguistic features stood out as strong discursive forms to inform the situated meaning in the discourse.

## DESCRIPTION OF USE OF MODALS

Modality is one of the linguistic features that came out prominent. It is a semantic category that deals with the kind of attitude or judgments expressed by a speaker towards a proposition (Downing & Locke, 2006; Greenbaum, 1996). Broadly, these attitudes can be classified into two types: epistemic (or extrinsic) and deontic (or intrinsic) modality. Although, the same types of modal verbs are used to express the two types of modal meanings, our study focused on the types of modal verbs which were used to enact power. In view of this, deontic modal meanings were considered. Deontic modality refers to the human control over a situation to suggest permission, intention, obligation, volition, necessity, and ability (Downing & Locke, 2006; Greenbaum, 1996). Ability is expressed through the use of *can* and *could*; permission is expressed through *can* and *may*; volition is through *shall*, *should*, and *will*; and obligation is achieved through *must* and *should*. The modal verbs used extensively by the three categories of participants—Speaker, Minority, and Majority—were *shall*, *should*, *must*, *could*, *can*, *may*, *might*, *will*, and *would* in different contexts and utterances. In the excerpts below, the various uses of deontic modality in the data are presented discussed.

## Excerpt 13

[222]**Speaker:** Honourable A1 (.) I think (.)I think we *must* try to observe some kind [223]of decorum in the house this morning (.) I hear words like night clubs (.) as far [224]as I know (.) words such as these (.) are unparliamentary (.) Honourable [225]A1 (.) I am not going to ask you to withdraw your statement, but I *will* want [226]you to be very decorous the next time you make such comments (.) *May* you proceed?

## Excerpt 14

[160]**Majority Member 1:** We are not students (.) and therefore (.) we *cannot* be in [161]a university (.) but we *can* only be in a state and for that matter a republic and [162]therefore, the republic is the Republic of University of Cape Coast and the [163]minority leader *must* take that education very (.) very (.) seriously because the [164]next time he does that I *will* personally (.) personally (.) personally (.) I*'ll* [165]personally (.) move a motion to pass a vote of no confidence in the minority [166]leader (.) [Cheers of hear, hear from the majority side & noo, noo from the [167]minority side.] He *shall* be removed from office (.) Mr. Speaker (.) on that note, [168]I *will* wish to say that the majority bench is prepared to debate this motion. [169]The majority bench is, is, is well poised to debate this motion very properly [170]and very well (.) therefore (.) on this note (.) I just *would* want to plead with all [171]members, as the Speaker has said to debate this motion with objectivity (.)

## Excerpt 15

[29]**Minority Leader:** Thank you very much Mr. Speaker (.) I for once thought I [30]was going to be on a lone road but I see my able chief whip coming in indicates [31]that the bench has been revamped (.) Mr. Speaker (.) I *wouldn't* be very [32]charitable today if the majority leader begins proposing (.) the moment he [33]begins proposing (.) I *will* be opposing Mr. Speaker (.) he *should* better start [34]following our procedures accordingly but as he duly said the . . . elected and [35]now an honourable member elect so definitely Mr. Speaker (.) I do second the [36]motion that we swear him in so that he *can* erh assume his constitutional [37]mandate to lead his constituent Mr. Speaker (.) I duly second the motion. [The [38]Minority Bench cheers hear, hear]

## INTERPRETATION OF THE USE OF MODALS

The use of deontic modality by the three groups of participants show the urge by each participant to control the discourse or utterance of the other. In excerpts 13, 14, and 15, the Speaker, the Majority Member 1, and the Minority Leader used *may, must, will, can, would,* and *should.* In excerpt 13, the Speaker employs *must* to place a strong obligation on the parliament to be decorous in its discourse. He uses *will* plus *want you to* place an obligation on, specifically, Honourable A1 to be decorous. *May* was used to grant permission to the acting Majority Leader (Honourable A1) to resume his contribution to the debate. Certainty, commitment and obligation were also expressed by a member of the Majority Bench through the use of *can/cannot, will/would,* and *must.* The use of *will* and *shall* point to certainty in commitment of the speaker to perform certain actions in the future whereas *must* mark a strong obligation on the part of the addressee. Similarly, the Minority Bench also expressed ability and obligation through the use of *can, would/ wouldn't, will,* and *shall.* The use of *will* in excerpt 15 marks certainty in commitment on the part of the speaker to perform the stated action in the future whereas *should* was used to mark strong obligation on the addressee to perform an expected behavior.

## TURN-TAKING

Turn-taking is an interactive discursive feature in many spoken discourses where participants are engaged in dialogues. The use of turn-taking was instrumental in determining how the participants marked power in the data. According to Gorjian and Habibi (2015), turn-taking plays an important role in organizing social interactions through controlling and regulating conversations. It regulates who speaks first and who speaks next depending on conversational cues given by interlocutors. The proceedings at the UCC Students' Parliament house, just like the discourse at any democratic parliament, is interactional in nature and therefore, employs the use of turn-taking to manage the discourse as to who speaks at what time during the interaction. In the data, it was observed that turn-taking was used as a feature to control the discourse at different levels. The Speaker controlled the turn of members in the house but there were also instances where members of the Majority and Minority Benches drew the Speaker's attention to the fact that they held a floor or that they flouted the conversational principle of turn-taking and took a turn. Members from the two benches sometimes took the turns from other members holding the floor by rising to their feet. The excerpts below illustrate some turn taking situations:

**Excerpt 16**

[16]**Speaker:** Honourable members (.) but before we go ahead I quickly want to [17]move to the majority side to advise the house . . . [Majority member stands] . . . [18]Honourable Majority Leader acting (.) you have the floor.

When the acting Majority Leader stood up, the Speaker understood by the discursive practices of parliamentary discourse that the Acting Majority Leader wanted to take the turn from him and the Speaker yielded the floor to the Acting Majority Leader.

**Excerpt 17**

[451]**Deputy Majority Leader:** Thank you very much Mr. Speaker . . . Mr. Speaker (.) [452]I am on my feet on a point of order and information seeking [Three members [453]of the minority bench rise] [458]**Minority Leader:** Mr. Speaker, we are on our feet on a total point of order (.) A [459]VERY BIG ONE (.)

In excerpt 17, three Minority members stood up and called for a point of order to take the turn from the Deputy Majority Leader, who was holding the floor. The three Minority Members were protesting the improper dressing of the Deputy Majority Leader who had stood up to take a turn from a Minority Member on the floor earlier.

## INTERPRETATION OF THE USE OF TURN-TAKING

Turn-taking and interruptions are considered part of interactions. As a basic tool in interaction, turn-taking varies between cultures and genres of communication. In parliamentary discourse, it is the Speaker who directs turn-taking and selects the speaker. Parliamentarians are not expected to self-select themselves to take turns. However, in that social context, and in adhering to the rules of conversation in parliamentary discourse, parliamentarians can, in exceptional cases, draw the attention of the Speaker to their desire to take the floor from the current speaker.

In the data, parliamentarians stood up to show their desire to take the floor from whoever was speaking. Though that was not the preferred discourse marker for taking turns, both the Majority and Minority Benches employed standing up to take turns from the opposition bench. It is important to note that although they interrupted each other to take the floor, they always looked up to the Speaker to grant them the opportunity. That notwithstanding, the Minority Bench interrupted the Speaker and members of the Majority Bench more frequently.

The ideological import of exercising control over other speakers who hold the floor without waiting for one's turn is discussed later in the paper. Control and formulation of topics for debate were also identified as linguistic forms that spoke to the semantic production of the text analyzed.

## TOPIC CONTROL AND FORMULATION

The power to decide the subject for discussion is regulated in interactions by the orders of discourse in the particular genre. In parliamentary discourse, the Speaker has vested authority to control and formulate the topic for debate because in an interactional context where there are hierarchical ranks, the topic is controlled by the highest-ranking person (Mautner, 2016). There were instances of topic control and formulation in the data. It was the Speaker who controlled the four main sessions of the House: the address, opening statement, debate, and advice sessions. However, in some situations, members of the two benches wrung that power from the Speaker and controlled the topic. The excerpt below illustrates some instances:

**Excerpt 18**

[142]**Speaker:** Quickly honourable members (.) I want to move to the majority [143]bench to give as an opening statement . . . [Majority member stands] [144]Honourable A2, you have the floor. [145]**Majority Member 1:** Mr. Speaker (.) I'm honestly grateful for this [146]opportunity (.) Mr. Speaker (.) even before I give the opening statement from [147]the majority bench (.) I would want to beg your highness an opportunity even [148]if it is 30 seconds [Cheers of no, no from the minority bench] to orient or to [149]educate the minority leader [Cheers of hear, hear from the majority bench] on [150]a very important issue (.) Mr. Speaker (.) if I have the floor (.) may I go on?

In the above extract, the Acting Majority Leader had been called by the Speaker to give the opening statement but instead of doing that, he rather changed the topic by asking permission from the Speaker to educate the Minority Leader. The protest from the Minority Bench indicates their displeasure about the change of topic. Usually, members try to control the topic when they are seeking information from a colleague on the floor. They sometimes also digress from the motion of the House by bringing in other arguments as a form of educating the House.

## INTERPRETATION OF TOPIC CONTROL AND FORMULATION

Topic Control and Formulation of utterances of others was identified as a discursive feature in the discourse. When a participant changes the topic for the interaction, he or she indicates that he or she is in control of how the interaction should go. Palmer (1989) asserts that controlling what is said in an interaction shows interpersonal dominance. It marks the person as the dominant participant in the conversation. According to Fairclough (1989), formulation is a rewording of what has been said by oneself or others or what has been implied. Of the three groups in the house of parliament, the Speaker usually formulated what had already been said by members of either side. For example:

## Excerpt 19

[177]Mr Speaker, we as members of the minority bench STILL REFUSE to take his [178]education on the republic (.) We have refused (.) he should go back and let his [179]social studies lecturer or teacher teach him (.) when he refuses it in the [180]classroom that a republic is a country coming out of dictatorship or military [181]rule (.) Are we as a country coming out of dictatorship rule? No (.) so please [182]go back to your social studies teacher and learn (.) let him teach you (.) [183]**Speaker:** Honourable member, are you by any way insinuating that Ghana is not a republic?

## Explanation of Linguistic and Discourse Forms

Meanings of expressions that otherwise may sound very common need to be looked at with other lenses whenever individuals engage in discourse practices. Words are related in terms of meaning systems that the social orders of the discourse imbue them with. In addition, the meaning systems are themselves ideologically structured for marking effects of power. It has been observed by linguists such as Fairclough (2014) and Foucault (1972) that language is imbued with power and social interactions provide platforms for such powers, influential or institutional, to be manifested. The extensive use of declaratives, which invariably pointed to the extended talk time of the Minority Bench over the other participants, presented the Minority Bench as a powerful participant. The recognition as such defeats the discursive feature that the Minority will wield less power than the Majority or the Speaker. In the data, the Majority did not prove that it had voice, neither did the Speaker who was expected to have institutional control in the discourse. The use of threats by the Minority Leader (e.g., *I wouldn't be very charitable today if the majority leader begins proposing . . . the moment he beings proposing, I will be opposing . . .* , from excerpt 6) and expressions that put doubts on the Majority Leader's competence show the Minority as powerful. In excerpt 7, the Minority Leader arrogates to himself the power to question the utterance of the Majority Leader and to redirect the speaker to an action the Speaker should take. Again, the use of imperatives from the Minority Bench, with none from the Majority and only formulaic order from the Speaker, makes the Minority more in control of the discourse than the Speaker, who should have been. By showing that it has power because it controls the discourse, the Minority Bench dominates the discourse and shapes what is worthwhile to debate. The Minority Bench thus shapes the thoughts of non-parliamentarians who are there to listen to the debate.

## DOMINATION

Domination as a form of power abuse manifests itself through polarization where there is a positive presentation of one *self* and a negative *other* representation. The use of polarization as control mechanism is adopted by the two benches of the house in their struggle for agency and to portray each other negatively. The Majority Bench presented the Minority Bench as irresponsible and without focus while they described themselves as intelligent, knowledgeable, and well prepared. The Minority also presented the Majority as unintelligent, lousy, inferior, irresponsible, and ignorant while they presented themselves as intellectual, strong, and knowledgeable, in other words, quality researchers and members who are prepared for sittings. That is, both Benches discredited their opponents and emphasized their supposed credentials.

**Excerpt 20**

[126]**Minority Leader:** Mr. Speaker (.) I implore my honourable acting majority [127]leader today to do *due readings* as to which country qualifies to be called a [128]republic (.) that notwithstanding Mr. Speaker (.) for the sake of the public [129]gallery and then (.) the *intellectuals* on my bench (.) Mr. Speaker (.) I duly [130]second the motion that we debate/

**Excerpt 21**

[219]**Acting Majority Leader:** and after they have taken their sitting allowances (.) [220]they spend it in night clubs and they don't sleep early (.) and they don't wake [221]up early and come to the house (.)

In the two excerpts above, both benches insinuate that the other is not up to the task of serving as members of parliament. The discourse is couched in descriptions that question the intellectual capacity or the moral commitment of the opposing group. For a group to question one's capabilities suggests that, all else being equal, that group has knowledge beyond the group it is critiquing. The concept of power in relation to knowledge is discussed fully by Foucault. According to Foucault (1998), power comes from all spheres of life and is wielded by all people. In any given context, individuals will exert power because power is never the preserve of any particular group of people. It is rather the case that power resides and is constituted in accepted forms of knowledge, understanding, and what he calls "truths." In effect, what the opposing benches consider to be the truth about each other goes to support the assertion that each society has its own regime of truth. What the Majority considers to be the truth about the Minority may not be considered the truth by the Minority, and in the same vein, the Minority may construct the Majority in a way they consider to be true, but which the Majority may not accept to be the truth. However, the discursive formation of one group by the other depicts the group's power to construct the identity of the other in any way it prefers. This conceptualization of power runs parallel to van Dijk's (1989) concept of social power, where the individual draws from the power of the society to act in the society. In the case of the two benches in the UCC Students' Parliament, power has not traveled hierarchically from or to any of the groups. The two groups have, rather, "arrogated" to themselves the power to determine who has the capacity to be considered a good member of parliament. In doing so, the Benches control how each constructs its own identity and the identity of the opponent.

Further occurrences of domination were seen in the way turns were taken by some of the members of the parliament in relation to who was already on the floor or who had the legitimate permission from the Speaker to hold the floor. There were four instances where the Minority Bench took the turn from the Majority Bench, and also from the Speaker, and held the floor. Sacks et al. (1974), in discussing how speakers take and manage turns, said that "one party talks at a time, though speakers change, and though the size of turns and ordering of turns vary; that transitions are finely coordinated; that techniques are used for allocating turns" (p. 699). For transitions to be finely coordinated, it means each speaker will observe the conversational rules. As O'Donnell (1990) mentions, power is closely linked to floor-holding as well as topic control and interruptions. If one participant in a conversation decides to hold onto power or to interrupt other speakers when it is not his or her turn, the activity indicates the former is appropriating a powerful positioning. Interruptions done by the Minority, especially, were not just to talk but also to control the contributions of the Majority and Speaker, and thus to dominate the debate. In addition to linguistic and discourse forms, the context of the Parliament formed a hierarchical setting of power.

## CONTEXTUAL FEATURES THAT ENACT POWER

The graphological context for this study puts the Speaker in a position of power (on a higher platform) than all the other members of parliament and in a more "comfortable" chair. Before parliamentary proceedings, the Marshal announces the arrival of the Speaker for the members to rise. The Speaker is usually ushered in by the clerk and the leadership of the two benches. After the proceedings, the Speaker stands first and utters the clause "I rise" for proceedings to end. These practices portray the Speaker as the most powerful person in the parliament, and rightly so because the UCC House of Parliament is fashioned on the structure of the national parliament; and the 1992 Constitution of the Republic of Ghana (article 95) designates the Speaker as the highest ranking person in Parliament, in whose absence Parliament cannot do business unless there is a deputy Speaker in the chair.

The two Benches are separated as is done in most parliaments. In Ghana, just as it is in New Zealand and some European countries, the Majority Bench sits on the right-hand side of the Speaker while the Minority Bench is on the left of the Speaker. This system of arrangement dates to or replicates the old French Monarchy where the King's supporters sat on his right and his opponents sat on his left. On each of the Benches, the seating arrangement is done hierarchically. In the UCC House of Parliament too, the seating determines the hierarchical power of the member. First are the leaders of the two Benches, their deputies, chief whips and their deputies, ministers, and senior members or ranking members before all the other members. During a session when one wants to leave abruptly, the person bows to the Speaker before he leaves. In speaking, one stands up for him or her to be called. These practices are considered part of the discursive practices of parliamentary discourse and tend to communicate power and authority.

In addition to the seating, the dressing also adds social power to the rights and privileges of the person who wears it. The Speaker puts on attire which is different from the other members of Parliament. He puts on a wine-colored gown with a sash carrying the inscription *Speaker* on it to demonstrate his power in the house. The other members of the house attend sittings in any clothing of any color. All these nonverbal communications demonstrate the power that the Speaker wields.

These observations confirm van Dijk's (2003) view that parliamentary debates are not merely the discursive structures of such debates but also the structures of their contexts such as the setting and participants, and also context as a mental model. Though context is seen as a social situation in which discourse occurs, it is also important to recognize that the mental representations of such contexts contribute to the construction of the discourse in the situation. For parliamentary discourse, as shown in the data, it is instructive to note that participants are greatly influenced by the mental models they have built of the graphological settings of a parliament, and thus act accordingly, either as acting in governance or in opposition (van Dijk, 2006b). By acting in consonance with the Speaker, the Majority Bench indicates its group affinity with the Speaker of Parliament; on the other hand, when the Minority Bench acts as opposing the Speaker and the Majority, it acts in its interactional role as opponents of the government. The irony emanating from the data is that though the context and the graphological foregrounding of the Speaker should have made him the most powerful participant, the control of the discourse from the Minority Bench wrenches the power away from the Speaker leaving him only a ceremonial positioning. The ability for the Minority to act in this role, and thus change the focus of the debate as well as reformulate topics, marks situational power that cannot be ignored.

When Fairclough (1989) talks about power behind discourse, he asserts that discourses in themselves are imbued with power that manifests in routinization of the discourse, the genre, and the discursive practices. Parliamentary discourse itself has power behind it as a genre and as such, participants exploit this power to their gain. Sometimes, there is resistance to this appropriation because power is not absolute and can be contested. In the case of the discourse in the data, there was not much resistance from any group. The Speaker did not resist the controlling and dominant utterances from the Minority, neither did the Majority. If there was any resistance, it came from the Minority that used its turns to change topics and formulate them to dominate the Majority Bench. One interesting instance where there was no resistance to the Speaker's utterance though it showed bias was when the sitting had to be adjourned.

## Excerpt 22

[786]**Speaker:** Honourable members (.) at long last the motion has been seconded (.) [787]and quickly (.) I want to put the motion to debate [to vote] (.) as many as those [788]who agree that more has been said and therefore we have to adjourn sittings (.) [789]till we meet here in the chambers next week (.) Wednesday, May I hear you say [790]aye? . . . [Members respond aye] As many as those who say that there is still more [791]to be debated and therefore we still have to continue sitting here (.) regardless [792]of any circumstance (.) geographical (.) climatic or any other (.) May I hear [793]you say nay? . . . [Members respond, nay] Per the ears of the speaker (.) [794]honourable members (.) before I declare the outcome of the results (.) we [795]have a short caucus after rising up (.) The ayes have it (.) I rise (.)

The use of the expression *per the ears of the Speaker* indicates that the Speaker himself knew he was being biased and controlling yet the two Benches did not resist the domination. It could be explained that the two Benches did not resist it because they recognized the utterance as formulaic and granted in genre.

## CONCLUSION

This study sought to investigate the discursive features that are employed to enact power and domination in the University of Cape Coast Students'

House of Parliament. The study revealed that Students' Parliamentarians from the two different Benches as well as the Speaker in their discourse used declaratives, interrogatives, and imperatives in varying degrees. The variation in the use of these clause types pointed to power differentials among the participants with the Minority bench standing out as more powerful against what pertains in the national parliament where the majority usually have voice due to sheer numbers. Deontic modal verbs were also used in the data to enact power. For example, where *should* could have been used to mitigate the force of obligation, *must* was rather used to force strong obligation on the part of the listening participant. The positive *self*-representation and negative *other*-representation as well as the peculiar turn-taking and interruptions showed dominance from speakers, although much was not seen to connote manipulation as suggested by van Dijk (2006a). In the area of the contextual features, as discussed in the literature, the distinction of the Speaker's attire in addition to the graphological setting—the Speaker's sitting position and the seating arrangements of parliamentarians in the UCC Students' Parliament—marks power relations because of the mental models attached to the hierarchical setting.

A systematic attention to the study of the UCC pseudo-parliamentary discourse has implications for Critical Discourse Analysis because the ideological and unequal standing of groups in parliament seems to shift from what pertains in national parliaments. Fairclough's (1989) theory of power and van Dijk's (2006a) theory of social power, applied as analytical frameworks for this paper, point to some similarities in power relations in students' parliamentary discourse as a pseudo-political discourse like could be found in national political discourse, but there are other related issues that need to be studied for pseudo-parliamentary discourse. Considering that literature is limited in this genre, it is important for the power behind such discourses that are not in the mainstream parliamentary discourse to be studied for the good of social and other political discourses and national governance. This paper opens a window to the phenomena of the discourse in student political discourse and calls for a study of such discourses in other contexts.

## REFERENCES

Appartaim, A. B. (2012). "Prominence and Rhythm in Ghanaian English Speech: A Study of Parliamentary Discourse." In D. F. Edu-Buandoh and A. B. Appartaim (eds.), *Between Language and Literature: A Festschrift for Professor Kofi Edu Yankson*, 56–75. Cape Coast: University Printing Press.

Atanga, L. (2012). "The Discursive Construction of a 'Model Cameroonian Woman' within the Cameroonian Parliament." *Equinox Publishing* 6(1): 21–45.

Bijeikiene, V., & A. Utka. (2006). "Gender-Specific Features in Lithuanian Parliamentary Discourse: An Interdisciplinary Sociolinguistic and Corpus Based Study." *SKY Journal of Linguistics* 19: 63–99.

Chilton, P. (2004). *Analysing Political Discourse: Theory and Practice*. London: Routledge.

Downing, A., & P. Locke. (2006). *English Grammar: A University Course*. New York: Routledge.

Fairclough, I., & N. Fairclough. (2013). *Political Discourse Analysis: A Method for Advanced Students*. London: Routledge.

Fairclough, N. (1989). *Language and Power*. New York: Longman Inc.

Fairclough, N. (2001). *Language and Power* (2nd ed.). London: Longman.

Fairclough, N. (2014). *Language and Power* (3rd ed.). London: Longman.

Foucault, M. (1972). *The Archaeology of Knowledge*. New York: Routledge.

Foucault, M. (1998). *The History of Sexuality: The Will to Knowledge* (vol. 1). London: Penguin

Gadavanij, S. (2002). "Intertextuality as Discourse Strategy: The Case of No-Confidence Debates in Thailand." *Leeds Working Papers in Linguistics and Phonetics* 9: 483–502.

Gee, J. P. (1996). *Social Linguistics and Literacies: Ideology in Discourses* (2nd ed.). Bristol, PA: Taylor and Francis.

Gorjian, B., & P. Habibi. (2015). "The Effect of Conversation Strategies on the Classroom Interaction: The Case of Turn Taking." *Journal of Applied Linguistics and Language Learning* 1(1): 14–23.

Greenbaum, S. (1996). *The Oxford English Grammar*. New York: Oxford University Press.

Hurford, J. R., B. Heasley, & M. B. Smith. (2007). *Semantics: A Coursebook* (2nd ed.). New York: Cambridge University Press.

Ilie, C. (2010). "Identity Co-construction in Parliamentary Discourse Practices." In C. Ilie (Ed.), *European Parliaments under Scrutiny: Discourse Strategies and Interaction Practices*, 57–59. Amsterdam: John Benjamins Publishing Company.

Johnstone, B. (2008). *Discourse Analysis* (2nd ed.). Malden, MA: Blackwell.

Mautner, G. (2016). *Discourse and Management: Critical Perspectives through the Language Lens*. London: Palgrave Macmillan.

Murphy, J. (2014). "(Im)Politeness in Political Discourse: The Case of Prime Minister's Questions in the UK Parliament." *Pragmatics & Society* 5(1): 76–104.

O'Donnell, K. (1990). "Difference and Dominance: How Labour and Management Talk Conflict." In Allen D. Grimshaw (ed.), *Conflict Talk: Sociolinguistic Investigations of Arguments in Conversations*, 210–240. Cambridge: Cambridge University Press.

Palmer, M. T. (1989). "Controlling Conversations: Turns, Topics and Interpersonal Control." *Communication Monographs* 56(1): 1–18.

Sacks, H., E. A. Schegloff, & G. Jefferson. (1974). "A Simplest Systematic for the Organization of Turn-Turn Taking for Conversation." *Language* 50(4): 696–735.

Shenhav, S. R. (2008). "Showing and Telling in Parliamentary Discourse: The Case of Repeated Interjections to Rabin's Speeches in the Israeli Parliament." *Discourse & Society* 19(2): 223–255.

Tsakona, V. (2012). "Linguistic Creativity and Institution Design: The Case of Greek Parliamentary Discourse." *Byzantine and Modern Greek Parliamentary Studies* 36(1): 91–109.

van Dijk, T. A. (1989). "Structures of Discourse and Structures of Power." *Annals of the International Communication Association* 12(1): 18–59.

van Dijk, T. A. (1997). "What Is Political Discourse Analysis?" In J. Blommaert & C. Bulcaen (eds.), *Journal of Linguistics*, 11–52. Amsterdam: John Benjamins Publishing Company.

van Dijk, T. A. (2001). "Critical Discourse Analysis." In D. Schiffrin, D. Tannen, & H. E. Hamilton (eds.), *The Handbook of Discourse Analysis*, 352–314. UK: Blackwell Publishers Ltd.

van Dijk, T. A. (2003). "Knowledge in Parliamentary Debates." *Journal of Language and Politics* 2(1): 193–129.

van Dijk, T. A. (2006a). "Discourse and Manipulation." *Discourse and Society* 17(2): 359–383.

van Dijk, T. A. (2006b). "Discourse, Context and Cognition." *Discourse Studies* 8(1): 159–177.

Vasilescu, A. (2010). "Metastance in the Romanian Parliamentary Discourse: Case Studies." *Revue Roumaine de Linguistique* 55(4): 365–380.

Wodak, R. (2009). *The Discourse of Politics in Action: Politics as Usual*. UK: Palgrave Macmillan.

*Chapter Twelve*

# The Role of Music in Ghanaian Political Communication

## Kofi Agyekum, Joshua Alfred Amuah, and Hilarius Mawutor Wuaku

## ETHNOMUSICOLOGY AND POLITICS

One of the prominent objects of political communication about which there is a dearth of scholarly work is that of music. Researchers of popular music have drawn attention to this neglect (Obeng, 2012). The primary aim of this paper is therefore to draw attention to the prominent role of music in political communication in Ghana. We argue that music and political communication are inseparable and that in looking at the functions of music in political communication, we side with Street (2017) in emphasizing music as a vehicle for protest, propaganda, and resistance; and we add further that music is a vehicle for showing patriotism and undertaking political criticism. This paper is discussed under the broad spectrum of ethnomusicology as demonstrated by Agyekum (2017) and Yankah (see Yankah's work on Nana Kwame Ampadu for details). Agyekum (2007) noted that "[e]thno-music and folksongs are songs that relate the indigenous songs to the people's culture, cultural ideology, religion, belief systems and their worldview." Ethnomusicology, he surmised, is one of the avenues by which one can understand a people's language and culture as well as their behavior through their music.

Ethnomusicologists go beyond the form, description, structure, and analysis of the music, studying a society's music from an anthropological standpoint that encompasses the studied community's overall language and culture. Thus, working within an ethnomusicological framework enjoins the researcher to consider the functions of music and its interrelationship with other aspects of life including politics.

Agyekum (2017) notes that scholars in ethnomusicology see their profession as a field of knowledge that investigates, documents, and preserves music as a physical, psychological, aesthetic, and sociocultural phenomenon involving many aspects of human activities. These include language, history, social identity, gender, politics, economics, religion, indigenous knowledge, and creative and literary art forms. Working within an ethnomusicological framework thus requires us to discuss the use of music as the channel for political communication.

With respect to politics and how it is conceived, it is true to argue that politics is a resource material for musical composition and creativity both in oral and written literature (Agyekum, 2013; Finnegan, 2012; Obeng, 2012; Okpewho, 1992). Indeed, politics is a rich and sustainable context for musical texts and in so far as politics continues in the human experience, there will be political songs and other genres that intertwine political discourse.

Oral literature scholars like Finnegan (2012) and Okpewho (1992) devote some space in their work to folksongs and discuss various types of songs from political standpoints. For instance, Finnegan (2012) writes about what she terms "[t]opical and political songs." She asserts the use of songs as forms of indirection in commenting on delicate issues, especially those about traditional rulers and other people in higher positions. Finnegan (2012) therefore states,

> This indirect means of communicating with someone in power through the artistic medium of a song is a way by which the singers hope to influence, while at the same time avoiding the open danger of speaking directly. The conventionality of the song makes it possible to indicate publicly what could not be said privately or directly to a man's face. (p. 268)

For his part, Emielu (2016, p. 45) discusses the role of music and musicians in political participation, grouping his studied musicians into three categories as follows:

1. Musicians who, through their music, speak to or speak about issues of politics and governance, pushing forward certain ideological positions or echoing popular dissent and/or public opinion
2. Musicians who combine their art with political activism
3. Musicians appropriated or contracted by a ruling government to either promote government programs and policies, gain cheap popularity needed to hold on to power, or rival opposition parties

He cited examples of these types of musicians from the African continent.[1]

# METHODOLOGY

The data for this paper were based on internet and library searches for materials on music and political communication from scholars in and outside of Ghana. We also searched for popular songs by Ghanaians that relate to political communication and collected songs from different categories of Ghanaian music. These included choral songs, patriotic songs, highlife, and the current hip-hop musical genre. Use of the different musical types was meant to help to trace the generational trend of political songs that relate to various political parties and governments/regimes. We searched for these songs from YouTube and from the gramophone record library at the Ghana Broadcasting Corporation.

We recorded, transcribed, translated, and analyzed twelve Ghanaian songs that are strongly related to politics with the view to determining how they communicate politically either in terms of patriotism, political campaigning, praising, criticism/satire, or resistance.[2]

## THE SOCIOCULTURAL AND POLITICAL ROLE OF MUSIC AND SONGS

Emielu (2016, p. 44) opines that "[a]ll throughout the history of mankind, music has lent itself for personal and group expressions of inner feelings whether for political, social or economic reasons." The above denotes the indispensability of music to the overall human experience. The music of a people embodies their language, culture, social life, religion, history, environment, and world view. Songs are used as a medium of information before the advent of writing. African music and songs were used to comment and report on historical and current affairs, as a medium for political pressure and propaganda, and to express public opinion. Finnegan (2012, p. 276) avers that "[s]ongs are now accepted by African political parties as a vehicle for communication, propaganda, political pressure, and political education." Political music is a doubled edged sword that can either praise politicians or criticize them, thereby highlighting the relationship between music (especially popular songs) and political communication. Politically oriented songs create awareness in the minds of the citizenry about the failures and successes of the regimes. In some instances, songs are transformed into patriotic songs for nation building and development (see Nyamnjoh & Fokwang, 2005). Ephraim Amu and J. H. K. Nketia, renowned Ghanaian ethnomusicologists, are noted for their patriotic songs in Ewe and Akan.

Due to the powerful nature of music and its use as a tool to create political education and awareness, as well as its ability to unearth maltreatment, maladministration, and inequality in societies, there is the tendency for some

songs to be censored from air play and even banned from public performances. Englert (2008, p. 11) posits that "Many political regimes throughout
Africa have responded with repression to pieces of popular music which they
perceived as containing criticism, fearing that the music would otherwise
become a site for resistance." She cites an example from Apartheid South
Africa, though Ghana also experienced music censorship during the regime
of Dr. Kwame Nkrumah and the period referred to as the *Culture of Silence*
during the military regime under Flt. Lt. J. J. Rawlings from 1981 to 1992.

In Ghana, both folk and contemporary music bring people together. For
instance, the patriotic song *Yɛn ara yɛn Asaase Ni*, "This Is Our Own Land"
and other songs in Akan were composed by the famed ethnomusicologist Dr.
Ephraim Amu. This song points to the sovereignty of Ghana and how pre-
cious it is to the present generation. Amu draws our attention to the core
values that can move the nation forward as well as those that draw us back.
He emphasized the fact that the country had been secured for us through the
blood of our ancestors and that we should continue from where they left off.
Amu elaborated the issues that were considered counter progressive to nation-building and thus stated:

> *Nimdeɛ ntraso, nkotokrane ne pɛsɛmenkomenya, Adi yɛn bra mu dɛm Ma yɛn
> asaase ho dɔ atɔ mu sɛ.*

> Exaggerated claims to knowledge [Know-it-All-Attitude] and sophistry and
> selfishness have dealt a scar to our national lives and caused our love for our
> country to sink and deviate from a rightful course, in an indescribable fashion.

After lamenting about the above retrogressive issues, Amu was hopeful that
all was not lost; however, whether Ghana could pick up again, progress, and
prosper came with a renewed sense of patriotism in the lives of Ghanaians.

Boadi (2004) did a detailed analysis of this song at a lecture organized by
the Ghana Academy of Arts and Sciences during the Sixth Ephraim Amu
Memorial Lecture in May 2004. On June 26, 2018, Nana Professor S. K. B.
Asante could not resist ending his lecture at the fifteenth edition of the same
memorial lecture series by requesting the choirs in attendance sing Amu's
*Yɛn ara yɛn asaase ni,* which he referred to as the nation's second national
anthem.

## Unity and Patriotic Songs

There are songs that that are believed to be capable of uniting Ghanaians and
are beneficial to them irrespective of different ethnicities. The national anthem was composed by the late Philip Gbeho. Listening to such patriotic
songs evokes a sense of nationalism and tones down the distinctiveness of
the various ethnicities. Nketia, a renowned ethnomusicologist, composed the

University of Ghana's anthem, and many other songs that have been learned in training colleges and secondary schools all over the country. Some of these songs are *Monkamfo no o Yɛn Wura e*, "You Should Praise Him Jesus," *Deɛ ɔman no*, "What the Nation Has," and *Nkyirimma nyɛ bi*, "The Future Generation Should Contribute." Most contemporary highlife songs are composed in Akan, but they are played and enjoyed by all Ghanaians because of their patriotic and cultural content. At parties, funerals, and weddings, irrespective of the locality, people admire and dance to these songs. Music thus becomes a binding and unifying force in a society.

National anthems communicate and create a sense of national identity, and in the case of Ghana, a sense of communality and collectiveness. They thus communicate "politically" for Ghanaians to see themselves as one people and one nation with a common heritage and destiny (see also Street, 2017, p. 6). Following is a renowned patriotic song by Daniel Asare.

*1. Ma ɔman yi ho nhia wo (Be Concerned about This Nation)*

| Text in Akan | English Translation |
| --- | --- |
| *Ma ɔman yi ho nhia,* | Be concerned about this nation |
| *Ghanaman yɛ wo ara wodze,* | Ghana as a nation is yours |
| *Dwene ɔman yi ho* | Think about this country |
| *Ma nka sɛ womfa ho.* | Do not be indifferent |
| *Momma yɛn nyinaa nso mu yɛmmoa.* | All hands on deck; Let's help! |
| *Obiara nyɛn'afam deɛ* | Let each person do his part |
| *Na ɔman yi bɛnya nkɔsoɔ* | So that there will be progress in this nation |
| *Ghana bɛtu mpon* | Ghana will develop |
| *Momma yɛn nyinaa nso mu* | All hands on deck |
| *Obiara nyɛ n'afam deɛ* | Let each person do his part |
| *Baako werɛ aduro a, Egu o* | When one person scratches the bark for medicine it scatters |
| *Tikor ɔnkɔ agyina* | One head cannot go into counselling |

This song calls on all citizens to contribute their quota to national development and to think about the country in order to help it develop. In particular, the song enjoins all Ghanaians to join hands to contribute collectively to the national welfare (or nation-building) since we cannot do so as individuals.

## Ephraim Amu and Political Songs

Amu contributed greatly to national patriotism and composed songs extensively using patriotic texts. His *Yɛn ara yɛn asaase ni*, mentioned earlier in this paper, was originally written in Ewe and later translated into Akan. This is because Akan is the most widely spoken language in Ghana both as a native language and also as a lingua franca for non-natives. As a very important patriotic song, Amu wanted it to reach a lot of the citizenry and hence rendering it in Akan was ideal. He also composed his *Dzɔdzɔenyenye doa dukɔ ɖe dzi*, "Righteousness Exalts a Nation" in his native language Ewe. The theme and title of this song were drawn from Proverbs 14:34 in the Bible and related more to nationalism in the Ghanaian perspective.

Amu calls on Ghanaian citizens to rise and cooperate in building our nation to gain a sustained and firm strength, growth, stability, and dignity. In stanzas 2 and 3 of the song, Amu entreats citizens to uphold hard work and vigilance. He indicates that hard work and perseverance result in a nation's growth and development. He also encourages citizens to hold on to vigilance that is vital to the security and stability of the nation. Below is the text of this song, which is structured in his usual strophic form.

*2. Song Text for Dzɔdzɔenyenye doa dukɔ ɖe dzi*

| Text in Ewe | English Translation |
|---|---|
| **Stanza 1** | |
| *Dumevio, dumegão,* | Citizens, both young and old, |
| *Mitso misɔ asi ɖe* | Rise; let's come together |
| *Mia dukɔaŋu mitui* | To build our nation |
| *Misɔasi ɖe mia dukɔa ŋu.* | Let's come together |
| *Mitui goŋ be ne likɛ tegbee* | To build our nation for stability. |
| *Dumevio, dumegão,* | Citizens, both young and old, |
| *Mitso misɔasi ɖe* | Rise; let's come together |
| *Mia dukɔa ŋu mitui* | To build our nation |
| *Misɔasi ɖe mia dukɔa ŋu* | Let's come together |
| *Mitui goŋ be nedze bubu ɖaa.* | To build our nation to attain dignity. |
| *Dzɔdzɔenyenye nanye gɔmeɖoɖoa.* | Righteousness should be the foundation. |

| | |
|---|---|
| *Dzɔdzɔenyenye nanye tutuɖedzia.* | Righteousness should be the building process |
| *Dzɔdzɔenyenye* | The same righteousness |
| *Ke nanye atsyɔɖoɖoa.* | Should be the fine-tuning. |
| *Mawu fe se si ɖu xexeame dzie* | The rule of God over the world |
| *Nye kpeɖoɖodzi faa na dukɔa be:* | Gives us assurance that |
| *Dzɔdzɔenyenye doa dukɔ ɖe dzi ɖaa.* | Righteousness always exalts a nation. |
| *Dumevio, dumegao,* | Citizens, both young and old, |
| *Mina midi dodoɖedzi na mia dukɔa.* | Let us wish our nation success. |
| *Mitso dzime ke di dodoɖedzi* | Let us from the bottom of our hearts |
| *Vavã na mia dukɔa tegbee* | Wish our nation the utmost upliftment. |
| *Dzɔdzɔenyenyemeleleɖ'asi mee* | It is holding on to righteousness that |
| *Dukɔa fe dodoɖedzi tso* | The upliftment of the nation |
| *Na daa (tegbee)* | Emanates forever |

**Stanza 2**

| | |
|---|---|
| *Dumevio, dumegão,* | Citizens, both young and old, |
| *Mitso misɔ asi ɖe* | Rise; let's come together |
| *mia dukɔaŋu mitui* | To build our nation |
| *Misɔasi ɖe mia dukɔa ŋu.* | Let's come together |
| *Mitui goŋ be ne likɛ tegbee* | To build our nation for stability. |
| *Dumevio, dumegão,* | Citizens, both young and old, |
| *Mitso misɔasi ɖe* | Rise; let's come together |
| *Mia dukɔa nu mitui* | To build our nation |
| *Misɔasi ɖe mia dukɔa ŋu* | Let's come together |
| *Mitui goŋ be ne likɛ tegbee.* | To build our nation for stability |
| *Dumevio, dumegão,* | Citizens, both young and old, |
| *Mitso misɔasi ɖe* | Rise; let's come together |
| *mia dukɔa ŋu mitui* | To build our nation |
| *Misɔasi ɖe mia dukɔa ŋu* | Let's come together |
| *Mitui goŋ be nedze bubu ɖaa.* | To build our nation to attain dignity. |

| | |
|---|---|
| *Kutrikuku nanye gɔmeɖoɖoa* | Hard work should be the foundation |
| *Kutrikuku nanye tutuɖedzia* | Hard work should be the building process |
| *Kutrikuku ke nanye atsyɔɖoɖoa* | The same hard work should be the fine-tuning. |
| *Mawu ƒe se si ɖu xexeame dzie* | The rule of God over the world |
| *Nye kpeɖoɖodzi ƒaa na dukɔa be:* | Gives us assurance that |
| *Kutrikuku kple tsitsiɖedzie zɔna ɖaa* | Hard work coexists with development. |
| *Dumevio, dumegãɔ,* | Citizens, both young and old, |
| *Mina midi dodoɖedzi na mia dukɔa* | Let us wish our nation success |
| *Mitso dzime ke di dodoɖedzi* | Let us from the bottom of our hearts |
| *Vavã na mia dukɔa tegbee* | Wish our nation the maximum success |
| *Kutrikukumeleleɖ'asi mee* | It is holding on to hard work that |
| *Dukɔa ƒe tsitsiɖedzi* | The growth of the nation |
| *Tsona ɖaa (tegbee)* | Emanates forever |

**Stanza 3**

| | |
|---|---|
| *Dumevio, dumegãɔ,* | Citizens, both young and old, |
| *Mitso misɔasi ɖe* | Rise; let's come together |
| *Mia dukɔa ŋu mitui* | To build our nation |
| *Misɔasi ɖe mia dukɔa ŋu* | Let's come together |
| *Mitui goŋ be ne likɛ tegbee* | To build our nation for stability |
| *Dumevio, dumegãɔ,* | Citizens, both young and old, |
| *Mitso misɔasi ɖe* | Rise; let's come together |
| *Mia dukɔa ŋu mitui* | To build our nation |
| *Misɔasi ɖe mia dukɔa ŋu* | Let's come together |
| *Mitui goŋ be nedze bubu ɖaa* | To build our nation to attain dignity |
| *Ŋudzɔnɔnɔ nanye gɔmeɖoɖoa* | Vigilance should be the foundation |
| *Ŋudzɔnɔnɔ nanye tutuɖedzia* | Vigilance should be the building process |
| *Ŋudzɔnɔnɔ ke nanye atsyɔɖoɖoa* | The same vigilance should be the fine-tuning. |
| *Mawu ƒe se si ɖu xexeame dzie* | The rule of God over the world |

| | |
|---|---|
| *Nye kpeɖoɖodzi faa na dukɔa be:* | Gives us assurance that |
| *Ŋudzɔnɔnɔ kple dedienɔnɔe* | It is vigilance and security |
| *zɔna ɖaa* | That always coexists. |
| *Dumevio, dumegão,* | Citizens, both young and old, |
| *Mina midi dodoɖedzi na mia dukɔa* | Let us wish our nation success |
| *Mitso dzime ke di dodoɖedzi* | Let us from the bottom of our hearts |
| *Vavã na mia dukɔa tegbee* | Wish our nation the maximum success |
| *Ŋudzɔnɔnɔmeleled'asi mee* | It is holding on to vigilance that |
| *Dukɔa fe dedienɔnɔ* | The security, stability of the nation |
| *Tsona ɖaa (tegbee)* | Emanates forever |

The major themes in this song are righteousness, hard work, collaboration, nation-building, and vigilance. According to the composer these are the key components that help to ensue national prosperity, security, stability, and dignity for our nation (Ghana). In terms of hard work, he states as follows: "[H]ard work should be the fine-tuning"; something that leads to perfection. The composer makes it clear that for nation building and growth, all hands of the citizenry ought to be on deck and that nobody should sit on the fence. This is seen in the lines that state, "To build our nation for stability, citizens, both young and old should rise and let us all come/work together." These are foregrounded in each of the stanzas. We find this recurring in the first ten lines of each stanza. The composer also talks about righteousness, spiritual upliftment, and hard work. He feels that from a natural law point of view, if people are righteous, work hard and are uplifted spiritually, they will definitely prosper. He emphasizes the fact that righteousness should form the foundation of the nation-building process and the fine-tuning of nation building and development. He surmises that it is the laws of God that control the world, thereby concretizing the notion that righteousness exalts a nation. The statements below exemplify and support the above-mentioned assertions.

*Mawu fe se si ɖu xexeame dzie Nye kpeɖoɖodzi faa na dukɔa be. Kutrikuku kple tsitsiɖedzie zɔna ɖaa Dukɔa fe tsitsiɖedzi Tsona ɖaa (tegbee) Kutrikukumeleleɖ'asi mee*

The rule of God over the world gives us assurance that hard work coexists with development. It is holding on to hard work that the growth of the nation emanates/hinges on forever.

There is a comment on national development that emanates from the people's heart. This is done using expressives and the desirative verb *wish*. It is stated as follows *Mina midi dodoḍedzi na mia dukɔa. Vavã na mia dukɔa tegbee Mitso dzime ke di dodoḍedzi.* "Let us wish our nation success. Let us from the bottom of our hearts wish our nation the utmost upliftment." Downing and Locke (2006, p. 139), aver that "we organise our mental contact with the world by means of mental processes. Mental processing involves *cognition, perception, affectivity,* and *desideration.*" They remark that the verbs that fall under these four main types are "cognition" (*know, understand, believe, doubt, remember,* and *forget*), "perception" (*see, notice, hear, feel,* and *taste*), "affectivity" (*like, love, admire, miss,* and *hate*), "desideration" (*hope, want, desire,* and *wish*). The success of the nation is intrinsic and generated from the citizens but not from foreigners.

## Music for Propaganda, Campaigns, and Slogans

Songs cannot be separated from political propaganda, campaigns, and slogans. All the political parties in Ghana from pre- and post-independence to date employ music to heighten their campaigns. In the 1969 general elections, the Progressive Party (PP), led by Dr. Busia, used political slogans. We heard slogans like PP, *Party Papa*, which became a household slogan and there was the perception that it was one of the tools that helped the party to win the election.

When Nkrumah was overthrown on February 24, 1966, there were jubilations in most parts of United Party's (opposition) stronghold, especially in the Ashanti Region of Ghana. Songs were therefore composed to highlight his presumed tyrannical and cruel rule, especially with reference to the Preventive Detention Act (PDA). People rented cars and traveled to places amid songs of innuendoes and invectives. One song even attacked the Ghanaian currency *cedi* that had Nkrumah's head as one of the emblems. The song was simply *Sidi, Kwasea bi tiri da so!,* "Cedi; There Is the Head of a Fool on It!" Kwame Nkrumah, the star of Africa, was by this song referred to as a fool. This discursive strategy heightened the power of music in political discourse.

Campaign songs have featured prominently in the Fourth Republic of Ghana, dominated by the National Democratic Congress (NDC) and New Patriotic Party (NPP). We have musicians who have openly attached themselves to these parties and have therefore composed campaign songs for them. Some of these campaign and propaganda songs are either for the presidential candidates or for the parties' slogans, themes, and/or manifestos. They are meant to project and promote these parties higher than their opponents with the ultimate aims of making these parties household names and the view to helping them to win more votes. The songs are part of party branding, rebranding, and marketing; and they are persuasive tools for attracting votes in elections.

In the Ghanaian set up, such songs include Jewel Ackah's song for the NDC, *Ehe Ejɔ Bɔdɔɔ*. This means that "everything will be smooth throughout," from the beginning to the end (lit. smoothness galore). This song is a rendition of the Methodist Hymn (MHB: 821) "Stand Up Stand Up for Jesus" that maintains the tune and changes the words.

In the 2000 election, Mr. J. A. Kufuor, the then presidential candidate of the New Patriotic Party (NPP), adopted the gospel song *Ewuradze kasa*, "Lord Speak" by Cindy Thompson as one of the songs played on the campaign trail. The song was an innuendo to indicate that Ghanaians were fed up with the president's regime and that God should speak for the anticipated "positive" change. In the 2012 and 2016 elections, another renowned Ghanaian musician, Daddy Lumba, composed a song titled *Nana ɔyɛ winner*, "Nana Is a Winner," for the presidential candidate of the NPP. Daddy Lumba thus joined the party on their campaign trail and performed this song on stage to the admiration of all party leaders and their supporters. During the 2016 elections, the NDC, the then-ruling party, had a song *ONAPO* to support the incumbent John Dramani Mahama. According to one of our Ga lecturers at the School of Performing Arts, Legon, *Oh! Nii Sowa, ONAPO* means "You will not get it; it is beyond your reach." This implies that the presidential candidate of the New Patriotic Party was not going to win the election; the presidency was far beyond his reach.

Street (2017) postulates that "[p]arties and politicians at least devote care and attention to the music that accompanies their campaigns and select music that in some sense 'speaks' to their manifesto." In an earlier study, Street (2003) discussed how political movements and authorities like the Nazis, South Africans, Zairians, and Kenyans employed popular music as a powerful tool in their political propaganda. He posited as follows:

> More recently, nationalist movements have exploited music's propaganda powers, as have elected and aspirant politicians. In the late-1960s and 1970s, President Mobuto of Zaire made extensive use of bands such as OK Jazz to sing his praises and in Kenya Daniel Arap Moy sponsored musicians who celebrated him in songs that became national hits. (pp. 115–116)

The above is in conformity with what happens in the traditional courts of the Akans, Dagombas, Somalians, Yorubas, and Hausas, where praise poets and griots chant appellations for the chiefs to portray their political feats, especially in wars.

## Persuasive Songs Meant to Avoid Sociopolitical Conflicts

When wars break out among people, music and songs can be employed to either intensify and protract the war or to bring about peace. People listen to the lyrics of these songs and are persuaded to resort to conflict resolution. During Ghana's 2000 general elections, most people were afraid that there was going to be war. Yaw Sarpong and the Asomafo Group had a song titled *Momma yɛn Nyinaa Mmom, Abatoɔ yi mu*, "Let Us All Unite, in This Election."

This song narrated the wars in Angola, Sierra Leone, Namibia, and Liberia and showed video clips of the consequences of these wars. This song was played over and over, and people could relate it to what would happen to Ghana if Ghanaians did not handle the elections very well. The National Peace Council of Ghana adopted the song and used it during the 2008 general elections. Other songs on peace contributed immensely to drawing people's attention to the effects of conflict as compared to peace. In the end, Ghana had a peaceful election in 2008, despite what people perceived as a dangerous and precarious situation in the country at the time. This depicts the "magical" power of language and songs in times of precarious and pensive political situations. The songs below talk about blessing, peace, and unity which are the cornerstone for nation building.

Emmanuel Obed Acquah composed the song "We Need Peaceful Election." He is a renowned scholar who holds a master of philosophy degree in music theory, composition, and ethnomusicology. The lyrics of the song are quoted below:

3. *"We Need Peaceful Election" by E. O Acquah*

**Text in English**
It is time; it is time now
To exercise your franchise, Ghanaians;
Let's see it as great responsibility,
An election free of provocation with healthy rivalry;
For WE HAVE NO OTHER PLACE TO STAY
Than our motherland Ghana.
Let UNITY AND PEACE prevail in this election.
For WE ARE ONE PEOPLE
To build a better Ghana.
Political leaders, all churches and individuals,
Institutions in Ghana; Let us agree.

In the above song, Acquah admonishes Ghanaians about the need to exercise our franchise and stay away from provocation behavior and rivalry because we do not have any place like Ghana. He encourages Ghanaians to be united and to build a better nation. The song points to patriotism and is influenced by election violence in other African countries that had brought about wars. It touches on voting as a civic responsibility in a democratic nation.

*Hyira Ghana* is a composition written by Michael K. Amissah.[3] *Hyira Ghana* is a request from Amissah for God to bless Ghana with peace in times of troubles. Elections in parts of Africa are characterized by wars and famine, cited from Kenya and Liberia that experienced protracted wars because of misunderstanding in election results. For God to spare Ghanaians from the wrath of wars, Amissah wrote *Hyira Ghana*. In the song, Amissah speaks about unity and development in Ghana.

*4. Hyira Ghana (Bless Ghana) by M. K. Amissah*

| Text in Fante | English Translation |
|---|---|
| *Egya Nyame hyira Ghanaman* | Father Lord bless Ghana |
| *Egya Nyame hyira Ghanamba* | Father Lord bless Ghanaians |
| *Na ma hɛn koryɛ.* | And grant us unity, |
| *Na asomdwee na mpontu* | Peace and development |
| *Dom hɛn asomdwee.* | Grant us peace |
| *Hyira Ghanaman hyira Ghanamba* | Bless the nation Ghana, bless Ghanaians |
| *Ghanamba, hyira hɔn dwumadzi* | Ghanaians, bless their activities |
| *Ghanaman, nhyira hom* | The nation Ghana, bless them |

The major messages here are; blessing, unity, peace and development. The verb *hyira,* "bless," and its nominal *nhyira,* "blessing," are found in five out of the eight lines in the song. In lines 1–2 and 6–8 the word *hyira* is in an imperative form used as a request and as supplication for God to help the country and the citizens, as in *Ghanaman,* "the nation," and *Ghanamba,* "citizens." The notion of blessing is found in the opening and closing lines to depict its importance in the musical piece. The word *asomdwoe,* "peace," is mentioned in lines 4 and 5, while *koryɛ,* "unity," and *mpontu,* "development," are encountered only in lines 3 and 4. We can deduce from the text that blessing is foregrounded in the song, and it presupposes that when the nation and the people are *blessed,* they will have *peace, unity,* and development. The verb *dom,* beginning line 5, loosely translated as "grant" or "favor," is derived from the nominal *adom,* "grace," which is granted to people for no work done. By extension, God should grant Ghana peace and that will imply that we Ghanaians can work for it, but the results rest on God's grace.

*Abatoɔ mmerɛ*, "Election Time," was composed by Godfred Sackey. It could be argued that Sackey had a background in traditional music such as *asafo*, "war songs"; *akɔm*, "priesthood/shrine songs"; *mboguo*, "folktale aside songs"; and *fɔntɔmfrɔm*, "a special palace drum genre" since he observed the performances of such ensembles at most times.

## 5. Abatoɔ Mmerɛ by Godfred Sackey

| Text in Twi | English Translation |
|---|---|
| *Asomdwee, asomdwee* | Peace! Peace! |
| *Asomdwee na yehwehwɛ (ampa)* | We are truly craving for peace |
| *Asomdweɛ, asomdwee,* | Peace! Peace! |
| *Asomdwee na yɛhwehwɛ (daa)* | We are always craving for peace |
| *Yɛmfa asomdwee ntena,* | Let's live in Peace |
| *Na ɔman Ghana ye baako pɛ* | Because there is one and only one Ghana |
| *Asomdwee na yɛrehwehwɛ,* | We are seeking Peace |
| *ɔman Ghana hia asomdwee!* | The nation Ghana needs peace |
| *Oh! momma yenngyaa mpaapaamu* | Oh let's stop DIVISENESS |
| *Ne nitan (ɛne) mansotwe bebree* | And hatred and the senseless litigations |
| *Ne ebufuo ne kasa bɔne yi, de ɔko ba,* | Anger and vulgar language promote wars |
| *Oh, Ghanamanfoee meyɛ Asanteni,* | Oh Ghanaians, I am an Ashanti, |
| *Meyɛ Fanteni, meyɛ Gonjani enti deɛn?* | I am a Fante; I am a Gonja, so what? |
| *Meyɛ Angloni, meyɛ Akyemni enti deɛbɛn?* | I am an Anglo; I am an Akyem, so what? |
| *Momma yengyaa mansotwe yi,* | Let's stop all litigations |
| *Momma yengyaa ebufuo yi* | Let's stop all these anger |
| *Na yɛmfa kroyɛ ntena* | And live in unity |
| *Na Ghana betu mpon oo onua ee* | And Ghana will see development. |
| *Eyɛ asomdwee man* | It's a peaceful country |
| *Enti ɛsɛ sɛ yɛbɔ ho ban oo (onua)* | So let's protect it, brother |
| *NDC or NPP, Oh whether PPP or* | NDC or NPP, Oh whether PPP or |
| *PNC yes whether CPP or APC* | PNC; yes whether CPP or APC, |

| | |
|---|---|
| *Yɛn nyinaa yɛ ade baako* | We are all one! |
| *Enti yɛmfa asomdwee ntena ɔman yi mu!* | So, let's stay in peace in the country |
| *Sɛ ɔko ba Ghana a* | When there is war in Ghana |
| *ɛhen na wo bɛkɔ, ɛhen na wo bɛkɔ o?* | Where will you go? Where will you go? |
| *NDC or NPP, Oh whether PPP or* | PNC yes whether CPP or APC |
| *NDC or NPP, Oh whether PPP or* | PNC yes whether CPP or APC |
| *Yɛn nyinaa yɛ ade baako* | We are all one |
| *Enti yɛmfa asomdwee ntena ɔman yi mu!* | So, let's stay peacefully in the country |
| *Yɛn nyinaa yɛ ade baako* | We are all one |
| *Enti yɛmfa asomdwee ntena ɔman yi mu!* | So, let's stay peacefully in the country |
| *Ghana Osee! Yee Ghana Osee! Yee,* | Ghana; Hurray! Hurray! Hurray! |
| *Yee aye!* | Hurray! Hurray! Hurray! |
| *Osee! Yee Ghana, Osee! Yee,* | Ghana; Hurray! Hurray! Hurray! |
| *Ghana Yee aye!* | Ghana; Hurray! |

In the song *Abatoɔ mmerɛ*, Sackey speaks about peace in times of elections. He opens the song with the word *peace* and encourages Ghanaians to live in peace because Ghanaians have nothing but Ghana. He speaks against ethnic inclinations or party affiliations because we all live under the Ghanaian umbrella. No matter one's ethnicity, one is first and foremost a Ghanaian. He points out that though we may belong to different parties, since we are all Ghanaians, we must live in peace. The song comments on rich values and condemns vices that will tear the country apart. The values are *peace, unity, patriotism,* and *development.* To achieve all of these, the song advises the citizens to eschew the vices that border on *divisiveness, litigation, anger,* and hate speech.

The song "We Need Peace" indeed speaks about the need to live in peace and harmony. In this song, Koranteng Amoah code-switches between three Ghanaian languages; Akan-Twi, Ewe, and Ghanaian English. He makes Ghanaian English the principal language for the song. The motive behind the code-switching of languages is to identify unity, love, and peace as major weapons for nation building. The song establishes the fact that no matter Ghanaians' multi-ethnicity, Ghanaians are of the same national heritage and therefore there is no need to allow elections to tear us (them) apart. He further indicates that whether one belongs to Party "A" or Party "B," we are all fighting for the same course, Ghana's prosperity. In the song, he pleads for all to put Ghana first before their unique ethnicities and try to protect Ghana. Apart from peace and protection, other themes found in the song include love, development, and stability.

## 6. "We Need Peace" by Amoah Koranteng Addo

Amoah Koranteng Addo holds a master of arts degree in music (see Agordoh, 2004). In the Western Region, he paired with Entsuah Mensah and formed several Vocal Bands, which compelled him to write so many social songs for keeping wakes.

### Text in English

Peace, we need everlasting peace and unity
We need love we need everlasting love citizens of Ghana
Before and after the election you must put Ghana first.
First remember to protect the love for our motherland
It's our sole responsibility to put Ghana first
Remember to protect our respected nation
My friend; remember to protect this nation
Remember to protect this noble democracy
N. P. P. or N. D. C. whether C. P. P. or P. N. C.
If U' re an Ashanti man or an Ewe man we are all the same
And G. C. P. P. or D. F. P. we are all the same
Let us be one, God Bless our motherland
*Mawu Neyra wo miade-nyigba* (God bless you, Our Motherland)
*Oh, Mawu Neyra wo mia de-nyigba* (Oh God bless you, Our Motherland)
*Oh, yɛn ara y'asase ni* (Oh this is our own land)
*Mawu neyra wo miade nyigba* (God bless you, Our Motherland)
*Na ebetu mpon aa n'e betu mpon aa* (It will develop, and it will develop)
*Ghana n'e betu mpon oo Ghana mmae n'e fri asomdwoe* (And Ghana will
    develop;
Ghanaians it will emanate from peace)
We need, we need PEACE Ghana
We need to stand firm to protect our land
Ghana, we need to stand firm to protect our land
We need, we need, we plea, we need, we need ability
We need protection, we need our land
*Ghana bɛyɛ yie Ghana bɛyɛ yie.* (Ghana will develop; Ghana will develop)

## Music as Satirical Communication in Politics

In all societies, there are songs of insults that challenge the governments in office and give satirical comments on sociopolitical issues. These songs are politically effective weapons that draw people's attention to some social misdeeds. They may address the works of past governments and chiefs and compare their government(s) with the current ones or others.[4]

We see here that songs are modes of political indirection, and if the songs were to be normal utterances in speech, they could bring about conflicts but such songs as the medium of communication, reduce the level of conflicts. As in all forms of innuendo and indirection, the targeted groups are not directly mentioned in the songs, but they can infer that the songs are commenting on their behavior. In discussing the use of music as a form of indirection in political communication, Finnegan (2012) postulates that

> [t]his indirect means of communicating with someone in power through the artistic medium of a song is a way by which the singers hope to influence while at the same time avoiding the open danger of speaking directly. The conventionality of the song makes it possible to indicate publicly what could not be said privately or directly to a man's face. (p. 268)

It is possible to use songs to comment on delicate and offensive issues that otherwise would have been face-threatening acts. Examples of such songs are found in the Apɔɔ songs of the people of Takyiman in the Brong Ahafo of Ghana. Below is an example of Apɔɔ song:

### 7. Ridiculing the Ashanti

| Text in Akan | English Translation |
| --- | --- |
| *Asantefɔɔe* | Hey Ashantis! |
| *Konkukon* | Konkukon (sound of a gongon) |
| *Mokyiri mo kurom* | You hate going to your town |
| *Konkukon* | Konkukon (sound of a gongon) |
| *Mo ni ne mo se* | Your fathers and mothers (Fuck you all!). |
| *Konkukon* | Konkukon (sound of a gongon) |

The expression *konkukon* is an attention-getter telling the Ashantis to listen. In the above Apɔɔ festival song, the people of Takyiman in the Brong Ahafo region, who are Bonos, are insulting the Asantes from the Ashanti region of Ghana, who have settled among them. According to Asihene (1980, p. 36), "Almost all Apɔɔ songs are abusive to individuals but especially to the Ashantis who defeated the Bonos." In the above song, musicians are insulting the Ashantis and their parents and also asking them to go back to their hometowns. Among the Akans, if one settles at a place for a long period without visiting home, he is considered irresponsible. Asihene (1980, p. 36) mentions other short songs that insult the Ashantis, cited as follows:

*Song 8*

> *Susuampa ara ne dwae e. Asantefoɔ monhwɛ yie*
> Beware of your pride Ashantis

> *Moamma Takyiman aduane ayɛ mo dɛ.*
> You have loved the food of Takyiman

The above-cited song is intended to ridicule the Ashantis, meaning that despite their bravery at war and their arrogance, they can be bought with the delicious food from Takyiman, hence they should be reasonable. These songs of political insults are not unique to the Bono. Swahili political songs and lampoons have also been reported, as well as Somali songs of attack on the sultan in those days (see Finnegan, 2012, pp. 266–267). Songs can be used positively to bring about unity among members of trade unions and laborers and to agitate against the unfair treatment by their employers. This is what really happened among African Americans when they were on the plantations in America. Their negro spiritual songs helped them to comment on their hard times and to criticize their masters without direct confrontation. Those songs made them identify themselves as in-group members. The slaves employed songs to convey secret codes as forms of communication and to help boost the morale of their fellow slave workers. One such songs titled "Walk with Me Lord" was sung during very stressful and strenuous days when they were in despair.

In Ghana, any time workers demonstrate to demand increase in wages and fair conditions of service or ask for firing of incompetent officials, they sing through the major streets of Ghana and most of their songs are composed to comment on the current government/administration; the songs are used as voices to let them be heard. Here is a popular slogan song normally sung by demonstrators to indicate that if their demands are not met there will be chaos:

*Song 9*

> *Yɛn ani abere, yɛn ani abere koɔ*
> We are pissed-off! we are terribly pissed-off!

## Songs for Political Protest, Resistance, Agitation, and Criticism

There are certain songs that are used as a medium of political protest and agitation. They are meant to create awareness in the minds of the people about the political atmosphere and thereby to articulate the political sentiments of the period. Political musicians hide by the ambiguity, indirectness, and rhythm of their songs to move the masses; the mobility of music reaches the masses and draws attention to political malfeasance (see Street, 2017, p. 3). During the struggle for independence in most modern and traditional African societies, songs were composed on topical issues to highlight the situations of oppression and suppression and the attitude of the masters. This same phenomenon was used during the struggle for political independence by African colonial societies against the apartheid system and during the Arab spring in early 2011. Undoubtedly, music speaks louder during political protest and agitation, and is thus an effective tool for political struggles and agitations.

In discussing the role of music in political movements and political resistance, there are records of the frontal role of music, especially how musicial instrumental in the expression of resistance and the organization of opposition to the regime. Ward (1998) studied the relationship between music and the civil rights movement in the United States and stated that "the music offers a glimpse into the state of black consciousness and the struggle for freedom and equality at a given moment" (p. 6).[5] In Ghana, during the reign of Dr. Kwame Nkrumah, the Young Pioneer movement adhered to Nkrumaism and the composition of songs to create awareness of socialism. One popular song is seen in the following.

*Song 10: "Work and Happiness"*

**Text in English**
Work and Happiness (4 times)
Yes, I must confess
It will bring success
For beautiful Ghana
United farmers and workers of Africa,
God will bless you wherever you are
Work and Happiness
Yes, I must confess
All must give their best
For beautiful Ghana

This song attaches happiness in work to productivity and the need for all Ghanaians irrespective of where they find themselves to work with zeal and enthusiasm and to give their best so that Ghana will be the best place to live because of its beauty.

During the reign of the Acheampong's military regime (1972–1978), various songs were composed in English and the Ghanaian languages to create awareness and drum home his policies on Operation Feed Yourself (OFY) and Self-reliance. The renowned folk musician Agya Koo Nimo's song below was one of the adopted songs for OFY.

*Song 12: M'afuo Yi Yɛ Ɔbrɛ Adwuma*

| Text in Akan | English Translation |
|---|---|
| *M'afuo yi yɛ ɔbrɛ adwuma* 2x. | My farming is a tiresome job |
| *Ei ebuoo* | It is not easy |
| *Obi se dɔ di a,* | If one advises you to farm and feed yourself |
| *Na ɔnyɛɛ wo* | Then he has not insulted you |

The above song drew people's attention to OFY and Self-reliance to indicate that even though farming is a tedious venture, it is never an insult to farm. People bought into the program and there was abundant food for export and domestic consumption in Ghana during that period. People in the cities and urban centers embarked on backyard gardening and harvested organic vegetables and other food crops.

There are certain satirical songs and lampoons that are meant to bring shame on culprits and to discourage future misconduct. Other satirical songs are innuendo-driven and full of verbal assault, not only toward individuals but also toward current governments and their maladministration.[6] There is the effective use of humor, metaphor, and parody through songs (Obeng, 2012). Yankah (1997) states, "Political critique under these conditions is handed over to the singer of tales, a culturally revered voice of the dominated who creatively manipulates cultural symbolism to convey themes celebrating the resilience of the deprived and exposing the gluttony of the dominant" (p. 54). In most cases, some of these songs are styled in the form of stories full of indirection and ambiguity and the composers can defend themselves when called upon to do so. Creative artists could and do naturally deny any political motivation and claim that their works are purely fictional. The use of indirection in songs is a face-saving mechanism aimed at avoiding face-affront and open confrontation.

Agyekum (2007) records that "[t]here is a popular song by one composer Asebu Amanfi of Kumasi entitled *Ka na wu na nsɛmfoo yɛ ahi* (literally), 'Say it and die, for nasty issues are very irritating.' This implies that sometimes it is better to be candid (i.e., make one's voice to be heard directly) even if this would lead to your death" (p. 175). This song was composed during the Provisional National Defence Council (PNDC) military regime under Flt. Lt. J. J. Rawlings from 1981 to 1992. This period was labeled the "culture of silence" in Ghanaian political history. It was a time when social and political conditions prevailing in the country brought about various political protests and media complaints.

During the first republic of Ghana, Nana Ampadu, a renowned highlife artist, composed a song, *Ebi te yie, ebi nso nte yie*, "Some Are Well-Seated, but Others Are Not." This depicted the situation where most people were suffering, and others were benefiting. He portrayed this in the form of a meeting of the animal kingdom where animals like the leopard were tramping on the "animal-rights" of the smaller animals like the antelope; this song had similar inferencing as George Orwell's *Animal Farm* (see Yankah, 1997). Such satirical songs can only become popular when played constantly in the media, especially on the radio.

The use of the media and songs has been a strong tool in Ghanaian political commentary. There have been various instances where certain politically motivated songs have played important roles in political campaigns either positively or negatively. Most of the parties adopt Gospel songs and modify the words; this depicts the political power of gospel songs.

Hip-hop and highlife music have been used as avenues to comment on sociopolitical issues. A paper by Clark (2012) highlights the sociopolitical role of hip-hop in Accra and Dar es Salaam. The paper traces the genesis of in both Ghana and Tanzania after the regimes of Dr. Kwame Nkrumah and Julius Nyerere. Clark argues that it was the political exigencies of those periods that served as the impetus for these creative artists. Hip-hop allowed the youth to participate and raise their voices to comment on social, political, and economic issues in their countries. Clark (2012) discusses the lyrics by these hip-hop artists and asserts the following:

> Hip hop artists in both Accra and Dar es Salaam have utilized hip hop to respond to the conditions in their respective countries, albeit in different ways. Many artists have delivered thought provoking lyrics, providing a discourse on living conditions, political corruption, greed, and ineffective political policies. In Ghana many of the lyrics are reflections on society and the behavior of Ghanaians themselves. (p. 30)

Clark (2012) cited the use of hip-hop by the Ghanaian artists Sarkodie and A Plus and the relationship between their music and political discourse. He remarked the following about the works of A Plus:

> One of the few Ghanaian hip hop artists to speak out openly on political issues, calling out officials by name, is A Plus. He has, in fact, released an album or

song every election cycle since 2000, including the albums *Freedom of Speech* and *Letter to Parliament*. His song "Osono Ate Ahwe" ("Political Review") addresses the election of President John Atta Mills in 2008. The song criticizes President Mills, saying that since his regime the prices for commodities have gone up and the value of the Ghanaian cedi has gone down. A Plus also comments on the greed that exists in the government, and corruption in the political process. . . . In fact, A Plus has gained a reputation among Ghanaians for his political commentary, discussing issues most Ghanaian artists choose not to. (p. 30–31)

The title of one of A-Plus's song is *Mesuro mpo na merekeka yi o*, "Even Though I Am Afraid, I Am Still Saying It." He knew that he was going to be bashed by politicians and their supporters, but he still gathered the courage to voice out his sentiments. Obeng's 2012 work is also based solely on A Plus's song *Agye gon*, which is a strong political criticism rendered via directness, indirectness, and satire.

Hip-hop artists belong to the youth group and their songs are therefore double edged; they speak to the politicians for them to know the political, economic, and social problems as well as the decadence in the country and their impact on the society. They also use their songs to speak directly to the youth who are primarily affected by such social menaces as unemployment, corruption, greed, and poverty. In effect, the few hip-hop artists are the voices of the majority of the voiceless and the vulnerable youth. These songs are on audio and video, YouTube, Facebook, and other online portals; some for free download. It makes their music accessible to a large portion of the youth, both nationally and internationally.

## SUMMARY

In this paper we have outlined the major role of music in political communication and demonstrated that music and politics are inseparable. The music-politics synergy points to the fact that the sound of music communicates political ideas and inspires political actions (Street, 2007). The general trend is that if songs are well managed and articulated, they can ward off conflicts and animosity among groups and uphold and/or augment people's political communication, awareness, and participation. When music and songs are well composed, they can bring about peace more than what long speeches may do. One advantage of music is that it sticks very well in the minds of the people.

We have identified the use of music in political protest, agitation, and resistance. Also elucidated is the role of music and satire in political propaganda, political praises, and patriotism. We have seen that music is used as a political tool to express the nation's political ideology and thereby move the people into political action either to support a political regime or to rise against it if it is not performing well. We thus agree with Street (2017) in saying that "music is a site both of the exercise of power and of resistance to it; it provides a voice for the powerful and for the powerless. How it is organized and used has consequences for the communication of politics" (p. 10).

Even though music can bring about peace and provide entertainment, if songs are not well handled, innuendo and invective songs can create and inflame passions and bring about conflicts. If people compose songs to cast insinuation against other groups, the opponent groups compose harsher counter-insinuating songs; music then is used as a verbal duel that potentially triggers and heightens wars in times of conflict.

In this paper twelve major songs on political communication were discussed. They were in Ghanaian English, Ewe, and Akan. These languages were selected because they are the most widely spoken languages in Ghana. The idea for composing these political songs in these languages is to reach many people, to drum home political messages, and to achieve or score political points.

## NOTES

1. For instance, Collins (2010, pp. 91–92) has documented how the first president of Ghana, Dr. Kwame Nkrumah, sponsored highlife bands and offered free training for musicians in the service of the state.

2. We conducted interviews on some musicians like Agya Koo Nimo and looked at the works of Prof. John Collins of the University of Ghana. We considered their views about the role of music in political communication.

3. He holds a master of arts degree in music (see Agordoh, 2004). In the Western Region, he paired with Entsuah Mensah and formed several vocal bands that compelled him to write so many social songs for keeping wakes.

4. Finnegan (2012, p. 266) states among others that "[a]t the local level, public singing can take the place of the press, radio and publication as a way of expressing public opinion and bringing pressure to bear on individuals. . . . In doing that, established chiefs can be criticized in this way—the medium of song being used for what cannot be said directly."

5. Wicke (1992) writes that "[r]ock musicians were instrumental in setting in motion the actual course of events which led to the destruction of the Berlin wall and the disappearance of GDR" (p. 81). See also Street (2003, p. 124).

6. In some cases, hymns of Christian songs have been used for political agitations to avoid direct confrontations. During the apartheid regime in South Africa, separatist churches used hymns to express political sentiments, agitations, and aspirations that they could not have done or communicated through other political forms. One of the most popular hymns was *Nkosi Sikele' iAfrica*, "God Bless Africa." This song became popular with the African National Congress (ANC). In Ghana, during the imprisonment of Nkrumah by the colonial administration, a popular Methodist hymn like *"Lead Kindly Light, amid Encircling Gloom"* was frequently sung (Finnegan, 2012, p. 275).

# REFERENCES

Agordoh, A. A. (2004). *Evangelical Presbyterian Church, Ghana and Her Musical Tradition*. Accra: Royal Gold Publishers.
Agyekum, K. (2007). "The Negative Role of Silence in Akan Communication." *Issues in Intercultural Communication* 2(1): 159–178.
Agyekum, K. (2013). *Introduction to* Literature (3rd ed.). Accra: Adwinsa Publications.
Agyekum K. (2017). "Proverbs in Akan Music: A Case Study of Alex Konadu's Lyrics." Paper presented at *School of Languages International Conference II* at the University of Ghana, Legon, October 24–26, 2017.
Asihene, E. V. (1980). *Apoo Festival*. Tema: Ghana Publishing.
Boadi, L. A. (2004). "The Poetry of Ephraim Amu." A Paper presented at the *Sixth Ephraim Amu Memorial Lecture May 2004*. Accra: Black Mark Limited.
Clark, M. K. (2012). "Hip Hop as Social Commentary in Accra and Dar es Salaam." *African Studies Quarterly*, 13(3): 23–46.
Collins, J. (2010). "Highlife and Nkrumah's Independence Ethos." *Journal of Performing Arts* 4(1): 89–100.
Downing, A., and P. Locke. (2006). *English Grammar: A University Course* (2nd ed.). London: Routledge.
Emielu, A. (2016)." Music and politics in Africa: The role of popular musicians. *Eyo Journal of the Arts and Humanities* 2(1): 43–49.
Englert B. (2008). "Popular Music and Politics in Africa: Some Introductory Reflections." *Stichproben. Wiener Zeitschrift für kritische Afrikastudien* 14(8): 1–15.
Finnegan, R. (2012). *Oral Literature in Africa* (2nd ed.). Cambridge: Open Book Publishers.
Nyamnjoh, F. B.; J. Fokwang. (2005). "Entertaining Repression: Music and Politics in Postcolonial Cameroon." *African Affairs* 104/415: 251–274.
Obeng, S. G. (2012). "Speaking the Unspeakable through Hiplife: A Discursive Construction of Ghanaian Political Discourse." In Toyin Falola & Fleming Tyler (eds.), *Music and Politics in Africa*, 296–315. New York: Rutledge.
Okpewho, I. (1992). *African Oral Literature: Backgrounds, Character, and Community*. Bloomington: Indiana Univ. Press.
Slaves in Society: https://historyengine.richmond.edu/episodes/view/4844. Retrieved on August 10, 2018.
Street, J. (2003). "'Fight the Power': The Politics of Music and the Music of Politics." In *Second in Occasional Series on Politics and Culture*, 113–130. Oxford: Blackwell Publishing.
Street, J. (2017). "Music as Political Communication." In K. Kenski and K. H. Jameison (eds.), *The Oxford Handbook of Political Communication*, 1–14. Oxford: Oxford University Press.
Ward, B. (1998) *Just My Soul Responding: Rhythm and Blues, Black Consciousness and Race Relations*. London: UCL Press.
Wicke, P. (1992). "'The Times They Are A-changing': Rock Music and Political Change in East Germany." In R. Garofalo (ed.), *Rockin' the Boat: Mass Music and Mass Movements*. Boston: South End Press.
Yankah, K. (1997). "Nana Ampadu, the Sung-Tale Metaphor, and Protest Discourse in Contemporary Ghana." In J. K. Adjaye and A. R. Andrew (eds.), *Language , Rhythm and Sound: Black Popular Cultures into the Twenty-First Century*, 54–73. Pittsburgh: University of Pittsburgh Press.

## Chapter Thirteen

# President Akufo-Addo's Address to the Nation on the US-Ghana Military Cooperation Agreement

*A Political Communicative Functional and Framing Analytic Approach*

Etse Sikanku, Frank Kofi Boadi, Halisa Aziz, and Nana Kwame Osei Fordjour

The grand promise of democracy includes an open society where free speech thrives, transparency is entrenched, and political communication is enhanced (Gyimah-Boadi, 2001; Eko, 2003). The connection or relationship between the presidency and the people is one of the important aspects of democratic governance, if we agree that politics is about the people (Gyimah-Boadi, 2001). In many democracies, speeches have become an important way for presidents and politicians to communicate directly with the public. This is crucial in the "march towards" democratic consolidation, transparency, and open governance.

Among, the variety of choices available for citizens to hear from their president(s), none is more important than direct speech events such as televised addresses where citizens get to see and hear from the president directly rather than through the reported texts of journalists (Lerman, 1985).

This is not surprising because deliberation and openness constitute some of the enduring ideals of democracy (Huntington, 1992). Indeed, Africa's turn towards democratization was expected to yield several dividends such as inclusion, economic development, stability, security, and pluralization, among others (Gyimah-Boadi, 2008; Gadzekpo, 2004). Years have passed since the wave of democratic reforms swept across Africa in the 1990s. All across the continent, efforts are being made toward democratic consolidation despite challenges.

Perhaps more than any other form of modern governance, democracy presents citizens with crucial avenues for participating, not just in the election of their leaders, but also in tracking the governance process between elections (Abdulai & Crawford, 2010). Media and communication channels have been acknowledged as critical agents in functional democracies (Gadzekpo, 2007; Kasoma, 1997); and the role of the media and communication in democratic politics and attendant key institutions, such as the presidency, or events cannot be underestimated. Communication and media help to keep citizens informed while providing platforms for debate and other forms of political, juridical, and social discourse (Tettey, 2001; Oquaye, 2000; Ansu-Kyeremeh & Karikari, 1998; Gyimah-Boadi, 2009).

## ON DEFINING POLITICAL COMMUNICATION

Political communication has been broadly defined as the role of communication in the political process (Association of Accredited Public Policy Advocated in Europe, 2016). According to McNair (2011), political communication can be defined as "purposeful communication about politics" (p. 4). For his part, Adetunji (2006) sees politics as a "discursive domain" (p. 177). Denton and Woodward (1990) identify political communication as "pure discussion about the allocation of public resources (revenue), official authority (who is given the power to make legal, legislative and executive decision), and official sanction (what the state rewards or punishes)" (p. 4).

According to Blumler and Gurevitch (1995), the core elements of political communication include political institutions, the media, audience orientation, and the relationship between communication and culture. McNair (2011) has defined political communication as "all forms of communication undertaken by politicians and other political actors" (p. 4). There is also some agreement among scholars about the intentionality or the purposeful nature of political communication (Semetko & Scammell, 2012). Political communication also involves symbolic, stylistic, and nonverbal cues, as well as speech (McLeod, Kosicki, & McLeod, 2002). For Strömbäck, Ørsten, and Aalberg (2008), political communication can be described as a "continuous relationship between political institutions and actors, media institutions and actors, and people as citizens, voters and media consumers" (p. 11).

Democratization in Africa offers various ways where political communication finds expression. More than ever before, politicians and citizens have an array of avenues to transmit information as well as to engage in discussions in the "marketplace of ideas" through media platforms. These twin roles of the media as a forum and as an information provider is therefore critical to the quality of democracy. However, political communication also includes all other forms of communication from political actors, including speeches, press conferences, and live television broadcasts.

## DEMOCRACY AND POLITICAL COMMUNICATION IN GHANA

Ghana has experienced seven successive elections since the return to democratic governance in the early 1990s. The country has been hailed as a bastion of democratic renewal in Africa, despite continuing challenges. Specifically, Ghana has experienced transfer of power from incumbents to an opposition party, such as occurred in 2000, 2008, and 2016. In a volatile geopolitical region where elections sometimes spell doom and conflict, Ghana's record is often recognized as exemplary.

After about a decade of military rule under the leadership of Flt. Lt Jerry John Rawlings, Ghana held multiparty elections in 1992. This was symptomatic with the "wave" of democratization that was reverberating all across Africa. Former military ruler, Jerry John Rawlings morphed into a political party candidate and won the 1992 elections (albeit under disputed circumstances) with his newly formed National Democratic Congress (NDC). The main opposition party was the New Patriotic Party (NPP) led by Professor Adu-Boahen. President Rawlings won a second term in 1996 with John Agyekum Kufuor as head of the opposition party. In 2000, Ghana experienced its first transfer of power from one political party to an opposition party when John Agyekum Kufuor beat the NDC's John Evans Atta-Mills after a second round of voting. President Kufuor won a second term in 2004. Professor John Evans Atta-Mills and the NDC won the 2008 elections, defeating the NPP's Nana Addo Dankwa Akufo-Addo and bringing about another transfer of power from an incumbent to the opposition. Professor Mills passed away in 2012 before the general elections and his vice president, John Mahama, took over as president and presidential candidate and won the 2012 elections (though the results were disputed and only "affirmed" after a protracted Supreme Court battle). In 2016, Nana Addo Dankwa Akufo-Addo triumphed over the NDC's John Mahama, bringing about the third instance where political transitions occurred between an incumbent and the opposition.

Throughout these regimes or administrations, political communication has emerged as a central part of Ghana's democratic politics (Tettey, 2001; Gadzekpo, 2007). The practice of political communication often takes place in various forms with the crucial goal of serving as a link between political authority and citizens (Norris, 2000; Negrine & Stanyer, 2007). In Ghana, much like in other democracies, political communication manifests in several forms, such as advertisements, press releases or press statements, speeches, and television broadcasts, among others. This has been further enhanced through the liberalization of the media and the communication space—a major feature of Ghana's developing democracy. Ghana now has one of the continent's most open and pluralized media spaces. In fact, in 2016, Ghana ranked highest among African nations on the World Press Freedom Index. During campaigns and in the process of governance, politicians and the presidency make use of various communication tools, channels, and messages in order to reach the public.

As noted earlier, the main object of this study is an elucidation of the content of a televised presidential address by President Nana Addo Dankwa Akufo-Addo on an important issue of national concern and controversy. Communication has become an important means through which politicians keep in touch with their citizens. On one end of the spectrum in any democratic system are the politicians who seek political office and who govern when they win, and on the other end are the citizens who vote and form the governed or the audience. The crucible, channel, or connective tissue that bridges these two ends of the spectrum—politicians and citizens—in touch with each other is communication and the media. This study will advance the scholarly research into political communication in Ghana, where there is limited and sometimes not-so-timely research in the discipline.

## THE PRESIDENTIAL ADDRESS AND ITS BACKGROUND

Joy FM, a leading radio station in Ghana, broke the news on March 20, 2018, that the government had sent a "secret document" to Parliament that contained a military cooperation between Ghana and the United States, which included setting up of a military base in Ghana. This set off a wave of outrage on the airwaves and within the public sphere with many Ghanaians expressing their angst and visceral displeasure about the issue.

Government officials granted interviews to the news media denying the establishment of any such military base, but many were unsatisfied. The crescendo of opposition only increased and media discussions were characterized with fierce arguments and debates on both sides of the issue. Ghana First, a nongovernmental organization, organized a demonstration that caught on with a wide section of the Ghanaian population. Many demonstrators held placards with pointed messages demonstrating their opposition to the agreement. The assurances from the defense and communication ministers that the deal was no different from previous agreements seemed like a drop in an ocean and did little to assuage emotions, which had run extremely high.

It was therefore not surprising when the presidency announced that President Akufo would address the nation. On April 5, 2018, Ghana's President

Nana Addo Dankwa Akufo-Addo addressed the nation in a televised speech on the national broadcaster, Ghana Television (GTV), and other major television networks. The address took place at 8 p.m. The televised address was held against the backdrop of fierce public debate and controversy regarding a military cooperation agreement between Ghana and the United States referred to as *the US-Ghana Military Cooperation Agreement* or the *Defense Cooperation Agreement* (DCA). There was public outrage surrounding this agreement because of public suspicion that the agreement could lead to the establishment of a U.S. military base in Ghana. There were also concerns that the deal was lopsided and gave too much room to the U.S. military to operate in Ghana. President Akufo-Addo sought to address these concerns in a televised medium to the nation. This was only the second time the president was addressing the nation in such a manner since he took over from the previous administration on January 7, 2017, thus emphasizing the political import of the speech.

## OBJECT OF STUDY

The main objective of this paper is to analyze the president's television address from a media and communicative purpose in order to (a) find out the dominant themes emerging from the speech; (b) synthesize and analyze the various strategies employed by the president to repair or manage his image following the public backlash; and (c) examine the functions of the speech using the various elements identified in Benoit's theory on the functions of political communication. This paper does not seek to analyze the agreement nor state arguments in favor or against previously discussed suspicions about this agreement.

This research is significant because of the paucity of original and systematic research in Ghana, particularly when it comes to political communication. While the functional theory of political communication and framing have been frequently applied to studies in media and communication within the political space globally, very limited studies have employed the functional theory of political communication and framing concepts in Ghana. Most of the existing studies using the theory have been within the domain of media coverage, political debates, campaign news and political advertisement. As far as we know, this is the first application of Benoit's theory to a presidential television address in Ghana. Communication has become an essential part of governance with politicians often interested in transmitting messages directly to the public. It is important to ascertain in a scholarly manner how political communication functions in an emerging democracy and a socio-politico-cultural setting different from those of the developed democracies. This study will thus help to deepen our understanding of the role and functions of political speeches and how politicians use communicative tools such as speeches to frame public issues while providing fresh analytical insights into political communication in Ghana.

As Ghana seeks to develop and entrench democracy, research agendas must begin to move toward examining the role and functions of the communication messages that have become such an intrinsic part of multiparty democracy in Ghana. This research thus makes a pivotal contribution to scholarship in Ghana by helping to deepen our understanding of political messages, the frames employed in communicating such messages, and the messages' functional roles. Beyond that, the strength of this study is evidenced by the application of well-tested political communication theories (framing, image repair, and the functions of political communication) with respect to a televised presidential speech in Ghana—the first such exercise.

## CONCEPTUAL FRAMEWORK

### Framing

Framing involves selecting and highlighting certain aspects of an issue in order to promote certain aspects of political and social reality. Framing is one of the most useful theories employed in academic studies focusing on speech, text and media messages (Bateson, 1972; Entman, 1993; Sikanku, 2013). Frames are sponsored by social and political actors (Chong & Druckman, 2013; van Dijk, 2000). This means that politicians and government officials are constantly involved in shaping, perpetuating, and constructing issues of discourse within the public sphere. To be sure, politicians are constantly focused on selling their messages to the public through speeches, the news media, and other communicative channels. In order to do this, they rely on dominant frames to anchor and sell their messages (Lagerwerf, Boeynaems, van Egmond-Brussee, & Burgers, 2014). To successfully unpack and interrogate any communication material, scholars have relied on framing theory (de Vreese, 2003; van Dijk, 2000). Though framing is often used in the analysis of information presented through the news media, it has also been empirically applied to all forms of text including political speeches (Sikanku, 2013).

Frames help to construct issues, define narratives, and influence public perception. (Lakoff, 2004; Scheufele, 1999). They serve as the lens or prism through which the public are informed and come to understand issues within the public sphere (Reese, 2001; Carragee & Roefs, 2004; Wolfsfeld, 1997). In other words, framing is the essence of political communication. Pan and Kosicki (2001) perceive frames as revealing a "point of view, which is shared on some level and communicable. It organizes our experiences and renders meaning to such organized information . . . a conceptual framework for examining the details of how issues are conceptualized in public discourse" (p. 181). This role of frames in helping to construct social reality has gained support within the academy (Entman & Rojecki, 1993; Chong & Druckman, 2013; Dimitrova & Connolly-Ahern, 2007; Durham, 2007).

The role of framing in political communication is seen in light of the fact that communication professionals and politicians latch onto frames as a central organizing framework to present information (Tankard, 2001; Pan & Kosicki, 2001). In a similar fashion, frames help to present complex and controversial information for public consumption and persuasion. This is often done through the use of key words, labels, projecting values, rhetorical devices, catchphrases, colloquial expressions, idioms, and metaphorical constructions, among others. The study will help to ascertain how President Akufo-Addo framed his response to the controversy surrounding the U.S.-Ghana military cooperation agreement.

Previous scholars have contributed to our understanding of framing by explicating the term as the way in which communication materials are presented or characterized through the use of devices such as catchphrases, metaphors, appeal to moral claims, and key words. Frames are also ascertained through repetitive phrasing or patterns in discourse. Politicians and the media employ frames to put forth their arguments in public debates. This is manifested through patterns or themes, labels and foregrounding word choices, ideological postulations, major terms, and phrasing (Chong & Druckman, 2007; Baker, 2010).

In this study we will be seeking the major rubric that the televised address used to define the news discourse on the bilateral agreement. This present research seeks to contribute to our understanding of political messages by bringing to light the major narrative techniques employed by the president to address a heated political debate and public controversy.

## Image Restoration Theory

Image repair strategies refer to the various strategies employed to address issues of national embarrassment, controversy, or debate. Presidents are likely to face various high and low points during their time in office. Just like any institution, the presidency may employ various strategies to address low points such as an issue of public embarrassment or major scandals. This may also involve issues that cause public outrage and widespread national controversy. Image restoration theory is deemed appropriate to examine this topic because the theory is premised on the foundation that an attack or issue of public concern is deemed offensive and a government, institution or a body can be identified and held responsible (in this case, that would be the Akufo-Addo regime).

Furthermore, image restoration strategies are often used to address how individuals or institutions respond to accusations, controversies, or acts deemed unpalatable by the public. Benoit (2007) put forth five categories of image restoration strategies: denial, evasion of responsibility, reducing offensiveness, corrective action, and mortification. He states,

> Denial and evasion of responsibility address the first component of the persuasive attack, rejecting or reducing the accused's responsibility for the act in question. Reducing offensiveness and corrective action, the third and fourth broad category of image restoration, concern the second component of persuasive attack: reducing offensiveness of the act attributed to the accused. The last general strategy, mortification, tries to restore an image by asking forgiveness. (p. 179)

Denial occurs when a politician refuses to accept responsibility, refuting or rejecting accusations. Evasion of responsibility occurs when an individual blames other parties. This occurs in four different ways. First is provocation where the accused justifies what happens by presenting it as an appropriate response to something that happened or was said. The second form is defeasibility when the accuser says there is nothing else that could be done about the situation, that is, a certain lack of control over the situation. The third strategy is characterizing the incident under consideration as an *accident,* which is to claim that what happened was clearly not on purpose. And then there is finally evasion of responsibility, which can be achieved by asserting that the general good or a good reason or intent necessitated the action.

Reducing offensiveness is the next major image restoration strategy. This particular strategy has six facets. It is generally used to reduce the seriousness or threat that may be present. The politician could tout their achievements or say positive things about themselves, try to reduce negative feelings, resort to differentiation where they say it is not as serious as another situation which they may bring up, attack the accuser to reduce their credibility, place the issue within a more favorable context, and then compensate.

The next major image restoration strategy is corrective action. With this strategy, steps are taken to address the issue, redeem the situation, and to ameliorate the crisis or issue at hand. The last, but not the least approach, is mortification where full responsibility is taken, and an apology is rendered.

Five methods were also suggested by Benoit to bolster efficient image restoration efforts. Important among these is persuasive rhetoric where words and speeches are used to enable the public support of a particular course of action. When individuals or institutions are at fault, they should immediately admit it. If the reason for the situation goes beyond the accused, it is important that blame is rightfully apportioned. There are situations that may be out of control and those should immediately be noted. One of the ways to alleviate a crisis and restore one's image is to also announce plans to solve or address the problem. While corrective action and minimizing seriousness may not always improve the situation, it is important to note that a combination of methods may work together.

As noted earlier, this study will analyze the president's speech to ascertain if any of these image restoration strategies were employed.

## Functional Theory of Political Communication

This study employs the functional theory of political communication as one of the theoretical frameworks for the present research. Research analyzing varying forms of political communication has often used this theory as a conceptual bedrock for such scholarly and systematic investigations (Benoit, 2007; Lee & Benoit, 2009; Benoit & Harthcock, 1999; Benoit & Sheafer, 2006; Padgett, 2009). The functional theory of political communication posits that politicians seek to influence the public or persuade them using three strategies in political discourse: acclaiming, attacking, and defending. According to the theory all these functions can happen on either a policy or a character issue (Benoit, Stein, & Hansen, 2005; Benoit, 2011).

In acclaiming, candidates seek to tout their achievements of self-praise in order to make their message and persona appealing to the citizens. Attack statements are statements that purport to weaken the arguments of opposition candidates, their personalities, or their records in order to decrease the preference of opposing candidates while increasing the stock of the individual attacking. In politics, political actors, normally engage in defense in order to refute various forms of attack within the public space (Cho & Benoit, 2005, 2006; Benoit & Airne, 2009). For instance, when the defense cooperation agreement was made public, the government came under various forms of attack, particularly from the biggest opposition party, the National Democratic Congress. As the target of these attacks, the president and his government could have possibly employed defense statements to ward off such attacks.

This theory asserts that acclaims are the safest or best choices for candidates because they are progressive and positive, and also, they accentuate the best qualities of a politician without necessarily highlighting or foregrounding drawbacks (Benoit, Brazeal, & Airne, 2007; Benoit & Airne, 2009). When attacks are used, they become helpful in reducing the appeal of opposing arguments or politicians by highlighting weaknesses. However, previous research has shown that voters turn to find disparaging statements and political attacks repulsive. Generally, too many attacks can undermine the strength of a speech (Benoit & Sheafer, 2006; Padgett & Brunner, 2009). The literature also reveals that defense statements are the least effective. This is because in defending a statement, political actors are likely to reference the attack, thereby reminding voters of the initial liability. In addition, defense statements do not necessarily add to the positive framing or highlighting of

the strengths or achievements of politicians (Benoit, Leshner, & Chattopadhyay, 2007; Benoit, Stein, & Hansen, 2005; Benoit & Hansen, 2004).

The functional theory of political communication has been applied to
various types of political communication all over the world (Benoit, 2007,
2011; Benoit, Brazeal, & Airne, 2007), but its application is limited in Ghana. The available studies employing the theory have applied it within the
context of social media messages (Fordjour, 2014) and political debates
(Boateng, 2014). Using the functional theory of political campaign discourse
as the bases for the analysis of candidates' Facebook posts, Fordjour's (2014)
research found that posts by the two leading candidates John Dramani Mahama (NDC) and Nana Addo Danquah Akufo-Addo (NPP) during the 2012
election campaign focused mainly on acclaims followed by attacks. Defenses
were rarely employed and only used by John Dramani Mahama. Boateng's
(2014) research also made similar findings. Acclaims dominated utterances
of the all candidates in the debate, followed by attacks and then defenses.
Boateng's (2014) research also made similar findings. Acclaims dominated
the utterances of all candidates in the debate, followed by attacks, and then
defenses.

This study will further contribute to examining the theory within the
Ghanaian political context by applying it to a televised presidential address.
Such repeated studies will help to confirm the applicability and provide
further insights into the explication of the concept in different political domains.

## METHODOLOGY

As noted earlier, the major concerns of this study were three-fold: to investigate the major frames used by President Akufo-Addo in his televised address
to the nation concerning a Ghana-U.S. military cooperation agreement, to
ascertain the image restoration theories used, and to analyze the speech using
the functional theory of political communication. In order to achieve these
objectives, content analysis and textual analysis were employed as methodological and analytical tools. Content analysis and textual analysis are relevant
for this research because they are reliable, valid procedures for analyzing
anybody of text.

### Textual Analysis

In general, textual analysis is a research method used in communication
studies to better understand texts by examining their content, unearthing
themes and making meaning. Scott (1990) posits that textual analysis involves comprehending "a text by understanding the frame of reference from

which it was produced" (p. 31). This underscores why the specific textual analytic technique of framing is used in this study.

According to Fairclough (2003), texts normally spoken or written are seen as part of social events. President Akufo-Addo's address to the nation was an event—a television broadcast event—that constituted part of the president's communication to the nation on a major issue of national debate. The speech, acting as a medium for communication, will be analyzed to ascertain the various frames or themes that were used to articulate or represent that president's thoughts, language, and ideology to the nation.

The specific form of textual analysis used is *framing analysis*. This approach is guided by the concept of communication framing, which serves as an entry point for analyzing speeches (Sikanku, 2013; Dimitrova & Connolly-Ahern, 2007). Politically and sociologically, understanding texts or speeches is of fundamental importance to a democratic process, where information and communication constitute an important aspect of deliberative governance. According to Garzone and Viezzi (2002), seeking to understand or make meaning of contemporary discourse requires the examination and unearthing of various frames employed in language use, such as speeches. Pan and Kosicki (1993) state that framing helps to understand how politicians "take an increasingly proactive approach to amplify their views of what an issue is about" (p. 55). They go further to posit that frames and themes play similar roles in texts, concluding that "a theme is also called a frame" (p. 59). This is similar to Entman's (1993) postulation on framing that states that frames can be established through the "presence or absence of certain keywords or stock phrases, stereotyped images, sources of information, and sentences that provide thematically reinforcing clusters of fact or judgment" (p. 52). Themes or frames are determined through areas of emphasis, use of key words, quotes, propositions implied, strategies used, storylines, narratives, background information presented, exemplars, and word choices (Gamson & Modigliani, 1989; Pan & Kosicki, 1993; Entman, 1993). These approaches, put together, will help to examine the speech under consideration in order to determine frames employed and image restoration strategies used by the president in his address.

## Content Analysis

The textual analytic method used here was supported by content analysis that helped to quantitatively examine the extent to which President Akufo-Addo used the various elements of the functional theory of political communication, namely: acclaims, attacks, and defenses. Wimmer and Dominick (2003) define content analysis as a research method for systematically examining the content of information. Content analysis is used in examining data or texts in order to unearth variables and concepts of elements in any communicative body of text. In this regard, content analysis becomes useful, particularly when examining the presence of the various elements or functions of political communication.

Content analysis is often employed by communication scholars to examine any form of communication or written text such as media content, press releases, and speeches (Wimmer & Dominick, 2003; Sikanku, 2011, 2014; Neuendorf, 2002). When content analysis is used in research, the goal is often to determine the presence of certain components or features in a text, which is one of the goals of this study: to examine the presence of acclaims, attacks, and defenses President Akufo-Addo used in his speech.

## RESULTS AND DISCUSSION

This section presents the results of the study and a discussion of it from textual and content analysis perspectives. The goal of this research was to investigate dominant frames used and image repair strategies employed, as well as to examine the political communicative function of the address.

### Dominant Themes Present in the President's Address

The first research question centered on the identification and explication of the dominant themes present in President Akufo-Addo's televised address. Communication scholars have long recognized the importance of frames in defining issues and persuading citizens on important matters of national concern. Four major frames emerged from the textual analysis of the president's speech. These frames are presented and discussed below.

### Deepening Democracy

In this address, the president sought to portray the process of signing the agreement in question as one that enhanced Ghana's democracy. He established this frame by employing various constituents of democracy such as "belief in the people" or people-centered governance and "openness." The president primarily cast himself as someone with trust, confidence, and "faith" in the people of Ghana. Here the key word or label he latches onto is "democracy," thereby espousing an ideological view of governance.

> You cannot claim to believe in democracy unless you have faith in the people, faith in their inherent goodness, and faith in their capacity to make the right decisions, given the right information. . . . [I]t is this faith that propels me to lead an open and transparent government.

He then cast the executive's involvement of parliament as a symbol of open and accountable governance. From a framing perspective, the interpretive devices used here were a key word and a phrase, namely "scrutiny" and "accountable governance," respectively. Specifically, he noted,

> I decided that, under my watch, any such agreements should be subject to the appropriate scrutiny of the people's representatives in Parliament, in consonance with the requirements of accountable governance and the teachings of the Constitution.

He further sought to burnish his democratic frame by alluding to this move as evidence of transparency and another key element of democracy—citizens' right to know.

> I take what has happened not to be symptomatic of the hazards of democracy, but a show of the strength of democracy in action. We are seeing being displayed before our very eyes, not the triumph of disorder, but the value of openness in governance, and of the need, the crucial need, for the people to be fully and accurately informed.

He further supported this frame by defending his government's policy to subject signing the agreement to public knowledge of both wide and limited accessibility, rather than to follow precedence in signing secretly, a demonstration of openness and transparency. Linguistically, President Akufo-Addo makes use of contrasts to drive home his point (for example, "hazards of democracy" vs. "strength of democracy" and "not the triumph of disorder" vs. "the value of openness in governance"). The president's attempt to shape the public narrative about this controversial issue by casting or framing it in a positive light is even more direct and straightforward in the following statement:

> It is my firm belief that the case for openness and transparency in our governance has been clearly demonstrated, and the argument conclusively settled by these events.

The president went further to portray and defend the military cooperation agreement and the deliberative process in signing the agreement as an embodiment and benefit of the democratic ideal.

> But for this decision to be open about this Agreement, how else would we, the people of Ghana, have ever known that for several decades, Ghana has had defense and security co-operation collaborations with the United States of America. . . . [W]e have provided them with facilities for the movement of personnel and equipment to help some of our neighbors who were facing security and health challenges. . . . [S]ubmitting this Agreement to open scruti-

ny now allows us to clear the unhealthy fog that has clouded our relations with
the United States of America.

The president's framing of the issue is consistent with the various explica-
tions of framing which allude to the fact that political actors tend to persuade
voters by projecting and emphasizing certain ideals as a "central organizing
framework" (Gamson & Modigliani, 1989, p. 2) in an attempt to take control
of an issue of public discourse and to shape everyday reality (Tuchman,
1978).

## Veiled Attacks

President Akufo-Addo for most parts of the speech either rebutted or attacked his opponents and called on Ghanaians to challenge their actions. The
president's initial attack described his political opponents as "hypocrites"
with duplicitous character and cast them as projecting anti-American sentiments. The president saw value in exposing these "frontline" politicians. He
also asserted that they were "misleading" Ghanaians with the aid of sections
of the media.

> But we have to take issue with the front-line politicians who have sought to
> mislead the people in this blatant manner, and those who, for mischievous
> purposes, leaked the document destined for the scrutiny of Parliament prema-
> turely to a section of the media, who then went on to describe it as a "secret
> document."

He maintained that the opposition's assertions amounted to a "cynical manipulation of reckless self-seekers" who through falsehood blatantly confused
people. According to him, the opposition had called for the overthrow of
Ghana's democracy and were seeking to destabilize the peace Ghanaians
enjoyed. He noted,

> Surely, [he says], this is the kind of cynical manipulation by reckless self-
> seekers, which, in the fullness of time, the people of Ghana will acknowledge
> and condemn. And I am sure that as the facts become clear and widely avail-
> able, and as the people come to terms with the evidence, they will reject the
> falsehood and deliberate attempts to destabilize our peaceful country.

The apparent attacks by the president show that politicians embrace certain
narratives in order not only to define issues but also reduce the social support
of opposing arguments through attacks. This intent is once again achieved
through the use of labels and stock phrases such as "reckless self-seekers."
This is consistent with McNair's (2011) view of political communication as
purposeful or targeted and Pan and Kosicki's (1993) view of projecting point
of view in forceful ways.

## Comparisons (Us vs. Them, Past vs. Present)

The speech followed a noticeable trait in Ghanaian politicking: consistent comparisons of records, where political actors point fingers at each other for being better, worse, or no different at something. The president's speech framed his NPP party, in some instances, as having behaved better than the NDC in handling the agreement, and in other instances having acted no different from what the NDC had done in the past. The president suggested that his government had done better than the NDC, who had been secretive with such agreements. He took credit for being transparent and affirmed that

> the case for openness and transparency in our governance has been clearly demonstrated, and the argument conclusively settled by these events.

He also legitimized the demand of Ghanaians for better governance by calling out his party's electoral victory over the NDC.

> After all, you, the Ghanaian people, had voted massively for change; therefore, there was simply no way my government would ever keep hidden from you, the people, agreements of such a nature.

## Enhancing Bilateral Relations, Sovereignty, and National Image

One of the dominant frames emerging from a textual analysis of the speech was that of international relations. The president used this theme or frame to defend the agreement and he assured the nation that their sovereignty was not being trampled upon.

> I will never be the President that will compromise or sell the sovereignty of our country.

He said the conditions under which the agreement was signed were no different from conditions bestowed on embassies, high commissions, and other international organizations operating in Ghana. He insisted that the agreement was in keeping with the norms of international diplomacy. Clearly, the president sought to assuage the fears of Ghanaians by situating the agreement within the international relations frame. The fact that conversations about the agreement still linger suggests he may not have been successful.

## Human Rights Defender

The president was personal, using this frame to allay fears and to build trust. The implicit strategy here is for the president to portray himself as someone sympathetic and as a key supporter of individual rights. He observed,

Everything I have done, since assuming the great honor and privilege of serving you as President of the Republic, demonstrates that I remain focused on building a self-reliant, free, prosperous Ghana, which will be able to make her own unique contribution to the growth and development of Africa and the world.

In concluding, the president sounded inspirational, nationalistic, and high-minded:

Let us rise above them, and build the Ghana of our destiny, the land of freedom, justice, progress and prosperity. May God bless us all, and our homeland Ghana, and make her great and strong.

## Image Repair Strategies Employed by the President in His Speech

An observation of the president's speech points to the fact that he employed *denial* as an image repair strategy. Specifically, he simply and directly denied the purported intention to establish a military base in Ghana. The president was very emphatic in his use of this strategy stating,

So let me state with the clearest affirmation that Ghana has not offered a military base and will not offer a military base to the United States of America.

It is conceivable that he would be so forceful, especially in response to the accusations amplified by the opposition, about the fact that his government had granted permission for the establishment of a military base to the U.S. government. There is no evidence of the president's attempt to shift blame in his use of the denial repair strategy.

The president also *evaded responsibility*, thereby employing one of the four tactics of evasion. He used the good intention tactic by providing reasons for his government's decision to sign the agreement. The three excerpts below provide credence to the above-mentioned fact:

1. The creeping threat to the peace of the region, had not disappeared . . . and, therefore, the need had arisen for continuing with our co-operation[;]
2. The Co-operation Agreement, which has subsisted, which we have approved can only enhance the global effort to preserve the peace in our region[; and]
3. Ghana has had very fruitful relations with a range of foreign embassies and major international institutions. . . . All these agencies enjoy similar conditions as those which the Co-operation Agreement offers to the U.S. military here.

Furthermore, the president sought to *reduce offensiveness* using various components of differentiation and transcendence. In particular, in bolstering his claim, he reminded Ghanaians of his political life as a freedom fighter and sought to advance his reputation as a defender of Ghana's rights:

> I have stood with you, the Ghanaian people, all my adult life, fighting for our individual and collective rights. Everything I have done, since assuming the great honor and privilege of serving you as President of the Republic, demonstrates that I remain focused on building a self-reliant, free, prosperous Ghana, which will be able to make her own unique contribution to the growth and development of Africa and the world.

He also bolstered his reputation as someone who respects the patriots and sovereignty of Ghana saying,

> I respect deeply the memory of the great patriots whose sacrifice and toil brought about our independence and freedom.

Another evident use of bolstering is gleaned from his statement committing to "never be the President that will compromise or sell the sovereignty of our country."

The president, as previously highlighted in identifying the themes/frames employed, sought to reduce any offensive intent by casting the agreement as part of Ghana's contributions to regional peace and to fighting the threat of instability in the region. He also alluded to the fact that it was in keeping with Ghana's impressive peacekeeping record. He attempted to reduce the extent of offensiveness (apparent or implied) through minimization by stating,

> The conditions of the Agreement mirror closely the conditions under which Ghana participates in peace-keeping operations under the United Nations. When our troops go on most peacekeeping duties, they do not carry their national passports, they carry their military identity.

In effect, Ghanaians also enjoy similar privileges as military operatives in foreign lands. The president also relied on differentiation, comparing and distinguishing between the manner in which the agreement was signed, secretly, by previous governments and his government's decision to subject it to public scrutiny and parliamentary debate. This repair strategy is consistent with the findings earlier explained in his *us* vs. *them* frame.

There is also evidence of the use of transcendence in the president's speech. He framed the agreement within the broader context of deepening democracy and international relations. He also attacked the accuser. As identified in his veiled attack frame, the president's focus was the opposition and the media. The term "accuser" in this case could also be broadened to include some section of the Ghanaian population who had been swayed by and believed the accusations of the opposition and the media.

## Extent of Acclaims, Attacks, or Defense Strategies Employed by the President That Are in Tandem with the Functional Theory of Political Communication

One of most relevant theories in the examination of political communication/ discourse is the functional theory of political communication (Benoit, 2007, 2011). The theory posits that political communication/discourse can either seek to establish preference through acclaims, attacks, or defense (Benoit, 2011; Benoit & Sheafer, 2006). Here, the theory is applied to Nana Akufo-Addo's televised address.

In all, there were fourteen (36 percent) cases of acclaims, thirteen (33 percent) statements that sought to defend the president's position, and the president attacked twelve (31 percent) times. This analysis indicates that President Akufo-Addo used acclaims slightly more than defense. This is not surprising, but it is consistent with Benoit's (2007) theory, which postulates that incumbents use acclaims more than attacks or defenses. Presidents use acclaims to talk about their achievements, accomplishments, and positive records in office in order to solidify their image in a credible way. Here is an example of a statement of acclaim:

> I decided that, under my watch, any such agreements should be subject to the appropriate scrutiny of the people's representatives in Parliament, in consonance with the requirements of accountable governance and the teachings of the Constitution.

However, defense, which is seen to have more drawbacks than any of the three functions, was the second highest for Nana Akufo-Addo. This signals that indeed, the president felt his back against the wall, and realized he had to do some damage control, image repair of defending the position or decision taken. Here is an example of a defense statement:

> No suggestion had ever been made that the United States of America had abused any of the privileges or concessions granted under any of these agreements.

The last function, *attacks*, is normally used to reduce the potency of an opponent's arguments in order to paint the attacker in a good light. This function is seen to have fewer drawbacks than defenses and was the least used. Here is an example of an attack statement:

Surely, this is the kind of cynical manipulation by reckless self-seekers, which, in the fullness of time, the people of Ghana will acknowledge and condemn and reject the hypocrisy of the nay-sayers who led our country into bankruptcy and the worse economic record of modern Ghanaian history.

## CONCLUSION

This research constitutes an early effort to deepen our understanding of the content and role of political speeches or addresses in Ghana. The significance of this research is seen because it fills the gap in political communication research in Ghana by examining a presidential address to the nation in a systematic and scholarly manner, using relevant concepts—something which is lacking in the media and communication literature. Our analysis sought to assess the address from three dimensions: the dominant frames used, the image repair strategies employed, and the functions of political communication.

We identified five major frames employed by the president in his address to the nation, namely, (a) deepening democracy, (b) veiled attacks, (c) comparisons, (d) enhancing bilateral or international relations, and (e) his history as a human rights defender. In the deepening democracy frame, the president saw the cooperation agreement and the process of signing it as one that was open and transparent thus enhancing the country's democratic processes. Since frames tend to give insights into the broader ideals regarding any communicative material, President Akufo-Addo's use of key words such as "open," "transparent," and "accountable" indicate that his emphasis on these democratic ideological tenets was employed to appeal to the wider Ghanaian public. In the second frame of veiled attacks, the president strongly denounced his political opponents and characterized or framed their posture as deleterious or destructive to the country's progress. He framed them as "nation wreckers" who want to "destabilize" the nation's peace. In the third frame of comparisons, the president sought to project the decision as a good one by comparing the record of his party to that of the opposition party, the National Democratic Congress (NDC). Here, the president focused his rhetorical strategy by pitting the ruling New Patriotic Party (NPP) against the NDC and then framing the NPP as the better of the two. This demonstrates that the politics of equalization or the comparison of records is a rife and recurring phenomenon in Ghana when it comes to political debates as well as controversy projection and resolution. With respect to the fourth frame, enhancing bilateral relations, sovereignty, and national image, the president framed the cooperation agreement with the United States as a way to bolster Ghana's standing within the international community by citing Ghana's commitment to peacekeeping efforts. Here, the president contextualizes the controversy in reference to a specific historical, nationalistic, and global frame by referring to Ghana's peacekeeping reputation and international image. In the final frame, his history as a human rights defender, the president sought to burnish his reputation as a champion of individual rights.

The image repair strategies used by the president included denial, evasion of responsibility, and reduction of offensiveness. He denied the setting up of a military base, he evaded responsibility by comparing it to previous regimes and highlighting the positive aspects of the agreement, and he reduced offensiveness by highlighting his reputation as a human rights and democracy champion, placing it within the wider context of international peace and security and then finally purporting that the process leading up to the agreement was transparent and open.

The study also found the functional theory of political communication applicable to Ghanaian political discourse. In all, acclaims dominated President Akufo-Addo's speech, followed by defenses and attacks. This is consistent with the literature that states that incumbents normally use acclaims more than any other function of political communication (Benoit, 2007, 2011; Benoit & Harthcock, 1999). These findings are also similar to findings by Boateng (2014) and Fordjour (2014) where acclaims dominated the political discourses, examined though a departure from both research studies is that defenses were used more by President Akufo-Addo in this study than in the two previous studies reviewed. This is perhaps because the president was facing widespread criticism on a controversial issue and so felt he had to make defense statements to justify policy decisions taken.

Speeches and public discussions or debate over national issues are important aspects of any functioning democracy. Communication and framing are important because the content and manner of information provision can shape public perception, behavior, and attitudes within the political system, particularly when it comes to national security discourse. This study constitutes one of the first attempts to analyze a nationally televised address in Ghana systematically using concepts from the political communication literature: framing, image restoration, and the functions of political communication.

This study marks a major contribution to the extant literature on political communication in Ghana. Future research can also extend the study into different parts of Africa's political landscape to understand language use, strategies, and framing appeals by the political figures. A third area of future research would also be a possible extension to different forms of political communication such press conferences, press releases, and other forms of speeches within the political arena in Ghana and Africa. This would make important contributions to assessing the overarching frames and underlying ideologies, as well as to deconstructing narratives and systematically examining discursive strategies in political communication.

# REFERENCES

AALEP. (2016). "Association of Accredited Public Policy Advocates to the European Union." Retrieved online from http://www.aalep.eu/taxonomy/term/1380.

Abdulai, A., & G. Crawford. (2010). "Consolidating Democracy in Ghana: Progress and Prospects?" *Democratization* 17(1): 26–67.

Adetunji, A. (2006). "Inclusion and Exclusion in Political Discourse: Deixis in Olusegun Obasanjo's Speeches." *Journal of Language and Linguistics* 5(2): 1475–8989.

Amoakohene, M. I. (2004). "Researching Radio Audiences in an Emerging Pluralistic Media Environment: A Case Study for the Focus Group Discussion (FGI) Method." *African Media Review* 12(2): 25–40.

Ansu-Kyeremeh, K., & K. Karikari. (1998). *Media Ghana: Ghana Media Overview, Practitioners and Institutions.* Legon, Ghana: School of Communication Studies Press.

Baker, P. (2010). "Representations of Islam in British Broadsheet and Tabloid Newspapers 1999–2005." *Journal of Language and Politics* 9(2): 310–338.

Bateson, G. (1972). *Steps to an Ecology of Mind: Collected Essays in Anthropology, Psychiatry, Evolution, and Epistemology.* San Francisco: Chandler Publishing Co.

Benoit, W. L. (2007). "Communication in Political Campaigns." New York: Peter Lang.

Benoit, W. L. (2011). "A Functional Analysis of the 2011 English Language Canadian Prime Minister Debates." *Contemporary Argumentation & Debate* 32: 45–69.

Benoit, W. L., & D. Airne. (2009). "Non-Presidential Political Advertising in Campaign 2004." *Human Communication* 12(1): 91–117.

Benoit, W. L., L. Brazeal, & D. Airne. (2007). "A Functional Analysis of Televised US Senate and Gubernatorial Campaign Debates." *Argumentation and Advocacy* 44(2): 75–89.

Benoit, W. L., & G. J. Hansen. (2004). "Presidential Debate Watching, Issue Knowledge, Character Evaluation, and Vote Choice." *Human Communication Research* 30(1): 121–144.

Benoit, W. L., G. J. Hansen, & R. L. Holbert. (2004). "Presidential Campaigns and Democracy." *Mass Communication & Society* 7(2): 177–190.

Benoit, W. L., & A. Harthcock. (1999). "Functions of the Great Debates: Acclaims, Attacks, and Defenses in the 1960 Presidential Debates." *Communication Monographs* 66(4): 341–357.

Benoit, W. L., G. M. Leshner, & S. Chattopadhyay. (2007). "A Meta-Analysis of Political Advertising." *Human Communication* 10(4).

Benoit, W. L., & T. Sheafer. (2006). "Functional Theory and Political Discourse: Televised Debates in Israel and the United States." *Journalism & Mass Communication Quarterly* 83(2): 281–297.

Benoit, W. L., K. A. Stein, & G. J. Hansen. (2005). "*New York Times* Coverage of Presidential Campaigns." *Journalism & Mass Communication Quarterly* 82(2): 356–376.

Bloomberg, M., J. Mosier, D. Chartrand, & A. Engelman. (2012). *Twitter Messaging in the 2012 Presidential Election: A Textual Analysis.* (Unpublished graduate research study.) Manhattan, KS: Kansas State University.

Blumler, J. G., & M. Gurevitch. (1995). *The Crisis of Public Communication.* London: Routledge.

Blumler, J. G., & D. McQuail. (1968). *Television in Politics: Its Uses and Influence.* London: Faber & Faber.

Boateng, E. (2014). *A Functional Analysis of the Televised 2012 Presidential Debates in Ghana.* (Unpublished Master's Thesis.) Ghana: The School of Communications Studies, University of Ghana.

Carragee, K., M., & W. Roefs. (2004, June). "The Neglect of Power in Recent Framing Research." *Journal of Communication* 54(2): 214–233. doi:10.1111/j.1460-2466.2004.tb02625.x.

Cho, S., & W. Benoit. (2005). "Primary Presidential Election Campaign Messages in 2004: A Functional Analysis of Candidates' News Releases." *Public Relations Review* 31(2): 175–183.

Cho, S., & W. Benoit. (2006). "2004 Presidential Campaign Messages: A Functional Analysis of Press Releases from President Bush and Senator Kerry." *Public Relations Review* 32(1): 47–52.

Chong, D., & J. Druckman. (2007). "Framing Theory." *Annual Review Political Science* 10: 103–126.

Chong, D., & J. Druckman. (2011). "Identifying Frames in Political News." In *The Sourcebook for Political Communication Research*, 26. New York: Routledge.

Chong, D., & J. Druckman. (2013). "Counter Framing Effects." *The Journal of Politics* 75(1): 1–16.

Denton, R. E., Jr., & G. C. Woodward. (1990). *Political Communication in America*. New York: Praeger.

de Vreese, C. H. (2003). *Framing Europe: Television News and European Integration*. Amsterdam: Aksant.

Diamond, L. (1997). *Consolidating the Third Wave Democracies*. Baltimore, MD: Johns Hopkins University Press.

Diamond, L. (2008). *The Spirit of Democracy: The Struggle to Build Free Societies throughout the World*. New York: Times Books.

Dimitrova, D., & C. Connolly-Ahern. (2007). "A Tale of Two Wars: Framing Analysis of Online News Sites in Coalition Countries and the Arab World during the Iraq War." *Howard Journal of Communications* 18(2): 153–168.

Durham, F. D. (2007). "Framing the State in Globalization: The *Financial Times'* Coverage of the 1997 Thai Currency Crisis." *Critical Studies in Media Communication* 24(1): 57–76.

Eko, L. (2003). "Freedom of the Press in Africa." *Encyclopedia of International Media and Communications* 2: 95–116.

Entman, R. (1993). "Framing: Toward Clarification of a Fractured Paradigm." *Journal of Communication* 43(4): 51–58.

Entman, R. M., & A. Rojecki. (1993). "Freezing Out the Public: Elite and Media Framing of the U.S. Anti-Nuclear Movement." *Political Communication* 10(2): 155–173.

Fairclough, N. (2003). *Analyzing Discourse: Textual Analysis for Social Research*. New York: Routledge.

Fordjour, N. K. O. (2014). *The Use of Facebook in the 2012 Presidential Campaign: A Content Analysis of John Dramani Mahama and Nana Addo Dankwa Akufo-Addo.* (Unpublished master's dissertation.) Ghana: The School of Communication Studies University of Ghana.

Gadzekpo, A. (1997). "Communication Policy in Civilian and Military Regimes: The Case of Ghana." *Africa Media Review* 11(2): 31–50.

Gadzekpo, A. (2004). "Strengthening Media Coverage of Development Issues. Report on One-Day Workshop with Student Journalist." Media Capacity Enhancement Program. Accra: Ghana.

Gadzekpo A. (2007). "The Difficulties of Democratic Deepening in Different Political Environments: The Case of Ghana Wilton Park Conference WP874." In *Democracy, Politics and Development*. West Sussex, Britain: Wiston House.

Gamson, W. A., & Modigliani, A. (1989). "Media Discourse and Public Opinion on Nuclear Power: A Constructionist Approach." *American Journal of Sociology*, 95(1), 1–37.

Garzone, G., & M. Viezzi, M. (eds.). (2002). *Interpreting in the 21st Century: Challenges and Opportunities*. Amsterdam/Philadelphia: John Benjamins.

Gyimah-Boadi, E. (2001). "A Peaceful Turnover in Ghana." *Journal of Democracy* 12(2): 103–107.

Gyimah-Boadi, E. (2008). "Ghana's Fourth Republic: Championing the Africa Democratic Renaissance?" *CDD-Ghana Briefing Paper* 8(4). Accra: Ghana.

Gyimah-Boadi, E. (2009). "Another Step Forward for Ghana." *Journal of Democracy* 20(2): 138–152.

Huntington, S. P. (1992). *The Third Wave: Democratization in the Late Twentieth Century*. Norman and London: University of Oklahoma Press.

Kasoma, F. P. (1997). "The Independent Press and Politics in Africa." *International Communication Gazette* 59: 295–310.

Lagerwerf, L., A. Boeynaems, C. van Egmond-Brussee, & C. F. Burgers. (2015). "Immediate Attention for Public Speech: Differential Effects of Rhetorical Schemes and Valence Framing in Political Radio Speeches." *Journal of Language and Social Psychology* 34(3): 273–299.

Lakoff, G. (2004). *Don't Think of an Elephant: Know Your Values and Frame the Debate.* White River Junction: Chelsea Green Publishing.

Lee, C., & W. L. Benoit. (2009). "A Functional Analysis of Presidential Television Spots: A Comparison of Korean and American Ads." *Communication Quarterly* 52(1): 115–132.

Lerman, C. L. (1985): "Media Analysis of a Presidential Speech: Impersonal Identity Forms in Discourse." In T. A. Dijk (ed.), *Discourse and Communication: New Approaches to the Analyses of Mass Media Discourse and Communication*, 185–216. Berlin: Lüderitz & Bauer.

McLeod, D. M., G. M. Kosicki, & J. M. McLeod. (2002). "Resurveying the Boundaries of Political Communication Effects." In J. Bryant & D. Zillmann (eds.), *Media Effects: Advances in Theory and Research*, 215–267. Mahwah, NJ: Lawrence Erlbaum.

McNair, B. (2011). *An Introduction To Political Communication* (5th ed.). London: Routledge.

Mosier, J. (2013). *E-mails, Propaganda, and the 2012 Presidential Elections: A Content Analysis.* (Unpublished master's thesis.) Manhattan, KS: Kansas State University.

Negrine, R., & J. Stanyer (eds.). (2007). *The Political Communication Reader.* London: Routledge.

Neuendorf, K. (2002). "The Content Analysis Guidebook." Thousand Oaks, CA, and London: Sage.

Norris, P. (2000). *A Virtuous Circle: Political Communications in Postindustrial Societies.* Cambridge: Cambridge University Press.

Oquaye, M. (2000). "The Process of Democratization in Contemporary Ghana." *Commonwealth Comparative Politics* 38(3): 53–78.

Padgett, J., & B. R. Brunner. (2009). *Topics of* New York Times *Coverage of the 2004 and 2008 Presidential Campaigns.* Thesis/dissertation: Auburn University.

Pan, Z., & G. Kosicki. (1993). "Framing Analysis: An Approach to News Discourse." *Political Communication* 10(1): 59–79.

Pan, Z., & G. M. Kosicki. (2001). "Framing as a Strategic Action in Public Deliberation." In S. D. Reese, O. H. Gandy Jr., & A. E. Grant (eds.), *Framing Public Life: Perspectives on Media and Our Understanding of the Social World*, 35–66. Mahwah, NJ: Lawrence Erlbaum Associates.

Reese, S. D. (2001). "Introduction." In S. D. Reese, O. H. Gandy, & A. E. Grant (eds.), *Framing Public Life: Perspectives on Media and Our Understanding of the Social World*, 1–31. Mahwah, NJ: Erlbaum.

Scheufele, D. A. (1999). "Framing as a Theory of Media Effects." *Journal of Communication* 49(4): 103–122.

Scott, J. (1990). *A Matter of Record, Documentary Sources in Social Research.* Cambridge: Polity Press.

Semetko, H. A., & M. Scammell. (2012). "The Expanding Field of Political Communication in the Era of Continuous Connectivity." In H. A. Semetko & M. Scammell (eds.), *The SAGE Handbook of Political Communication*, 1–5. London: Sage Publications.

Sikanku, E. G. (2011). "Inter-Media Influences among Ghanaian Online and Print News Media: Explicating Salience Transfer of Media Agendas." *Journal of Black Studies* 42(8): 1320–1335.

Sikanku, E. G. (2013). *Barack Obama's Identity Construction and International Media Representations during the 2008 Presidential Election: A Discursive and Comparative Framing Analysis.* Unpublished doctoral dissertation. http://ir.uiowa.edu/etd/4911/.

Sikanku, E. G. (2014). "Consolidating Inter-Media Agenda Setting Research in Ghana: A Study of Associational Relationships among Wire, Online and Print News Media." *Journal of Black Studies* 45(5): 396–414.

Strömbäck, J., M. Ørsten, & T. Aalberg. (2008). "Political Communication in the Nordic Countries." In J. Strömbäck, M. Ørsten, & T. Aalberg (eds.), *Communicating Politics: Political Communication in the Nordic Countries*, 11–24. Göteborg: Nordicom.

Tankard, J. W. (2001). "The Empirical Approach to the Study of Media Framing." In S. D. Reese, O. H. Gandy, & A. E. Grant (eds.), *Framing Public Life: Perspectives on Media and Our Understanding of the Social World*, 95–106. Mahwah, NJ: Erlbaum.

Tettey, W. J. (2001). "The Media and Democratization in Africa: Contributions, Constraints and Concerns of the Private Press." *Media Culture & Society* 23(1): 5–31.

Trammel, K. D. (2006). "Blog Offensive: An Exploratory Analysis of Attacks Published on Campaign Blog Posts from a Political Public Relations Perspective." *Public Relations Review* 32: 402–406.

Tuchman, G. (1978). *Making News: A Study in the Construction of Reality*. New York: Free Press.

van Dijk, T. (1998). "Opinions and Ideologies in the Press." In A. Bell & P. Garrett (eds.), *Approaches to Media Discourse*, 21–63. Malden, MA: Blackwell.

van Dijk, T. A. (2000). "On the Analysis of Parliamentary Debates on Immigration." In M. Reisigl and R. Wodak (eds.), *The Semiotics of Racism: Approaches in Critical Discourse Analysis*, 85–104. Vienna: Passagen Verlag.

Wen, W. C. (2014). "Facebook Political Communication in Taiwan: 1.0/2.0 Messages and Election/Post-Election Messages." *Chinese Journal of Communication* 7(1): 19–39.

Wicks, H. R., A. Bradley, G. Blackburn, & T. Fields. (2011). "Tracking the Blogs: An Evaluation of Attacks, Acclaims, and Rebuttals Presented on Political Blogs during the 2008 Presidential Election." *American Behavioral Scientist* 55(6): 651–666.

Wimmer, R. D., & J. R. Dominick. (2003). *Mass Media Research: An Introduction*. Belmont, CA: Thomson/Wadsworth.

Wolfsfeld, G. (1997). *Media and Political Conflict: News from the Middle East*. Cambridge: Cambridge University Press.

*Chapter Fourteen*

# Language and Liberty in the Ghanaian Political Ecology

## *An Overview*

## Samuel Obeng

An important aspect of the intersection between language and liberty is free speech and how censorship can put a stranglehold on the free flow of information from the governing elite (the powerful) to the mass of the population (the powerless) and vice versa. Censorship may even put an iron grip on the free flow of information among the citizenry. The object of this chapter is to recapitulate and extend my earlier studies on free speech and the entwining of language and liberty in the Ghanaian political sphere. The initial part of the paper deals with a general synthesis and analysis of the concepts of *censorship* and *free speech* and a determination of the extent to which Ghanaian political actors, critics and the media have enjoyed them or been denied them within Ghana's post-independence political domain. The second part of the paper recapitulates and extends my earlier work on liberty and how Ghanaian political actors, social commentators, journalists and the news media have used language in its (liberty's) pursuit. Also elucidated is the extent to which language and liberty find reality in each other. The paper ends with a brief conclusion.

## CENSORSHIP AND FREE SPEECH IN GHANA

An essential facet of the Universal Declaration of Human Rights (UDHR) is the inherent right of every individual to freedom of opinion and expression, what I would like to refer to here as both *positive* and *negative communica-*

*tive liberty*. In some of my previous work on language, politics and liberty (Obeng, 2018a 2019), I noted that in working within the theory of *language and liberty*, researchers ought to confirm the fact that liberty is a legal, political, and philosophical concept (Date-Bah, 2008), and that language is used to express the aforementioned notions and their associated philosophies; thus, I argue that liberty hinges on language to become authentic. Based on the philosophical exposition of Sir Isaiah Berlin (1960) on liberty as the bedrock of my theory, I contend that liberty must be considered from two viewpoints, namely, *liberty from* (which Berlin refers to as negative liberty) and *liberty to* (which he refers to as positive liberty). Whereas *positive liberty* secures the right of persons to partake in governance and to share in the political power of their communities and hence includes the right to autonomy and sovereignty at the various levels of a political entity, *negative liberty* entails the safeguard of individuals and minorities from the intrusions of the government and other persons or institutions into their fundamental freedoms. In writing about liberty and freedom of speech, the UDHR declares,

> Everyone has the right to freedom of opinion and expression; this right includes freedom to hold opinions without interference *[negative liberty]* and to seek, receive and impart information and ideas through any media and regardless of frontiers *[positive liberty]*.

The above UDHR declaration of comprehensive human rights enjoins governments and social institutions to guarantee individuals their freedom of association, information, human development, equal access, and participatory rights, among others. Specifically, individuals must have the right to protest peaceably and to assemble freely to deliberate issues related to their lives. Every individual must also have the right to seek information and/or knowledge and to be informed or be provided with information needed to function as a normal and efficient being. Governments and social institutions are obliged to provide individuals access to the cultural mores of their communities and to allow the citizenry to develop freely based on those cultural mores. Furthermore, the citizens of a polity, according to this declaration, must have equal access to broad and unlimited resources such as housing, health, and education at their disposal to function competently. For their part, the citizens must be able to do same for each other.

However, a systematic observation of governance issues in various countries points to governments use of violence (physical, mental, emotional, social, financial, somatic, etc.) against news producers and journalists who question certain behaviors of people in power or news producers and journalists who are perceived by the powerful as not agreeing with the policies of governing institutions. Some politically powerful actors also use intimidation in the form of bullying, property destruction, threats, and calling the news media *fake news*—and by that prejudicing the minds of the citizenry against such news media. These and other schemes are used to intrude on the liberty of journalists and opposition political actors and to consequently mute their voices.

Furthermore, the enactment of repressive legislations via decrees, executive orders, and parliamentary majorities to ignore or suppress minority opinions often limit or deny individuals access to information production and distribution. For example, during Ghana's First Republic, the promulgation of the *Preventive Detention Act* led to the incarceration of opposition political actors who dared challenge President Nkrumah and his Convention Peoples Party government. This led to the muting of the voices of the incarcerated actors. Indeed, during the 1966 coup of by the NLC aided by the CIA and the subsequent rule of the Progress Party there was repression and intrusion of individual liberties with the Trade Union Congress (TUC) and some media outlets such as the *Evening News* being banned. Komla Gbedema, an important CPP political actor, was banned from political activities.

In general, governments engage in censorship via the suppression of so-called opposition newspapers, censor and destroy essential resources needed by the media to function adequately, and blacklist journalists and news media they view as non-friendly via exclusionism (as occurred in the United States in 2018 when some journalists of CNN were prevented from attending news briefings/conferences in the White House and were also told they could not ask questions at news conferences). Other governments also organize boycotts of so-called opposition news media, and in extreme cases, outlaw such newspapers. Governmental control in classifying news into *fake* and *non-fake* (as is the current practice in the United States), not only leads to communicative abuse but also to a denial of knowledge, education, and hence proper participation in governance. The question is this: How effective is a democracy if the populace is uninformed, not because they are illiterate, but because of a denial of their negative liberty via intrusion by a government and a prevention of their ability to competently participate in processes that affect their social, cultural, matrimonial, and networking lives (i.e., their positive liberty)?

It is common knowledge that in Ghana, certain songs were at some point banned because they were viewed as anti-government (see Agyekum et al., chapter 12, in this volume); some journalists were openly criticized or banned from doing their work; and some books and newspapers have been known to be banned or put out of business (see this volume) because they were viewed as anti-government. For example, after the 1966 coup, the *Evening News* was banned and books by Nkrumah were burnt. There were times in Ghana's political history (as well as that of other countries, developed and Third World) that some radio and TV stations were prohibited from broadcasting and thus from exercising their right of participating in the sociopolitical affairs of the country. Such oppressive behavior on the part of the elite and powerful have created monopolies for government owned newspapers, *Daily Graphic* and *Ghanaian Times* (either directly or indirectly) and led to the infringement on the free speech of the victims given that they have been denied voice with some ending up dead in jail. This course of action has also denied the mass of the population their God-given unalienable right to make decisions based on non-biased objective facts.

Barring of the voice of the opposition, denying them the right to exercise their right to participate in the governance of the nation via the creation of government or government-centered ideologically biased way of information content and information flow, leads to communicative, linguistic, sociohistorical, and financial imbalance since the citizenry become puppets rather than rational human beings. Indeed, as Amoakohene and Ansu-Kyeremeh note in chapter 7, there are situations where the governed may not even understand the language in which they are governed. Given that communication is not complete if messages do not reach addressees, such governments fail in their communicative enterprise. An important discourse-pragmatic question worth asking is this: What use does communication have if the media through which messages and news are communicated are not and cannot be understood by the target of the messages and news? During Ghana's First Republic, some government officials and so-called party faithfuls or functionaries charged with relaying and explaining President Nkrumah's policies to the citizenry failed in their jobs because they themselves had problems understanding the incomprehensible and bombastic expressions that Nkrumah used. It is often rumored for "comic relief" that there were some who said that despite the fact they did not understand Nkrumah's speeches, they preferred what he said to that of J. B. Danquah (the opposition leader), which they understood! Inability to understand government policies led to massive corruption on the part of government functionaries since it was alleged that some interpreted Nkrumah's socialist agenda to mean what in Akan became known as *di bi na menni bi*, "Equity in looting (government funds)." Even though there is no way of corroborating this folk etymology-based discourse token, the fact that it has become part and parcel of Ghana's historical and political folk discourse points to what happens or could happen if the mass of the population or even a portion of those in power are denied their linguistic and communicative rights: those of communicating and being communicated to in a language they can understand.

Furthermore, use of economic constraints (either monetary, pecuniary, commercial, or fiscal) to bankrupt the powerless (especially those in opposition), squeeze out such individuals and the media from exercising their free speech is quite common, not just in emerging markets and democracies but also in so-called developed democracies, especially in the Western World. Besides financial pressures, social pressures are also used to deny the media their professional communicative right to keep the citizenry informed. In Ghana, the news and media imbalance (resulting from censorship and fear of imprisonment), especially in the First Republic (1960–1964) and Second Republic (the late 1970s) as well as from the 1980s to the early 2000s, led to journalists and the mass of the population *giving up on words*, what came to be called the *Culture of Silence* by Professor Adu Boahene, a distinguished historian and university professor turned politician who led efforts to speak the unspeakable. To give up on words does not necessarily mean remaining silent because one has nothing to say, but rather remaining silent for fear of what might happen if one speaks up given the fact that one is perceived as not being on the side of the government. Inability to counteract bias is as dangerous as, if not more dangerous than, intrusion on one's right to existence. In fact, during the periods of Ghana's "political communicative silence" noted above, some Ghanaians exerted pressure for the restoration of liberty by calling for democratization in political participation in particular, and communication in general. For example, during the First Republic headed by President Nkrumah, Dr. J. B. Danquah fought not just for his liberty to speak his mind and to make known the views of his party, but for the liberty of the Ghanaian nation. He saw it as a personal and professional responsibility to draw President Nkrumah and his CPP government's attention to their intrusion of Ghanaians' liberty through its restriction on free speech and wanton imprisonment by Nkrumah of people who held dissenting views. It is important to note that there are those who hold the view that Nkrumah acted the way he did because of threats on his life.

In Danquah's letters from his jail cell to Nkrumah and the speaker of Ghana's National Assembly, as demonstrated in the next section of this paper, Danquah appropriated the strongest linguistic and discursive tools to challenge the illegality of his incarceration and called for a restoration of rule of law and due diligence in Ghanaian jurisprudence in dealing with the citizenry. He also called for equal political participation for those in power as well as those in the opposition.

On the above same topic, Ansu-Kyeremeh and Karikari (1998) and Amoakohene (2012; and also chapter 10 in this volume) painstakingly explicate and exemplify the above-mentioned situation by noting how the General Acheampong's Supreme Military Council and Flight Lieutenant Rawlings's Armed Forces Revolutionary Council (AFRC) regimes denied Ghanaians' their communicative liberty by stifling and regulating the media with the view to using them to fulfill their political objectives of building consensus and support of the electorate and to ensuring electoral victory without paying attention to the public's liberty. Indeed, during the AFRC and Provisional National Defense Council (PNDC) eras, news media that wrote against the policies and practices of the regimes were "shit-bombed" (that is, had toilet waste dumped in their offices and premises) in an attempt to silence them. In

Ghana, the population's right to receive information from journalists and the news media was often encumbered by both internal governmental forces (as elucidated above) and external forces.

Furthermore, past economic sanctions and external financial forces (via the World Bank, International Monetary Fund, and others) and business entities have at one point in time or another held the mass of the Ghanaian population hostage via repressive economic policies that limited the nature and extent of information or news that was made available to them (the Ghanaian citizenry). Specifically, the harsh economic situation created by these international financial institutions and businesses made it impossible for private persons to import broadcasting and news printing materials for producing and distributing news. Denying access to varied information creates a situation where only the governments could purchase such materials. Such a situation led to monopoly in the production and distribution of news and consequently made the citizenry unable to participate sensibly in governance because they were unable to separate personal belief from fact and to separate truth from untruth. It also negatively impacted their ability to create and maintain constructive criticism and to scrutinize facts dumped on them by the government and the so-called powerful and elite.

Also linked to the external financial and entrepreneurial encumbrance is the often-biased reportage by external news organizations about what is happening in Ghana. Given that the intelligentsia sometimes mistakenly classify "foreign" news by, for example, the British Broadcasting Corporation, Cable News Network (CNN), or the Voice of America as authentic, and in view of the fact that the mass of the population's linguistic and communicative competence in the English language can be called into question, presentation of falsehood by external news media (which may be due to cultural misunderstanding) could constitute the basis of misinformation and hence, miscommunication, leading to biased judgement of what is happening in the country. This has the potential to negatively impact, not only positive governance but also the liberty of the polity. To mitigate this canker, it is incumbent upon Ghanaian governments to help install individuals' linguistic and communicative rights through education in the official language (English language) and, most importantly, to enact national policies that require the government to communicate with the people in all forty-four indigenous Ghanaian languages.

It must be noted that for the past decade and a half, the private Ghanaian media houses (TV and radio stations) have significantly improved access to news by the general mass of the population by broadcasting in the local languages of wider communication; notably Akan, but also in Ga-Dangme and Ewe. Other national languages namely Dagaare, Dagbani, Hausa, Gonja, Gruene, and Nzema have had news disseminated through them. Note, however, that the overall quantity of information that is shared in the English language compared to those of the local languages is unbalanced. This unbalanced situation only serves to keep the mass of the population from becoming active participants in the nation's governance. Thus, the fact that the mass of the population receives inadequate and sometimes poor information from the elite and powerful limits the masses' participation and makes the elite and powerful believe that everything they do is right. Indeed, there is the tendency for those in power to assume, wrongly, that the powerless either have no ideas related to governance or are incapable of participating in the "complex" discourses that take place in Parliament. In Ghana's current Parliament (2018) there is a female parliamentarian who sometimes becomes the laughingstock of Parliament because of her less-than-perfect English communicative competence. Thus, even when English (the "gatekeeper") allows one to "slip through" the gate of Parliament, once in Parliament, English becomes a stranglehold on such a political actor by not only intruding on the actor's negative liberty but also by indirectly preventing her from participating in the affairs of her community (Parliament) and thus adequately representing her constituency.

Another consequence of the elite and powerful controlling the production and distribution of news is the creation of a situation whereby what they consider as newsworthy is often not relevant to the target audience. For example, of what relevance is the execution of a drug dealer in the Philippines or the Oscars in Los Angeles to the peasant farmer in a Ghanaian village? Thus, cognizant of the fact that the nature of news communicated by the elite and powerful to the mass of the population is often not relevant to the lifestyle of mass of the population, a social barrier is created, making the powerful unable to relate to the masses and vice-versa. To avert this situation, it is essential for the powerful to pay attention to the cultural congruency of what counts as news and the appropriate way(s) of delivering such news to the people.

Another common strategy of denial of free speech and the intrusion on individuals' liberty involves deception and distortion whereby governments and their accomplices replace news and facts deemed true with erroneous facts, stretched truths (which involve *selection* whereby only certain aspects of news deemed relevant by the news producer are broadcast to the people), and fabrication (also known as plain falsehoods). Closely associated with the above-mentioned assertion is the use of government-owned media to propagate fear, announce public planned executions (as happened during the AFRC and PNDC eras as well as the NLC period), and summon segments of the population to appear before citizens' vetting committees, as happened during the dictatorships of Rawlings's AFRC and PNDC regimes, during which time the government infringed on the civil liberties of the citizenry given the exaggerated fear it created and the extent to which use of the media prevented people from freely participating in their own social lives, their economic activities, and their free participation in the running of govern-ment. Via radio, print media, and TV announcements, people's liberties were known to have been intruded upon cognizant of the fact that some were barred from political participation and incarcerated. Undeniably, during the AFRC and PNDC eras, decisions about incarceration and property seizure were announced via radio, TV, and the print media, and affected individuals had little to no way of speaking up and seeking justice. The denial of free speech and its accompanying access to legal representation and information that could help exonerate incarcerated individuals is known to have resulted in the death of many a political prisoner with the most prominent one being Dr. J. B. Danquah, the doyen of Ghanaian politics.

Some government-owned media and their journalists have also been known to resort to crisis journalism whereby they engage in selection (a form of lying mentioned earlier in this section) by concentrating mainly on report-ing about members of the opposition party's failures, mistakes and unimpact-ful activities leaving out their successes, achievements, and impactful deeds. This is known to have created hatred toward those in opposition and prevent-ed them from bringing their full potential to bear on governance. For exam-ple, Dr. J. B. Danquah was wrongly accused of aiding and abetting the British to delay Ghana's independence and this resorted in his harassment by a section of the population. There were times that people not only hooted at him but also threw bottles and stones at him because of this wrong accusa-tion. Thus, this act by the government infringed on both his and his party's liberty by denying them voice and action in Ghana's political ecology.

Also, Ghana's history during the late 1970s and the 1980s demonstrates instances where speech was monopolized by parties in power through the use of so-called patriotic songs to commemorate and celebrate the anniversary of coup d'états (such as those of President Rawlings's AFRC and PNDC), during which time no real national socioeconomic or even cultural import are given prominence by such governments. Such songs and parades served as a painful reminder to those hurt by the coup d'états, distorted truth and reality, and paid little to no attention toward the feelings and personal comfort of those hurt by such events. Thus, the mass of the population was not part of the decision-making process regarding information production and distribu-tion; they were mere objects or targets of government communication propa-ganda. Ensuring the people's liberty via democratization of the news media and political communication at that point in time would have ensured that the wants and the needs of the public were addressed.

However, President Rawlings's National Democratic Congress govern-ment's decision to finally allow and empower private individuals to own and operate private radio and TV stations helped to diversify news production and dissemination, acts that encouraged the production of divergent opinions and gave the mass of the population the opportunity to choose what to say and where, what to watch or read, as well as what to listen to and in what language. Thus, people's liberties regarding news production and distribution were largely protected, and this helped build, nurture, and strengthen Ghana's democratic institutions. By democratizing the mass media, there was broader access to communication and the citizenry had avenues to air their views and to receive feedback from the political actors and media professionals. Furthermore, the participation of the citizenry in the production and dissemination of information gave rise to community participation in decision making and in the implementation of their ideas given that they became part of the democratic governance, even if minimally.

## LANGUAGE, POLITICS, AND LIBERTY IN GHANA

As elucidated earlier in this paper, in Obeng (2018a, 2019), I established the fact that in working within my theory of *language and liberty*, it is incumbent upon scholars and/or researchers to establish the fact that liberty has its roots on a nation's law, politics, and overall philosophical orientations, and that liberty depends on language to become a reality. Following Sir Isaiah Berlin, I argue that liberty should be viewed from two perspectives—*negative liberty*, which entails the safeguard of individuals and minorities from the intrusions of the government and other persons or institutions into their fundamental freedoms), and *positive liberty*, which safeguards the right of persons to contribute to the governance of their communities, to be autonomous and sovereign, and to share in the political power of such communities.

Following Date-Bah's (2008) argument and recommendation for there to be legal and material conditions put in place in a country's constitution and in judicial precedent to ensure and maintain individuals' liberty, I argue that these protections must be made available to the mass of the population in a language(s) they can understand and function in competently. As Ghana's political experience teaches us, and as succinctly explicated and exemplified by Date-Bah (2008), failure to enshrine a Bill of Rights in Ghana's constitution created a situation in which President Nkrumah and his CPP government felt they were not or could not be subjected to law, a belief that led to their infringement on the negative and positive liberties of members of the opposition party. In fact, their promulgation of the *Avoidance of Discrimination Act, 1957 (C.A. 38)*, also known as the *Preventive Detention Act*, made the opposition party illegitimate and hence led to the creation of a one-party state; President Nkrumah therefore saw nothing wrong with incarcerating his "enemies." Thus, as Date-Bah (2008) painstakingly elucidates, the absence of a tradition of subjecting government to law emboldened President Nkrumah to engage in human right abuses through what Date-Bah refers to as *parliamentary supremacy* provided for in Ghana's Independence Constitution of 1957. This made Nkrumah not only an authoritarian but also despotic given that he and the Ghanaian National Assembly dominated by the CPP did not tolerate divergent views.

Moreover, I have also noted in some of my earlier works that by fighting for their liberty and the liberty of the people they represent, political actors in opposition, public critics and pundits, as well as journalists put their careers and their lives at risk. I noted, however, that strategies exist for the protection of their positive and negative liberty. Thus, I have elucidated and exemplified some of the discursive strategies employed in challenging the validity of claims and actions of the powerful (Obeng, 2018a, 2019). I also demonstrated the entwining between language, politics, law, and liberty in Ghana. In particular, using some of the letters written by Dr. J. B. Danquah, the doyen of Ghanaian politics (Rahman, 2007) from his jail cell to President Nkrumah and the Speaker of Ghana's National Assembly (see Danquah, 1970), I showed that besides the sociopolitical ecology within which Danquah's letters were written, the letters' content and grammatical values (*expressive values*), their ideological-alignment (*experiential values*), and their *usages or collocations* showed relationships between Danquah and Nkrumah (*relational values*) and that all the above impacted the production and interpretation of responses to the letters (see Fairclough [1989] for explication of the above italicized discourse pragmatic strategies).

Unearthing how language and liberty impact one another enjoins us to find out what kind of language that actors seeking liberty use, especially the sentence types (e.g., active-passive, commands, statements, or questions), the specific content and grammatical words, and the discourse-pragmatic markers (especially, inferencing, speech act types, and politeness markers, among others) used by them. Finally, the language used by actors to either control news production and dissemination or to seek liberty and justice is essential to determine the extent of strength of the bond between language and liberty.

Among the grammatical markers described in my earlier works (Obeng, 2018a, 2019) as being used to seek liberty are *factivity formulae* like, *as you know*, *we all know*, and *you will recall*, which presuppose the truth of a complement clause that follows them (Kiparsky & Kiparsky, 1979). Use of such syntactic frames makes it impossible for the target of the messages to vigorously challenge the assertions and claims made. Other syntactic features employed in the fight for liberty includes the use of conditional sentences, political pronouns (usually *us* versus *them*, also referred to as inclusive and exclusive pronouns), physical verbs denoting destruction/harassment/injury, collocation, as well as adverbs and adverbial constructions that describe the extent of oppression and how badly/urgently the victims need liberty (Obeng, 2018a, 2019). Indeed, there are occasions when the seeking of liberty is done via the use of graphological features such as the use of uppercase letters to show emphasis and/or to demonstrate one's frustration at the denial of liberty. For example, to demonstrate his frustration at the fact that the Ghanaian Parliament was intentionally, with the support of the president, passing "bogus" laws in order to permanently infringe on his liberty, Danquah used uppercase letters to put emphasis on his message as shown below:

> Under the Constitution, the President has a Cabinet of persons who, together with him, constitute the Executive of the Government of Ghana, with collective responsibility, and they together, as constituting an "it," are not "private persons," but are parts of an institution—the Government of Ghana.

The use of uppercase letters for emphasis is documented in Obeng (2000a, 2000b) as being widely used in Ghanaian political communication done through graffiti.

Some of the discourse-pragmatic markers that index the entwining of language and liberty are *contrastive pairs* also called *antithetic constructions*, deferential modes of address and reference, various politeness strategies, candor, glittering generalities, emotional valence, intertextuality, and delegitimization of each other's action, leading to the creation of an "other" worldview. Ghanaian political actors also engage in inferencing whereby the target of an utterance is not mentioned but could be easily made out via reasoning, deduction or extrapolation.

Sometimes Ghanaians seeking liberty employ candor by openly and unequivocally expressing their mistreatment and their right to be free from intrusions from the State and other institutions, as well as by requesting the right to participate in the process of governance and to share in the political power of the state/polity in which they live. At other times they seek liberty via the use of literary features like situational and dramatic irony (Obeng, 1997, 2016) whereby the victims of oppression describe their situation through oblique allusions and verbal indirectness. As Obeng (2016) elucidates, Ghanaian fighters for liberty such as Danquah, Hawa Ogede Yakubu, Adu Boahen, P. K. K. Quaidoo, and many others often communicate through the voices of others via indirectness, intertextuality, dialogism (also referred to here as polyvocality or doublewordedness) to give credence and evidentiality to their assertions, complaints, or protests. Dialogism, used by Ghanaians who seek liberty, has often involved references to history and historical events, traditional Ghanaian axioms, and biblical characters and events. For example, biblical intertextuality was appropriated by Mrs. Hawa Ogede Yakubu (1995), an independent Member of Parliament for Bawku-Central constituency in Ghana, when she spoke at a seminar at Abokobi, a suburb of Accra, on the theme of the debate, "The Economic Reality and Family Planning in Ghana." During her speech, she quoted John 19:17 and referenced Jesus being made to carry his cross in order to imply that President Rawlings had lost control of Ghana and was being rendered useless by corrupt minis-

ters of state. Danquah, in a similar fashion referenced Psalm 119:18 in his
criticism of Ghana's executive branch of government, the judiciary, and the
legislature (Ghana's National Assembly) for ignoring judicial due process
and intruding on his and others' liberty. As noted in Obeng (2016, 2018a),
through the voice of the Psalmist, Danquah bemoaned the fact that inatten-
tion to the laws regarding liberty led to wrongful incarceration of the weak
and defenseless and to the trampling on their negative and positive liberty.
The biblical allusion disclosed the power inequality and social injustice in
Ghanaian society of that era as well as the political tension in Ghana during
Ghana's First Republic.

A systematic observation to the above discussion points to the fact that
the fight for liberty becomes reality through language. Also, one's understanding of the law on liberty and on politics as well as the recognition of
rights and the need to object to the powerful voices' illegitimate actions all
help make the fight for liberty a reality. There is no doubt that power relations are deeply rooted in culture, politics, and ideology, and an actor's
effective use of language helps to produce and reproduce the tools for fighting for liberty.

Fairclough's *ideological common sense*, which affects the "meanings of
linguistic expressions, conventional practices of speaking and writing, and
the social subjects and situations of discourse" (Fairclough, 1989, ix) also
impacts how and the extent to which language and liberty index each other in
the Ghanaian political ecology. An argument made by Fairclough (1989) that
does not hold or is not applicable to the Ghanaian political ecology is his
argument that the less conscious interactants are of ideological assumptions,
the more effective they are at reproducing language and its associated power
within discourse, and in perpetuating the underlying relationships between
language and power (see also Obeng, 2018b). Journalists, social commentators, and political actors are aware of the stratified makeup of Ghanaian
culture and its underlying ideological common sense. This awareness influences their lexical and syntactic choices and renditions as well as the nature
of explanations and/or interpretations given to their own texts and to those of
others. However, I would like to maintain and reemphasize the fact that
Fairclough's argument of variation in ideologies is capable of restricting the
scope of ideological common sense and thereby creating relationships between discourses of the subjugated and those in control. An observation of
the Ghanaian political ecology during the First Republic (from July 1, 1960,
to February 24, 1966) indicates that President Nkrumah's voice, which was
the governing or powerful voice, "made" ideological assumptions associated
with it to become enfranchised, and accordingly the lone "legitimate" voice.
It is important to note, however, that the dominated voices (such as those of
Danquah, William Ofori-Attah, Emmanuel Obetsebi-Lamptey, Ebenezer
Arko-Adjei, and others) continued to play a resistant role even from jail

despite their voices being contained by Nkrumah. A similar situation happened during the dictatorships of the AFRC and the PNDC, during which times the dominated voices such as those of the late Professor Paul Ansah of the then School of Journalism and Mass Communication at Legon, Professor Albert Adu Boahen of Legon's History Department, and Elizabeth Ohene (a renowned Ghanaian journalist) played resistant roles in their quest for liberty for the Ghanaian population.

Indeed, the language behavior in Ghana's political ecology, as measured in terms of Danquah, Adu Boahen, Paul Ansah, Elizabeth Ohene, and many others' candor, is complexly in sync with their stance and perception of liberty and its relation to power and ideology. As elucidated in my earlier works on liberty, citizens' knowledge of how language relates to liberty and political power entails "implicit and deep understanding of how particular linguistic and discourse-pragmatic forms can be used to perform pragmatic tasks like criticism, complaint, disagreement, request or apology and the norms of the discourse ecology, the goals of the political actors, and the actors' ideological preferences and expectations regarding how such pragmatic tasks must be performed" (Obeng, 2019); it is not just a litany of correspondences between particular discourse and/or linguistic forms and liberty.

Furthermore, the dominated Ghanaian voices' strategy of protesting injustice visited upon them by dominant persons or institutions amplifies power imbalance within the Ghanaian discourse ecology. In particular, in the Ghanaian sociopolitical context, the dominant voices often expect the dominated voices to assume a more submissive and deferential role as elucidated in my work on juridical discourse (Obeng, 2018b). The dominant actors could be angered by the dominated voices' refusal to be muted and this has sometimes led to perpetual incarceration and even death, in extreme cases, of the dominated voices/persons (Obeng, 2018a, 2019). Thus, via their challenge of power in the search for liberty and the unyielding response of the powerful, we observe the discursive entwining of language and liberty in Ghana's polity.

## CONCLUSION

A close observation of the Ghanaian political context suggests the occurrence of censorship and hence the denial of free speech at various times in Ghana's history. We also observed that even when free speech was denied, Ghanaians often found ways to resist the powerful and to speak their minds.

Also, I have demonstrated that an observation of the interconnectedness between language and liberty in the Ghanaian political ecology shows Ghana's languages and linguistic situation, its politics, history, law, and culture as impacting each other in a web of constellation all shaping the fight for liberty. Liberty for all Ghanaians is made a reality not only by the dominant voices, but also by the voices of the dominated Ghanaian political actors, social commentators, and journalists irrespective of their unique philosophical and ideological orientations, their histories, and their sociocultural distinctiveness. All such voices view Ghana's democratic development, the constitution of order, and associated economic development as a function of the exercise by all Ghanaians contributing their unique abilities and potentials to molding liberty for all. Thus, Ghanaians view the intrusion on their negative and positive liberty by the dominating or dominant political forces or voice(s) as blocking them from playing their unalienable role in the socioeconomic and political life of Ghana. These dominated persons and institutions perceive such an intrusion as unacceptable; consequently, they appropriate linguistic and discursive strategies to resist domination and to fight for *liberty from* (protection from the intrusions of the government and others into their fundamental freedoms) and *liberty to* (what Sir Isaiah Berlin [1960] refers to as a guarantee of the right to participate in the process of government and to share in the political power of one's community or state). Ghanaians continue to fight for the right to self-determination at the various levels of the Ghanaian polity and political process. Language has and will continue to make the fight for liberty possible. For its part, liberty has become reality through language.

## REFERENCES

Agyekum, Kofi, Joshua A. Amuah, & Hilarius M. Wuaku. (2019). "The Role of Music in Ghanaian Political Communication." In Samuel Gyasi Obeng and Emmanuel Debrah (eds.), *Ghanaian Politics and Political Communication*, chapter 12. London: Rowman & Littlefield International.
Amoakohene, Margaret I. (2012). *Political Communication in Ghana's Emerging Democracy.* Saarbrücken, Germany: LAP Lambert Academic Publishing.
Amoakohene, Margaret I. (2019). "How Much Communication Is in Ghanaian Presidents' State of the Nation Addresses?" In Samuel Gyasi Obeng and Emmanuel Debrah (eds.), *Ghanaian Politics and Political Communication*, chapter 10. London: Rowman & Littlefield International.
Amoakohene, Margaret I., & Kwasi Ansu-Kyeremeh. (2019). "When Government Is Unaware It Is Incommunicado." In Samuel Gyasi Obeng and Emmanuel Debrah (eds.), *Ghanaian Politics and Political Communication*, chapter 7. London: Rowman & Littlefield International.
Ansu-Kyeremeh, Kwasi, & Kwame Karikari. (1998). *Media Ghana: Ghanaian Media Overview, Practitioners and Institutions.* Legon, Accra: School of Communication Studies Press.
Berlin, Isaiah. (1960). *Four Essays on Liberty.* Oxford: Oxford University Press.
Danquah, Joseph Boakye. (1970). *Journey to Independence and After—1947–1965.* Accra: Waterville Publishing House.
Date-Bah, Samuel Kofi. (2008). *On Law and Liberty in Contemporary Ghana.* Accra: Ghana Academy of Arts and Sciences.
Fairclough, Norman. (1989). *Language and Power* (2nd ed.). Language and Social Life Series, edited by Christopher N. Candlin. London and New York: Longman.

Kiparsky, Paul, and Carol Kiparsky. (1979). "Fact." In Donna Jo Napoli and Emily Norwood Rando (eds.), *Syntactic Argumentation*, 328–368. Washington, DC: Georgetown University Press.

Obeng, Samuel Gyasi. (1997). "Language and Politics: Verbal Indirection in Political Discourse." *Discourse and Society* 8(1): 49–83.

Obeng, Samuel Gyasi (2000a). "Doing Politics on Walls and Doors: A Linguistic Analysis of Graffiti in Legon [Ghana]." *Multilingua* 19(4): 337–365.

Obeng, Samuel Gyasi. (2000b). "From Praise to Criticism: A Pragmalinguistic Discussion of Metaphors in African Political Rhetoric." *Contact, Variation, and Culture* 2: 73–88.

Obeng, Samuel Gyasi. (2016). "Biblical Intertextuality in Ghanaian Political Text and Talk." *Issues in Political Discourse Analysis* 5 (1): 23–46.

Obeng, Samuel Gyasi. (2018a). "Language and Liberty in Ghanaian Political Communication: A Critical Discourse Perspective." *Ghana Journal of Linguistics* 7(2): 199–224.

Obeng, Samuel Gyasi. (2018b). *Conflict Resolution in Africa: Language, Law and Politeness in Ghanaian (Akan) Jurisprudence*. Durham, NC: Carolina Academic Press.

Obeng, Samuel Gyasi. (2019). "Grammatical Pragmatics: Language, Power and Liberty in African (Ghanaian) Political Discourse." *Discourse and Society* 33(5).

Rahman, Ahmad A. (2007). "The Watson Commission and the Coussey Committee." In Ahmad A. Rahman, *The Regime Change of Kwame Nkrumah*, 143–182. New York: Palgrave Macmillan. doi:10.1057/9780230603486_7.

Yakubu, Hawa Ogede. (May 5, 1995). "Rawlings to Carry His Cross." *Ghana Review International*.

# Index

www.ingramcontent.com/pod-product-compliance
Lightning Source LLC
Chambersburg PA
CBHW021809270326
41932CB00007B/120